The Hebrew Book of Matthew

"The Original Gospel"

English Translation

Hebrew Text Version (HTV)

Miles R. Jones, Ph.D.

First Edition © Copyright 2025 Miles R. Jones
ISBN # 978-1-957488-15-8

"Yehovah gave the Word; Great was the company of those that published it!"
Psalm 68:11

Great Publishing Company

Benai Emunah Institute
121 Mountain Way Drive
Kerrville, Texas 78028

830-257-7414

Dedicated

to the untold numbers of Messianics who, over centuries, laid their lives on the line and were often imprisoned, tortured, and martyred - to preserve the Hebrew words of Yeshua Ha Mashiach – and to the magnificent team of current Messianic scholars of Benaï Emunah Institute who put their all into this Spirit-filled translation of Hebrew Matthew that you hold in your hands.

Table of Contents

04 .... Acknowledgements
05 .... Hebrew Book of Matthew Format
07 .... Editor's Commentary
26 .... Editor's Preface to Hebrew Matthew
28 .... Hebrew Matthew Preface by Jerome
35 .... Hebrew Matthew Chapter 1
45 .... Hebrew Matthew Chapter 2
56 .... Hebrew Matthew Chapter 3
63 .... Hebrew Matthew Chapter 4
73 .... Hebrew Matthew Chapter 5
95 .... Hebrew Matthew Chapter 6
108 .... Hebrew Matthew Chapter 7
120 .... Hebrew Matthew Chapter 8
135 .... Hebrew Matthew Chapter 9
151 .... Hebrew Matthew Chapter 10
169 .... Hebrew Matthew Chapter 11
182 .... Hebrew Matthew Chapter 12
204 .... Hebrew Matthew Chapter 13
229 .... Hebrew Matthew Chapter 14
241 .... Hebrew Matthew Chapter 15
257 .... Hebrew Matthew Chapter 16
269 .... Hebrew Matthew Chapter 17
280 .... Hebrew Matthew Chapter 18
295 .... Hebrew Matthew Chapter 19
308 .... Hebrew Matthew Chapter 20
322 .... Hebrew Matthew Chapter 21
341 .... Hebrew Matthew Chapter 22
359 .... Hebrew Matthew Chapter 23
377 .... Hebrew Matthew Chapter 24
399 .... Hebrew Matthew Chapter 25
417 .... Hebrew Matthew Chapter 26
446 .... Hebrew Matthew Chapter 27
472 .... Hebrew Matthew Chapter 28
480 .... Editor's Final Comments

Acknowledgements

Miles R. Jones, PhD., Chief Editor
Jonathan Felt, Chief Archivist
Patrick J. McGuire, Creative Director
Janet Thurgood, Marketing
Ronit Mor, N.D., Hebrew Editor
Katrice Addison, Translation Team Leader
Vincent Pace, Assistant Archivist
Nigel Lloyd-Jones, Manuscript Transcription
Rae Lloyd Jones, Book Editor
Drew Sartorius, Webmaster
Catherine Jones, BEI Chaplain

BEI Team Leaders:
Anita Tadeuszow, Pamela Miller, Anita Burke,
David Lewis, Johannes Verboom, Julie Lansford

BEI Board:
Miles Jones, Doug & Janette Harrington,
Geoff & Lianne Haber

Manuscript Scholars:
Jailenne Denisse Ayala, Alan F. Esselbach, Brooke Chabert, Bruce S. Busa, Carson Loga, Christine Herron, David Geering, Debbie Taylor, Drew Sartorius, Ebben Jones, Elizabeth Wright, Geoff Haber, John Lansford, John Wilkerson, Lianne Haber, Mickaël Chabert, Mihail Motzev, Regina Jones, Tami Yeakley

Hebrew Book of Matthew Format

Each chapter of the book is in two sections, the first is the basic Hebrew Text Version (HTV). The second section has each verse with the closest of the several Hebrew manuscripts text that represents the full meaning of the verse. Then the HTV in English followed by any editor note and for comparison to the Greek text in English we have included the King James Version (KJV) text. Some verses will include a clip from the manuscript and/or an editor's note.

Matthew 5:17

Clip from manuscript

Freiburg Hebrew Manuscript

אַל תַּחְשְׁבוּ שֶׁבָּאתִי לְהָפִיר אֶת-הַתּוֹרָה אוֹ-אֶת־
הַנְּבִיאִים לֹא בָּאתִי לְהָפִיר כִּי-אִם-שֶׁאֲמַלֵּא

Modern Hebrew with vowel points

HTV: **At that time Yeshua the Messiah said to his disciples, "Do not think - I came that I might breach (break) the Torah - or the prophets. I came not that I might fulfill (complete or end) but rather that I might fill (the Torah) to overflowing, *abundantly* overflowing!"**

Hebrew Text Version

Note: The verse uses two verbs meaning *overflowing* one after the other. This is common in Hebrew for emphasis. We do not do this in English. We will instead use an emphatic word like: *very, greatly,* or in this case *abundantly.*

Another meaning for the double emphasis is to clarify the meaning of the word לְהָפִיר which is used once negatively in the sense of *end* or *fulfill*, and the second time meaning *fill to overflowing*. This literary device is called *perinamosia*, using two words from the same root in the same sentence for emphasis.

Editor's notes

KJV: Think not that I am come to destroy the law, or the prophets: I am not come to destroy, but to fulfil.

King James Version

The Benai Emunah Institute's team has meticulously transcribed each Hebrew manuscript from the scribe's hand written text into modern Hebrew text. Then they have compared each manuscript to autenticate the content of the verse between each manuscript. An interlinear chart is created to break down every word and the various meanings of the word's usage. Below is an example of the interlinear chart for Matthew 5:17 from the Freiburg Hebrew Manuscript.

The Hebrew Book of Matthew

אַל תְּחָשְׁבוּ שֶׁבָּאתִי לְהָפִיר אֶת-הַתּוֹרָה אוֹ-אֶת-
הַנְּבִיאִים לֹא בָאתִי לְהָפִיר כִּי-אִם-שֶׁאֲמַלֵּא

Freiburg Hebrew Manuscript

Matt. 5:17	אַל	תְּחָשְׁבוּ	שֶׁבָּאתִי	²לְהָפִיר	³אֶת- הַתּוֹרָה	אוֹ-3אֶת- הַנְּבִיאִים
Freiburg HGC & STM	'al no.don't neg part (immediate prohibition)	techash'yu think v Nif'al fut 2mp	shebaetiv that I came v Pa'al 1s	l'hafiyr that I might breach, break prep	et-ha'torah the Torah ddo-nfs	o-at-han'veem or-you-the-prophets nmp

לֹא	בָאתִי	²לְהָפִיר	כִּי-אִם-שֶׁאֲמַלֵּא	כִּי-אִם-⁴שֶׁאֲמַלֵּא
lo' not part	va'tiy I came v Pa'al 1s	l'hafiyr that I might fill, complete, overflowing prep	kiy'im-sham'leh for this reason that I might fill to overflowing v Pi'el fut 1s	sheh'amalei' for that I fill rel part

BEI Archives

The Benai Emunah Institute has created an extensive archive of the translations with notes and interlinear charts which is available for researchers to study. The archive is available on a subscription basis for scholars through the Benai Emunah Institute at **WritingOfGod.com**

Abbreviations of Manuscripts used in translation:

HTV: Hebrew Text Version of The Hebrew Gospels

HGV: Hebrew Gospels from Catalonia Vat. Ebr. 100

FRB: Freiburg Brit Hadashah, Freiburg HS-314

GHM: Gaster Hebrew Manuscript, Rylands MS. 1616

CNT: Cochin Hebrew New Testament, Cambridge Oo.1.32

STM: Shem Tov Manuscript, Hebrew Matthew Vat. Ebr. 101

DuT: DuTillet Hebrew Matthew, BNP Paris Ms. 132

MHM: Munster Hebrew Manuscript of Matthew pub. 1537

Editor's Commentary
Dr. Miles R. Jones
Benai Emunah Institute

The Hebrew Book of Matthew is the cornerstone of Christianity - although it was not called "Christianity" until later. Those who followed Yeshua the Messiah were called "The Way!" (See Acts 9:2, 19:9, 19:23, 22:4, 24:14, 24:22.). They were also called **Nazareans** "Notzrim" after their teacher Yeshua, aka the Nazarene. Matthew was published in 40 AD, less than ten years after the crucifixion.

The followers of Yeshua "**were first called <u>Messianics</u> in Antioch**" (Hebrew Acts 11:26). Luke and Acts were written about 50 AD - granted there is much argument about that date. The first known reference to the "**Chrestians**" was by Nero who became Emperor after Luke's writings - and it was later still before the "Chrestians" became officially known as "Christians." That was beyond the time of Luke. In Hebrew Acts 12:4, Herod seized Peter in order to put him to death, "**intending after Passover to bring him forth to the people**." In the Greek and English Bibles, it usually says "<u>Easter</u>" which did not become an official Christian holiday, replacing Passover, until the fourth century under Emperor Constantine - who founded the Greco-Roman Church - and divorced it from the Jews and Messianics.

And so, the story begins. In the first century, Yehovah - God of the Hebrews - sent his son Yeshua the Messiah to bring his Word and New Covenant doctrines, in Hebrew, to the world. Matthew and Luke were originally written in Hebrew and published in the first half of the first century. They were translated by the Greeks - who tweaked them to support the emerging Greek Church doctrine. The new Greek Church needed four things: A <u>Greek God</u> (Theos), a <u>Greek Christ</u> - (Jesus), <u>Greek Scripture</u>, and

Greek doctrine. The Greeks rejected the Torah and the Covenant of Yehovah. This came to be called *Replacement Theology* and is still the operant doctrine of the Christian Church.

Yehovah became Theos (Deus, Dios, or LORD). Yeshua became Jesus. The New Covenant became the New Testament - and the Torah was replaced by Greek doctrine - a revision of the Word rather breath-taking in its extent! Words like "Christian" and "Easter" were backdated into the Bible to authenticate them - the names "Yehovah, Yeshua, Messianic, Torah and Menorah" vanished from the Word.

I must state here that I absolutely believe that God's Word is sacred and inerrant! It is Man's changes to the Word that leave me aghast. **The Hebrew Book of Matthew is the only eye-witness account of the Messiah by an Apostle!** Luke and Mark did not know the Messiah in his lifetime. John - although it is the sacred Word - was written by Greek editors, presumably from writings John had left behind and the notes and testimonies of those who knew him. "This is the disciple who testified of these things, and wrote these things - and **we know that his testimony is true**" (John 21:24). Who might this "**we**" be? They are John's Greek editors. That makes it a second-hand account. It was supposedly written in the last days of his life 90-100 AD in Greek-speaking Ephesus. There is no clear or compelling evidence of the date, origin, or even of John as the author of the *Fourth Gospel*. It is distinctly different from the other gospels.

Of Matthew, however, there is no such doubt. There are 75 attestations in the early church literature that Matthew was the author of the first Gospel and it was written in Hebrew. There are 80 quotations from *The Hebrew Gospel* cited in those writings by two dozen early church fathers, such as: **Papias** (60-130 AD), **Irenaus** (130-200 AD), **Pantaenus** (c. 190 AD), **Hegessipus** (c. 180 AD), **Hippolytus** (170-236 AD), **Origen** (185-254 AD), **Eusebius** (260-340 AD), **Ephrem** the Syrian (306-373 AD), **Didymus** (310-398 AD), **Epiphanius** (315-403 AD), **Jerome** (345-419 AD) who translated *The Hebrew Gospel* into Greek and Latin, and **Nicephorus Xanthopoulus** of Constantinople (c.1320). So, *The Hebrew Gospel* survived there until the 14th century. All of these witnesses, and others, had seen *The Hebrew Gospel* before it became rare and then disappeared! The fuller versions of those early church fathers' testimonies are in Appendix C. Today, 2000 years later, theologians now claim otherwise:

> The working hypothesis of modern scholarship is that an **erroneous judgement about the existence of an original** *Hebrew Gospel* entered the bloodstream of the church as early as Papias, and that veneration for ancient testimony caused the error to be transmitted and elaborated - <u>rather than rectified and uprooted</u>.
> - Adam Findley, "Byways in Early Christian Literature"

Doctrinal Markers of Hebrew Matthew

I have stated that changes were made to *The Hebrew Gospels* in order to support Greco-Roman doctrines. Here are my premises:

1. The Gospels were Hebrew in origin.
2. There are numerous changes in the Greek Gospels.
3. Many of those changes support the new Greek doctrines.

As you might imagine, each of these logical premises are in dispute. Let's start with the Hebrew origin. The "chosen people" of Yehovah were the Hebrews. Yeshua was the begotten son of Yehovah. All of his words and all of his disciples and all of the gospel writers were Hebrew. He was sent specifically to the Hebrew people of Israel. It is a Hebrew story. That foundation is unavoidable.

Regardless of whether any particular book of the New Testament comes down to us in Hebrew or Greek - it does not change the fact that practically every word originating from

Yeshua's mind and mouth was in Hebrew. Number two, the Greek gospels were changed - they are different - not only from the Hebrew but from each other.

There are approximately 100 surviving Hebrew manuscripts of all, or part of, **The Brit Hadashah** (*Hebrew New Covenant* - known to us as the *New Testament*). There are 5000 surviving Greek manuscripts. There are 10,000 surviving Latin manuscripts. There are (almost) zero versions of any of them which are identical. **The reality is that all of these manuscripts will have Hebrew elements - and all of them will all have Greek elements.** They will also have elements that come from other cultures they have passed through such as Latin or English. This is called "**Acculturation**."

The task of the Benai Emunah Institute has been to determine what degree of Hebrew or Greek elements are predominant in each manuscript and what they tell us. We do this by establishing "*markers*" of The Hebrew texts. An example of one such marker is Matthew 5:18, "Not one yod from Torah… will pass away." A *marker* says something in Hebrew that is not in the Greek.

Number three, most changes from the Hebrew to the Greek support the new doctrines. That is why *The New Covenant* in Hebrew is now called *The New Testament*. **The Greeks rejected Yehovah's Torah and His Covenant - deeming them 'dead legalism'!**

Some Arguments against *The Hebrew Gospels*

1) Divine providence has given us the New Testament in Greek.

Since the Greek Scriptures are given from God - the Hebrew Scriptures are not - therefore, the Hebrew is not authoritative. This is the basic premise of Replacement Theology, also called Supersessionism. In order to believe this, you must put more faith in Man than in God. *The Hebrew Gospel* was first. So, say all the church fathers.

2) The Hebrew Gospels are a myth! They don't exist.

Not according to the many early church fathers who commented upon them in writing - not a single one denied *The Hebrew Gospel*.

3) Any Hebrew Gospel manuscript is translated from Greek, or Latin.

There were no Greek or Latin converts to Yeshua the Messiah when *The Hebrew Gospel* was first written.

4) The Gospels were first written in Aramaic.

This is a 'red herring' - an argument that sends you off in the wrong direction - to a dead end! There is no evidence of Aramaic gospels before the fourth century.

5) No one in Israel spoke Hebrew anymore in the first century. The Israelites all spoke Greek. This is patently ridiculous, linguistically speaking!

6) All the Israelites spoke Aramaic.

True - but the Hebrews still spoke and wrote in Hebrew - as proven by the Dead Sea Scrolls from that period.

7) Yeshua and his Apostles quoted from the Greek Septuagint (the Greek O.T.) when citing the Old Testament.

Please, they would have been stoned - the Greeks were hated in Israel.

However, quotes from the Old Testament given in the New Testament are different! The name of God - YHVH - was scrubbed from the Greek N.T. Yeshua and his Apostles would never substitute the name of a Greek god for Yehovah - **It would not happen!**

In my books *Sons of Zion vs Sons of Greece* and *Messianic Church Arising!* - I have repudiated in detail all of these arguments. In this Editor's Commentary on Hebrew Matthew it is not appropriate to fight all these battles again point by point. I recommend the reader obtain those books for the complete story of The Hebrew Gospels and the survival of the Messianic Church throughout the centuries. I have summarized the arguments and included in the appendices the original discourse. These appendices are subject to updates - so they are provided digitally for free at: **https://revelationofthemonth.com/appendices**

Appendix D describes briefly all of the manuscripts used in this compilation of The Hebrew Book of Matthew, including where you can find them and some of their distinguishing Hebrew markers. The testimonies of the early church fathers are summarized in Appendix C. The all-important arguments proving the authenticity of The Hebrew Gospels as coming from a first century source are in Appendix B. Last, but not least, the evidence and history of the Name of God is in Appendix A.

Critical information on the names of Yehovah and Yeshua <u>on the next three pages</u> are inserted from our publication of ***The Hebrew Book of Revelation***:

In the Hebrew Cochin manuscript of Revelation 1:8,

יִהְיֶה	הֹוֶה	הָיָה	יְהֹוָה
Who will be	**Who is**	**Who was**	**Yehováh**

The name of Yehovah and His son Yeshua are both subjects of debate. The publication **of *The Hebrew Book of Revelation*** along with related research on the sacred Names should resolve that debate. Below are displayed the appearance of **the Sacred Name of Yehovah with correct vowel markings in ten manuscripts of <u>The Hebrew New Testament</u>!** It demonstrates the Messianic (Jewish-Christian) assemblies' desire to preserve and sanctify the true Name of Yehovah as directed by Yeshua in ***The Hebrew Gospels*** in John 17:6-26:

"I have manifested Your Name unto the men you have given me… I have declared unto them Your Name - and I will declare it!"

Editor's Commentary

This was fulfillment of the prophecy in Psalms 22:22,
"I will declare Your Name to my brethren!"

Thanks to Janice Baca for much of the work done on the Name of God.

Thanks to the work of Nehemia Gordon in the *Old Testament* and my own research in the *New Testament* - there should be no more question. Dr. Gordon has now discovered the Name of *Yehováh* with correct vowels in hundreds of manuscripts, thousands of times. But, ingrained views on such a heated debate seldom go away with the mere discovery of evidence. It has become an article of faith to many. Sooner or later, it will sort itself out. The evidence is now definitive.

The correct given name of *Yeshua*, in Hebrew, is also debated. Many scribes used the short (Aramaic) version *Yeshu*, while others attached the shortened root form of Yehovah's name *Yah*, or *Yahu*. This renders a variant name for Yeshua -*Yehoshua*. One has even used the Grecian form of the name Yeshua with a final Greek /s/ - *Yeshuas*.

The Hebrew Book of Matthew

Here is the breakdown of their usage in 20 Hebrew N.T. texts:

Manuscripts	Form	Hebrew
Freiburg 314, Neofiti 33, Augsburg, Yeates, Uppsala 31, Uppsala 32, Add.170, Shepreve 16.A.II, 2 Peter British Library, Vat Ebr 530, Udine Ebr 3, Marsaille MS 24-25	**Yeshua** used in 12 of 20 = **60%** manuscripts	יֵשׁוּעַ
Shem Tov Vat Ebr 101, Cambridge Oo.1.32, Guenzburg 363, Cambridge Oo.1.16.2, Matthew Russia Ms D101	**Yeshu** used in 5 of 20 mss =**25%**	יֵשׁוּ יְשׁוּ
Sloane Hazon 273, Paris 131	**Yehoshua** used in 2 of 20 mss =**10%**	יְהוֹשֻׁעַ
HGC Vat Ebr 100	**Yeshuas** used in 1 of 20 mss = **5%**	יֵשׁוּאַס

From Hazon & Cochin manuscripts Hebrew Revelation 1:8:

*"I am the Aleph and the Tav, the First and the Last -
says Yehovah Elohim - (Hazon Ms.)
Who is, Who was, and Who will be - the Almighty."
(Cochin Ms.)*

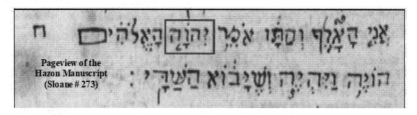

Pageview of the Hazon Manuscript (Sloane # 273)

The Hebrew text uses the name of God, **Yehovah**, with the correct vowel pointing - as do most Messianic texts.

The Battle Lines are Drawn

The establishment of the Greco-Roman Church by Constantine in the fourth century formed the battle lines between the Hebrew perspective and the Greek. The Greek Church and its descendants, including the Reformation churches, have all but obliterated the Hebrew perspective. Whatever the foundations of your faith -

Editor's Commentary

you deserve to know the original story! The return to the original Hebrew text only serves to strengthen faith not weaken it!

One example serves to illustrate these differences:

*"This is **my blood of the New Covenant** which is poured out for many..."* **Hebrew Matthew 26:28.**

*"This is **my blood of the New Testament**..."* **Greek Matthew 26:28**

In Jeremiah 31:31 it speaks of a New Covenant relationship between Yehovah and His followers. In Hebrew, the New Testament is called the ***Brit Hadashah*** - **The New Covenant.**

In the Greek text there is no **New Covenant** - it is called the **New Testament!**

And so the Torah (or Tanakh) - the ***Old Covenant*** - becomes the ***Old Testament*** in Greek. Without truly understanding the Covenant relationship between Yehovah and His followers - including Gentiles - the Bible is likely to be an undecipherable mystery to most.

There is a difference! A *Covenant* is a legally binding contract between God and His people - a *Testament* is not! The Greeks did not want to buy into the Torah with all of its strange laws and statutes. They came to describe the Torah as ***"dead legalism!"*** **But it is impossible to separate the Torah from the Covenant! The Covenant is an oath to obey the Torah.** Perhaps the main difference between a Testament and a Covenant is that one is not sworn to obey a Testament. The Greeks wanted to create their own doctrines. So, they changed the name of Yehovah to a Greek name (expressly forbidden in the Bible). They changed the name of His son to Greek. They rewrote the O.T. and N.T. to have their own Scripture. **That is how the Hebrew Covenant became a Greek Testament.** In modern times, many texts are going back to the original meaning of *Covenant* - a good first step!

The changes to ***Hebrew Matthew*** made by the Greco-Roman

church will be covered in the footnotes to the text. There are two major types of changes - changes made by mistake and changes made on purpose. Let us deal with mistakes first.

In the genealogy given in Matthew 1:17 - it concludes with,

> "So the generations from Abraham to David are fourteen generations - and from David until the exile into Babylon are fourteen generations, and from the exile in Babylon until Christ are fourteen generations" (Matthew 1:17).

This is a nice neat set of generations: 14, 14, 14. The problem is when you count the generations from the exile in Babylon to Yeshua the Messiah - there are only 13. Try it yourself - but remember that Joseph and Myriam are of the same generation and cannot be counted as two generations. In the **Hebrew** DuTillet and Munster manuscripts we have the generation of Avner (Abner)[1] included in the last set of names from the exile to the birth of Yeshua the Massiah - completing the final set of generations to 14.

This is clearly a scribal error, done by a lackadaisical scribe who simply made a mistake in translating it into Greek. However, that error has lasted almost two thousand years giving the lie to biblical accuracy for anyone who bothered to count the generations. Numerous times in the history of the Gospels, the Hebrew has provided correction to the Greek manuscripts. This is one of those times. Here is another:

Hebrew Matthew 11:12
"From the days of John, the Baptist until this day - **the kingdom of heaven is flashing forth in strength - and mighty men seize upon it!**"

Greek Matthew 11:12

---

[1] Also refer to: The Corrected King James Version: Matthew, 2nd ed., Kennedy, 2022, pp.80-85. Old Hebrew Matthew Gospel, Schonfield, 2014/1927, pp.26-29.

"And from the days of John the Baptist until now - **the kingdom of heaven suffers violence, and the violent take it by force!**"

So, Yehovah's kingdom of heaven is being taken over by violent men? **Really?** How did those violent men get into heaven to seize it? This is a reflection of earthly warfare not spiritual warfare.

"We are receiving a kingdom that cannot be shaken!" (Hebrews 12:28)

It also has no meaning within the context of the discourse about John the Baptist. This is simply very poor translation by the Greeks!

The "it" that is "flashing forth" is the "Light of the World" - Yeshua (John 1:1). This happened in the time of John the Baptist, in the immediate past. John is only six months older than Yeshua. Something has just begun. What did John do? John baptized Yeshua, beginning his ministry - releasing the "Light of the World" (Yeshua) bursting forth from the kingdom of heaven! Those mighty men of God that Yeshua had prepared (the disciples) seized upon it with joy, not violence. However, the mistakes continue to pile up.

In *Hebrew Matthew* 11:16,

"Who does this generation resemble? It resembles children sitting in the market - who call out to their friends (*to play*):"

Yeshua describes children at play who invent scenarios of war, weddings, festivals, or funerals and blow their toy flutes and dance, or sing, and all who come into their playground must play their childish games, even though their actions are imaginary. Yeshua is delivering a dramatic condemnation of the religious leaders of their generation. They are like children. "Behold! We sang to you and you did not dance!" Yeshua treated the priests' imaginary godly authority and feigned wisdom as childish games.

The priests, however, were deeply offended and gravely threatened that Yeshua would not play the game.

In *Hebrew Matthew* 11:19, Yeshua completes his metaphor of this generation and their leaders as foolish children by saying that whenever Yehovah sends his anointed ones, the priests condemn and persecute them - even kill them! The Hebrew parable ends with:

> **"Therefore, foolish children are judging the wise!"**
> **Hebrew Matthew 11:19**
> **"But wisdom is justified by her children." ???**
> **Greek Matthew 11:19**

Clearly the Greeks did not understand these Hebrew verses and by translating them badly - produced a nonsensical conclusion!

Purposeful Changes to the Greek Text

The second type of changes are purposeful. Most of these are very obvious - such as the substitution of words that no longer have a place in the new Greek doctrine. *Torah* being changed to *law* is a prime example. *Torah* is specific - *law* is ambiguous. Yeshua was a Torah teacher. In the Sermon on the Mount that is perfectly clear: Yeshua the Messiah said to his disciples,

> "Do not think - I came that I might destroy the **Torah** -
> or the prophets. I came not that I might fulfill *it* (the
> **Torah**) but rather that I might fill *it* (the **Torah**)
> to overflowing, *abundantly overflowing!*"
> *(Hebrew Matthew 5:17)*

> "Truly, I am telling you, until heaven and earth pass
> away - not one yod from **Torah**, nor even the tip of a
> yod, will pass away - until all of these words are carried
> out." (*Hebrew Matthew`5:18)*

Such a direct crystal-clear statement of Yeshua's purpose is dismantled with only two strokes. First, one must get rid of that pesky word *Torah*. The Greeks were not interested in following **Torah**. Done! - The word *Torah* is now "*law*" which mostly means whatever you want it to mean. Second, define the word "*fulfil*" to mean finish, end, complete. Not in this context -Yeshua's words specify it in the negative. **"I have not come to destroy!"** The mistranslation of this verse is then applied to all of God's royal law in the Bible. Thousands of verses are rendered moot at one stroke. Yeshua, it is claimed, has replaced the Old Covenant with the New Testament. **The law of God – Torah - is dead!** Of course, what happens in reality is that theologians cherry-pick the Old Testament. Take what you want and leave the rest. It leaves believers with a deeply schizophrenic church.

The Gentile Church is straddled between two archetypes: the Hebrew Yeshua the Messiah, a Messianic Rabbi who upholds Torah – and the Greek Jesus, the *Christ* - which means *anointed by God* – who has come to free us from the bondage of God's law - Torah!

The result, 2000 years of trying to get rid of the Hebrew Messiah and his Messianic followers so the Greek Christ can be the undisputed king - and the Greek doctrines the undisputed law - and the Greek Church the undisputed throne of God's kingdom on earth!

This is neither to diss - nor dismiss Jesus. Untold millions have been saved reaching out to that name. Praise God! Yeshua and Jesus are the same historical person. Their archetypes, however, are distinctively different. An archetype is our sense of who they are? What is their message? And what is the goal of their mission? For example, is the Messiah Hebrew or Greek? Was he sent to minister to all of us or only to the "lost sheep of Israel"? Was the Messiah's goal to create a new church and do away with the old one? You will find answers to many of these questions in the pages of ***The Hebrew Book of Matthew***.

Matthew 7:21-23 is just such an example. When the word "law" is substituted for "Torah" - then putting the Torah back in the N.T. yields some stunning reassessments.

> "Not all who say to me 'Lord, Lord', shall enter the kingdom of heaven... Many will say to me on that day, 'Lord, Lord, did we not prophesy in your name? - And in your name did we not cast out demons from men? - And in your name perform many mighty deeds?' "

> **"Then I myself shall profess to them, I never knew you! Depart from me -All you who are without Torah (law-less)!"**

For many Gentile readers this may be a bitter pill to swallow. We have been raised to believe Yeshua died to free us from the bondage of the law. In the words of Messianic author Daniel Gruber:

> The problem is that **Christianity - as a 'New Covenant Religion,'** has defined itself in opposition to the Jewish people for seventeen hundred years. All Jewishness has been removed from the major Church creeds. After countless attempts to annihilate the Jewish people and any connection with them - and after almost unceasing Catholic, Protestant, Orthodox, and Evangelical theological denunciation of the Jewish people and what God has given to them - Such an understanding of **Christianity is not possible!**[2]

So many believers today are recognizing the Hebraic Roots of their faith and making efforts to try and understand them.

> "You, being a wild olive, were grafted in among them (the chosen people) and became partaker with them of the rich root of the olive tree.' (Romans 11:17).

---

2   Gruber, Daniel. 2005: p.190, **Separation of Church & Faith**, vol 1. Elijah Publishing.

Were we grafted in for the purpose of destroying the tree? There are difficult questions on both sides of the divide that must be asked and answered by the true Word of the Messiah.

As a result, *The Hebrew Gospels* have become the most forbidden books in the history of humankind! It is not hard to understand that they go against Greek doctrine. Yeshua teaches the **Torah**!

> "You yourselves have heard what it said in the ancient **Torah**, 'You shall not commit adultery!'" (Hebrew Matthew 5:27).

Then Yeshua proceeds to fill the **Torah** to "overflowing, abundantly overflowing" by teaching the spirit of the law alongside the letter of the law.

> "But I tell you that anyone who would see a woman alone - in order to lust - has already committed the act of adultery in his heart." (Matthew 5:28).

> "The Torah says, 'Whosoever divorces his wife, must give to her a writ of divorce'" or else the husband as well as the wife become adulterers. (Matthew 5:33)

And so it continues, "You have heard that the **Torah** says, "An eye for an eye - and a tooth for a tooth!" This is guidance from Deuteronomy 19:21 on fair judgment for punishment. Yeshua puts it in context. In fighting with men in the earthly battle, a tit-for-tat is one thing. However, in fighting evil in the supernatural realm - supernatural entities cannot be killed by earthy weapons. They can only be defeated and bound by the light and love of God - His weapons of war!

> "The weapons we fight with are not the weapons of the world" (2 Corinthians 10:4).

Yeshua is correcting the oral Torah which interprets the verse in Deuteronomy out of context.

Related to this is Hebrew Matthew 5:43, Yeshua says,

"Moreover Yeshua said to his disciples, "You have heard the **Torah** says, 'You must love your neighbor as yourself - but hate your enemy!'

Yeshua is correcting the oral Torah again - because the written **Torah** does not say anywhere to "hate your enemy." In fact, kindness and fair treatment are called for in the written **Torah** - especially concerning captured enemies.

Commandments of Men

Yeshua had a running battle going on with the Pharisees concerning their oral Torah "takanot" *commandments of men* - which are proclaimed as the sacred word. Matthew 15:9, "They teach as tradition the commandments of men!" The Pharisees claimed secret wisdom passed down from Mount Sinai through the oral tradition of the sages. This oral Torah is said by them to be as accurate, and as sacred, as the written tradition. God had given it to them alone to interpret the true meaning of the word of God.

Yeshua is often taught to us as the epitome of meekness (which rhymes with weakness). I just watched a movie called *The Last Supper* where Yeshua was portrayed as a diminutive, somewhat delicate, and definitely meek personage who was terrified of the upcoming torture he must endure. When he goes before the high priest Caiphas he appears as bloody and beaten in both body and spirit.

Yeshua truly does have humility and a gentleness of heart and spirit - but there is another side to the Messiah. In the pages of *The Hebrew Book of Matthew* - Yeshua is fierce! He speaks truth to power with the absolute confidence there is nothing they can do that would stop the hard truths he is revealing to them.

In Matthew 23:2, it says
"The scribes and the Pharisees sit in Moses seat:"
In **Greek** Matthew 23:3, it says

"All therefore whatsoever <u>they</u> bid you observe, that observe and do; but do not ye after their works: for they say, and do not."

In **Hebrew** Matthew 23:3, it says

"**All that <u>Moses</u> taught you - guard it, do it, and make it happen!** The priests tell you to observe their commands - but do not follow them, because - the things they teach - they do not observe them."

The entire Chapter 23 of Matthew is a blistering condemnation of the Sadducees and Pharisees! **"Woe to you scribes and Pharisees - hypocrites!** you shut off the kingdom of heaven from men - You do not enter there yourselves, nor allow others to come in." (23:13). You steal widow's homes ...and for this reason you shall receive damnation!" (23:14) **Yet in the Greek version, you are told to obey these corrupt priests - who have just been damned to Hell by Yeshua - rather than obey Moses.**

Yeshua is only getting warmed up. He calls them evil-doers and gold-diggers, focusing on the trivial but ignoring the Torah - its judgement, grace and faith. They are posing as righteous but inside are the epitome of iniquity and corruption (23:27-28). They are putting heavy burdens on believers - burdens which they would not lift a finger to do themselves (23:4). They are guilty, in this generation, of spilling the blood of Yehovah's prophets just as their forefathers did.

They are fleeing the judgment of Hell and the house of Israel will be desolate, because the blood of the prophets then & now is upon their heads (23:31-38). They have slain Zachariah the father of John the Baptist. This is only made clear in *The Hebrew Gospel!*

In **Hebrew** Matthew 23:35, it says

"That upon you may come all the righteous blood shed upon the earth, from the blood of righteous Abel, **unto the blood of Zachariah, <u>blessed son</u>,** whom you slew between the sanctuary and the altar."

In **Greek** Matthew 23:35, it says

"**Unto the blood of Zacariah, <u>son of Berechiah</u>,** whom you slew between the sanctuary and the altar."

If we are speaking of **"Zachariah, blessed son"** then this incident is a blistering condemnation of this generation and its leaders, as well as the Greek translators, and even today's religious leaders. Clearly, this judgment is not simply against the Hebrew priests but all religious leaders, past and future - who manipulate and mislead believers and prevent them from entering heaven because they are leading them astray (23:13).

Can you see why religious leaders would want to mute that judgment?

However, if we are looking through the perspective of **"Zachariah, son of Berechiah,"** then this entire dialog is relegated to six hundred years previously. That is when the book of Zachariah was written, starting with the words **"Zachariah, son of Berechiah."** So Yeshua's profound judgment of the leaders of that generation - one of the most important chapters in the New Testament - is dismissed as no longer relevant to today's generation of leaders.

A couple of small tweeks are all it takes to nullify the entire chapter which is now often interpreted as referring only to the religious leaders six centuries before Yeshua.

The Hebrew Book of Matthew is replete with verses that add to our understanding of the Hebrew perspective taught from Yeshua's own Hebrew words. Regardless of your faith tradition - You have a right to know the true words of Yeshua from *The Hebrew Gospels*.

It should not be thought that I oppose the King James Version of the Bible. The KJV is the best, most used, and strongest exemplar of the Majority Text of the Bible which comes from the Received Text which I most certainly endorse. These Hebrew differences, however, were made so early in the history of Christianity - they predate even the best of the Roman Catholic and Greek Orthodox manuscripts of the Bible - from the fourth century - whereas *The Hebrew Gospel of Matthew* springs from the first century. (See

Appendices B & C.) This introduction is, of necessity, only the tip of the iceberg. The real treasure awaits you as you go through the verses of *The Hebrew Gospel of Matthew* one by one and compare then to the work of the Greeks.

Methodology of Translation

Whenever *The Hebrew Gospel* has new information to add to the Gospel - that is a treasure! For example, how many wise men were there - those who came to worship the young Messiah? Search your Greek-English Bible. It is not there. It is, however, in *The Hebrew Book of Matthew* 2:16, "When Herod saw that the **three** Magi scorned the king (*by not returning to report*) - he was very angry!" There are many more examples like this in *The Hebrew Book of Matthew*. Often enough a verse will include information or phrasing from two sources. This is the basic nature of a compilation. Take the best from all sources available. Sometimes the final translation will differ from the Greek because the Hebrew words, which came first, reveal a meaning which clearly makes more sense in the context.

All Bible translations are done by compilation. No single manuscript is perfect. Things are added or omitted. If a verse is omitted, should one leave it blank in the translation? Or should one look at other reliable manuscripts and use them to arrive at a complete translation? If something is added, should one consult other reliable versions to determine if it belongs or not? We believe researchers should cast their net wide enough to capture all of the elements of *The Hebrew Gospel* - rather than focus on a solitary source. To this end we have scoured the world to find and obtain all the extant manuscripts of *The Hebrew Gospels*. The result is the finest translation possible, inspired by the Holy Spirit and all the Messianic scribes who for two millennia have laid their lives on the line to protect the Word!

The Hebrew Book of Matthew

Preface to Hebrew Matthew
HGC Vat. Ebr. 100
Editor's Comments on Jerome's Preface - by Dr. Miles R. Jones

Jerome was born in Roman Dalmatia (now Croatia) in 340 AD. He was converted to Christianity in 366, and quickly became renowned for his intellect and prodigious accomplishments in translation and theological commentary. He became secretary to Pope Damasus and was commissioned by him to translate the entire Bible into Latin in 380 AD.

He read and wrote in Hebrew, Greek, and Latin.

He translated The Hebrew Gospel of Matthew into Greek and Latin. He called it "the authentic fountainhead of the Word" and cited the critical need to return to the source in view of the many corrupt versions of Scripture that were circulating in his day. He was widely criticized, even by Pope Damasus, for translating from the Hebrew rather than the Greek versions of the day.

Editor's Commentary

Jerome has been described as the "most ruthless of all the church fathers." He was briefly excommunicated due to his severe, often vitriolic, criticism of other shining stars of the Church such as Ambrose and Augustine, among many others. He was clearly a hater of men - as well as being a lover of books. He did not stray from Church doctrine. Jerome was famous for a defense of Mary, the mother of Yeshua - as a perpetual virgin - despite the fact she had several children. The Church claimed these as children of a previous marriage by her husband Joseph. Keep this in mind as you read his Preface.

Jerome's work, though focusing on religious topics, is not Holy Writ! It does not deserve the status of sacred and inerrant. He is clearly championing the doctrinal politics of the fourth century. The Hebrew Gospels predate Jerome's Preface and translation by centuries. So Jerome's work was done long after the original Hebrew manuscripts and reflect the acculturation of his times. Even so, Jerome's Preface, written in Hebrew - done at the time of his translation of The Hebrew Gospel into Latin - clearly states the Gospel of Matthew was originally written in the Lashon Ha Chodesh - the Holy Tongue (Hebrew).

When there are prefaces included in The Hebrew Gospel manuscripts - they also typically mention the Hebrew origin of the Gospel - a crucial fact that is always missing in Jerome's prefaces when published in Latin and Greek. This is the first time Jerome's Hebrew prefaces of Matthew (also Mark and Luke) will be published in English.

The Hebrew Book of Matthew

בס״ד אתחיל דא

ש׳ מתיאו   כאשר דרש ראשונה
              העוונגיאו הוא דיבר
להעתיק בנצור דרוש

לתילוס · כתב זה העוונגי׳ בלשון הקדש מן
בדין שינה ש׳ אחר · כן מייב דרוש אמונה
העיונגי׳ לקיים המצות עד היוס · (נש
שרגם כתבן והאיונגי׳ לבד ארצנה יש /
עדות אמת · כי הם הצדו מעונת השלש
באומנה חלק · העולם · ודרך ה׳אל היא בד׳
אופנים שנשאה דריסת האיונגי׳ · ויחם
אנשי שהיה כתב בד׳ מין מות הוברח שעתו
כנגד הרשעת · ונצבור זה היו האיונגי׳ ה׳
האחרים הבל שלא היו מקובלים · כי השם
איננו דויגד שהמספך למשלה אמור יהיה
מעגבד בעבור כח שבועשם · האיונן לישוש
נראים בד׳ אגרות · ואומנם הארס מייב
הבן מעם שדוחנות · מתיאו רומן יעירד
ארם · כי הוא נצר ראשונה מהעלרות ישו
משיח · מרקן יש לן יערך אריה · כי
רבר מעהתמיה · לוקא יש לן יערך
עגל · כי דבר מתעלדות השגי לים שמקריבים
הכהנים · יואן יש לן יעדת נשר · כי מעב
עצמת השבועות מעשין האלהות. ישאנ׳
משיח שמנעא הם מרבדים · אדם היה · איש
עלך מצבתו לה · עגל נקרב · אריה שקס חי
אחר מינתב · נשר שנטה לטמיס · כן אדם
דומי מעשות · עגל ולחית · אריה מלכות
נשר שבועת ענין האלהות :

Matthew Preface by Jerome
Hebrew Text Version (HTV)

¹ With the help of heaven, I will begin this. ² Saint Matthew, when he first preached the gospel, he wanted to copy it for the fallen ones, (the lost of Israel). ³ The evangelist (Matthew) wrote this in the holy tongue (Hebrew) as a memorial which he left for his brothers. ⁴ The true evangelical faith is needed to uphold the Scriptures against the heretics. ⁵ Although many wrote the Gospel - only four had the true testimony - because they spoke the faith of the Trinity in *these* four eternal Gospels.

⁶ The way of God is (*exemplified by*) four wheels that carry the message of the Gospel. ⁷ He (*Yehovah*) divided mankind into four apostate sects - *but evangelicals* (N.T. Gospel believers) were confirmed to carry God's favor - in their time. ⁸ For the sake of this, they were the evangelists of God - so the vain empty speech (*teachings*) of others were not accepted (*but rejected*).

⁹ Since God takes pleasure in that exalted number *(four)* - He said it (*the four Gospels*) shall be put forward and exalted for the sake of their powerful (*covenant)* promise. ¹⁰ The evangelists are seen in four ways - and one is obliged to understand what they represent.

¹¹ Matthew represents the shape of man - because he first spoke of the genealogy of Yeshua the Messiah. ¹² Mark has the image of a lion - because he spoke of the resurrection (*of the lion of Judah*). ¹³ Luke has the image of a calf - for he spoke regarding the calves that are offered by the priests over the generations. ¹⁴ John has the image of an eagle - because he wrote the sayings which are the words of the divine Yeshua the Messiah about whom they speak.

¹⁵ Adam (and the son of Adam - the son of Man) was a man born of a virgin - a calf sacrificed - a lion who rose up alive after his death - an eagle who went up to heaven. ¹⁶ The Son of Adam (Man) represents humanity - calf the priesthood - lion kingship - eagle the divine promise.

The Hebrew Book of Matthew

Matthew Preface: 1

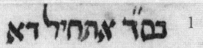

Hebrew Gospel from Catalonia - HGC Vat. Ebr. 100

(בסיעתא דשמיא) בס״ד אתחיל דא

HTV: With the help of heaven, I will begin this.

> Note: It is an ancient tradition among the orthodox, whether Jews or Messianics, to consecrate anything written - to God in heaven - by putting this acronym at the top of the page.

Matthew Preface: 2

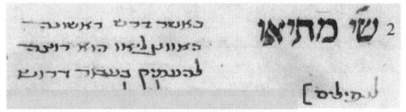

HGC Vat. Ebr. 100

ש׳ מתיאו כאשר דרש ראשונה האוונגליאו הוא רויצה להעתיק בעבור דרוש לנפילים

HTV: Saint Matthew, When he first preached the gospel, he wanted to copy it for the fallen ones,* *(the lost of Israel).*

> *Note: In Matthew 15:24, However, he (Yeshua) responded and said, "I was not sent - except to the lost sheep of the House of Israel."

Matthew Preface: 3

כתב זה האונגילי בלשון הקדש כמו זכרון שיניח לְ אחיו

HTV: The evangelist (Matthew) wrote this in the holy tongue* (Hebrew) as a memorial which he left for his brothers.

*Note: The "holy tongue" always refers to **Hebrew**. This is a *"marker"* of the Hebrew Gospel manuscripts. The Preface, when there is one, often mentions the Hebrew origin of the text.

Matthew Preface: 4

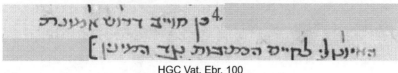

HGC Vat. Ebr. 100

כֵּן חוֹיב דרוש אמונת האיונגלי לקיים הכתיבות נגד חמינין

HTV: **The true evangelical faith is needed to uphold the Scriptures against the heretics.**

Note: **This Preface is not Holy Writ.** It is written by Jerome in the fourth century and clearly reflects the demands of the Greco-Roman Church which outlawed anything other than its own doctrines and language.

Matthew Preface: 5

ועם שֶׁרַבִּים כתבו האיונגלי לבד ארבעה יש עדות אמת

HTV: **Although many wrote the Gospel - only four had the true testimony - because they spoke the faith of the Trinity in *these* four eternal Gospels.***

*Note: Jerome is politicking for the decrees of the new church of Constantine in the fourth century - mandating the Trinity and the canon of only four Gospels - both brand new concepts.

Matthew Preface: 6

ודרך האל היא בד אופנים שנושאה דרישת האיונגלי

HTV: **The way of God is (*exemplified by*) four wheels that carry the message of the Gospel.**

Note: Jerome is using Ezekiel's wheel - his vision of the four faces of Yehovah as his justification for the canonization of these four gospels as the only authorized word of God. (See Ezk 1:1-21)

Matthew Preface: 7

HGC Vat. Ebr. 100

ויחז אנושי שהיה מת בד' מיני מות הוכדח שנותו בעד הרשתם.

HTV: **He (*Yehovah*) divided mankind into four apostate sects - *but evangelicals* (N.T. Gospel believers) were confirmed to carry God's favor - in their time.**

> Note: Jerome is commenting on those falling away from the true word - apostate sects which he does not elaborate upon.
>
> However, *The Dictionary of Biblical Imagery* specifies "There are at least four distinct images in Scripture of the concept of apostasy. All connote an intentional defection from the faith." These are called *dead* sects by Jerome below:

Matthew Preface: 8

ובעבורזהההיוהאיונגליהואחריםהבלשלאהיומקובלים

HTV: **For the sake of this, they were the evangelists of God - so the vain empty speech (*teachings*) of others were not accepted (*but rejected*).**

Matthew Preface: 9

כי השם איניט רוצה שהמספר למעלה אמוד יהיה מועבר בעבור כח שבועתם

HTV: **Since God takes pleasure in that exalted number (*four*) - He said it (*the four Gospels*) shall be put forward and exalted for the sake of their powerful (*covenant*) promise.**

Matthew Preface: 10

האיונגלישטש נראים בד' צורות ואותם האדם חייב הבין מה שרומזות

HTV: **The evangelists are seen in four ways - and one is obliged to understand what they represent.**

> Note: These are the four images of the faces of God in Ezekiel's wheel, his vision of the Almighty.

Matthew Preface: 11

מתיאו רומז צורת אדם כי הוא דבר ראשוכה מתולדות ישו משיח.

HTV: **Matthew represents the shape of man - because he first spoke of the genealogy of Yeshua the Messiah.**

Matthew Preface: 12

מרקו יש לו צורת אריה כי דבר מהתחיה.

HTV: **Mark has the image of a lion - because he spoke of the resurrection (*of the lion of Judah*).**

> Note: The reference is to Yeshua - the Lion of Judah who rose from the dead after crucifixion.

Matthew Preface: 13

לוקא יש לו צורת עגל - כי דיבר מתולדות העגלים שמקריבים הכהנים.

HTV: **Luke has the image of a calf - for he spoke regarding the calves that are offered by the priests over the generations.**

Matthew Preface: 14

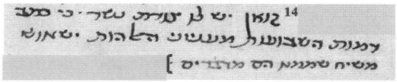

HGC Vat. Ebr. 100

The Hebrew Book of Matthew

זואן יש לו צורת נשר - כי כתב דמות השבועות מעשני האלוהות ישואש משיח שממנו הם מדברים.

HTV: **John has the image of an eagle - because he wrote the sayings which are the words of the divine Yeshua the Messiah about whom they speak.**

> Note: The Messianic Church accepted these new doctrines - but to no avail. They were considered competition by the new church and **declared heretic**. By the end of the fourth century any Scripture in Hebrew was heresy. It was called *Judaizing* - and ***Judaizing* was punishable by death.**

Matthew Preface: 15

אדם היה איש נולד מבתולה עגל נקרב אריה שקם חי אחר מיתתו נשר שעלה לשמים.

HTV: **Adam* (& the son of Adam - the son of Man) was a man born of a virgin - a calf sacrificed - a lion who rose up alive after his death - an eagle who went up to heaven.**

> *Note: Adam in Hebrew also means "man" since Adam was the first man. So, the *son of Adam* is also the *son of Man*. The genealogical factor is primary here. Adam was disobedient to God. It required the son of Adam to come - the son of Man (Yeshua) who was without sin to sacrifice himself to put us back in right standing with Yehovah. Without that knowledge - verses like this tend to get lost in translation.

Matthew Preface: 16

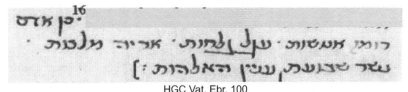

HGC Vat. Ebr. 100

בן אדם רומז אנושות - עגל גלחות - אריה מלכות - נשר שבועת עניין האלהות.

HTV: **The Son of Adam (Man) represents humanity - calf the priesthood - lion kingship - eagle the divine promise.**

Matthew Chapter 1

קפיטולו ראשון כפי ש׳ מתיאן׳

¹ The First Chapter According to Saint Matthew: This is the book of the generations of the Messiah - son of David - son of Abram.

² Abram fathered Isaac, Isaac fathered Jacob, Jacob fathered Judah and his brothers.

³ Judah fathered Peres and Zerah from Tamar - Peres fathered Chetsron, Chetsron fathered Aram.

⁴ Aram fathered Aminadab, Aminadab fathered Nahshon, Nahshon fathered Salmon.

⁵ Salmon fathered Boaz from Rahab, Boaz fathered Obed, Obed fathered Jesse.

⁶ Jesse fathered David King of Israel, David King of Israel fathered Solomon from the wife of Uriah.

⁷ Solomon fathered Rehoboam, Rehoboam fathered Aviah, Aviah fathered Asha.

⁸ Asha fathered Jehosaphat, Jehosaphat fathered Joram, Joram fathered Uzziah.

⁹ Uzziah fathered Jotash, Jotash fathered Ahab, Ahab fathered Hezekiah.

¹⁰ Hezekiah fathered Manasseh; Manasseh fathered Amon; Amon fathered Josiah.

¹¹ Josiah fathered Jeconias and his brothers in the Babylonian exile.

¹² And his brother in exile in Babylon - Jeconias fathered Shealthiel, Shealthiel fathered Zerubabel.

¹³ Zerubbabel begat Abihud; Abihud begat

Avner; Avner begat Eliakim; Eliakim begat Azzur;

¹⁴ Azor fathered Zadok, Zadok fathered Achim, Achim fathered Elihud.

¹⁵ Eliud fathered Eliezar, Eliezar fathered Nathan, Nathan fathered Jacob.

¹⁶ Jacob fathered Joseph, betrothed of Myriam (Mary), from whom was born Yeshua who is called Messiah.

¹⁷ Therefore, all the generations from Abram to David are 14 (generations), and from that time until the Babylonian exile *are* 14 (generations), and from the Babylonian exile to Yeshua *are* 14 (generations).

¹⁸ And the genealogy of Yeshua the Messiah was this: When Yeshua the Messiah had come to pass, the mother of Yeshua the Messiah - Miriam, betrothed of Joseph, in the name of God - before they came together - she conceived by the Holy Spirit.

¹⁹ Joseph, being righteous, did not want to hand her over - as an unmarried female - *to be put* to death! For a time, she went into hiding. Going secretly, she left.

²⁰ While he considered this, the angel of God appeared to Joseph in a dream and said, "Joseph, son of David, fear not to take Myriam as your wife - she has conceived and become pregnant by the Holy Spirit."

²¹ And she shall give birth to a son, and call his name Yeshua (salvation) because he will save (*yoshia*) his people from their sins.

²² All this was done to fulfill the spoken word of God (El) which He spoke through the hand (*voice*) of the prophet.

²³ Behold! A virgin shall conceive and give birth to a singular son - and his name shall be Immanuel - meaning: "Yehovah *is* with us."

²⁴ When Joseph arose from his dream, he did that which the angel of God had commanded - and he took (Myriam) *as* his wife.

²⁵ And he (Joseph) did not know her (Myriam) until she gave birth to the son, and he called him Yeshua.

Matthew Chapter 1
HTV with translator notes and KJV comparison

Matthew 1:1

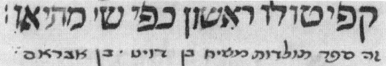
HGC Vat. Ebr. 10

קפיטולו ראשון כפישי מתיאו זה ספר תולדות משיח בן דויט בן אבראם.

HTV: The First Chapter According to Saint Matthew: This is the book of the generations of the Messiah - son of David - son of Abram.

KJV: The book of the generation of Jesus Christ, the son of David, the son of Abraham.

Matthew 1:2

אבראם הוליד ישאק ישאק הוליד יקוף יקוף הוליד יודא ואת אחיו.

HTV: Abram fathered Isaac, Isaac fathered Jacob, Jacob fathered Judah and his brothers.

KJV: Abraham begat Isaac, and Isaac begat Jacob, and Jacob begat Judas and his brethren.

Matthew 1:3

יודא הוליד פרש וזרא מתמר פרש הוליד חצרון חצרון הוליד אראם.

HTV: Judah fathered Peres and Zerah from Tamar - Peres fathered Chetsron, Chetsron fathered Aram.

KJV: And Judas begat Phares and Zara of Thamar; and Phares begat Esrom; and Esrom begat Aram;

37

The Hebrew Book of Matthew

Matthew 1:4

אראם הוליד אמינדאף אמינדאף הוליד נאשון נאשון הוליד שלמון.

HTV: **Aram fathered Aminadab, Aminadab fathered Nahshon, Nahshon fathered Salmon.**

KJV: And Aram begat Aminadab; and Aminadab begat Naasson; and Naasson begat Salmon;

Matthew 1:5

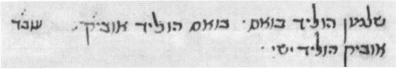

HGC Vat. Ebr. 100

שלמון הוליד בואז בואז הוליד עובד עובד הוליד ישי.

HTV: **Salmon fathered Boaz from Rahab, Boaz fathered Obed, Obed fathered Jesse.**

Note: The mention of Rahab is in every Hebrew manuscript, except the HGC. Rahab is described as an innkeeper. She is not described as a "*harlot*" in the vast majority of Hebrew manuscripts of the New Testament. For example, the George Howard translation of the Shem Tov Manuscript is taken from eight extant Hebrew versions.

Six of the eight say " Rabab" whereas only the two from the Bodleian Library say "Rahab the harlot." So the translation from Eusebius, "Rahab the harlot," in the fourth century which supposedly came from the Greek Septuagint is not backed up by the vast majority of Hebrew mss of the Matthew genealogy, nor is it in the King James version of the Bible.

KJV: And Salmon begat Booz of Rachab; and Booz begat Obed of Ruth; and Obed begat Jesse;

Matthew 1:6

HGC Vat. Ebr. 100

ישי הוליד דויט דויט מלך ישרא דויט מלך ישרא הוליד שלמה מאשת אוריאש.

HTV: **Jesse fathered David King of Israel, David King of Israel fathered Solomon from the wife of Uriah.**

KJV: And Jesse begat David the king; and David the king begat Solomon of her *that had been the wife* of Urias;

Matthew 1:7

שלמה הוליד רחבעם רחבעם הוליד אביה אביה הוליד אשא.

HTV: **Solomon fathered Rehoboam, Rehoboam fathered Aviah, Aviah fathered Asha.**

KJV: And Solomon begat Roboam; and Roboam begat Abia; and Abia begat Asa.

Matthew 1:8

אשא הוליד יושפט יושפט הוליד יורם. יורם הוליד עוזיה.

HTV: **Asha fathered Jehosaphat, Jehosaphat fathered Joram, Joram fathered Uzziah.**

KJV: And Asa begat Josaphat; and Josaphat begat Joram; and Joram begat Ozias;

Matthew 1:9

אוזיאש הוליד יותאש יותאש הוליד אקאז אקאז הוליד איזקיאש.

HTV: **Uzziah fathered Jotash, Jotash fathered Ahab, Ahab fathered Hezekiah.**

KJV: And Ozias begat Joatham, and Joatham begat Achaz, and Achaz begat Ezekias;

Matthew 1:10

חזקיה הוליד מנשיש מנשיש הוליד אמון אמון חזקיה יאשיה.

HTV: **Hezekiah fathered Manasseh; Manasseh fathered Amon; Amon fathered Josiah.**

KJV: And Ezekias begat Manasses; and Manasses begat Amon; and Amon begat Josias;

Matthew 1:11

יאשיה הוליד יקוניאש ואחיו בגלות בבל.

HTV: **Josiah fathered Jeconias and his brothers in the Babylonian exile.**

KJV: And Josias begat Jechonias and his brethren, about the time they were carried away to Babylon:

Matthew 1:12

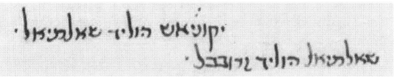
HGC Vat. Ebr. 100

ואחיו בגלות בבל יקוניאש הוליד שאלתיאל שאלתיאל הוליד זרובבל.

HTV: **And his brother in exile in Babylon - Jeconias fathered Shealthiel, Shealthiel fathered Zerubabel.**

KJV: And after they were brought to Babylon, Jechonias begat Salathiel; and Salathiel begat Zorobabel;

Matthew 1:13

זרובבל הוליד אביאוט אביאוט הוליד אבנר אבנר הוליד אליקים אליקים הוליד אזור.

HTV: **Zerubbabel begat Abihud; Abihud begat <u>Avner</u>; <u>Avner</u>* begat Eliakim; Eliakim begat Azzur;**

> Note: Greek -English Bibles have only 13 generations between the Exile and the birth of Yeshua. The Hebrew DuTillet and Munster **Hebrew mss. read Avner (Abner)** as the missing name which completes the number of 14 generations. See Matthew 1:17 where they are all counted.
>
> Also refer to: The Corrected King James Version: Matthew, 2nd ed, Kennedy, 2022, pp80-85. Old Hebrew St. Matthew's Gospel, Schonfield, 2014/1927, pp26-29. Which validate the Hebrew.

KJV: And Zorobabel begat Abiud; and Abiud begat Eliakim; and Eliakim begat Azor;

Matthew 1:14

אזור הוליד צדוק צדוק הוליד אקים אקים הוליד אליאוט.

HTV: **Azor fathered Zadok, Zadok fathered Achim, Achim fathered Elihud.**

KJV: And Azor begat Sadoc; and Sadoc begat Achim; and Achim begat Eliud;

Matthew 1:15

HGC Vat. Ebr. 100

אליאוט הוליד אלעזר אלעזר הוליד נתן נתן הוליד יקוף.

HTV: **Eliud fathered Eliezar, Eliezar fathered Nathan, Nathan fathered Jacob.**

KJV: And Eliud begat Eleazar; and Eleazar begat Matthan; and Matthan begat Jacob;

Matthew 1:16

יקוף הוליד יושאף ארוז מרים שממנה נולד ישאוש שקרוי משיח.

HTV: **Jacob fathered Joseph, betrothed of Myriam (Mary), from whom was born Yeshua who is called Messiah.**

KJV: And Jacob begat Joseph the husband of Mary, of whom was born Jesus, who is called Christ.

Matthew 1:17

HGC Vat. Ebr. 100

אם כן כל תולדות מאברם עד דויט הם יד׳ ומדוד עד בבל הם יד׳ ומגלות בבל עד ישוש יד׳.

HTV: **Therefore, all the generations from Abram to David are 14 (generations), and from that time until the Babylonian exile** *are* **14 (generations), and from the Babylonian exile to Yeshua** *are* **14 (generations).**

> Note: Count the three sets of generations in your Bible - you will find they number 14, 14, & 13, Myriam and Joseph are a single generation not two generations. The "lost" generation is not lost in the Hebrew, **which includes Avner** (Mt.1:13) to complete the final set of 14 generations.

> Note 2: Papias in the 2nd century wrote that ***The Gospel according to the Hebrews*** were the *Logia,* 'sayings' or proverbs of Yeshua. In the Shem Tov and the HGC every time his name is mentioned or Yeshua says something - a new chapter is begun to highlight whatever he says. The verse and chapter number we are used to in our modern N.T. are in the margin to the left.

KJV: So all the generations from Abraham to David *are* fourteen generations; and from David until the carrying away into Babylon *are* fourteen generations; and from the carrying away into Babylon unto Christ *are* fourteen generations.

Matthew 1:18

ותולדת ישואש משיח היתה זאת וכאשר אם ישועש משיח היתה ארוסה זאת היא מריאה ויוסף טרם השם התחברם היא הרתה מהקדש רוח.

HTV: And the genealogy of Yeshua the Messiah was this: When Yeshua the Messiah had come to pass, the mother of Yeshua the Messiah - Miriam, betrothed of Joseph, in the name of God - before they came together - she conceived by the Holy Spirit.

KJV: Now the birth of Jesus Christ was on this wise: When as his mother Mary was espoused to Joseph, before they came together, she was found with child of the Holy Ghost.

Matthew 1:19

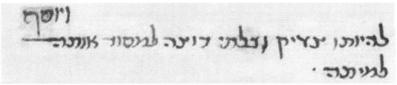

HGC Vat. Ebr. 100

Chapter 1

ויוסף להיותו צדיק לבלתי רוצה למסור אותה למיתה ורוצה לכת בהחבא עזבה.

HTV: Joseph, being righteous, did not want to hand her over - as an unmarried female - *to be put* to death! For a time, she went into hiding. Going secretly, she left.

> Note: This is one of the significant differences between the Greek and Hebrew Gospel. The ultimate penalty for adultery, even among the betrothed, was being stoned to death. It was the same for men or women although I doubt that it was applied equally. The Greeks had little restraint, or shame, in sexual matters. They could not comprehend the Hebrew perspective. Myriam goes, privately, to Elisheva as Gabriel had told Myriam of her miraculous pregnancy.

KJV: Then Joseph her husband, being a just *man*, and not willing to make her a public example, (*put her to shame*) was minded to put her away privily.

Matthew 1:20

ובעיד היותו מחשב זה מלאך השם נראה אל יוסף בחלום אמר יושאף בן דויט אל תירא לקחת מרים אשתך מי מה שהרתה הרתה מרוח קדש.

HTV: While he considered this, the angel of God appeared to Joseph in a dream and said, "Joseph, son of David, fear not to take Myriam as your wife - she has conceived and become pregnant by the Holy Spirit."

KJV: But while he thought on these things, behold, the angel of the Lord appeared unto him in a dream, saying, Joseph, thou son of David, fear not to take unto thee Mary thy wife: for that which is conceived in her is of the Holy Ghost.

Matthew 1:21

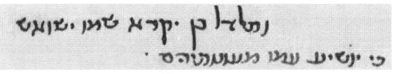

HGC Vat. Ebr. 100

ותלדו בֵן יקרא שמו ישועש כי יושיע עמו מעואתיהם.

The Hebrew Book of Matthew

HTV: **And she shall give birth to a son, and call his name Yeshua (salvation) because he will save*** (*yoshia*) **his people from their sins.**

> *Note: This is called **perinamosia** - when a sentence uses two words from the same root word. In this case, ישוע *Yeshua* which means **salvation**, and יושיע *yoshia* which means "*he will save*." It is internal rhyme meant to be both beautiful and memorable. It is also a marker of Hebrew origin as most perinamosia is lost in translation - as below in the KJV.

KJV: And she shall bring forth a son, and thou shalt call his name JESUS: for he shall save his people from their sins.

Matthew 1:22

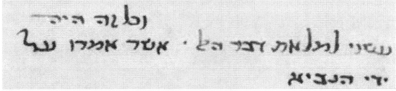
HGC Vat. Ebr. 100

וכל זה היה עשוי למלאת דבר האל אשר אמרו על ידי הנביא.

HTV: **All this was done to fulfill the spoken word of God (El) which He spoke through the hand (*voice*) of the prophet.**

> Note: "By the hand of" is a misunderstood Hebrew idiom meaning "by the actions" of the prophet, which includes his actions, voice and his written words.

KJV: Now all this was done, that it might be fulfilled which was spoken of the Lord by the prophet, saying,

Matthew 1:23

HGC Vat. Ebr. 100

הנה העלמה תהר ויולדת בן אחד ויהיה שמו עמנואל רל השם יהיה עמנו.

HTV: **Behold! A virgin shall conceive and give birth to a singular son - and his name shall be Immanuel - meaning: "Yehovah *is* with us."**

Note: The words *ben ehad* בן אחד mean a *singular son* - in the sense of special, unlike any other. See Isaiah 7:14, often times spelled Emmanuel in English.

KJV: Behold, a virgin shall be with child, and shall bring forth a son, and they shall call his name Emmanuel, which being interpreted is, God with us.

Matthew 1:24

וכאשר קם יוסף מחלומו עשה כאשר צוה מלאך האל ויקח אשתו.

HTV: **When Joseph arose from his dream, he did that which the angel of God had commanded - and he took (Myriam) *as* his wife.**

KJV: Then Joseph being raised from sleep did as the angel of the Lord had bidden him, and took unto him his wife:

Matthew 1:25

שעושי תארק אוהו ןבה הדליש דע העדי אלו.

HTV: **And he (Joseph) did not know her (Myriam) until she gave birth to the son, and he called him Yeshua.**

KJV: And knew her not till she had brought forth her firstborn son: and he called his name JESUS.

Matthew Chapter 2
Hebrew Text Version (HTV)

[1] When Yeshua was born in Bethlehem, in the land of Judea, in the days of King Herod - behold! Messengers (ambassadors) from the East came to Jerusalem,

[2] Saying, "Where is the king of the Jews who was born - because

we ourselves saw his star in the east - and we came, with offerings, to bow before him!"

³ And it came to pass, when Herod heard their words, he was alarmed, and every man of Jerusalem with him.

⁴ He (Herod) gathered all his chief priests and wise men of the people - and asked them (the messengers) with great diligence - the time when the star (birth of the Messiah) appeared to them.

⁵ They (the wise men) said, "in Bethlehem, of Judah - so it was written by the prophet…"

⁶ "You, Bethlehem, in Judah, are not insignificant among the thousands of Judah. From you (Bethlehem) to Me (Yehovah) a king will come forth and be a shepherd (Messiah) to my people Israel."

⁷ Then Herod secretly called the magicians and wisemen (from afar) and learned from them at what time a star had appeared to them.

⁸ He (Herod) sent them away to Bethlehem, and he said to them, "Go inquire carefully about the young boy to know (where he is), and when you find him whom you seek, return to me that I may go to worship before him."

⁹ When they heard the king›s words, they went their way and going before them was the star they saw in the east, until it stood *still* over the place where the (boy) child was.

¹⁰ When they saw the star, they rejoiced with great joy!

¹¹ And they came to the house - and found the boy with Mary his mother - and they bowed before him, and opened their treasures, and gave him gold, frankincense, and myrrh.

¹² And the angel warned them not to return to Herod - so they returned to their kingdom by another route.

¹³ After their (the wisemen) departure - the angel of God (EL) appeared in a dream to Joseph, and told him "Get up and take the child and his mother and flee to Egypt (Mitsrayim) and stay there until I come to you - because Herod will want the boy *in order* to destroy him."

¹⁴ Then he (Joseph) got up in the night, took the child and his mother, and went to Egypt (Mitzraim).

¹⁵ and he remained there until the death of Herod - to fulfill the word of God (EL), who said through the prophet, "I myself

Chapter 1

called my son out of Egypt (Mitzraim)."

¹⁶ When Herod saw that they (the wisemen) scorned the king *(by not returning to report)* - he was very angry - and ordered *his soldiers* to kill all the male children in Bethlehem and all the surrounding areas since the child was born according to the time he asked of the wisemen.

¹⁸ "And loud voices of weeping and crying out could be heard in Ramah - Rachel was crying for her sons and did not take comfort because they are gone."

¹⁹ And when Herod died - the angel of Yehovah appeared to Joseph in a dream *while* in Egypt (Mitzrayim).

²⁰ He (the angel) said to him (Joseph), "Get up and take the child and his mother and go to the Land of Israel - because the one who wanted to kill the boy is dead."

²¹ And he (Joseph) got up and took the child and his mother and went to the Land of Israel.

²² And it came to pass when he (Joseph) heard that Archelaus was ruling in place of Herod, his father, in the land of Judea - he was afraid to go there and was warned in a dream to go to the land of Galilee.

²³ And he sojourned in the province of Nazareth - so that the prophecy which said - "he will be called Nazarene" - would be fulfilled.

Matthew Chapter 2
HTV with translator notes and KJV comparison

Matthew 2:1

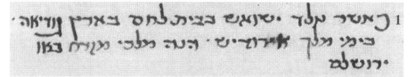

HGC Vat. Ebr. 100

כאשר נולד ישואש בבית לחם - בארץ *גודיאה - בימי מלך
אירודיש - הנה מלכי מזרח באו ירושלם

The Hebrew Book of Matthew

HTV: **When Yeshua was born in Bethlehem, in the land of Judea, in the days of King Herod - behold! Messengers* (ambassadors) from the East came to Jerusalem,**

> Note: These were not *kings* as it is commonly translated. The same root word מלך (*MLK*) can mean **angel, messenger, or king**. A messenger of God is often an angel. Kings base their authority on the "divine right of kings." That is to say, I (the king) have authority over you because I am the messenger - the very voice - of God. In this case, the word **ambassadors** would be more appropriate. In fact, they were descendants of Daniel's astronomers, called Magi.

KJV: Now When Jesus was born in Bethlehem of Judea in the days of Herod the king, behold, Now behold, there came wise men from the east to Jerusalem,

Matthew 2:2

אומרים אנה הוא מלך היהודים שנולד כי אנחנו ראינו כוכבו במזרח ובאנו עם מנחות

HTV: **Saying, "Where is the king of the Jews who was born - because we ourselves saw his star in the east - and we came, with offerings, to bow before him!"**

KJV: Saying, where is he that is born King of the Jews? For we have seen his star in the east, and are come to worship him.

Matthew 2:3

ויהי כשמוע אירודש דבריהם עמד נבהל וכל אנושי ירושלם עמו

HTV: **And it came to pass, when Herod heard their words, he was alarmed, and every man of Jerusalem with him.**

KJV: When Herod the king had heard *these things*, he was troubled, and all Jerusalem with him.

Matthew 2:4

יקבץ 4
כל ראשי כהנים וסופרים של העם וישאל להם היכן נולד
משיח :

Gaster Ms. 1616

Chapter 2

וקבץ כל ראשי כהנים וסופרים של העם ושאל להם היכן נולד משיח

HTV: He (Herod) gathered all his chief priests, scribes and wise men of the people - and asked them (the Magi) with great diligence - the time when the star* (signaling the birth of the Messiah) appeared to them.

*Note: The "King" star (Jupiter) was the brightest star (actually a planet) in the sky and the obvious choice as the harbinger of the coming king.

KJV: And when he had gathered all the chief priests and scribes of the people together, he demanded of them where Christ should be born.

Matthew 2:5

נישיח ׃ 5. הם אמרו בבית לחם דיהודה וכך כתיב בנביא ׃

Gaster Ms. 1616

הם אמרו בבית לחם דיהודה וכן כתיב בנביא

HTV: They (the wise men) said, "in Bethlehem, of Judah - so it was written by the prophet…"

Note: This was the prophecy of Micah 5:2, see notes in following verses.

KJV: They said to him, in Bethlehem of Judea: for thus it is written by the prophet,

Matthew 2:6

ואתה בית לחם של יהודה לא *היות צעיר באלפי יהורה ממך לי
יצא מלך ומרעה לעמי ישראל

HTV: "You, Bethlehem, in Judah, are not insignificant among the thousands of Judah. From you (Bethlehem) to Me (Yehovah) a king will come forth and be a shepherd (Messiah) to my people Israel."

KJV: And thou Bethlehem, in the land of Judea, art not the least among the princes of Judea: for out of thee shall come a Governor, that shall rule Israel.

49

Matthew 2:7

Gaster Ms. 1616

ועתה הרודס בסתר קרא לחרטומים וחכמים ולמד מהם באיזה זמן נראה להון כוכב

HTV: Then Herod secretly called the Magi (wisemen) and learned from them at what time a star had appeared to them.

> Note: Daniel had studied the stars and these wisemen/magicians were the descendants of his disciples tasked with a multi-generational mission, after the rebuilding of Jerusalem, which was accomplished by Herod, they were to watch for a star prophesying the birth of the King of the Jews. These men were astronomers, often called magicians in biblical and ancient records.

KJV: Then Herod, when he had privily called the wise men, inquired of them diligently what time the star appeared.

Matthew 2:8

וישלחם לבית לחם ויאמר להם לכו שאלו מהילד בתבונה ובדעת וכמוצאכם אותו שובו אל מפני שאלך והשתחות לפניו

HTV: He (Herod) sent them away to Bethlehem, and he said to them, "Go inquire carefully about the young boy to know (where he is), and when you find him whom you seek, return to me that I may go to worship before him."

KJV: And he sent them to Bethlehem, and said, Go and search diligently for the young child, and when ye have found him, bring me word again, that I may come and worship him also.

Matthew 2:9

HGC Vat. Ebr. 100

ובשומעם דברי המלך הלכו לדרכם והיה הולך לפניהם הככב
אשר ראו במזרח עד שעמד על המקום אשר הילד שם

HTV: **When they heard the king's words, they went their way and going before them was the star they saw in the east, until it stood *still* over the place where the (boy) child was.**

*Note: The "King" star (Jupiter) went into retrograde motion appearing to stand still for some time. This happened December 25 of 2 BC according to our analysis of the Star of Bethlehem in *Sons of Zion vs Sons of Greece*, p.128. It appeared to the east of Bethlehem low on the horizon.

KJV: When they had heard the king, they departed; and, lo, the star, that they saw in the east, went before them, til it came and stood over where the child was.

Matthew 2:10

וכראותם הככב שמחו שמחה גדולה

HTV: **When they saw the star, they rejoiced with great joy!**

KJV: When they saw the star, they rejoiced with exceeding great joy.

Matthew 2:11

ויבאו בבית וימצאו הילד עם מריאה אמו וישתחוו לפניו ויפתחו
אוצרותיהם ויתנו לו זהב ולבונה ומירא

HTV: **And they came to the house - and found the boy with Mary his mother - and they bowed before him, and opened their treasures, and gave him gold, frankincense, and myrrh.**

KJV: When they were come into the house, they saw the young child with Mary his mother, and fell down; and worshiped him: and when they had opened their treasures, they presented unto him gifts; gold, frankincense, and myrrh.

Matthew 2:12

והמלאך הזהירם שלא ישובו לאירודיש וישובו למלכותם בדרך
אחרת

HTV: **And the angel warned them not to return to Herod - so, they returned to their kingdom by another route.**

KJV: And being warned of God in a dream that they should not return to Herod, they departed into their own country another way.

Matthew 2:13

HGC Vat. Ebr. 100

ואחרי שובם נראה מלאך השם בחלום אל יוסף ויאמר לו קום ולקחת הילד ואמו וברחת למצרים וישבת שם עד בואי אליך כי עתיד הוא שאירודיש ירצה הילד להכבידו

HTV: **After their (the Magi's) departure - the angel of God (EL) appeared in a dream to Joseph, and told him "Get up and take the child and his mother and flee to Egypt (Mitzrayim) and stay there until I come to you - because Herod will want the boy** *in order* **to destroy him."**

KJV: And when they were departed, behold, the angel of the Lord appeareth to Joseph in a dream, saying, Arise, and take the young child and his mother, and flee into Egypt, and be thou there until I bring thee word: for Herod will seek the young child to destroy him.

Matthew 2:14

אז קם ניקח הילד ואמו לילה וילך למצרים

HTV: **Then he (Joseph) got up in the night, took the child and his mother, and went to Egypt (Mitzraim).**

KJV: When he arose, he took the young child and his mother by night, and departed into Egypt:

Chapter 2

> ויעמוד שם עד מות אירודיש למלאת דבר האל שאמר על־ידי
>
> *HGC Vat. Ebr. 100*

ויעמוד שם עד מות אירודיש למלאת דבר האל שאמר על־ידי הנביא אני קראתי לבני ממצרים

HTV: and he remained there until the death of Herod - to fulfill the word of God (EL), who said through the prophet, "I myself called my son out of Egypt (Mitzraim)."

Note: Hosea 11:1 "When Israel was a child I loved him - and out of Egypt I called my son." Also Numbers 24:8.

KJV: and was there until the death of Herod: that it might be fulfilled which was spoken of the Lord by the prophet, saying, Out of Egypt have I called my son.

Matthew 2:16

ויהי כראות אירודש שהלעיגו ממט שלשת המלכים היה מאד כעוז וצוה להמית כל הילדים הנמצאים בבית לחם ואת כל הסביבות מעת שהילד היה צוד לפי הזמן ששאל למלכים

HTV: When Herod saw that <u>the three Magi</u> scorned the king *(by not returning to report)* - he was very angry - and ordered *his soldiers* to kill all the male children in Bethlehem and all the surrounding areas since the child was born according to the time he asked of the Magi.

KJV: Then Herod, when he saw that he was mocked of the wise men, was exceeding wroth, and sent forth, and slew all the children that were in Bethlehem, and in all the coasts thereof, from two years old and under, according to the time which he had diligently enquired of the wise men.

Matthew 2:17

אז נשלם מה שאמר ירמיה הנביא

53

The Hebrew Book of Matthew

HTV: Then it was fulfilled what Jeremiah the prophet spoke,

KJV: Then the word was completed that Yermiyahu (Jeremiah) the prophet said,

Matthew 2:18

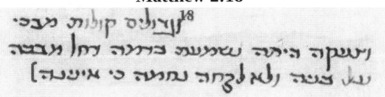

HGC Vat. Ebr. 100

וגדולים קולות מבכי וצעקה היתה נשמעת ברמה רחל מבכה על בניה ולא לקחה נחמה כי אינינה

HTV: "And loud voices of weeping and crying out - could be heard in Ramah - Rachel was crying for her sons and did not take comfort because they are gone."

> Note: Jeremiah 31:15, "This says Yehovah, a voice was heard in Rama, lamentation *and* bitter weeping - Rachel weeping for her children, refusing to be comforted for her children, because they are no more."

KJV: In Rama was there a voice heard, lamentation, and weeping, and great mourning, Rachel weeping for her children, and would not be comforted, because they are not.

Matthew 2:19

וכאשר אירודיש מת מלאך השם נראה לו בחלום אל יוספף מצרים

HTV: And when Herod died - the angel of Yehovah appeared to Joseph in a dream *while* in Egypt (Mitzrayim).

KJV: But when Herod was dead, behold, an angel of the Lord appeareth in a dream to Joseph in Egypt,

Matthew 2:20

ואמר לו קום וקח הילד ואמו ולך לארץ ישראל כי מת אותו שרוצה להמית הילד

Chapter 2

HTV: **He (the angel) said to him (Joseph), "Get up and take the child and his mother and go to the Land of Israel - because the one who wanted to kill the boy is dead."**

KJV: Saying, Arise, and take the young child and his mother, and go into the land of Israel: for they are dead which sought the young child's life.

Matthew 2:21

ויקם ויקח הילד ואמו ויבא לארץ ישראל

HTV: **And he (Joseph) got up and took the child and his mother and returned to the Land of Israel.**

KJV: And he arose, and took the young child and his mother, and came into the land of Israel.

Matthew 2:22

קיהי כאשר שמע כי ארכיליוס היה מולך תחת אירודיש אביו בארץ גודיאה פחד ללכת שס ונזהר בחלום ללכת לארץ גלליאה

HTV: **And it came to pass when he (Joseph) heard that Archelaus was ruling in place of Herod, his father, in the land of Judea - He was afraid to go there and was warned in a dream to go to the land of Galilee.**

KJV: But when he heard that Archelaus did reign in Judaea in the room of his father Herod, he was afraid to go thither: notwithstanding, being warned of God in a dream, he turned aside into the parts of Galilee:

Matthew 2:23

ויגר במדינת נאזריט שתהיה נשלמת הנבואה שאמרה הוא יקרא שמו נאזריוש

HTV: **And he sojourned in the province of Nazareth - so that the prophecy which said - "he will be called Nazarene" - would be fulfilled.**

KJV: And he came and dwelt in a city called Nazareth: that it might be fulfilled which was spoken by the prophets, He shall be called a Nazarene.

Matthew Chapter 3
Hebrew Text Version (HTV)

¹ At that time, came John (Yohanan) the Baptizer (Immerser) - into the wilderness of Judea, preaching…

² Proclaiming, "Repent - for the kingdom of heaven draws near!"

³ This is the One of whom was spoken, according to the prophet Isaiah, who said, "The voice of One crying in the wilderness - prepare you the way of Yehovah - make straight His Royal Way!"

⁴ (*Yohanan*) John's garments were of camel's hair and the belt which girded his waist *was* of leather; his food* *was* locusts and wild honey.

⁵ And all the inhabitants of Jerusalem, and all Judea, and all the country around the Jordan - went out to him.

⁶ So they could be baptized of him (John) in the Jordan - confessing their sins!

⁷ And after he had seen many Pharisees and Sadducees coming to his baptism, he said to them, "Seed of vipers, who now has revealed to you to flee from the wrath to come?"

⁸ Make fruit worthy of repentance (Teshuvah)!

⁹ Do not say among yourselves, behold, we have the Father Abraham - for I tell you that Elohim can bring forth out of these stones sons of Abraham.

¹⁰ For the axe has already been placed at the root of the tree - Every tree that does not bear good fruit shall be cut down and cast into the fire.

¹¹ I baptize you in the waters of repentance - but he who is to come after me (Yeshua) - that one is mightier than I. I do not deserve to carry his shoes. He will baptize you with the Holy Spirit and with fire.

¹² He (Yeshua) who *has* in his hand the winnowing fan to purge his threshing floor. He will gather together the wheat into his barn and the chaff he will burn with fire which will never be extinguished.

Chapter 3

¹³ Then came Yeshua from Galilee to the Jordan - unto John - in order to be baptized by him.

¹⁴ But John forbade him, saying, "I have need to be baptized of you - and *yet* you come to me?"

¹⁵ And Yeshua answered and said to him, "Allow it now - because the dew *of heaven* rests upon us." And then he allowed him.

¹⁶ Then Yeshua was baptized and immediately rose up out of the waters - and behold, the heavens were opened - and he saw the Spirit of Elohim descend and come upon him like a dove!

¹⁷ Behold, a voice came from heaven, saying "This is my beloved son - in whom I am well pleased."

Matthew Chapter 3
HTV with translator notes and KJV comparison

Matthew 3:1

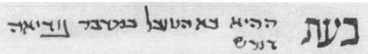

Hebrew Gospels from Catalonia HGC

בעת ההיא בא הטובל במדבר גודיאה דורש

HTV: At that time, came John (Yohanan) the Baptizer (Immerser) - into the wilderness of Judea, preaching...

Note: We are told this is Yohanan, called John in English, in verse 4 below.

KJV: In those days came John the Baptist, preaching in the wilderness of Judaea,

Matthew 3:2

ואומר עשות תשובה כי המלכות שמים יי מתקרבת

HTV: Proclaiming, "Repent - for the kingdom of heaven draws near!"

KJV: And saying, Repent ye: for the kingdom of heaven is at hand.

57

The Hebrew Book of Matthew

Matthew 3:3

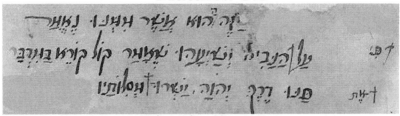

Freiburg Hebrew Manuscript

זֶה הַהוּא אֲשֶׁר מִמֶּנּוּ נֶאֱמַר עַל פִּי הַנָּבִיא יְשַׁעְיָהוּ שֶׁאָמַר קוֹל קוֹרֵא בַּמִּדְבָּר פַּנּוּ דֶּרֶךְ יְהוָה יַשְּׁרוּ-אֶת-מְסִלּוֹתָיו

HTV: This is the One of whom was spoken, according to the prophet Isaiah, who said, "The voice of One crying in the wilderness - prepare you the way of Yehovah - make straight His Royal Way!"

Note: The Old Testament reference is to Isaiah 40:3, preparing the royal way not making a roadway.

KJV: For this is he that was spoken of by the prophet Esaias, saying, The voice of one crying in the wilderness, Prepare ye the way of the Lord, make his paths straight.

Matthew 3:4

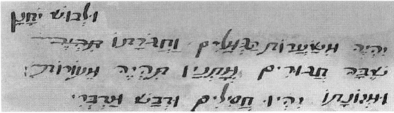

Freiberg Hebrew Manuscript

וּלְבוּשׁ יָחָנָן יִהְיֶה מִשַּׂעֲרוֹת הַגְּמַלִּים וַחֲגֹרָתוֹ שֶׁבָּהּ חֲגוּרִים מָתְנָיו תִּהְיֶה מְעוֹרוֹת : וּמְזוֹנָתוֹ יִהְיוּ חֲסִילִים וּדְבַשׁ מַדְבָּרִי

HTV: (Yohanan) John's garments were of camel's hair and the belt which girded his waist *was* of leather; his food* *was* locusts and wild honey.

Note: In the Dead Sea Scrolls the Essenes wrote that locust was a clean food if it was roasted. They were also renowned for their date trees and date honey. There are many other indicators that John was among the Essenes as he grew up in the wilderness.

Chapter 3

KJV: And the same John had his raiment of camel's hair, and a leathern girdle about his loins; and his meat was locusts and wild honey.

Matthew 3:5

וַיֵּצְאוּ אֵלָיו כָּל-יוֹשְׁבֵי יְרוּשָׁלַיִם וְכָל-יְהוּדָה וְכָל-מְדִינָה אֲשֶׁר בִּסְבִיב יַרְדֵן

HTV: **And all the inhabitants of Jerusalem, and all Judea, and all the country around the Jordan - went out to him.**

KJV: Then went out to him Jerusalem, and all Judaea, and all the region round about Jordan,

Matthew 3:6

וַיִּטָּבְלוּ מִמֶּנּוּ בַּיַּרְדֵן מוֹדִים אֶת חַטָּאוֹתֵיהֶם

HTV: **So they could be baptized of him (John) in the Jordan - confessing their sins!**

KJV: And were baptized of him in Jordan, confessing their sins.

Matthew 3:7

וְאַחֲרֵי שֶׁרָאָה רַבִּים פְּרוּשִׁים וְצַדּוּקִים בָּאִים אֶל טְבִילָתוֹ וַיֹּאמֶר לָהֶם הַזֶּרַע הָאֶפְעִים מִי-נָא-הִרְאָה לָכֶם לִבְרוֹחַ מֵחָרוֹן הֶעָתִיד

HTV: **And after he had seen many Pharisees and Sadducees coming to his baptism, he said to them, "Seed of vipers, who now has revealed to you to flee from the wrath to come?"**

KJV: But when he saw many of the Pharisees and Sadducees come to his baptism, he said unto them, O generation of vipers, who hath warned you to flee from the wrath to come?

Matthew 3:8

Freiburg Hebrew Manuscript

59

The Hebrew Book of Matthew

עֲשׂוּ פְּרִי שֶׁרָאוּי לִתְשׁוּבָה

HTV: **Make fruit worthy of repentance (Teshuvah)!**

Note: Teshuvah means *return* to Yehovah and his Torah. John is accusing the Pharisees and Sadducees of not being righteous before Yehovah, not following His law. In other words, get right before God, convicted of your own sin, before coming for cleansing.

KJV: Bring forth therefore fruits meet for repentance:

Matthew 3:9

אַל תֹּאמְרוּ בֵּינֵיכֶם הִנֵּה יֵשׁ לָנוּ הָאָב אַבְרָהָם : כִּי אֲנִי אוֹמֵר לָכֶם שֶׁהָאֱלֹהִים יָכוֹל לְהוֹצִיא מֵאֵלּוּ הָאֲבָנִים בְּנֵי אַבְרָהָם

HTV: **Do not say among yourselves, behold, we have the Father Abraham - for I tell you that Elohim can bring forth out of these stones sons of Abraham.**

KJV: And think not to say within yourselves, We have Abraham to *our* father: for I say unto you, that God is able of these stones to raise up children unto Abraham.

Matthew 3:10

Freiburg Hebrew Manuscript

כִּי כְּבָר הוּשַׂם הַגַּרְזֶן אֶל שׁוֹרֶשׁ הָאִילָן : כָּל-אִילָן שֶׁלֹּא יַעֲשֶׂה פְּרִי טוֹב הוּא יִכָּרֵת וְיֻשְׁלַךְ בָּאֵשׁ

HTV: **For the axe has already been placed at the root of the tree - Every tree that does not bear good fruit shall be cut down and cast into the fire.**

KJV: And now also the axe is laid unto the root of the trees: therefore every tree which bringeth not forth good fruit is hewn down, and cast into the fire.

Chapter 3

Matthew 3:11

אֲנִי טוֹבֵל אֶתְכֶם בַּמַּיִם לִתְשׁוּבָה אֲבָל אֲשֶׁר עָתִיד לָבוֹא אַחֲרַי הַהוּא גִּבּוֹר מִמֶּנִּי אֵינִי רָאוּי שֶׁאֶשָּׂא לוֹ-אֶת-נְעָלָיו הַהוּא יִטְבּוֹל אֶתְכֶם בָּרוּחַ הַקָּדוֹשׁ וּבָאֵשׁ

HTV: I baptize you in the waters of repentance - but he who is to come after me (Yeshua) - that one is mightier than I. I do not deserve to carry his shoes. He will baptize you with the Holy Spirit and with fire.

KJV: I indeed baptize you with water unto repentance: but he that cometh after me is mightier than I, whose shoes I am not worthy to bear: he shall baptize you with the Holy Ghost, and *with* fire:

Matthew 3:12

אֲשֶׁר בְּיָדוֹ הַמִּזְרֶה וְיַטְהִיר אֶת-גָּרְנוֹ וְיַקְבִּיץ אֶת-חִטָּה בַּאֲסָמוֹ וְאֶת-מוֹץ יִשְׂרוֹף בָּאֵשׁ שֶׁלֹּא יִכְבֶּה

HTV: He (Yeshua) who *has* in his hand the winnowing fan to purge his threshing floor. He will gather together the wheat into his barn and the chaff he will burn with fire which will never be extinguished.

KJV: Whose fan *is* in his hand, and he will thoroughly purge his floor, and gather his wheat into the garner; but he will burn up the chaff with unquenchable fire.

Matthew 3:13

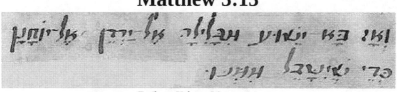

Freiburg Hebrew Manuscript

וְאָז בָּא יֵשׁוּעַ מִגָּלִילָה אֶל-יַרְדֵּן אֶל-יוֹחָנָן כְּדֵי שֶׁיִּטָּבֵל מִמֶּנּוּ

HTV: Then came Yeshua from Galilee to the Jordan - unto John - in order to be baptized by him.

KJV: Then cometh Jesus from Galilee to Jordan unto John, to be baptized of him.

The Hebrew Book of Matthew

Matthew 3:14

אָמְנָם יוֹחָנָן יִמְנַע אוֹתוֹ לֵאמֹר אֲנִי צָרִיךְ לְהִטָּבֵל מִמְּךָ וְאַתָּה בָא אֵלַי

HTV: But John forbade him, saying, "I have need to be baptized of you - and *yet* you come to me?"

KJV: But John forbad him, saying, I have need to be baptized of thee, and comest thou to me?

Matthew 3:15

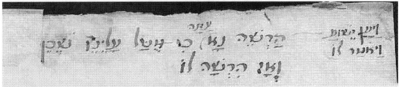

Freiburg Hebrew Manuscript

וַיַּעַן יֵשׁוּעַ וַיֹּאמֶר לוֹ הַרְשֵׁה נָא עַתָּה כִּי-מַטַּל עָלֵינוּ שָׁכֵן וְאָז הִרְשָׁה לוֹ

HTV: And Yeshua answered and said to him, "Allow it now - because the dew *of heaven* rests upon us." And then he allowed him.

> Note: The "dew of heaven" refers to the divine favor of Yehovah, especially in bringing forth crops of grain, grapes, etc. Salvation is often referred to in the Brit Hadashah as the gathering of grain that is ripe. The "dew of heaven" is used in Genesis 27:28 & 39, Haggai 1:10, Deut 33:13.

KJV: And Jesus answering said unto him, Suffer *it to be so* now: for thus it becometh us to fulfil all righteousness. Then he suffered him.

Matthew 3:16

וְיֵשׁוּעַ נִטְבַּל וּמִיָּד עָלָה מִמַּיִם וְהִנֵּה הַשָּׁמַיִם נִפְתְּחוּ לוֹ וַיִּרְאֶה אֶת רוּחַ הָאֱלֹהִים יוֹרֵד כַּיּוֹנָה וּבָא עָלָיו

HTV: Then Yeshua was baptized and immediately rose up out of the waters - and behold, the heavens were opened - and he saw the Spirit of Elohim descend and come upon him like a dove!

KJV: And Jesus, when he was baptized, went up straightway out of the water: and, lo, the heavens were opened unto him, and he saw the Spirit of God descending like a dove, and lighting upon him:

Matthew 3:17

וְהִנֵּה יָצְאָה קוֹל מִשָּׁמַיִם לֵאמֹר הַזֶּה הַהוּא בְּנִי הֶחָבִיב אֲשֶׁר בּוֹ רָצִיתִי

HTV: Behold, a voice came from heaven, saying "This is my beloved son - in whom I am well pleased."

KJV: And lo a voice from heaven, saying, This is my beloved Son, in whom I am well pleased.

Matthew Chapter 4
Hebrew Text Version (HTV)

¹ Then Yeshua the Messiah was brought by the Holy Spirit into the wilderness to be tempted by Satan.

² And (*Yeshua*) fasted forty days and forty nights and afterwards was hungry.

³ The Tempter drew near and said to him (*Yeshua*), "if you are the Son of God, therefore command these stones to become bread!"

⁴ Then (Yeshua) answered and said to him, "It is written, 'Man will not live by bread alone - but by every word which is spoken from the mouth of Yehovah."

⁵ Then Ha-Satan brought him up to the Holy City and set him (Yeshua) on the height of the House of the Sanctuary.

⁶ And he (Satan) said to him, "If you are the Son of God, cast yourself down. For it is written that His angels will guard you and protect you - lest your feet stumble on a stone."

⁷ Yeshua said to him again - "It is written that you shall not tempt Yehovah your God!"

⁸ Then Ha-Satan continued and took him up to a very high mountain, and he showed him all the kingdoms of the world and their glory.

⁹ He (Ha-Satan) said to him, "Behold, I will give them all to you, if you will fall on the ground and worship me!"

¹⁰ Then Yeshua said to him, "Go away Ha-Satan, for it is

written, "You shall worship Yehovah Elohim, and Him alone you shall serve!"

¹¹ Then Ha-Satan left him, and the angels came and served him.

¹² Indeed, when Yeshua heard that John was delivered into prison, he went to Galilee.

¹³ And he left the city of Nazareth, and he came and lived in the city of Capernaum, which is on the seashore in the region of Zebulon and Naphtali;

¹⁴ So that what was said - according to the mouth of Isaiah the prophet - would be fulfilled:

¹⁵ "In the land of Zebulun, and the land of Naphtali - the way of the sea across the Jordan - Galilee of the Gentiles;"

¹⁶ "The people walking in darkness have seen a great light, and those who dwell in the shadow of death have seen a light shine upon them." (from Isaiah 9:2)

¹⁷ From then on, Yeshua began to preach to many, saying, "Return in repentance, for the kingdom of heaven draws near!"

¹⁸ Yeshua walked by the Sea of Galilee and saw two brothers, Simon called Cephas, and Andrew his brother - who were casting a net into the sea because they were fishermen.

¹⁹ Then (Yeshua) he said to them, "Follow me and I will make you fishers of men."

²⁰ At once, they left the nets and followed after him.

²¹ And (Yeshua) went on from there and saw two other brothers Jacob (Ya'akov) son of Zebedee and John (Yohanan) his brother, in the ship with their father Zebedee preparing their nets, and he called them.

²² And promptly they *too* left their nets and followed after him.

²³ Yeshua went round and round all the Galilee, teaching in synagogue after synagogue, preaching to many the good news of the kingdom - healing every disease and all that ailed the people.

²⁴ Report of him went throughout all Syria, and they brought him all their sick and afflicted of various diseases, and those tormented with demons, and also those who had disabled limbs, and he healed them.

²⁵ And many people came to him from Galilee and Decapolis and Jerusalem and Judea and beyond the Jordan.

Matthew Chapter 4
HTV with translator notes and KJV comparison

Matthew 4:1

Freiburg Hebrew Manuscript

וְאָז הוּבָא יֵשׁוּעַ מֵהָרוּחַ בְּמִדְבָּר כְּדֵי שֶׁיְנָסֶה מִשָּׂטָן

HTV: Then Yeshua the Messiah was brought by the Holy Spirit into the wilderness to be tempted by Satan.

Note: The words "*Holy Spirit*" are in both the Shem Tov Manuscript (STM) and the Hebrew Gospels from Catalonia (HGC). In the Freiburg it says "*Spirit.*"

KJV: Then was Jesus led up of the Spirit into the wilderness to be tempted of the devil.

Matthew 4:2

וּמִשָּׁצָם אַרְבָּעִים יָמִים וְאַרְבָּעִים לֵילוֹת וְאַחֲרֵי כֵן יִרְעַב

HTV: And (*Yeshua*) fasted forty days and forty nights and afterwards was hungry.

KJV: And when he had fasted forty days and forty nights, he was afterward an hungred.

Matthew 4:3

וַיִּקְרַב אֵלָיו הַמְנַסֶה וַיֹאמַר לוֹ אִם אַתָּה הַבֵּן הָאֱלֹהִים אֱמוֹר נָא שֶׁאֵלוּ הָאֲבָנִים תֵּעָשֶׂינָה לֶחֶם

HTV: The Tempter drew near and said to him (*Yeshua*), "if you are the Son of God, therefore command these stones to become bread!"

KJV: And when the tempter came to him, he said, If thou be the Son of God, command that these stones be made bread.

Matthew 4:4

וַיַּעַן וַיֹּאמֶר הִנֵּה כָּתוּב לֹא בַּלֶּחֶם לְבַדּוֹ יִחְיֶה הָאָדָם כִּי אִם עַל כֹּל דָּבָר אֲשֶׁר רוֹצֵא מִפִּי יְהֹוָה

HTV: **Then (Yeshua) answered and said to him, "It is written, 'Man will not live by bread alone - but by every word which is spoken from the mouth of Yehovah."**

KJV: But he answered and said, It is written, Man shall not live by bread alone, but by every word that proceedeth out of the mouth of God.

Matthew 4:5

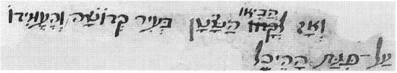
Freiburg Hebrew Manuscript

וְאָז הֵבִיאוּ הַשָּׂטָן בְּעִיר קְדוֹשָׁה וְהֶעֱמִידוֹ עַל-פִּנַּת הַהֵיכָל

HTV: **Then Ha-Satan brought him up to the Holy City and set him (Yeshua) on the height of the House of the Sanctuary.**

> Note: The Temple in Hebrew Scripture is often referred to as the House of God, House of Prayer, etc. There is an inner Temple called the Sanctuary or Holy of Holies.

KJV: Then the devil taketh him up into the holy city, and setteth him on a pinnacle of the temple,

Matthew 4:6

וַיֹּאמֶר לוֹ וְאִם אַתָּה הַבֵּן אֱלֹהִים הַשְׁלֵיחַ עַצְמְךָ מִלְמַעְלָה לְמַטָּה הִנֵּה כָּתוּב כִּי-מַלְאָכָיו יְצַוֶּה לָךְ וְעַל כַּפַּיִם יִשָּׂאוּנֶּךָ פֶּן-תִּגֹּף בָּאֶבֶן רַגְלְךָ

HTV: **And he (Satan) said to him, "If you are the Son of God, cast yourself down. For it is written that His angels will guard you and protect you - lest your feet stumble on a stone."**

Chapter 4

KJV: And saith unto him, If thou be the Son of God, cast thyself down: for it is written, He shall give his angels charge concerning thee: and in *their* hands they shall bear thee up, lest at any time thou dash thy foot against a stone.

Matthew 4:7

Freiburg Hebrew Manuscript

וַיֹּאמֶר לוֹ יֵשׁוּעַ עוֹד-כָתוּב לֹא-תְנַסֶּה אֶת יְהוָה אֱלֹהֶיךָ

HTV: Yeshua said to him again - "It is written that you shall not tempt Yehovah your God!"

KJV: Jesus said unto him, It is written again, Thou shalt not tempt the Lord thy God.

Matthew 4:8

וְהוֹסִיף הַשָּׂטָן וּלְקָחוֹ בְהַר מְאֹד רָם וְהִרְאָה לוֹ כֹל מַמְלְכוֹת הָעוֹלָם וְאֶת-כְּבוֹדָן

HTV: Then Ha-Satan continued and took him up to a very high mountain, and he showed him all the kingdoms of the world and their glory.

KJV: Again, the devil taketh him up into an exceeding high mountain, and sheweth him all the kingdoms of the world, and the glory of them;

Matthew 4:9

וַיֹּאמֶר לוֹ הִנֵּה אֵלּוּ כֻלָּם לְךָ אֶתֵּן אִם תִּפּוֹל עַל אֶרֶץ וְתִשְׁתַּחֲוֶה אוֹתִי

HTV: He (Ha-Satan) said to him, "Behold, I will give them all to you, if you will fall on the ground and worship me!"

KJV: And saith unto him, All these things will I give thee, if thou wilt fall down and worship me.

67

Matthew 4:10

Freiburg Hebrew Manuscript

אָז-אָמַר יֵשׁוּעַ לֵךְ-לְךָ הַשָׂטָן כִּי כָתוּב אֶת-יְהֹוָה אֱלֹהֶיךָ תִּשְׁתַּחֲוֶה וְלוֹ לְבַדּוֹ תַעֲבוֹד

HTV: Then Yeshua said to him, "Go away Ha-Satan, for it is written, "You shall worship Yehovah Elohim, and Him alone you shall serve!"

KJV: Then saith Jesus unto him, Get thee hence, Satan: for it is written, Thou shalt worship the Lord thy God, and Him only shalt thou serve.

Matthew 4:11

אָז הֵנִיחוֹ הַשָׂטָן וְהִנֵּה הַמַלְאָכִים קָרְבוּ וְעָבְדוּ לוֹ

HTV: Then Ha-Satan left him, and the angels came and served him.

KJV: Then the devil leaveth him, and, behold, angels came and ministered unto him.

Matthew 4:12

אָמְנָם כַּאֲשֶׁר יֵשׁוּעַ שָׁמַע אֲשֶׁר יוֹחָנָן נִמְסַר בְּבֵית אֲסִירִים הוּא הָלַךְ בְּגָלִילָה

HTV: Indeed, when Yeshua heard that John was delivered into prison, he went to Galilee.

KJV: Now when Jesus had heard that John was cast into prison, he departed into Galilee;

Matthew 4:13

וְעָזַב אֶת עִיר נָזֶרֶת הִנֵּה בָא-וַיֵּשֶׁב בְּעִיר כְּפַר-נַחוּם שֶׁבְּחוֹף הַיָּם בִּגְבוּלֵי זְבֻלוֹן וְנַפְתָּלֵי

HTV: And he left the city of Nazareth, and he came and lived in the city of Capernaum, which is on the seashore in the region of Zebulon and Naphtali;

Chapter 4

KJV: And leaving Nazareth, he came and dwelt in Capernaum, which is upon the sea coast, in the borders of Zabulon and Nephthalim:

Matthew 4:14

שֶׁיִמָּלֵא מָה שֶׁנֶּאֱמַר עַל פִּי יְשַׁעְיָהוּ הַנָּבִיא

HTV: **So that what was said - according to the mouth of Isaiah the prophet - would be fulfilled:**

KJV: That it might be fulfilled which was spoken by Esaias the prophet, saying,

Matthew 4:15

Freiburg Hebrew Manuscript

אֶרֶץ זְבָלוּן אֶרֶץ נַפְתָּלִי דֶּרֶךְ הַיָּם עֵבֶר הַיַּרְדֵּן גְּלִיל הַגּוֹיִם

HTV: **"In the land of Zebulun, and the land of Naphtali - the way of the sea across the Jordan - Galilee of the Gentiles;"**

Note: The verse comes from Isaiah 9:1.

KJV: The land of Zabulon, and the land of Nephthalim, *by* the way of the sea, beyond Jordan, Galilee of the Gentiles;

Matthew 4:16

הָעָם הַהֹלֵךְ בַּחֹשֶׁךְ רָאָה אוֹר גָּדוֹל וּלְיוֹשְׁבִים בְּאֶרֶץ צַלְמָוֶת אוֹר נָגַהּ עֲלֵיהֶם

HTV: **"The people walking in darkness have seen a great light, and those who dwell in the shadow of death have seen a light shine upon them."** *(from Isaiah 9:2)*

KJV: The people which sat in darkness saw great light; and to them which sat in the region and shadow of death light is sprung up.

Matthew 4:17

וּמִכָּאן הִתְחִיל יֵשׁוּעַ לִדְרֹשׁ לְרַבִּים לֵאמֹר הָשִׁיבוּ בַּתְּשׁוּבָה כִּי קָרְבָה מַלְכוּת הַשָּׁמַיִם

HTV: **From then on, Yeshua began to preach to many, saying, "Return in repentance, for the kingdom of heaven draws near!"**

KJV: From that time Jesus began to preach, and to say, Repent: for the kingdom of heaven is at hand.

Matthew 4:18

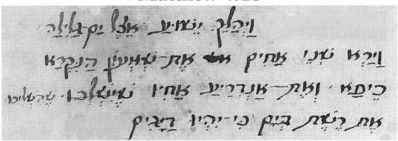
Freiburg Hebrew Manuscript

וַיֵּלֶךְ יֵשׁוּעַ אֵצֶל יָם-גָּלִילָה וַיַּרְא שְׁנֵי אַחִים אֶת-שִׁמְעוֹן הַנִּקְרָא כֵּיפָא וְאֶת-אַנְדְּרֵיעַ אָחִיו שֶׁהִשְׁלִיכוּ אֶת רֶשֶׁת בְּיָם כִּי יִהְיוּ דַיָּגִים

HTV: **Yeshua walked by the Sea of Galilee and saw two brothers, Simon called Cephas, and Andrew his brother - who were casting a net into the sea because they were fishermen.**

> Note: The name Cephas is actually from the Aramaic name *Kaypha* - rock or stone. This is often translated by the Greek word *Petros* which comes down to us as Peter.

KJV: And Jesus, walking by the sea of Galilee, saw two brethren, Simon called Peter, and Andrew his brother, casting a net into the sea: for they were fishers.

Matthew 4:19

וַיֹּאמַר לָהֶם בֹּאוּ נָא-אַחֲרַי וַאֲעֶשֶׂה לִהְיוֹתְכֶם דַּיְּגֵי הָאֲנוֹשִׁים

HTV: **Then (Yeshua) he said to them, "Follow me and I will make you fishers of men."**

Chapter 4

KJV: And he saith unto them, Follow me, and I will make you fishers of men.

Matthew 4:20

וְהֵמָה מִיָּד עָזְבוּ אֶת רְשָׁתוֹת וַיִּרְדְּפוּ אַחֲרָיו

HTV: At once, they left the nets and followed after him.

KJV: And they straightway left *their* nets, and followed him.

Matthew 4:21

Freiburg Hebrew Manuscript

וְהָלַךְ מִכַּאן הָלְאָה וַיַּרְא שְׁנֵי אֲחֵרִים אַחִים אֶת-יַעֲקוֹב בֶּן זְבְדִי וְיוֹחָנָן אָחִיו בִּסְפִינָה עִם אֲבִיהֶם זְבְדִי מְסַדְּקִים אֶת רְשָׁתוֹתֵיהֶם וַיִּקְרָא אוֹתָם אֵלָיו

HTV: And (Yeshua) went on from there and saw two other brothers Jacob (Ya'akov) son of Zebedee and John (Yohanan) his brother, in the ship with their father Zebedee preparing their nets, and he called them.

Note: The sons of Zebedee were Jacob, called James, and John his brother.

KJV: And going on from thence, he saw other two brethren, James *the son* of Zebedee, and John his brother, in a ship with Zebedee their father, mending their nets; and he called them.

Matthew 4:22

וְהֵמָה מִיָּד עָזְבוּ אֶת-רְשָׁתוֹת וַיִּרְדְּפוּ אַחֲרָיו

HTV: And promptly they *too* left their nets and followed after him.

KJV: And they immediately left the ship and their father, and followed him.

71

Matthew 4:23

Freiburg Hebrew Manuscript

וְהָלַךְ יֵשׁוּעַ סָבִיב סָבִיב בְּכֹל גָלִילָה מְלַמֵּד בְּכֹל כְּנֶסֶת וּכְנֶסֶת שֶׁלָהֶם מְדָרֵשׁ לְרַבִּים אֶת-בְּשׂוֹרָה שֶׁל מַלְכוּת רוֹפֵא אֶת-כָּל-חוֹלִי וְכֹל מַכְאוֹב בָּעָם

HTV: Yeshua went round and round all the Galilee, teaching in synagogue after synagogue, preaching to many the good news of the kingdom - healing every disease and all that ailed the people.

Note: The Hebrew word, *besora* or *besorot,* means "good news" but is translated as *gospel.*

KJV: And Jesus went about all Galilee, teaching in their synagogues, and preaching the gospel of the kingdom, and healing all manner of sickness and all manner of disease among the people.

Matthew 4:24

וַתֵּצֵא שְׁמוּעָה מִמֶּנּוּ בְּכֹל-סוּרְיָה וְהֵבִיאוּ אֵלָיו כֹּל חוֹלִים בִּמְשָׁנִים חֳלָיִים וְעִנוּיִים וַאֲשֶׁר בָּהֶם שֵׁדִים וְגַם אֶת הַמְשׁוּ עִם וּנְשׁוּלֵי אֲבָרִים וְהִרְפְּאָם

HTV: Report of him went throughout all Syria, and they brought him all their sick and afflicted of various diseases, and those tormented with demons, and also those who had disabled limbs, and he healed them.

KJV: And his fame went throughout all Syria: and they brought unto him all sick people that were taken with divers diseases and torments, and those which were possessed with devils, and those which were lunatick, and those that had the palsy; and he healed them.

Matthew 4:25

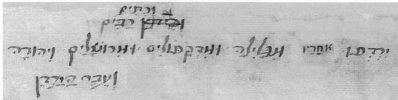

Freiburg Hebrew Manuscript

וְכִתִּים רַבִּים יִרְדְפוּ אַחֲרָיו מִגָּלִילָה וּמִדְּקָפּוֹלִיס וּמִירוֹשָׁלַיִם וִיהוּדָה וְעֵבֶר הַיַּרְדֵּן

HTV: And many people came to him from Galilee and Decapolis and Jerusalem and Judea and beyond the Jordan.

Note: The Decapolis is a region of ten Greek towns east of Galilee in Syria, only one (Scythapolis) was west of the Jordan in Israel proper.

KJV: And there followed him great multitudes of people from Galilee, and *from* Decapolis, and *from* Jerusalem, and *from* Judaea, and *from* beyond Jordan.

Matthew Chapter 5

Hebrew Text Version (HTV)

¹ When Yeshua saw the groups of people, he went up on the mountain, and when he sat down - then his disciples drew near to him.

² He opened his mouth and he taught, saying,

³ "Blessed are the humble in spirit, for theirs is the kingdom of heaven."

⁴ "Blessed are the humble, for they shall inherit the earth."

⁵ "Blessed are the mourners, for they will be comforted."

⁶"Blessed are those *who* are hungry and thirsty for righteousness - for they will be satisfied!"

⁷ "Blessed are those who are compassionate, for they will receive compassion."

⁸ "Blessed are the pure in heart, for they shall see God!"

⁹ "Blessed are the partners of peace, for they shall be called sons of God."

¹⁰ "Blessed are the sufferers - persecuted because of *their* righteousness - for to them is the kingdom of heaven."

¹¹ "Blessed are you when people curse you, persecute you, and say all manner of evil against you - falsely - for my sake!"

¹² "Be happy and rejoice! Your reward is great in heaven because they also persecuted the prophets who were before you."

¹³ "Behold! You are the salt of the earth! Indeed, if the salt loses its essence - it is nothing. Therefore, it is good for nothing - since it will be thrown out and trampled under the feet of men."

¹⁴ "You are *the* light of the world. It is not possible to hide the city placed upon a mountain!"

¹⁵ "Neither do you light the candle and put it under a bushel - but on the Menorah - In order to enlighten everyone in the house!"

¹⁶ "Therefore, shine your light before men. Let them see your good deeds, and they will praise your Father, who is in heaven."

¹⁷ At that time Yeshua the Messiah said to his disciples, "Do not think - I came that I might breach (break) the Torah - or the prophets. I came not that I might fulfill (complete or end) but rather that I might fill (the Torah) to overflowing, *abundantly overflowing!*"

¹⁸ "Truly, I say unto you, until heaven and earth pass away - not one yod from Torah, nor even the tip of a yod, will pass away - until all of these words are carried out."

¹⁹ "For this reason, whoever will take away one of the smallest of these commandments and teach that *to* men - that one will be called small in the kingdom of heaven. But anyone who will practice and teach truly - will be called great in the kingdom of heaven."

²⁰ I say to them (scribes and teachers of Torah), "Do not add to the law any more than is written in the book - and by doing this - scribes will ascend to heaven."

²¹ "You have heard what was said *in the Torah*, 'you shall not murder', because whoever murders will be held accountable."

Chapter 5

²² "Truly, I say unto you that anyone who angrily accuses his brother alone, *without witness,* will be liable to judgment *by* the law. Whoever says to his brother that he is worthless ('Raca') - he will be liable to the congregation. But whoever says to his brother, 'You are a fool!' - that person will be in danger of hell fire ('Gehinnom')."

²³ "Therefore, when you go to bring your gift to the altar - and you remember your brother has anything against you,"

²⁴ Leave your gift there and go! Be reconciled with your brother - and after that come and bring near your gift."

²⁵ "Reconcile with your adversary while you are still with him on the way - so that your adversary will not hand you over to the judge - and the judge hand you over to the servant (*of the court*) - and throw you in prison."

²⁶ "Truly I tell you, you will not leave there until you have paid the last penny."

²⁷ Yeshua said to his disciples, "You yourselves have heard what was said in the ancient Torah, 'You shall not commit adultery!'"

²⁸ "But I tell you that anyone who would see a woman alone - in order to lust - has already committed the act of adultery in his heart!"

²⁹ "If your right eye becomes a snare to you - Gouge it out and hurl it from you! Because it profits you more to destroy one member - considering the whole body will *otherwise* be sent to hellfire (in Gehinnom)."

³⁰ "If your right hand will be a snare to you - Cut it off and hurl it from you! Because that is more useful - that one lose one member - considering *otherwise* your whole body will be sent to hell (Gehinnom)!"

³¹ Moreover, Yeshua Mashiach said to his disciples, "The Torah says, 'Whosoever divorces his wife, must give to her a writ of divorce.'"

³² "Indeed, I am saying to you, that everyone who sends away his wife from his house - unless for the sake of adultery - that one shall make her commit adultery - and whoever is the sender commits adultery."

³³ "Again, you have heard that which was said *in the Torah* -

'You shall not swear falsely!' Surely you shall give to Yehovah your vow.' "

³⁴ "Truly, I am saying to you, that you shall not swear by anything at all. Not by the heavens - because that is the throne of God,"

³⁵ "Nor by the earth, for it is the footstool of His feet, and not by Jerusalem - for that is the city of God."

³⁶ "You shall not swear by your head, because you are not able to make one hair white or black."

³⁷ "Let your word(s) be 'yes' *meaning* 'yes' - or 'no' *meaning* 'no' - because anything else is-from-evil."

³⁸ "You have heard that the Torah says, 'An eye for an eye - and a tooth for a tooth!' " (Deut. 19:21)

³⁹ "Indeed, I tell you do not rebel against evil because if someone strikes you on the right cheek, give to him the other one also."

⁴⁰ "To the one who wants to fight with you in court and take your shirt - let him have the coat as well."

⁴¹ "Whoever would command you to go a thousand steps with him, go another two thousand."

⁴² "Whoever asks anything of you, give it to him. If he wants to borrow from you - do not refuse it from him."

⁴³ Moreover Yeshua said to his disciples, "You have heard that the Torah says, 'You must love your neighbor as yourself - but hate your enemy!' "

⁴⁴ "Indeed, I say to you, 'You will love your enemies and be good to those who will hate you - instead - pray for your persecutors and abusers.' "

⁴⁵ "So that you may be children of your Father - who is in heaven - who causes the sunrise to shine upon the good and the bad - and who makes it rain upon the righteous and upon the unrighteous."

⁴⁶ "If you *only* love your loved ones - what then will be your reward? Are not the tax collectors also doing this?"

⁴⁷ "And if you have agreement and peace only with your brother - are not the Gentiles also doing this?"

⁴⁸ "Therefore, you must be without blemish - as your heavenly Father is without blemish."

Matthew Chapter 5
HTV with translator notes and KJV comparison

Matthew 5:1

Freiburg Hebrew Manuscript

וּמִשֶּׁ-יֵּשׁוּעַ רָאָה אֶת-הַכִּתִים הוּא עָלָה בָהָר וְכַאֲשֶׁר יָשַׁב אָז יִקְרְבוּ אֵלָיו הַתַּלְמִידָיו

HTV: When Yeshua saw the groups of people, he went up on the mountain, and when he sat down - then his disciples drew near to him.

KJV: And seeing the multitudes, he went up into a mountain: and when he was set, his disciples came unto him:

Matthew 5:2

וְהוּא פָּתַח אֶת-פִּיהוּ וַיְלַמְּדָם לֵאמֹר

HTV: He opened his mouth and he taught, saying,

KJV: And he opened his mouth, and taught them, saying,

Matthew 5:3

אַשְׁרֵי הָאֶבְיוֹנִים בְּרוּחַ כִּי לָהֶם מַלְכוּת הַשָּׁמַיִם

HTV: "Blessed are the humble in spirit, for theirs is the kingdom of heaven."

Note: In some Hebrew manuscripts it says the "kingdom of God."

KJV: Blessed *are* the poor in spirit: for theirs is the kingdom of heaven.

Matthew 5:4

אַשְׁרֵי הָעֲנָוִים

כִּי הֵמָה יִקְנוּ אֶת הָאָרֶץ

Freiburg Hebrew Manuscript

אַשְׁרֵי הָעֲנָוִים כִּי הֵמָה יִקְנוּ אֶת הָאָרֶץ

HTV: **"Blessed are the humble, for they shall inherit the earth."**

Note: In Matthew 28:18-19, Yeshua says, "I have been given all authority **in heaven and on earth**" which he then gives to his followers to go and baptize all the nations of the earth. These two blessings to the humble - Matthew 5:3 (heaven) and 5:4 (earth) - are given to those followers who have humbled themselves before Yehovah as Yeshua has done.

KJV: Blessed *are* they that mourn: for they shall be comforted.

Matthew 5:5

אַשְׁרֵי הַסּוֹפְדִים כִּי הֵמָה יְנָחֲמוּ

HTV: **"Blessed are the mourners, for they will be comforted."**

Note: Apparently verses 4 & 5 were reversed in the Freiburg manuscript.

KJV: Blessed *are* the meek: for they shall inherit the earth.

Matthew 5:6

אַשְׁרֵי הָרְעֵבִים וְהַצְּמֵאִים אֶת-הַצֶּדֶק כִּי הֵמָה יִשְׂבְּעוּ

HTV: **"Blessed are those *who* are hungry and thirsty for righteousness - for they will be satisfied!"**

KJV: Blessed *are* they which do hunger and thirst after righteousness: for they shall be filled.

Matthew 5:7

אַשְׁרֵי הָרַחֲמָנִים כִּי הֵמָה יִמְצְאוּ אֶת-רַחֲמִים

HTV: **"Blessed are those who are compassionate, for they will receive compassion."**

KJV: Blessed *are* the merciful: for they shall obtain mercy.

Matthew 5:8

אַשְׁרֵי הַבָּרֵי לֵבָב כִּי הֵמָה יִרְאוּ אֶת-הָאֱלֹהִים

HTV: "Blessed are the pure in heart, for they shall see God!"

KJV: Blessed *are* the pure in heart: for they shall see God.

Matthew 5:9

אַשְׁרֵי הַנִּלְוִים לְשָׁלוֹם כִּי הֵמָה יִקָּרְאוּ בְנֵי הָאֱלֹהִים

HTV: "Blessed are the partners of peace, for they shall be called sons of God."

KJV: Blessed are the peacemakers: for they shall be called the children of God.

Matthew 5:10

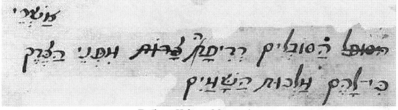
Freiburg Hebrew Manuscript

אַשְׁרֵי הַסוֹבְלִים רְדִיפָה מִפְּנֵי הַצֶּדֶק כִּי לָהֶם מַלְכוּת הַשָּׁמַיִ

HTV: "Blessed are the sufferers - persecuted because of *their* righteousness - for to them is the kingdom of heaven."

KJV: Blessed *are* they which are persecuted for righteousness' sake: for theirs is the kingdom of heaven.

Matthew 5:11

אַשְׁרֵיכֶם כַּאֲשֶׁר אֲנוֹשִׁים יְקַלְּלוּכֶם וְיִרְדְּפוּכֶם וְיֹאמְרוּ כָל רָעָה
כְּנֶגְדְּכֶם אָמְנָם כּוֹזְבִים בַּעֲבוּרִי

The Hebrew Book of Matthew

HTV: **"Blessed are you when people curse you, persecute you, and say all manner of evil against you - falsely - for my sake!"**

KJV: Blessed are ye, when *men* shall revile you, and persecute *you*, and shall say all manner of evil against you falsely, for my sake.

Matthew 5:12

שִׂמְחוּ וְגִילוּ כִּי שְׂכַרְכֶם גָּדוֹל בַּשָּׁמַיִם כִּי-כֵן-גַּם אֶת-הַנְּבִיאִים אֲשֶׁר הָיוּ לִפְנֵיכֶם רָדְפוּ

HTV: **"Be happy and rejoice! Your reward is great in heaven because they also persecuted the prophets who were before you."**

KJV: Rejoice, and be exceeding glad: for great *is* your reward in heaven: for so persecuted they the prophets which were before you.

Matthew 5:13

Freiburg Hebrew Manuscript

הִנֵּה אַתֶּם מֶלַח הָאָרֶץ אָמְנָם אִם הַמֶּלַח יִתָּפֵל בְּאֵיזֶה דָּבָר נָא יִמָּלַח אֵינוּ הוּא יוֹעִיל עוֹד לִמְאוּמָה כִּי אִם שֶׁיְּשַׁלַּךְ לַחוּצָה וְיֵרָמֵס מֵרַגְלֵי אֱנוֹשִׁים

HTV: **"Behold! You are the salt* of the earth! Indeed, if the salt loses its essence - it is nothing. Therefore, it is good for nothing - since it will be thrown out and trampled under the feet of men."**

> *Note: Salt was of the highest value in ancient times. It was essential to the flavoring and even more important - the preservation of food. It was rare and expensive. Yeshua is referring to preserving and using the Holy Spirit they are given.

KJV: Ye are the salt of the earth: but if the salt have lost his savour, wherewith shall it be salted? it is thenceforth good for nothing, but to be cast out, and to be trodden under foot of men.

Matthew 5:14

אַתֶּם יֵשׁ אוֹר הָעוֹלָם אִיאֶפְשָׁר לְהַסְתֵּר הָעִיר הַשׂוּמָה עַל הָהָר

HTV: **"You are *the* light of the world. It is not possible to hide the city placed upon a mountain!"**

KJV: Ye are the light of the world. A city that is set on a hill cannot be hid.

Matthew 5:15

Freiburg Hebrew Manuscript

וְאֵין מַדְלִיקִים אֶת הַנֵּר וְשָׂמִים אוֹתוֹ תַּחַת אֵיזֶה כְּלִי כִּי-אִם-עַל-הַמְּנוֹרָה כְּדֵי שֶׁיָּאִיר לְכֹל הַיּוֹשְׁבִים בְּבַיִת

HTV: **"Neither do you light the candle and put it under a bushel - but on the Menorah - In order to enlighten everyone in the house!"**

Note: Yehovah Himself taught us how to make the Menorah (Exodus 25:31-40) and endowed it with a powerful spiritual significance.

Salt of the earth = Light of the world = Menorah enlightening everyone! This is a three-fold metaphor originating with the giver of light Himself.

KJV: Neither do men light a candle, and put it under a bushel, but on a candlestick; and it giveth light unto all that are in the house.

Matthew 5:16

וְכֵן יָאִיר גַּם-אוֹרְכֶם לִפְנֵי הָאֲנָשִׁים כְּדֵי שֶׁיִּרְאוּ אֶת-טוֹבִים מַעֲשֵׂיכֶם וַיְהַדְּרוּ אֶת אֲבִיכֶם אֲשֶׁר בַּשָּׁמַיִם

HTV: **"Therefore, shine your light before men. Let them see your good deeds, and they will praise your Father, who is in heaven."**

KJV: Let your light so shine before men, that they may see your good works, and glorify your Father which is in heaven.

Matthew 5:17

Freiburg Hebrew Manuscript

אַל תְּחָשְׁבוּ שֶׁבָּאתִי לְהָפִיר אֶת-הַתּוֹרָה אוֹ-אֶת-הַנְּבִיאִים לֹא בָאתִי לְהָפִיר כִּי-אִם-שֶׁאֲמַלֵּא

HTV: At that time Yeshua the Messiah said to his disciples, "Do not think - I came that I might breach (break) the Torah - or the prophets. I came not that I might fulfill (complete or end) but rather that I might fill (the Torah) to overflowing, *abundantly** overflowing!"

Note: The verse uses two verbs meaning *overflowing* one after the other. This is common in Hebrew for emphasis. We do not do this in English. We will instead use an emphatic word like: *very, greatly,* or in this case *abundantly*.

Another meaning for the double emphasis is to clarify the meaning of the word לְהָפִיר which is used once negatively in the sense of *end* or *fulfill*, and the second time meaning *fill to over-flowing*. This literary device is called *perinamosia,* using two words from the same root in the same sentence for emphasis.

KJV: Think not that I am come to destroy the law, or the prophets: I am not come to destroy, but to fulfil.

Matthew 5:18

Freiburg Hebrew Manuscript

בֶּאֱמֶת אֲנִי אוֹמֵר לָכֶם עַד שֶׁיַּעֲבְרוּ שָׁמַיִם וָאָרֶץ לֹא יַעֲבוֹר מִתּוֹרָה יוֹד אֶחָד אוֹ עוֹקֶץ אֶחָד עַד שֶׁכֹּל הַדְּבָרִים יֵעָשׂוּ

HTV: "Truly, I say unto you, until heaven and earth pass away - not one yod from Torah, nor even the tip of a yod, will pass away - until all of these words are carried out."

Chapter 5

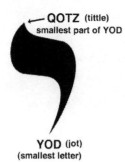

QOTZ (tittle) smallest part of YOD

YOD (jot) (smallest letter)

*Note: A *yod* is the smallest letter in the Hebrew alphabet, and a *qots yod* is a small serif. A serif, or tittle, is a decorative mark added to letters, in this case to the "tip of the yod."

The Greek to English translation is not trivial but a monumental one since it eliminates "Torah" from Scripture.

KJV: For verily I say unto you, Till heaven and earth pass, one jot or one tittle shall in no wise pass from the law, till all be fulfilled.

Matthew 5:19

לְפִיכָךְ אֲשֶׁר יָפִיר אַחַת מֵאֵלּוּ הַמִּצְוֹת הַקְּטַנּוֹת וִילַמֵּד אֶת-אֱנוֹשִׁים הַהוּא יִקָּרֵא קָטָן בְּמַלְכוּת הַשָּׁמַיִם מִכֹּל אֲחֵרִים אָמְנָם מִי שֶׁיַעֲשֶׂה וִילַמֵּד אוֹתָם הַזֶּה יִקָּרֵא גָּדוֹל בְּמַלְכוּת הַשָּׁמַיִם

HTV: **"For this reason, whoever will take away one of the smallest of these commandments and teach that *to* men - that one will be called small in the kingdom of heaven. But anyone who will practice and teach truly - will be called great in the kingdom of heaven."**

KJV: Whosoever therefore shall break one of these least commandments, and shall teach men so, he shall be called the least in the kingdom of heaven: but whosoever shall do and teach *them*, the same shall be called great in the kingdom of heaven.

Matthew 5:20

Cochin Gaster 1616

אומר להם שלא יוסיפו במשפט יותר שיש בספר או סופרים ובזה תזכו תעלון

HTV: **I say to them (scribes and teachers of Torah), "Do not add to the law any more than is written in the book - and by doing this - scribes will ascend to heaven."**

The Hebrew Book of Matthew

Note: The Cochin translation precisely follows the thread of the last three verses in this passage, Matthew 5:17-20, where it prohibits adding to or taking away from the Torah, God's royal law. The Greek translation, or addition, below - although true - changes the subject inappropriately.

KJV: For I say unto you, That except your righteousness shall exceed *the righteousness* of the scribes and Pharisees, ye shall in no case enter into the kingdom of heaven.

Matthew 5:21

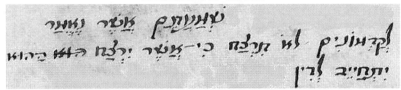
Freiburg Hebrew Manuscript

שְׁמַעְתֶּם אֲשֶׁר נֶאֱמַר לְקַדְמוֹנִים לֹא תִרְצַח כִּי-אֲשֶׁר יִרְצַח הַהוּא יִתְחַיֵּב לַדִּין

HTV: "You have heard what was said *in the Torah*, 'you shall not murder', because whoever murders will be held accountable."

Note: Greek-influenced manuscripts replace "**in the Torah**" with "to the ancients." However, enough Hebrew manuscripts have retained "**in the Torah**" to know this is the proper phrasing. (see verses 5:17, 27, 18, 31, 38, 43).

KJV: Ye have heard that it was said by them of old time, Thou shalt not kill; and whosoever shall kill shall be in danger of the judgment:

Matthew 5:22

Freiburg Hebrew Manuscript

אֲבָל אֲנִי אוֹמֵר לָכֶם אֲשֶׁר כֹּל יִקְצֹף שֶׁלְּבַד עַל אָחִיו הַהוּא יִתְחַיֵּב

Chapter 5

לְדִין וַאֲשֶׁר יֹאמַר לְאָחִיו רַקָא הוּא יִתְחַיֵּיב לְעֵדָה אֲבָל מִשֶׁיֹּאמַר לְאָחִיו אַתָּה כְּסִיל הַהוּא יִתְחַיֵּיב לַגֵּיהִנָּם הָאֵשׁ

HTV: **"Truly, I say unto you that anyone who angrily accuses his brother alone, *without witness*, will be liable to judgment *by* the law.[1]   Whoever says to his brother that he is worthless ('Raca') - he will be liable to the congregation. But whoever says to his brother, 'You are a fool!'[2] - that person will be in danger of hell fire ('Gehinnom')."**

[1]Note: Yeshua is speaking of three levels of authority: local law, congregation law, and the judgment of Yehovah. As in all his other comparisons, Yeshua is teaching Torah, "Be careful of your thoughts, for your thoughts run your life!" (Proverbs 4:23). The seed of murder is in an angry heart. Yehovah knows your thoughts and they will be judged as well as your actions. It does not say one will be thrown into hellfire - but think carefully about the truth of your words.

[2]Note: The word "fool" is variously translated as "impious one", "evil one", "deranged", "nothing", "sucker", "dupe", "ignoramus." So, it is not the word used that is the sin. The danger of hellfire applies when one is making a false accusation or witness. In Matthew 23:17, Yeshua calls the Sadducees and Pharisees "fools" but his accusation was absolutely true.

KJV: But I say unto you, That whosoever is angry with his brother without a cause shall be in danger of the judgment: and whosoever shall say to his brother, Raca, shall be in danger of the council: but whosoever shall say, Thou fool, shall be in danger of hell fire.

Matthew 5:23

לְפִיכָךְ כַּאֲשֶׁר תַּקְרִיב אֶת-מִנְחָתְךָ אֶל הַמִּזְבֵּחַ וְשָׁם תִּזְכּוֹר שֶׁלְאָחִיךָ מְאוּמָה כְּנֶגְדְּךָ

HTV: **"Therefore, when you go to bring your gift to the altar - and you remember your brother has anything against you,"**

KJV: Therefore if thou bring thy gift to the altar, and there rememberest that thy brother hath ought against thee;

Matthew 5:24

הַנִּיחַ שָׁם-אֶת-מִנְחָתְךָ וְלֵךְ וְהִתְפַּיֵּיס עִם-אָחִיךָ וְאַחֲרֵי כֵן בּוֹא וְהַקְרִיב אֶת מִנְחָתְךָ

HTV: **Leave your gift there and go! Be reconciled with your brother - and after that come and bring near your gift."**

KJV: Leave there thy gift before the altar, and go thy way; first be reconciled to thy brother, and then come and offer thy gift.

Matthew 5:25
אַתָּה תִּתְרַצֶּה עִם אוֹיְבְךָ בִּהְיוֹתְךָ עוֹד עִמּוֹ בְּדֶרֶךְ כְּדֵי שֶׁלֹּא יִמְסֹר אוֹתְךָ אוֹיִבְךָ לְדַיָּן וְהַדַּיָּן יִמְסָרְךָ לִמְשָׁרֵת וְתֻשְׁלַךְ בְּבֵית אֲסִירִים

HTV: **"Reconcile with your adversary while you are still with him on the way - so that your adversary will not hand you over to the judge - and the judge hand you over to the servant (*of the court*) - and throw you in prison."**

KJV: Agree with thine adversary quickly, whiles thou art in the way with him; lest at any time the adversary deliver thee to the judge, and the judge deliver thee to the officer, and thou be cast into prison.

Matthew 5:26
בֶּאֱמֶת אֲנִי אוֹמֵר לְךָ לֹא תֵצֵא מִכַּאן עַד-שֶׁתִּתֵּן אֶת-פְּרוּטָא הָאַחֲרוֹן

HTV: **"Truly I tell you, you will not leave there until you have paid the last penny."**

KJV: Verily I say unto thee, Thou shalt by no means come out thence, till thou hast paid the uttermost farthing.

Matthew 5:27
עוד אמר ישאוש לתלמידיו אתם שמעתם שהתורה הישנה אמרה לא תנאף

HTV: **Yeshua said to his disciples, "You yourselves have heard what was said in the ancient Torah, 'You shall not commit adultery!'"**

KJV: Ye have heard that it was said by them of old time, Thou shalt not commit adultery:

Matthew 5:28

אֲבָל אֲנִי אוֹמֵר לָכֶם אֲשֶׁר כֹּל מִי שֶׁיִּרְאֶה אִישָׁה לְבַד לְחַמְדָּהּ אֲשֶׁר הוּא כְּבָר נָאַף בְּלִבּוֹ

HTV: **"But I tell you that anyone who would see a woman alone - in order to lust - has already committed the act of adultery in his heart!"**

KJV: But I say unto you, That whosoever looketh on a woman to lust after her hath already committed adultery with her already in his heart.

Matthew 5:29

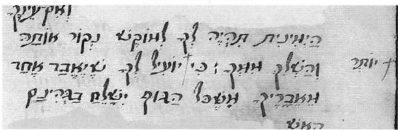
Freiburg Hebrew Manuscript

וְאִם-עֵינְךָ הַיְמִינִית תִּהְיֶה לְךָ לְמוֹקֵשׁ נָקוֹר אוֹתָהּ וְהַשְׁלֵךְ מִמְּךָ כִּי יוֹתֵר יוֹעִיל לְךָ שֶׁיֹּאבַד אֶחָד מֵאֵבָרֶיךָ מִשֶּׁכֹּל הַגּוּף יִשָּׁלַח בַּגֵּיהִנָּם הָאֵשׁ

HTV: **"If your right eye becomes a snare to you - Gouge it out and hurl it from you! Because it profits you more to destroy one member - considering the whole body will *otherwise* be sent to hellfire (in Gehinnom)*."**

> *Note: This is a metaphor not a prescription. Origin castrated himself, then later came to understand the truth - lust was not in the body but in the mind - still it must be cast out. Gehinnom refers to the valley of Hinnom where babies were sacrificed to Moloch by being burnt alive! This became the vision of hell to the Israelites. The word *Hell* came from *Gehinnom*.

KJV: And if thy right eye offend thee, pluck it out, and cast *it* from thee: for it is profitable for thee that one of thy members should perish, and not that thy whole body should be cast into hell.

Matthew 5:30

וְאִם יְמִינְךָ יִהְיֶה לְךָ לְמוֹקֵשׁ חֲתָכוֹ וְהַשְׁלֵךְ מִמְּךָ כִּי יוֹתֵר יוֹעִיל לְךָ שֶׁיֹּאבַד אֶחָד מֵאֵבָרֶיךָ מִשֶּׁכֹּל הַגּוּפְךָ יִשָּׁלַח בַּגֵּיהִנָּם

HTV: **"If your right hand will be a snare to you - Cut it off and hurl it from you! Because that is more useful - that one lose one member - considering *otherwise* your whole body will be sent to hell (Gehinnom)!"**

Note: *Yminekha* means "right" but by extension, means *"right hand"* (Gen 48:18, Ex 15:6 & 12).

KJV: And if thy right hand offend thee, cut it off, and cast *it* from thee: for it is profitable for thee that one of thy members should perish, and not *that* thy whole body should be cast into hell.

Matthew 5:31

עוד אמר ישאוש משיח לתלמידיו התורה אומרת המגרש אשתו יתן לה ספר כריתות

HTV: **Moreover, Yeshua Mashiach said to his disciples, "The Torah says, 'Whosoever divorces his wife, must give to her a writ of divorce.'"**

KJV: It hath been said, Whosoever shall put away his wife, let him give her a writing of divorcement:

Matthew 5:32

Freiburg Hebrew Manuscript

אֲבָל אֲנִי אוֹמֵר לָכֶם אֲשֶׁר כָּל-שֶׁיְשַׁלַּח אֶת-אִשְׁתּוֹ מִבֵּיתוֹ לוּלֵי בַעֲבוּר נְאוּף הַהוּא יַעֲשֶׂה שֶׁתִּנְאַף וַאֲשֶׁר אֶת הַמִּשְׁלָחָה יִקַּח הַהוּא מְנָאֵף

HTV: **"Indeed, I am saying to you, that everyone who sends away his wife from his house - unless for the sake of adultery - that one shall make her commit adultery - and whoever is the sender commits adultery."**

Note: The Greek version, from which the KJV is taken, seems to absolve the husband of any blame or harm due to his failure under the Torah to give his wife a writ of divorce so she can go on with her life and remarry. The Hebrew makes it clear the husband, as well, is committing adultery should he remarry. Yeshua is condemning husbands, who send their wives away, for their hard-heartedness.

KJV: But I say unto you, That whosoever shall put away his wife, saving for the cause of fornication, causeth her to commit adultery: and whosoever shall marry her that is divorced committeth adultery.

Matthew 5:33

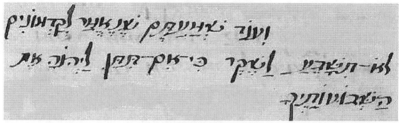

Freiburg Hebrew Manuscript

וְעוֹד שְׁמַעְתֶּם שֶׁנֶּאֱמַר לַקַּדְמוֹנִים לֹא-תִשָּׁבַע לַשֶּׁקֶר כִּי-אִם-תִּתֵּן לַיהוָה אֶת הַשְּׁבוּעוֹתֶיךָ

HTV: **"Again, you have heard that which was said *in the Torah** - 'You shall not swear falsely!' Surely you shall give to Yehovah your vow.' "**

*Note: Greek-influenced manuscripts replace "**in the Torah**" with "by the ancients." However, enough Hebrew manuscripts have retained "**in the Torah**" to know this is the proper phrasing. (see verses in Matthew 5:17, 18, 27, 31, 38, 43). Giving a vow to Yehovah is in Num 30:1-3.

KJV: Again, ye have heard that it hath been said by them of old time, Thou shalt not forswear thyself, but shalt perform unto the Lord thine oaths:

Matthew 5:34

אָמְנָם אֲנִי אוֹמֵר לָכֶם שֶׁמִּכֹּל וְכֹל לֹא תִשָּׁבְעוּ לֹא בַּשָּׁמַיִם כִּי-יֵשׁ- כִּסֵּא הָאֱלֹהִים

HTV: **"Truly, I am saying to you, that you shall not swear by anything at all. Not by the heavens - because that is the throne of God,"**

The Hebrew Book of Matthew

KJV: But I say unto you, Swear not at all; neither by heaven; for it is God's throne:

Matthew 5:35

Freiburg Hebrew Manuscript

וְלֹא בָאָרֶץ כִּי-הִיא-הֲדוֹם רַגְלָיו וְלֹא בִירוּשָׁלַיִם כִּי-הִיא-עִיר-הַמֶּלֶךְ הַגָּדוֹל

HTV: "Nor by the earth, for it is the footstool of His feet, and not by Jerusalem - for that is the city of God."

> Note: A scribal note in the margin of Eusebius' translation of the Septuagint says, "In **The Gospel according to the Hebrews,** it says '**city of God**.' " There are other scribal notes mentioning **The Hebrew Gospel(s)** indicating the scribes of that era knew it well. The other Hebrew manuscripts, HGC & STM, say the "**city of God**" rather than "the great king."

KJV: Nor by the earth; for it is his footstool: neither by Jerusalem; for it is the city of the great King.

Matthew 5:36

וְאַל תִּשָּׁבַע בְּרֹאשְׁךָ כִּי-אֵינְךָ יָכוֹל לַעֲשׂוֹת שַׂעֲרָה אַחַת לְבָנָה אוֹ שְׁחוֹרָה

HTV: "You shall not swear by your head, because you are not able to make one hair white or black."

KJV: Neither shalt thou swear by thy head, because thou canst not make one hair white or black.

Matthew 5:37

Freiburg Hebrew Manuscript

יְהִי מַאֲמַרְכֶם הֵן הֵן לֹא לֹא כִּי מָה שֶׁתְּיַתֵּר מֵאֵלֶּה דְּבָרִים הוּא-יֵשׁ-מֵהָרָעָה

HTV: **"Let your word(s) be 'yes'** *meaning* **'yes' - or 'no'** *meaning* **'no' - because anything else is-from-evil."**

> Note: Yeshua is saying, if your word is no good - why would your oath be any better. You need not swear by God to have His authority for your word to be true. He gives you that authority. In fact, He commands you to be truthful in all things. To be constantly calling on God for authority you already have - is off-putting to God.

KJV: But let your communication be, Yea, yea; Nay, nay: for whatsoever is more than these cometh of evil.

Matthew 5:38

אתם שמעתם שהתורה אומרת עין תחת עין שן תחת שן

HTV: **"You have heard that the Torah says, 'An eye for an eye - and a tooth for a tooth!'"** (Deut. 19:21)

KJV: Ye have heard that it hath been said, An eye for an eye, and a tooth for a tooth:

Matthew 5:39

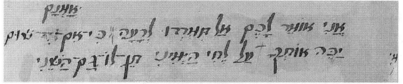
Freiburg Hebrew Manuscript

אֲמְנָם אֲנִי אוֹמֵר לָכֶם אַל תִּמְרְדוּ לְרָעָה כִּי אִם שׁוּם יַכֶּה אוֹתְךָ מִי עַל לְחִי הַיְמִינִי תֵן לוֹ גַם הַשֵּׁנִי

HTV: **"Indeed, I tell you do not rebel against evil because if someone strikes you on the right cheek, give to him the other one also."**

> *Note: In fighting with men in the earthly battle, a tit-for-tat is appropriate. In fighting *evil* in the supernatural realm - supernatural entities cannot be killed by earthy weapons, but they can be defeated and bound by the light and love of God, His weapons of war. "The weapons we fight with are not the weapons of the world" (2nd Cor 10:4).

KJV: But I say unto you, That ye resist not evil: but whosoever shall smite thee on thy right cheek, turn to him the other also.

Matthew 5:40

וּלְמִי שֶׁיִּרְצֶה לָרִיב אִתְּךָ בְּדִין וּלְקַחַת אֶת הַכֻּתֹּנֶת שֶׁלְּךָ הַנִּיחַ לוֹ גַם אֶת-הַמְּעִיל

HTV: "To the one who wants to fight with you in court and take your shirt - let him have the coat as well."

KJV: And if any man will sue thee at the law, and take away thy coat, let him have *thy* cloke also.

Matthew 5:41

Freiburg Hebrew Manuscript

וַאֲשֶׁר יַצְרִיחְךָ לְאֶלֶף פְּסָעִים הֵלֵךְ עִמּוֹ עוֹד אֲחֵרִים אֲלָפַיִם

HTV: "Whoever would command you to go a thousand steps* with him, go another two thousand."

*Note: The Romans coined the word "mile" from *mille passus*, one thousand paces. Any subject peoples were required to carry a Roman soldier's gear up to one mile when commanded.

KJV: And whosoever shall compel thee to go a mile, go with him twain.

Matthew 5:42

לְשׁוֹאֵל מִמְּךָ מְאוּמָה תִּתֵּן לוֹ וּמִי שֶׁיִּרְצֶה לִלְוֹת מִמְּךָ אַל תְּסִירֵהוּ מִמְּךָ

HTV: "Whoever asks anything of you, give it to him. If he wants to borrow from you - do not refuse it from him."

KJV: Give to him that asketh thee, and from him that would borrow of thee turn not thou away.

Matthew 5:43

Hebrew Gospels from Catalan (HGC Vat. Ebr. 100)

עוד אמר ישאוש לתלמידיו אתם שמעתם שהתורה אומרת
ואהבת לרעך כמוך ותכעיס אויבר אֶת אוֹיְבָךְ

HTV: **Moreover Yeshua said to his disciples, "You have heard that the Torah says, 'You must love your neighbor as yourself - but hate your enemy!'"**

Note: Yeshua is correcting what they have heard about the Oral Torah, because the written Torah does not say "hate your enemy." In fact, kindness and fair treatment are called for in the written Torah - specifically concerning captured enemies.

KJV: Ye have heard that it hath been said, Thou shalt love thy neighbour, and hate thine enemy.

Matthew 5:44

אָמְנָם אֲנִי אוֹמֵר לָכֶם אָהוֹב תֶּאֱהֲבוּ אֶת-אוֹיְבֵיכֶם וְתֵטִיבוּ לְאוֹתָם אֲשֶׁר יִשְׂנְאוּכֶם וְהִתְפַּלְלוּ תַּחַת רוֹדְפֵיכֶם וְעוֹשְׁקֵיכֶם

HTV: **"Indeed I say to you, 'You will love your enemies and be good to those who will hate you - instead - pray for your persecutors and abusers.'"**

KJV: But I say unto you, Love your enemies, bless them that curse you, do good to them that hate you, and pray for them which despitefully use you, and persecute you;

Matthew 5:45

כְּדֵי שֶׁתִּהְיוּ בְנֵי אֲבִיכֶם אֲשֶׁר הוּא-בַשָּׁמַיִם שֶׁמַּזְרִיחַ אֶת שִׁמְשׁוֹ עַל הַטּוֹבִים וְעַל הָרָעִים וּמַמְטִיר עַל צַדִּיקִים וְעַל בִּלְתִּי צַדִּיקִים

HTV: **"So that you may be children of your Father - who is in heaven - who causes the sunrise to shine upon the good and the bad - and who makes it rain upon the righteous and upon the unrighteous."**

KJV: That ye may be the children of your Father which is in heaven: for he maketh his sun to rise on the evil and on the good, and sendeth rain on the just and on the unjust.

Matthew 5:46

וְאִם אַתֶּם אוֹהֲבִים אֶת אוֹהֲבֵיכֶם אֵיזֶה נָא שָׂכָר יִהְיֶה לָכֶם הֲלֹא גַם הַמּוֹכְסִים עוֹשִׂים הַזֹּאת

HTV: "**If you *only* love your loved ones - what then will be your reward? Are not the tax collectors also doing this?**"

KJV: For if ye love them which love you, what reward have ye? do not even the publicans the same?

Matthew 5:47

וְאִם לְבַד לְאַחִיכֶם תַּקְדִּימוּ שָׁלוֹם הֲלֹא גַם הַגּוֹיִם עוֹשִׂים הַזֹּאת

HTV: "**And if you have agreement and peace only with your brother - are not the Gentiles also doing this?**"

KJV: And if ye salute your brethren only, what do ye more than others? do not even the publicans so?

Matthew 5:48

לְפִיכָךְ אַתֶּם תִּהְיוּ תְמִימִים כְּמוֹ גַם אֲבִיכֶם הַשְׁמֵימִי הוּא תָמִים

HTV: "**Therefore you must be without blemish - as your heavenly Father is without blemish.**"

KJV: Be ye therefore perfect, even as your Father which is in heaven is perfect.

Matthew Chapter 6
Hebrew Text Version (HTV)

¹ "Take heed and consider that you should not give your charity in order to appear righteous before men. If so, you surely will not *be* rewarded by your Father who *is* in heaven."

² "When you give charity do not make an effort to exalt *yourself* - do not sound a trumpet before you - as the hypocrites do in the assemblies and in the markets in order to show off to men. In truth I say to you that they have already received their reward."

³ "But if you shall give charity, do not let your left hand know what your right hand is doing,"

⁴ "In order that your righteous deeds may be in secret - your father who sees in the secret place - He shall repay you."

⁵ "When you pray, you shall not be like the hypocrites who take pains to pray standing in the assemblies - and at the corners of the markets - that they will be seen of men. Truly I say to you - they have already received their reward."

⁶ "But you, when you pray - you shall go into your room, closing the door - you will pray to your Father who is in the secret place and from the secret place, He will see and He will reward you."

⁷ "When you are praying, do not multiply your words as the Gentiles do - who think that they will be heard for this reason - if they speak many words."

⁸ "Do not be like them, for your Father - Who is in heaven - knows what you need before you ask."

⁹ "Pray in this manner - Our Father, who is in heaven - May Your name be glorified!"

¹⁰ "Your kingdom come. Your will be done. As it is in heaven - so shall it be on earth."

¹¹ "Give us this day our daily bread."

¹² "Forgive us our debts as we also forgive our debtors."

¹³ "Do not lead us into temptation - but deliver us from evil."

¹⁴ "If you forgive *others* their sins - your heavenly Father also

will forgive you - your sins."

¹⁵"But if you will not forgive men for their sins - likewise your Father will not forgive you - your sins."

¹⁶ "So when you fast, do not be like hypocrites hiding *behind* gloomy faces - so they appear to men *that* they fast. Truly - I say to you - they have already taken their reward."

¹⁷ "Indeed, if you yourself fast, anoint your head with oil, and wash your face."

18 "Do not show men that you are fasting, for your Father - who is in the secret place will see you from the secret place and reward you."

¹⁹ "Do not store up for yourselves treasures on the earth, where the moth and the mildew will eat *them*, and the thieves will dig up and steal."

²⁰ "If you build up your treasure in heaven - from there no moth or mildew will eat it and no thieves will dig it up and steal it."

²¹ "For where you put your treasure - your heart will be also."

²² "The lamp of the body exists in the eye - for if the eye is open - your whole body will be filled with light!"

²³ "Indeed, if it is evil - all your body will be in darkness. Behold - if the light in you becomes dark, how much darkness will be in you?"

²⁴ "No one can serve two masters - either he will hate the one and love the other - or tolerate one and despise the other. One cannot serve God and mammon."

²⁵ "Therefore, upon your portion, I tell you do not worry your soul regarding what you will eat - or what you will wear. Beloved, your soul is more precious than the clothing on your body."

²⁶ "Consider the birds in the heavens - because they do not sow nor gather into granaries - yet your heavenly Father provides for them. Are you not more precious than they are?"

²⁷ "Who of you - from his own wisdom - will be able to add one cubit to his stature?"

²⁸ "What would be *the point* worrying about your clothing? Let your eyes consider the lily of the field. It grows with no toil nor sewing of clothes."

²⁹ "Truly I say to you that Solomon - in all his glory - will not be dressed as one of them."

³⁰ "Even as God *clothes* the grass of the field today, which tomorrow will be thrown into the fire - how much more will He clothe you? Oh you of little faith!"

³¹ "For this reason, do not worry, saying - 'What will we eat?' And, 'What will we drink?' Or, 'What will we wear?' "

³² "Because all these things - the peoples seek - However, your Father knows that all these things are required for you."

³³ "First, seek the kingdom of Elohim and His righteousness - and then all of these things shall be added unto you."

³⁴ "Therefore, do not worry about tomorrow - because tomorrow will take care of itself - be satisfied with the concerns of today."

Matthew Chapter 6
HTV with translator notes and KJV comparison

Matthew 6:1

Freiburg Hebrew Manuscript

רְאוּ וְהִתְבּוֹנְנוּ שֶׁלֹּא תִּתְּנוּ אֶת צִדְקַתְכֶם לִפְנֵי אֲנוֹשִׁים כְּדֵי שֶׁתֵּרָאוּ מֵהֶם וְאִם-כֵּן לֹא-יִהְיֶה לָכֶם שׁוּם שָׂכָר אֵצֶל הָאָבִיכֶם אֲשֶׁר בַּשָּׁמַיִם

HTV: "Take heed and consider that you should not give your charity in order to appear righteous before men. If so, you surely will not *be* rewarded by your Father who *is* in heaven."

KJV: Take heed that ye do not your alms before men, to be seen of them: otherwise ye have no reward of your Father which is in heaven.

Matthew 6:2

וְכַאֲשֶׁר תִּתֵּן צְדָקָה לֹא-תִשְׁתַּדֵּל לְהָרִים קוֹל שׁוֹפָר לְפָנֶיךָ כְּמוֹ עוֹשִׂים הַחֲנֵפִים בַּכְּנֵסִיּוֹת וּבַשּׁוּקוֹת כְּדֵי שֶׁיִּתְהַדְּרוּ מֵאֲנוֹשִׁים בֶּאֱמֶת אֲנִי אוֹמֵר לָכֶם שֶׁכְּבָר לָקְחוּ אֶת-שְׂכָרָם

The Hebrew Book of Matthew

HTV: **"When you give charity do not make an effort to exalt *yourself* - do not sound a trumpet before you - as the hypocrites do in the assemblies and in the markets in order to show off to men. In truth I say to you that they have already received their reward."**

KJV: Therefore when thou doest *thine* alms, do not sound a trumpet before thee, as the hypocrites do in the synagogues and in the streets, that they may have glory of men. Verily I say unto you, They have their reward.

Matthew 6:3

וְאִם אַתָּה תִּתֵּן צְדָקָה לֹא תֵדַע שְׂמֹאולְךָ מָה תַעֲשֶׂה יְמִינְךָ

HTV: **"But if you shall give charity, do not let your left hand know what your right hand is doing,"**

KJV: But when thou doest alms, let not thy left hand know what thy right hand doeth:

Matthew 6:4

כְּדֵי שֶׁתִּהְיֶה צִדְקָתְךָ בְּסֵתֶר וְאָבִיךְ שֶׁיִּרְאֶה בְּסֵתֶר יְשַׁלֵּם לְךָ

HTV: **"In order that your righteous deeds may be in secret - your father who sees in the secret place - He shall repay you."**

Note: The "secret place" is cited by King David in Psalm 27:5 & 91:1.

KJV: That thine alms may be in secret: and thy Father which seeth in secret himself shall reward thee openly.

Matthew 6:5

וְכַאֲשֶׁר תִּתְפַּלְלוּ אַל תִּהְיוּ דּוֹמִים לַחֲנֵפִים אֲשֶׁר מִשְׁתַּדְּלִים לְהִתְפַּלֵּל עוֹמְדִים בַּכְּנֵסִיּוֹת וּבִפְנוֹת הַשְּׁוָקוֹת שֶׁיֵּרָאוּ מֵאֲנוֹשִׁים בֶּאֱמֶת אֲנִי אוֹמֵר לָכֶם הֵמָּה כְּבָר לָקְחוּ אֶת שְׂכָרָם

HTV: **"When you pray, you shall not be like the hypocrites who take pains to pray standing in the assemblies - and at the corners of the markets - that they will be seen of men. Truly I say to you - they have already received their reward."**

Chapter 6

KJV: And when thou prayest, thou shalt not be as the hypocrites *are*: for they love to pray standing in the synagogues and in the corners of the streets, that they may be seen of men. Verily I say unto you, They have their reward.

Matthew 6:6

וְאַתָּה אִם תִּתְפַּלֵּל תָּבוֹא בַחַדְרְךָ וְאַחֲרֵי שֶׁפֶּתַח נִסְגַּר אַתָּה תִּתְפַּלֵּל לְאָבִיךָ שֶׁהוּא בְּחֶסֶר וְאָבִיךָ אֲשֶׁר רוֹאֶה בְּסֵתֶר יִתֶּן לְךָ

HTV: **"But you, when you pray - you shall go into your room, closing the door - you will pray to your Father who is in the secret place and from the secret place, He will see and He will reward you."**

KJV: But thou, when thou prayest, enter into thy closet, and when thou hast shut thy door, pray to thy Father which is in secret; and thy Father which seeth in secret shall reward thee openly.

Matthew 6:7

Freiburg Hebrew Manuscript

וְכַאֲשֶׁר תִּהְיוּ מִתְפַּלְּלִים אַל תִּרְבּוּ אֶת-דִּבְרֵיכֶם כַּאֲשֶׁר עוֹשִׂים הַגּוֹיִם שֶׁחוֹשְׁבִים אֲשֶׁר יִשָּׁמְעוּ אִם-יַרְבּוּ אֶת-דִּבְרֵיהֶם לְפִיכָךְ

HTV: **"When you are praying, do not multiply your words as the Gentiles do - who think that they will be heard for this reason - if they speak many words."**

KJV: But when ye pray, use not vain repetitions, as the heathen *do*: for they think that they shall be heard for their much speaking.

Matthew 6:8

אַל תִּדְמוּ לָהֶם כִּי אֲבִיכֶם יוֹדֵעַ מַה לָכֶם צָרִיךְ לִפְנֵי שֶׁתִּשְׁאָלוּ׃

The Hebrew Book of Matthew

HTV: **"Do not be like them, for your Father - Who is in heaven - knows what you need before you ask."**

KJV: Be not ye therefore like unto them: for your Father knoweth what things ye have need of, before ye ask him.

Matthew 6:9

בְּאוֹפָן הַזֶה תִּתְפַּלְלוּ אָבִינוּ שֶׁבַּשָׁמַיִם יְקֻדַּשׁ שִׁמְךָ

HTV: **"Pray in this manner - Our Father, who is in heaven - May Your name be glorified!"**

KJV: After this manner therefore pray ye: Our Father which art in heaven, Hallowed be thy name.

Matthew 6:10

תָּבוֹא מַלְכוּתְךָ יְהִי רְצוֹנְךָ כְּמוֹ בַשָׁמַיִם וְכֵן בָּאָרֶץ

HTV: **"Your kingdom come. Your will be done. As it is in heaven - so shall it be on earth."**

KJV: Thy kingdom come. Thy will be done in earth, as *it is* in heaven.

Matthew 6:11

לַחֲמָנוּ הַתְּמִידִי תֶּן-לָנוּ הַיּוֹם

HTV: **"Give us this day our daily bread."**

KJV: Give us this day our daily bread.

Matthew 6:12

Freiburg Hebrew Manuscript

וּסְלַח לָנוּ אֶת חוֹבוֹתֵינוּ כְּמוֹ גַם אֲנַחְנוּ סוֹלְחִים לִמְחַיְּיבֵינוּ

HTV: **"Forgive us our debts as we also forgive our debtors."**

Note: Most Hebrew translations say "Forgive us our debts,'" but the Shem Tov manuscript says, "Forgive us our sins, as we forgive those who sin against us."

KJV: And forgive us our debts, as we forgive our debtors.

Matthew 6:13

Freiburg Hebrew Manuscript

וְאַל תָּבִיא אוֹתָנוּ בְּמַסָּה כִּי אִם תַּוְהַצִּילֵנוּ מֵהָרָעָה אָמֵן

HTV: "Do not lead us into temptation - but deliver us from evil."

Note: The epilogue to The Lord's Prayer "**For thine is the kingdom, and the power, and the glory**." is not in the Hebrew. There is nothing false - it simply wasn't in the original Hebrew or Greek texts. It was used in the Greek liturgy, the call and response from pastor to congregation. Because of that it was copied into Matthew in this verse and was so popular it was not removed.

KJV: And lead us not into temptation, but deliver us from evil: For thine is the kingdom, and the power, and the glory, forever. Amen.

Matthew 6:14

וְאִם תִּסְלְחוּ לָאֲנוֹשִׁים אֶת חוֹבוֹתֵיהֶם גַּם אֲבִיכֶם הַשְּׁמֵימִי יִסְלַח לָכֶם הוֹבוֹתֵיכֶם

HTV: "If you forgive *others* their sins - your heavenly Father also will forgive you - your sins."

KJV: For if ye forgive men their trespasses, your heavenly Father will also forgive you:

Matthew 6:15

וְאִם לֹא תִסְלְחוּ לָאֲנוֹשִׁים גַּם אֲבִיכֶם לֹא יִסְלַח לָכֶם אֶת חוֹבוֹתֵיכֶם

HTV: "But if you will not forgive men for their sins - likewise your Father will not forgive you - your sins."

KJV: But if ye forgive not men their trespasses, neither will your Father forgive your trespasses.

Matthew 6:16

וְכַאֲשֶׁר תָּצוּמוּ אַל תִּהְיוּ כַּחֲנֵפִים קוֹדְרִים הַמַּסְתִּירִים אֶת-פְּנֵיהֶם כְּדֵי שֶׁיֵּרָאוּ לַאֲנוּשִׁים צָמִים בֶּאֱמֶת אֲנִי אוֹמֵר לָכֶם שֶׁכְּבַר לָקְחוּ אֶת-שְׂכָרָם

HTV: "So when you fast, do not be like hypocrites hiding *behind* gloomy faces - so they appear to men *that* they fast. Truly - I say to you - they have already taken their reward."

KJV: Moreover when ye fast, be not, as the hypocrites, of a sad countenance: for they disfigure their faces, that they may appear unto men to fast. Verily I say unto you, They have their reward.

Matthew 6:17

אָמְנָם אַתָּה אִם-תָּצוּם מְשַׁח אֶת רֹאשְׁךָ וְרָחַץ אֶת פָּנֶיךָ

HTV: "Indeed, if you yourself fast, anoint your head with oil, and wash your face."

KJV: But thou, when thou fastest, anoint thine head, and wash thy face;

Matthew 6:18

שֶׁלֹּא תֵרָאֶה לַאֲנוּשִׁים צָם-כִּי-אִם לְאָבִיךָ אֲשֶׁר הוּא בְּחֶסֶד וְאָבִיךָ אֲשֶׁר יִרְאֶה בְּסֵתֶר הַהוּא יִתֵּן לָךְ

HTV: "Do not show men that you are fasting, for your Father - who is in the secret place will see you from the secret place and reward you."

KJV: That thou appear not unto men to fast, but unto thy Father which is in secret: and thy Father, which seeth in secret, shall reward thee openly.

Matthew 6:19

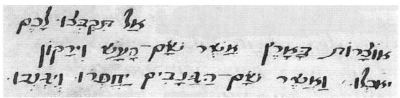

Freiburg Hebrew Manuscript

Chapter 6

אַל תִּקְבְּצוּ לָכֶם אוֹצָרוֹת בָּאָרֶץ אֲשֶׁר שָׁם הָעָשׁ וְיִדָּקוֹן יֹאכְלוּ וַאֲשֶׁר שָׁם הַגַּנָּבִים יַחְפְּרוּ וְיִגְנֹבוּ

HTV: **"Do not store up for yourselves treasures on the earth, where the moth and the mildew will eat *them*, and the thieves will dig up and steal."**

> Note: This is a reference to the afterlife where kings, pharaohs and the wealthy amass gold, silver and fine things to serve them after death. All of this is vain.

KJV: Lay not up for yourselves treasures upon earth, where moth and rust doth corrupt, and where thieves break through and steal:

Matthew 6:20

כִּי אִם קִבְצוּ לָכֶם אוֹצָרוֹת בַּשָּׁמַיִם שֶׁשָּׁם לֹא הָעָשׁ וְלֹא הַיְּרָקוֹן יֹאכְלוּ וְשֶׁשָּׁם הַגַּנָּבִים לֹא יַחְפְּרוּ וְלֹא יִגְנֹבוּ

HTV: **"If you build up your treasure in heaven - from there no moth or mildew will eat it and no thieves will dig it up and steal it."**

KJV: But lay up for yourselves treasures in heaven, where neither moth nor rust doth corrupt, and where thieves do not break through nor steal:

Matthew 6:21

כִּי אַיֵּה יִהְיֶה אוֹצָרְךָ שָׁם יִהְיֶה אַף לִבְּךָ

HTV: **"For where you put your treasure - your heart will be also."**

KJV: For where your treasure is, there will your heart be also.

Matthew 6:22

נֵר הַגּוּף יֵשׁ-עֵינֶךָ : כִּי אִם עֵינְךָ תִּהְיֶה פְּתוּחַ הִנֵּה כֹּל גּוּפְךָ יִהְיֶה בָּהִיר

HTV: **"The lamp of the body exists in the eye - for if the eye is open - your whole body will be filled with light!"**

KJV: The light of the body is the eye: if therefore thine eye be single, thy whole body shall be full of light.

The Hebrew Book of Matthew

Matthew 6:23

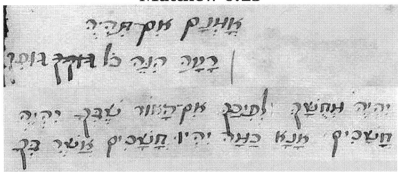

Freiburg Hebrew Manuscript

אָמְנָם אִף-תִּהְיֶה רָעָה הִנֵּה כֹּל גּוּפְךָ יִהְיֶה מְחָשָׁךְ לְפִיכָךְ אִם הָאוֹר שֶׁבְּךָ יִהְיֶה חֲשָׁכִים אָנָא כַּמָּה יִהְיוּ חֲשָׁכִים אֲשֶׁר בָּךְ

HTV: "Indeed, if it is evil - all your body will be in darkness. Behold - if the light in you becomes dark, how much darkness will be in you?"

> Note: Yeshua is using a metaphor of the eye as an outlet for the mind and its morality. If what you see provokes you to evil then your whole psyche and body is involved. Still, it is one thing to have a wrong impulse based on what you see - it is a much deeper darkness to act upon it.
> (See Proverbs 21:10 and Proverbs 22:9)

KJV: But if thine eye be evil, thy whole body shall be full of darkness. If therefore the light that is in thee be darkness, how great *is* that darkness!

Matthew 6:24

Freiburg Hebrew Manuscript

אֵין נִמְצָא שֶׁיּוּכַל לִשְׁנַיִם אֲדוֹנִים לַעֲבוֹד אוֹ-אֶחָד יִשְׂנָא וְהָאַחֵר יֶאֱהַב וְהָאֶחָד יִסְבּוֹל וְהָאַחֵר יִבְזֶה לֹא-תוּכְלוּ לַעֲבוֹד לֵאלֹהִים וּלְמָמוֹנָא

HTV: "No one can serve two masters - either he will hate the one and love the other - or tolerate one and despise the other. One cannot serve God and mammon."

Note: Mammon means riches, one of the desires of men. The beasts of the field do not seek after silver and gold. This is a weakness of Man.

KJV: No man can serve two masters: for either he will hate the one, and love the other; or else he will hold to the one, and despise the other. Ye cannot serve God and mammon.

Matthew 6:25

עַל מְנַת אֲנִי אוֹמֵר לָכֶם אַל תְּחוֹשְׁשׁוּ עַל נַפְשְׁכֶם מָה תֹּאכְלוּ וְלֹא עַל גּוּפְכֶם מָה תִּלַבְּשׁוּ הֲלֹא הַנֶּפֶשׁ הוּא יְקָרָה מֵהַגּוּף וְהַגּוּף יָקָר מִלְבוּשׁ

HTV: **"Therefore, upon your portion, I tell you do not worry your soul regarding what you will eat - or what you will wear. Beloved, your soul is more precious than the clothing on your body."**

KJV: Therefore I say unto you, Take no thought for your life, what ye shall eat, or what ye shall drink; nor yet for your body, what ye shall put on. Is not the life more than meat, and the body than raiment?

Matthew 6:26

הַבִּיטוּ נָא אֶל עוֹפוֹת הַשָּׁמַיִם כִּי אֵינָם זוֹרְעִים וְאֵינָם קוֹבְצִים לַאֲסָמִים וַאֲבִיכֶם הַשְּׁמֵימִי מְפַרְנְסָם הֲלֹא אַתֶּם יְקָרִים מִמֶּהֵם

HTV: **"Consider the birds in the heavens - because they do not sow nor gather into granaries - yet your heavenly Father provides for them. Are you not more precious than they are?"**

KJV: Behold the fowls of the air: for they sow not, neither do they reap, nor gather into barns; yet your heavenly Father feedeth them. Are ye not much better than they?

Matthew 6:27

מִי נָא מִמְּכֶם בְּבִינָתוֹ יוּכַל לְהוֹסִיף עַל קוֹמָתוֹ אַמָּה אֶחָד

HTV: **"Who of you - from his own wisdom - will be able to add one cubit to his stature?"**

KJV: Which of you by taking thought can add one cubit unto his stature?

Matthew 6:28

מַה תִּהְיוּ נָא-מְחוֹשְׁשִׁים עַל הַלְבוּשׁ תְּנוּ נָא עֵינֵיכֶם עַל חֲבַצֶּלֶת הַשָּׂדֶה אֵיכָה תִצְמַח כִּי-אֵין-טוֹרְחָה וְאֵין תּוֹפְרָה

HTV: "What would be *the point* worrying about your clothing? Let your eyes consider the lily of the field. It grows with no toil nor sewing of clothes."

KJV: And why take ye thought for raiment? Consider the lilies of the field, how they grow; they toil of not, neither do they spin:

Matthew 6:29

אֲבָל אֲנִי אוֹמֵר לָכֶם שֶׁשְּׁלֹמֹה אֵין יִהְיֶה בְּכֹל כְּבוֹדוֹ מְלֻבָּשׁ כְּאַחַת מֵהֶן

HTV: "Truly I say to you that Solomon - in all his glory - will not be dressed as one of them."

KJV: And yet I say unto you, That even Solomon in all his glory was not arrayed like one of these.

Matthew 6:30

וְאִם הָאֱלֹהִים אֶת-עֵשֶׂב הַשָּׂדֶה אֲשֶׁר הוּא הַיּוֹם וּלְמָחֳרָת יֻשְׁלַךְ בְּתַנּוּר כַּךְ יְלַבֵּשׁ כַּמָּה יוֹתֵר אֶתְכֶם הַקְּטַנֵּי אֱמוּנָה

HTV: "Even as God *clothes* the grass of the field today, which tomorrow will be thrown into the fire - how much more will He clothe you? Oh you of little faith!"

KJV: Wherefore, if God so clothe the grass of the field, which to day is, and to morrow is cast into the oven, *shall he* not much more clothe you, O ye of little faith?

Matthew 6:31

לְפִיכָךְ אַל תְּחוֹשְׁשׁוּ לֵאמוֹר מָה נֹאכַל וּמָה נִשְׁתֶּה אוֹ בְּמָה נִלְבָּשׁ

HTV: "For this reason, do not worry, saying - 'What will we eat?' And, 'What will we drink?' Or, 'What will we wear?' "

KJV: Therefore take no thought, saying, What shall we eat? or, What shall we drink? or, Wherewithal shall we be clothed?

Chapter 6

Matthew 6:32

כִּי כָל אֵלֶה דְבָרִים מְבַקְשִׁים הַגּוֹיִם כִּי אֲבִיכֶם יוֹדֵעַ כִּי כָל אֵלֶה דְבָרִים לָכֶם צְרִיכִים

HTV: "Because all these things - the peoples seek - However, your Father knows that all these things are required for you."

KJV: (For after all these things do the Gentiles seek:) for your heavenly Father knoweth that ye have need of all these things.

Matthew 6:33

Freiburg Hebrew Manuscript

עַל מְנָת בְּרִאשׁוֹנָה תְּבַקְשׁוּ אֶת-מַלְכוּת הָאֱלֹהִים וְצִדְקוֹ וְאָז אֵלֶּה דְבָרִים כֻּלָּם יִתּוֹסְפוּ לָכֶם

HTV: "First, seek the kingdom of Elohim and His righteousness - and then all of these things shall be added unto you."

KJV: But seek ye first the kingdom of God, and his righteousness; and all these things shall be added unto you.

Matthew 6:34

עַל כֵּן לֹא תְחוֹשְׁשׁוּ לְיוֹם מָחָר כִּי הַיּוֹם מָחָר הוּא יְחוֹשֵׁשׁ בַּעֲדוֹ כִּי תִסְתַּפֵּק לְיוֹם חֲשָׁשָׁה שֶׁלּוֹ

HTV: "Therefore, do not worry about tomorrow - because tomorrow will take care of itself - be satisfied with the concerns of today."

KJV: Take therefore no thought for the morrow: for the morrow shall take thought for the things of itself. Sufficient unto the day *is* the evil thereof.

Matthew Chapter 7

Hebrew Text Version (HTV)

¹ "Do not judge, and you will not be judged."

² "The judgment which you *make* is the same judgment which will be made against you - and the measure which you *take*, others will also *take* of you."

³ "Why do you see the chaff in your brother's eye - but what happens in your own eye - you do not see?"

⁴ "Or how *can* you say to your brother, 'Oh! my brother please *allow* me to *remove* the chaff from your eye' - yet you do not see the beam in your *own* eye?"

⁵ "Hypocrite! I beseech you - remove first the beam from your eye - so you can see to remove the chaff from the eye of your brother."

⁶ "Yeshua Mashiach said to his followers, "You must not speak the sacred writings before beasts - nor place the precious words before pigs - that they not trample them under foot and tear them apart."

⁷ "Ask of God and it shall be given to you. Seek and you shall find. Knock and the door shall b opened unto you."

⁸ "Every*one* that asks will receive. The one who seeks - he will find. To him who knocks - the door will be opened."

⁹ "Which man of you - if his son asks him for bread - will give him a stone?"

¹⁰ "Or if he asks for a fish - will you give him a snake?"

¹¹ "Therefore, since you - being fallible - know how to give good things to your children - So much more will your Father in Heaven give good things of the Spirit to those who seek Him."

¹² "All that you would want people to do for you - so will you do likewise for them. Upon this hangs the words of the Torah and the prophets."

¹³ Yeshua said to his followers, "Come! I pray you - enter into the narrow gate! For the wide gate and the broad way -

bring destruction to the many who go on it!"

¹⁴ "How straight and narrow is the gate - and difficult is the way that leads to life - and few are they who are walking in it"!"

¹⁵ "Beware of false prophets- who come to you in sheep's clothing - but inside they are ravenous wolves who will come to snatch you *away*!"

¹⁶ "From their fruits you shall know them. Does one gather grapes from thorns - or figs from briars?"

¹⁷ "Thus every good tree produces good fruit - but the bad tree produces evil fruit."

¹⁸ "Because the good tree can not produce bad fruit - nor the bad tree produce good fruit."

¹⁹ "Every tree that does not produce good fruit will be cut down and thrown into the fire!"

²⁰ "Therefore, you will surely know them from their fruits."

²¹ Yeshua Mashiach said to his followers, "Not all who say to me 'Lord, Lord', shall enter the kingdom of heaven. However, whosoever does the will of my Father, who is in heaven, shall enter."

²² "Many will say to me on that day, 'Lord, Lord, did we not prophesy in your name - and in your name did we not cast out demons from men - and in your name perform many mighty deeds!'"

²³ "And then I myself shall profess to them, 'I never knew you! Get away from me - All you workers of lawlessness!'"

²⁴ "Therefore, all who hear these words and do them - resemble a wise man who built his house upon the rock."

²⁵ "The rain fell, the floods came, the winds blew, but his house did not fall - for it was built upon the rock."

²⁶ "All who hear these words but do not do them - resemble the foolish man who built his house upon the sand."

²⁷ "The rain came down, the floods came, the winds blew - the house did fall - and great was its ruin!"

²⁸ And it came to pass, when Yeshua had said all these things - the crowds were astonished by his teaching…

²⁹ Because (Yeshua) taught them - with authority - not as the scribes and Pharisees.

The Hebrew Book of Matthew

Matthew Chapter 7

HTV with translator notes and KJV comparison

Matthew 7:1

Freiberg Hebrew Manuscript

אַל תִּשְׁפְּטוּ וְלֹא תִשָּׁפֵטוּ

HTV: "Do not judge, and you will not be judged."

KJV: Judge not, that ye be not judged.

Matthew 7:2

כִּי בְּמִשְׁפָּט אֲשֶׁר בּוֹ תִשְׁפְּטוּ בְּאוֹתוֹ גַם אַתֶּם תִּשָּׁפְטוּ וּבְמִדָּה שֶׁבָּהּ תָּמֹדּוּ בְּאוֹתָהּ אֲחֵרִים יָמֹדּוּ לָכֶם

HTV: "The judgment which you *make* is the same judgment which will be made against you - and the measure which you *take*, others will also *take* of you."

KJV: For with what judgment ye judge, ye shall be judged: and with what measure ye mete, it shall be measured to you again.

Matthew 7:3

מָה נָא אַתָּה רוֹאֶה מוֹץ בְּעֵין אָחִיךָ וְאֶת-קוֹרָה שֶׁבְּעֵינְךָ אֵינְךָ רוֹאֶה

HTV: "Why do you see the chaff in your brother's eye - but what happens in your own eye - you do not see?"

KJV: And why beholdest thou the mote that is in thy brother's eye, but considerest not the beam that is in thine own eye?

Matthew 7:4

אוֹ אֵיכָה אַתָּה אוֹמֵר לְאָחִיךָ אָנָא הֶאָחִי הָנִיחַ נָא שֶׁאוֹצִיא אֶת הַמוֹץ מֵעֵינֶךָ וְאַתָּה אֵין רוֹאֶה אֶת-הַקּוֹרָה בְּעֵינֶךָ

HTV: **"Or how *can* you say to your brother, 'Oh! my brother please *allow* me to *remove* the chaff from your eye' - yet you do not see the beam in your *own* eye?"**

KJV: Or how wilt thou say to thy brother, Let me pull out the mote out of thine eye; and, behold, a beam *is* in thine own eye?

Matthew 7:5

הֶחָנֵף הוֹצִיא נָא בְרִאשׁוֹנָה אֶת-הַקּוֹרָה מֵעֵינֶךָ וְאַחַר כַּךְ תִּרְאֶה לְהוֹצִיא אֶת הַמוֹץ מֵעֵין אָחִיךָ

HTV: **"Hypocrite! I beseech you - remove first the beam from your eye - so you can see to remove the chaff from the eye of your brother."**

KJV: Thou hypocrite, first cast out the beam out of thine own eye; and then shalt thou see clearly to cast out the mote out of thy brother's eye.

Matthew 7:6

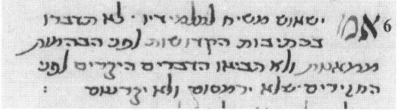
Hebrew Gospel from Catalonia

אמר ישאוש משיח תלמידים לא תדברו בכתיבות הקדושות לפני הבהמות ממאנות ולא הביאו הדברים היקרים לפני החזירים שלא ירמסוס ולא יקרעוס

HTV: **"Yeshua Mashiach said to his followers, "You must not speak the sacred writings before beasts - nor place the precious words before pigs - that they not trample them under foot and tear them apart."**

The Hebrew Book of Matthew

Note: Yeshua is speaking of men, not animals. Some men are clean minds (like nominal believers) but not inclined nor ready to be taught the truth of the sacred Word.

Others are unclean minds (like pagans) who would mock and destroy the sacred Word. The Hebrew makes it clear Yeshua is speaking of the sacred Word of God - not vague "holy *things*!"

KJV: Give not that which is holy unto the dogs, neither cast ye your pearls before swine, lest they trample them under their feet, and turn again and rend you.

Matthew 7:7

שַׁאֲלוּ נָא וְיִנָּתֵן לָכֶם דִּרְשׁוּ וְתִמְצָאוּ הַקִּישׁוּ פֶּתַח וְיִפָּתַח לָכֶם

HTV: **"Ask of God and it shall be given to you. Seek and you shall find. Knock and the door shall be opened unto you."**

KJV: Ask and it will be given to you; seek and you will find; knock and the door will be opened to you.

Matthew 7:8

כָּל שֶׁיִּשְׁאַל הוּא יִקַּח וְהַדּוֹרֵשׁ יִמְצָא וּלְמָקִישׁ פֶּתַח יִפָּתַח

HTV: **"Every*one* that asks will receive. The one who seeks - he will find. To him who knocks - the door will be opened."**

KJV: For every one that asketh receiveth; and he that seeketh findeth; and to him that knocketh it shall be opened.

Matthew 7:9

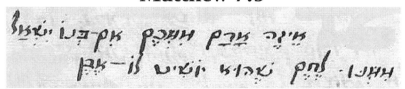

Freiberg Hebrew Manuscript

אֵיזֶה אָדָם מִמְּכֶם אִם בְּנוֹ יִשְׁאַל מִמֶּנּוּ לֶחֶם שֶׁהוּא יוֹשִׁיט לוֹ אֶבֶן

HTV: **"Which man of you - if his son asks him for bread - will give him a stone?"**

KJV: Or what man is there of you, whom if his son ask bread, will he give him a stone?

Matthew 7:10

אוֹ אִם יִשְׁאַל דָּגָה שֶׁיּוֹשִׁיט לוֹ הַנָּחָשׁ

HTV: **"Or if he asks for a fish - will you give him a snake?"**

KJV: Or if he ask a fish, will he give him a serpent?

Matthew 7:11

Freiberg Hebrew Manuscript

לְפִיכָךְ בִּהְיוֹתְכֶם רָעִים וְיוֹדְעִים לָתֵת לִבְנֵיכֶם דְּבָרִים טוֹבִים וְכָל שֶׁכֵּן אֲבִיכֶם אֲשֶׁר בְּשָׁמַיִם יִתֵּן דְּבָרִים טוֹבִים לְשׁוֹאֲלִים מִמֶּנּוּ

HTV: **"Therefore, since you - being fallible - know how to give good things to your children - So much more will your Father in Heaven give good things of the Spirit to those who seek Him."**

> Note: The word translated as "things" here is from Hebrew ***devarim*** which can mean "things" but has a definite spiritual aspect to it. ***Devarim***, for example also means "The Ten Commandments" The STM manuscript says Father will **"give His good Spirit"** so it is more than simply "things."

KJV: If ye then, being evil, know how to give good gifts unto your children, how much more shall your Father which is in heaven give good things to them that ask him?

The Hebrew Book of Matthew

Matthew 7:12

וְכֹל שֶׁתִּרְצוּ לַעֲשׂוֹת לָכֶם אֲנוֹשִׁים וְכֵן תַּעֲשׂוּ לָהֶם בְּזֹאת תְּלוּיָה הַתּוֹרָה וּנְבִיאִים

HTV: "All that you would want people to do for you - so will you do likewise for them. Upon this hangs the words of the Torah and the prophets."

KJV: Therefore all things whatsoever ye would that men should do to you, do ye even so to them: for this is the law and the prophets.

Matthew 7:13

בּוֹאוּ נָא בְּשַׁעַר דָּחִים כִּי שַׁעַר רוֹחָב וְדֶרֶךְ מְרוֹחָב אֲשֶׁר מֵבִיא לְשַׁחַת וְרַבִּים הוֹלְכִים בּוֹ

HTV: Yeshua said to his followers, "Come! I pray you - enter into the narrow gate! For the wide gate and the broad way - bring destruction to the many who go on it!"

KJV: Enter ye in at the strait gate: for wide is the gate, and broad *is* the way, that leadeth to destruction, and many there be which go in thereat:

Matthew 7:14

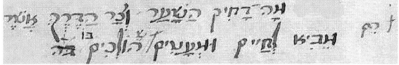
Freiberg Hebrew Manuscript

מַה-דְּחִים הַשַּׁעַר וְצַר הַדֶּרֶךְ אֲשֶׁר מֵבִיא לְחַיִּים וּמְעַטִּים הֵם שֶׁהוֹלְכִים בּוֹ

HTV: "How straight and narrow is the gate - and difficult is the way that leads to life - and few are they who are walking in it!"

KJV: Because strait *is* the gate, and narrow *is* the way, which leadeth unto life, and few there be that find it.

Chapter 7

Matthew 7:15

הִשָּׁתַמְּרוּ לָכֶם מִנְּבִיאֵי הַשֶּׁקֶר אֲשֶׁר בָּאִים אֲלֵיכֶם בְּמַלְבּוּשֵׁי הַצֹּאן בְּקִרְבָּם הֵם זְאֵבִים חֲטוּפִים

HTV: **"Beware of false prophets - who come to you in sheep's clothing - but inside they are ravenous wolves who will come to snatch you *away*!"**

KJV: Beware of false prophets, which come to you in sheep's clothing, but inwardly they are ravening wolves.

Matthew 7:16

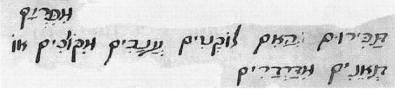

Freiberg Hebrew Manuscript

מִפֶּרְיָם תַּכִּירוּם הַאִם לוֹקְטִים עֲנָבִים מְקוֹצִים אוֹ תְאֵנִים מִדַּרְדָּרִים

HTV: **"From their fruits you shall know them. Does one gather grapes from thorns - or figs from briars?"**

Note: Neither grape vines nor fig trees have thorns, so if prophets are gathering their fruit from thorns that is a bad or evil source. But evil fruit produces evil results so you will know false prophets by their fruits.

KJV: Ye shall know them by their fruits. Do men gather grapes of thorns, or figs of thistles?

Matthew 7:17

וְכֵן כָּל אִילָן הַטוֹב מוֹצִיא פְּרִי טוֹב וְאִילָן הָרַע מוֹצִיא פְּרִי רָע

HTV: **"Thus every good tree produces good fruit - but the bad tree produces evil fruit."**

KJV: Even so every good tree bringeth forth good fruit; but a corrupt tree bringeth forth evil fruit.

Matthew 7:18

כִּי לֹא יוּכַל אִילָן הַטוֹב לְהוֹצִיא פְּרִי הָרַע וְאִילָן הָרַע לְהוֹצִיא פְּרִי הַטוֹב

The Hebrew Book of Matthew

HTV: "Because the good tree can not produce bad fruit - nor the bad tree produce good fruit."

KJV: A good tree cannot bring forth evil fruit, neither *can* a corrupt tree bring forth good fruit.

Matthew 7:19

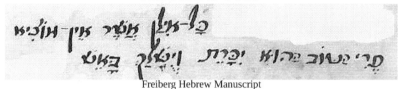
Freiberg Hebrew Manuscript

כָּל אִילָן אֲשֶׁר אֵין מוֹצִיא פְּרִי הַטוֹב הַהוּא יִכָּרֵת וְיָשְׁלַךְ בָּאֵשׁ

HTV: "Every tree that does not produce good fruit will be cut down and thrown into the fire!"

KJV: Every tree that bringeth not forth good fruit is hewn down, and cast into the fire.

Matthew 7:20

לְפִיכָךְ אַתֶּם תַכִּירוּם מִפִּרְיָם

HTV: "Therefore, you will surely know them from their fruits."

KJV: Wherefore by their fruits ye shall know them.

Matthew 7:21

לֹא כָל שֶׁיֹאמַר לִי הָאָדוֹן הָאָדוֹן הַהוּא יִכָּנֵס בְּמַלְכוּת הַשָׁמַיִם אֲבָל שֶׁיַעֲשֶׂה אֶת-הָרָצוֹן הָאָבִי שֶׁבַּשָׁמַיִם הַהוּא יִכָּנֵס בְּמַלְכוּת הַשָׁמַיִם

HTV: **Yeshua Mashiach said to his followers, "Not all who say to me 'Lord, Lord', shall enter the kingdom of heaven. However, whosoever does the will of my Father, who is in heaven, shall enter."**

KJV: Not everyone that saith unto me, Lord, Lord, shall enter into the kingdom of heaven; but he that doeth the will of my Father which is in heaven.

Matthew 7:22

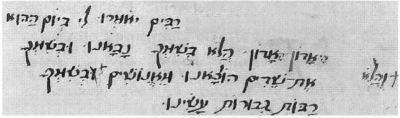

Freiberg Hebrew Manuscript

רַבִּים יֹאמְרוּ לִי בַיּוֹם הַהוּא הָאָדוֹן הָאָדוֹן הֲלֹא בְשִׁמְךָ נִבֵּאנוּ וּבְשִׁמְךָ אֶת-שֵׁדִים הוֹצֵאנוּ מֵאֲנוֹשִׁים וְהֲלֹא בְשִׁמְךָ רַבּוֹת גְבוּרוֹת עָשִׂינוּ

HTV: **"Many will say to me on that day, 'Lord, Lord, did we not prophesy in your name - and in your name did we not cast out demons from men - and in your name perform many mighty deeds!' "**

Note: See 2nd Thessalonians chapter two, which specifies the great "falling away" of those brethren who have chosen to accept lies rather than the truth. They chose unrighteousness. There will be great dangers, even death, for those who hold to truth. Many, if not most, may choose to talk the talk - but not walk the walk.

KJV: Many will say to me in that day, Lord, Lord, have we not prophesied in thy name? and in thy name have cast out devils? and in thy name done many wonderful works?

Matthew 7:23

Freiberg Hebrew Manuscript

וְאָז אֲנִי אוֹרֶה לָהֶם כִּי אֲנִי לְעוֹלָם לֹא הִכַּרְתִּיכֶם סוּרוּ מִמֶּנִּי כָּל הַפּוֹעֲלֵי עָוֶן

HTV: **"And then I myself shall profess to them, 'I never knew you! Get away from me - All you workers of lawlessness!' "**

Note: We are saved by grace through faith. It is the schoolmaster of Torah that keeps us on the path of righteousness. "Everyone who sins is breaking God's Torah - in fact, sin is the transgression of Torah!" (1John 3:4) So Yeshua is saying, "I never knew you - get away from me - all you who are without Torah! (law-less)" Something to consider. Most Bibles now translate this word as "lawlessness" rather than " iniquity."

KJV: And then will I profess unto them, I never knew you: depart from me, ye that work iniquity.

Matthew 7:24

לְפִיכָךְ כֹּל שֶׁשּׁוֹמֵעַ הָאֵלֶה דְבָרַי וְיַעֲשֶׂה אוֹתָם הַהוּא יִדָּמֶה לָאִישׁ חָכָם שֶׁבָּנָה אֶת בֵּיתוֹ עַל הַצּוּר

HTV: **"Therefore, all who hear these words and do them - resemble a wise man who built his house upon the rock."**

KJV: Therefore whosoever heareth these sayings of mine, and doeth them, I will liken him unto a wise man, which built his house upon a rock:

Matthew 7:25

וַיֵּרֶד מָטָר וְיָבוֹאוּ הַנְּהָרִים וְנָשְׁבוּ הָרוּחוֹת וְכָשְׁלוּ עַל אוֹתוֹ הַבַּיִת וְלֹא נָפַל כִּי יִהְיֶה בָּנוּי עַל הַצּוּר

HTV: **"The rain fell, the floods came, the winds blew, but his house did not fall - for it was built upon the rock."**

KJV: And the rain descended, and the floods came, and the winds blew, and beat upon that house; and it fell not: for it was founded upon a rock.

Matthew 7:26

וְכֹל שֶׁיִּשְׁמַע הָאֵלֶה דְבָרַי וְלֹא יַעֲשֶׂה אוֹתָם הַהוּא נִתְדַּמֶה לָאִישׁ כְּסִיל אֲשֶׁר בָּנָה אֶת-בֵּיתוֹ עַל הַחוֹל

HTV: **"All who hear these words but do not do them - resemble the foolish man who built his house upon the sand."**

KJV: And every one that heareth these sayings of mine, and doeth them not, shall be likened unto a foolish man, which built his house upon the sand:

Matthew 7:27

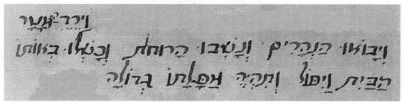

Freiberg Hebrew Manuscript

וַיֵּרֶד הַמָּטָר וַיָּבוֹאוּ הַנְּהָרִים וְנָשְׁבוּ הָרוּחוֹת וְכָשְׁלוּ בְאוֹתוֹ הַבַּיִת וַיִּפּוֹל וְתִהְיֶה מַפַּלְתּוֹ גְדוֹלָה

HTV: **"The rain came down, the floods came, the winds blew - the house did fall - and great was its ruin!"**

KJV: And the rain descended, and the floods came, and the winds blew, and beat upon that house; and it fell: and great was the fall of it.

Matthew 7:28

וַיְהִי כַּאֲשֶׁר יֵשׁוּעַ כָּלָה הָאֵלֶּה דְּבָרִים שֶׁהַכִּתִּים יִהְיוּ תּוֹמְהִים עַל לִימּוּדוֹ

HTV: **And it came to pass, when Yeshua had said all these things - the crowds were astonished by his teaching.**

KJV: And it came to pass, when Jesus had ended these sayings, the people were astonished at his doctrine.

Matthew 7:29

כִּי יִהְיֶה מְלַמְּדָם כְּאִילּוּ לוֹ מֶמְשָׁלֶת נִתְּנָה וְלֹא כְסוֹפְרֵיהֶם וּפְרוּשִׁים

HTV: **Because (Yeshua) taught them - with authority - not as the scribes and Pharisees.**

KJV: For he taught them as *one* having authority, and not as the scribes.

Matthew Chapter 8

Hebrew Text Version (HTV)

¹ When Yeshua came down from the mountain, great crowds of people followed after him.

² And a leper came, he bowed to him (Yeshua) and said "My Lord if you want - you are able to cleanse me."

³ Yeshua stretched out his hand and touched him, and he said, "Behold, I will it - be clean now!" And behold his leprosy was immediately cleansed.

⁴ And Yeshua said to him, "Look and beware! - that you do not tell anyone. Indeed, go and show yourself to the priest, and offer your sacrifice - which Moses commanded them (the priests) *to do* as a testimony."

⁵ When he (Yeshua) entered into Capernaum, a certain commander of hundreds [a Centurion] came to him - petitioning;

⁶ Saying, "My Lord, behold, <u>my son</u> is lying sick in bed in my house - paralyzed in his limbs and suffering greatly!"

⁷ And Yeshua said to him, "I will come and heal him."

⁸ And the Centurion answered and said, "My Lord I am not worthy that you should come under the roof of my home - but if you will say just one word - <u>my son</u> will be healed."

⁹ I am a man under authority - there are men of war under my dominion - when I say to one 'go!' he goes - and to another 'come' he comes - and to my servant 'do this', and he does.

¹⁰ When Yeshua heard these words, He said to his followers, "Truly I say to you, I have not found faith such as this in Israel."

¹¹ "I say to you, that many shall come from the east and the west - and sleep with Abraham, Isaac and Jacob - in the kingdom of heaven."

¹² "But many of the sons of the kingdom (*of Israel*) shall be cast into outermost darkness - there shall be wailing and gnashing of teeth."

¹³ Yeshua said to the centurion, "Go! and *what* you have

believed shall come to pass" - and the boy was healed at that same hour.

¹⁴ When Yeshua entered Peter's house - Behold, he saw his (Peter's) mother-in-law who lay suffering from a fever.

¹⁵ He touched her hand and the fever left her. Then she arose and served them.

¹⁶ After the sun went down - at twilight - they brought near to him many who were demon-possessed. He cast out the evil spirits by his word and he healed all of the sick,

¹⁷ in fulfillment of what had been spoken by (the mouth of) the prophet Isaiah, who said, "Surely our griefs he lifted - and our sorrows he carried!" (Isa. 53:4)

¹⁸ When Yeshua saw crowds of people all around him - he commanded the disciples *to prepare* to cross over the sea (*of Galilee*).

¹⁹ A certain scribe approached him and said, "Rabbi, I will follow after you wherever you go!"

²⁰ Yeshua said to him, "Behold - foxes have caves and birds have nests - but the son of Adam (Man), the son of the virgin, has no place where he can lay his head."

²¹ One of his followers said to him, "My lord, please allow me to remain so that I may first go bury my father."

²² Yeshua said to him, "Come follow after me! and let the dead (*in Spirit*) bury their own dead."

²³ After that - he went up into the boat - and his disciples followed after him.

²⁴ Behold, a great storm arose in the sea until the ship was covered by waves and he (Yeshua) was asleep.

²⁵ And the disciples approached him and woke him up saying, "Lord please save us, because we are perishing!"

²⁶ Yeshua said to them, "What are you afraid of - *you of* little faith?" Then he stood up and commanded the winds and the sea to be renewed - *and there was* great calm.

²⁷ The people were amazed saying, "Behold! - Who is this that the winds and the sea - listen and obey him?"

²⁸ When Yeshua passed over the sea to the other *side*, to the country of the Gergashites, a demon-possessed man came toward him from the tombs. He was exceedingly savage and

The Hebrew Book of Matthew

raging - *so much so* that no person was able to pass that way.

²⁹ "Behold!" they (the demons) shouted saying, "What are we to you - son of David - Yeshua Mashiach? Have you come here before the appointed time - to banish us?"

³⁰ There was, not too distant from them, a large herd of many pigs who were feeding.

³¹ The demons pressed upon him saying, "If you banish us from here my Lord - allow us to enter into the herd of pigs."

³² Yeshua Mashiach said to them, "GO!" And they went out and they entered every one of the herd - and the pigs rushed with a great loud noise into the sea and they died in the water.

³³ The shepherds who were keeping them (the pigs) saw this - they ran away and came into the city - and told all these things - and what happened to the demon-possessed man.

³⁴ The whole city came out to Yeshua Mashiach, and when they saw him, asked him to go away from their country.

Matthew Chapter 8

HTV with translator notes and KJV comparison

Matthew 8:1

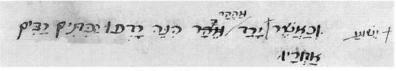

Freiburg Hebrew Manuscript

וְכַאֲשֶׁר יֵשׁוּעַ יָרַד מֵהָהָר הִנֵּה רָדְפוּ הַכִּתִּים רַבִּים אַחֲרָיו

HTV: When Yeshua came down from the mountain, great crowds of people followed after him.

KJV: When he was come down from the mountain, great multitudes followed him.

Matthew 8:2

וְהִנֵּה בָא שׁוּם אָדָם צָרוּעַ וַיִּשְׁתַּחֲוָה לוֹ וַיֹּאמַר הָאֲדוֹנִי אִם תִּרְצֶה אַתָּה תּוּכַל לְטַהֲרֵנִי

HTV: **And a leper came, he bowed to him (Yeshua) and said "My Lord if you want - you are able to cleanse me."**

KJV: And, behold, there came a leper and worshipped him, saying, Lord, if thou wilt, thou canst make me clean.

Matthew 8:3

וְיוֹשִׁיט יֵשׁוּעַ אֶת-יָדוֹ וַיִּגַּע אוֹתוֹ לֵאמֹר הִנֵּה אֲנִי רוֹצֶה הִטָּהֵר עַתָּה וּמִיָּד נִטְטָהֲרָה הַצָּרַעַת שֶׁבּוֹ

HTV: **Yeshua stretched out his hand and touched him, and he said, "Behold, I will it - be clean now!" And behold his leprosy was immediately cleansed.**

KJV: And Jesus put forth *his* hand, and touched him, saying, I will; be thou clean. And immediately his leprosy was cleansed.

Matthew 8:4

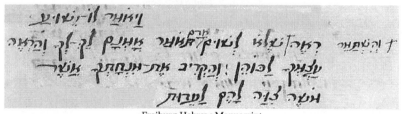
Freiburg Hebrew Manuscript

וַיֹּאמֶר לוֹ יֵשׁוּעַ רְאֵה וְהִשָּׁתַמֵּר שֶׁלֹּא לְשׁוּם אָדָם תֹּאמַר אָמְנָם לֵךְ- לֵךְ וְהַרְאֵה עַצְמְךָ לַכּוֹהֵן וְהַקְרִיב אֶת-מִנְחָתְךָ אֲשֶׁר מֹשֶׁה צִוָּה לָהֶם לְעֵדוּת

HTV: **And Yeshua said to him, "Look and beware! - that you do not tell anyone. Indeed, go and show yourself to the priest, and offer your sacrifice - which Moses commanded them (the priests)** *to do* **as a testimony."**

Note: See Leviticus 14 for the required official priestly ritual of sacrifice and certification that one is now clean. Matthew 11:5 cites "the blind see,

The Hebrew Book of Matthew

the lame walk, the lepers are cured, the deaf hear, the dead are raised to life, and the Good News is preached to the poor." These miraculous signs of the Messiah's coming are from references in the Tanakh; Isa 35:5-6, 42:6-7, 61:1, 63:1.

KJV: But go thy way, shew thyself to the priest, and offer the gift that Moses commanded, for a testimony unto them.

Matthew 8:5

וּמִשֶּׁנִכְנַס בִּכְפַר-נָחוּם בָּא אֵלָיו שׂוּם הַשַּׂר מֵאוֹת שׁוֹאֵל מִמֶּנּוּ

HTV: **When he (Yeshua) entered into Capernaum, a certain commander of hundreds [a Centurion] came to him - petitioning;**

KJV: And when Jesus was entered into Capernaum, there came unto him a centurion, beseeching him,

Matthew 8:6

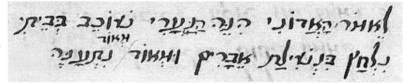

Freiburg Hebrew Manuscript

לֵאמֹר הָאֲדוֹנִי הִנֵּה הַנַּעֲרִי שׁוֹכֵב בְּבֵית י נִלְחַץ בִּנְשִׁילַת אֲבָרִים וּמְאֹד מְאֹד נִתְעַנֶּה

HTV: **Saying, "My Lord, behold, <u>my son</u> is lying sick in bed in my house - paralyzed in his limbs and suffering greatly!"**

Note: The Shem Tov, the HGC, and the DuTillet Hebrew manuscripts have *beni* "my son." In addition the Sahidic Coptic has "my son." The Freiberg, the Harley MS, Munster, and the Travancore-Cochin Hebrew MSS have "my boy," which can also refer to the Centurion's son. The Syriac Peshitta and Harklean texts both say "my child." The Old Latin has "puer" which can mean child, boy, youth, servant, slave, or bachelor. The Old Latin reading may be the key to understanding - the Hebrew was translated into Latin and the ambiguous Latin was then translated into Greek to read "servant," departing from the original Hebrew reading.

KJV: And saying, Lord, my servant lieth at home sick of the palsy, grievously tormented.

Matthew 8:7
וַיֹּאמֶר לוֹ יֵשׁוּעַ אֲנִי אָבוֹא וַאֲרַפֵּא אוֹתוֹ

HTV: **And Yeshua said to him, "I will come and heal him."**

KJV: And Jesus saith unto him, I will come and heal him.

Matthew 8:8
וַיַּעַן הַשַּׂר מֵאוֹת וַיֹּאמַר הָאֲדוֹנִי אֵינִי רָאוּי שֶׁתָּבוֹא תַּחַת קוֹרַת דִּירָתִי כִּי אִם אֱמוֹר לְבַד דָּבָר אֶחָד וְיֵרָפֵא הַנַּעֲרִי

HTV: **And the Centurion answered and said, "My Lord I am not worthy that you should come under the roof of my home - but if you will say just one word - <u>my son</u> will be healed."**

KJV: The centurion answered and said, Lord, I am not worthy that thou shouldest come under my roof: but speak the word only, and my servant shall be healed.

Matthew 8:9
הִנֵּה אַף אֲנִי אִישׁ נִשְׁתַּעֲבַד לְמֶמְשֶׁלֶת הָאַחֵר וְיֵשׁ לִי אַנְשֵׁי מִלְחָמוֹת וְאִם אָמַר לְזֶה לֵךְ וְהוּא הוֹלֵךְ וּלְאַחֵר אַתָּה בּוֹא וְהִנֵּה הוּא בָא וּלְעַבְדִּי עֲשֵׂה הַזֹּאת הִנֵּה הוּא עוֹשֶׂה

HTV: **I am a man under authority - there are men of war under my dominion - when I say to one 'go!' he goes - and to another 'come' he comes - and to my servant 'do this', and he does.**

KJV: For I am a man under authority, having soldiers under me: and I say to this *man*, Go, and he goeth; and to another, Come, and he cometh; and to my servant, Do this, and he doeth *it*.

Matthew 8:10
וּמִשֶּׁיֵּשׁוּעַ שָׁמַע הָאֵלֶּה דְּבָרִים הוּא אָמַר לְהַנִּמְשָׁכִים אַחֲרָיו בֶּאֱמֶת אֲנִי אוֹמֵר לָכֶם שֶׁלֹּא מָצָאתִי אֱמוּנָה כָּזֹאת בְּיִשְׂרָאֵל

HTV: **When Yeshua heard these words, He said to his followers, "Truly I say to you, I have not found faith such as this in Israel."**

The Hebrew Book of Matthew

KJV: When Jesus heard *it*, he marvelled, and said to them that followed, Verily I say unto you, I have not found so great faith, no, not in Israel.

Matthew 8:11

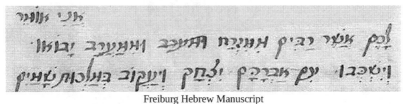
Freiburg Hebrew Manuscript

אֲנִי אוֹמֵר לָכֶם אֲשֶׁר רַבִּים מִמִּזְרָח וּמִמַּעֲרָב יָבוֹאוּ וְיִשְׁכְּבוּ עִם אַבְרָהָם יִצְחָק וְיַעֲקוֹב בְּמַלְכוּת שָׁמַיִם

HTV: "I say to you, that many shall come from the east and the west - and sleep with Abraham, Isaac and Jacob - in the kingdom of heaven."

> Note: Yeshua is prophesying about faith. Many from afar will sleep with the family of Abraham because they have been grafted into the family of faith through belief in the Son of Yehovah.
>
> They will lie down (figuratively) in the family tomb, and be with Abraham, Isaac and Jacob in heaven. It is about faith not geography. It is not exclusively for Israelites. This is about the faithful remnant, wherever they are.

KJV: And I say unto you, That many shall come from the east and west, and shall sit down with Abraham, and Isaac, and Jacob, in the kingdom of heaven.

Matthew 8:12

Freiburg Hebrew Manuscript

אֲבָל בְּנֵי הַמַּלְכוּת יִשְׁלְחוּ חוּצָה בַּחֲשָׁכִים הַחִיצוֹנִים שָׁם-תִּהְיֶה הַבֶּכָא וְחִרוּק שִׁנַּיִם

HTV: "But many of the sons of the kingdom (*of Israel*) shall be cast into outermost darkness - there shall be wailing and gnashing of teeth."

Chapter 8

Note: Conversely, Yeshua is saying that just because you are Israelite - does not mean you have a free ticket to the kingdom of heaven. There is evil and unbelief there. It is about faith not geography. See Romans 11:17-25, some natural branches are pruned for unbelief while some wild branches are grafted into the family of Abraham.

KJV: But the children of the kingdom shall be cast out into outer darkness: there shall be weeping and gnashing of teeth.

Matthew 8:13

וַיֹּאמַר יֵשׁוּעַ לְשַׂר-מֵאוֹת לֶךְ-לְךָ וִיהִי לְךָ כְּמוֹ שֶׁהֶאֱמַנְתָּ וְנִרְפָּא הַנַּעַר בְּאוֹתָהּ שָׁעָה

HTV: **Yeshua said to the centurion, "Go!, and *what* you have believed shall come to pass" - and the boy was healed at that same hour.**

KJV: And Jesus said unto the centurion, Go thy way; and as thou hast believed, *so* be it done unto thee. And his servant was healed in the selfsame hour.

Matthew 8:14

וְכַאֲשֶׁר יֵשׁוּעַ בָּא בְּבֵית כֵּיפָא הִנֵּה רָאָה אֶת חֲמוֹתוֹ שֶׁתִּשְׁכַּב וְתִתְלַחֵץ מִקְּדַחָה

HTV: **When Yeshua entered Peter's house - Behold, he saw his (Peter's) mother-in-law who lay suffering from a fever.**

KJV: And when Jesus was come into Peter's house, he saw his wife's mother laid, and sick of a fever.

Matthew 8:15

וַיִּגַּע אֶת-יָדָהּ וַעֲזָבָהּ הַקְּדַחָה וַתָּקָם וַתְּשַׁמֵּשׁ לָהֶם

HTV: **He touched her hand and the fever left her. Then she arose and served them.**

KJV: And he touched her hand, and the fever left her: and she arose, and ministered unto them.

Matthew 8:16

וְאַחֲרֵי שֶׁהַשֶּׁמֶשׁ נָטָה לַעֲרוֹב הֵמָה הִקְרִיבוּ לוֹ רַבִּים אֲשֶׁר בָּהֶם הַשֵּׁדִים וְגֵרֵשׁ אֶת-רוּחוֹת רָעִים בִּדְבָרוֹ וַיִּרְפָּא כָּל חוֹלִים

HTV: **After the sun went down - at twilight - they brought near to him many who were demon-possessed. He cast out the evil spirits by his word and he healed all of the sick,**

KJV: When the even was come, they brought unto him many that were possessed with devils: and he cast out the spirits with *his* word, and healed all that were sick:

Matthew 8:17

כְּדֵי שֶׁיִּמָּלֵא מָה שֶׁנֶּאֱמַר עַל פִּי יְשַׁעְיָהוּ הַנָּבִיא הָאוֹמֵר אָכֵן חֳלָיֵנוּ הוּא נָשָׂא וּמַכְאֹבֵינוּ סְבָלָם

HTV: **in fulfillment of what had been spoken by (the mouth of) the prophet Isaiah, who said, "Surely our griefs he lifted - and our sorrows he carried!"** (Isa. 53:4)

KJV: That it might be fulfilled which was spoken by Esaias the prophet, saying, Himself took our infirmities, and bare *our* sicknesses.

Matthew 8:18

וַיַּרְא יֵשׁוּעַ כִּתִּים רַבִּים בִּסְבִיבוֹ וַיְצַוֶּה אֶת-הַתַּלְמִידִים לַעֲבוֹר אֶת הַיָּם

HTV: **When Yeshua saw crowds of people all around him - he commanded the disciples *to prepare* to cross over the sea (*of Galilee*).**

KJV: Now when Jesus saw great multitudes about him, he gave commandment to depart unto the other side.

Matthew 8:19

וַיִּקְרַב שׁוּם סוֹפֵר וַיֹּאמַר לוֹ רַבִּי אֲנִי אָבוֹא אַחֲרֶיךָ לְכֹל מָקוֹם שֶׁאַתָּה תֵלֵךְ

HTV: **A certain scribe approached him and said, "Rabbi, I will follow after you wherever you go!"**

Chapter 8

KJV: And a certain scribe came, and said unto him, Master, I will follow thee whithersoever thou goest.

Matthew 8:20

וַיֹּאמֶר לוֹ יֵשׁוּעַ הִנֵּה לְשׁוּעָלִים נִמְצָאוֹת מְעָרוֹת וּלְעוֹפוֹת שָׁמַיִם קִנִּים אֲבָל לְבֶן הָאָדָם אֵין מָקוֹם אֲשֶׁר שָׁם יַטֶּה אֶת-רֹאשׁוֹ

HTV: **Yeshua said to him, "Behold - foxes have caves and birds have nests - but the son of Adam (Man), the son of the virgin, has no place where he can lay his head."**

KJV: And Jesus saith unto him, The foxes have holes, and the birds of the air *have* nests; but the Son of man hath not where to lay *his* head.

Matthew 8:21

Freiburg Hebrew Manuscript

וְאֶחָד מִתַּלְמִידָיו אָמַר לוֹ אָנָּא אֲדוֹנִי הַנִּיחַ לִי שֶׁבָּרִאשׁוֹנָה אֵלֵךְ וְאֶקְבּוֹר אֶת-אָבִי

HTV: **One of his followers said to him, "My lord, please allow me to remain so that I may first go bury my father."**

Note: This may well refer to the second burial. A body was allowed to decompose until only bone were left, then the bones were put into an ossuary box for reburial. This could be a lengthy process of many months. If so, Yeshua did not forbid him to honor his father's funeral, that was already done.

KJV: And another of his disciples said unto him, Lord, suffer me first to go and bury my father.

Matthew 8:22

וַיֹּאמֶר לוֹ יֵשׁוּעַ בּוֹא אַחֲרַי וְהַנִּיחָה שֶׁהַמֵּתִים יִקְבְּרוּ אֶת הַמֵּתֵיהֶם

HTV: **Yeshua said to him, "Come follow after me! and let the dead (*in Spirit*) bury their own dead."**

Note: Yeshua would have him focused on those who seek everlasting "life in the spirit."

KJV: But Jesus said unto him, Follow me; and let the dead bury their dead.

Matthew 8:23

וּמִשֶּׁעָלָה בַסְּפִינָה נִמְשְׁכוּ אַחֲרָיו הַתַּלְמִידָיו

HTV: **After that - he went up into the boat - and his disciples followed after him.**

KJV: And when he was entered into a ship, his disciples followed him.

Matthew 8:24

וְהִנֵּה תְּנוּעָה גְּדוֹלָה נִתְחַדְּשָׁה בַיָּם עַד שֶׁהַסְּפִינָה תְּכֻסֶּה מִגַּלִּים וְהוּא יִהְיֶה יָשֵׁן

HTV: **Behold, a great storm arose in the sea until the ship was covered by waves and he (Yeshua) was asleep.**

KJV: And, behold, there arose a great tempest in the sea, insomuch that the ship was covered with the waves: but he was asleep.

Matthew 8:25

Freiburg Hebrew Manuscript

וַיִּקְרְבוּ אֵלָיו הַתַּלְמִידָיו וַיְקִצוּהוּ לֵאמֹר אָנָא הָאָדוֹן הוֹשִׁיעֵנוּ כִּי אֲנַחְנוּ אוֹבְדִים

HTV: **And the disciples approached him and woke him up saying, "Lord please save us, because we are perishing!"**

Chapter 8

KJV: And his disciples came to *him*, and awoke him, saying, Lord, save us: we perish.

Matthew 8:26

וַיֹּאמֶר לָהֶם יֵשׁוּעַ מָה אַתֶּם יְרֵאִים הַקְּטַנֵּי אֱמוּנָה וְאָז קָם וַיְצַוֶּה לָרוּחוֹת וּלַיָּם וְנִתְחַדְּשָׁה הֲנָחָה גְדוֹלָה

HTV: **Yeshua said to them, "What are you afraid of - *you of* little faith?" Then he stood up and commanded the winds and the sea to be renewed -** *and there was great calm.*

King James Version (KJV): And he saith unto them, Why are ye fearful, O ye of little faith? Then he arose, and rebuked the winds and the sea; and there was a great calm.

Matthew 8:27

וְהִנֵּה הָאֲנוֹשִׁים יִתְמְהוּ לֵאמֹר אֵיזֶה הַזֶּה כִּי הָרוּחוֹת וְהַיָּם שׁוֹמְעִים לוֹ

HTV: **The people were amazed saying, "Behold! - Who is this that the winds and the sea - listen and obey him?"**

KJV: But the men marveled, saying, What manner of man is this, that even the winds and the sea obey him!

Matthew 8:28

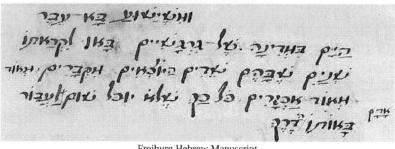

Freiburg Hebrew Manuscript

וּמִשֶּׁיֵּשׁוּעַ בָּא אֶל עֵבֶר הַיָּם בִּמְדִינָה שֶׁל גֵּרְגֵּשִׁיִּים בָּאוּ לִקְרָאתוֹ שְׁנַיִם שֶׁבָּהֶם שֵׁדִים הַיּוֹצְאִים מִקְּבָרִים מְאוֹד מְאוֹד אַכְזָרִים כֹּל כָּךְ שֶׁלֹּא יוּכַל שׁוּם אָדָם לַעֲבוֹר בְּאוֹתוֹ הַדֶּרֶךְ

131

The Hebrew Book of Matthew

HTV: **When Yeshua passed over the sea to the other *side*, to the country of the Gergashites, a demon-possessed man came toward him from the tombs. He was exceedingly savage and raging -** *so much so* **that no person was able to pass that way.**

> Note: In the Hebrew Gospel from Catalonia, it says "**one man**" possessed of "**many demons**." However, in the next verse it says "they shouted" to Yeshua. The demons shouting seem to have confused copyists and translators into thinking there were two men. However, in Mark 5:9, where the same story is told, it says one man. When Yeshua asked the demon his name, he said "Legion - for we are many." In the HGC the word "satan" is used to mean "demon" or "devil"

KJV: And when he was come to the other side into the country of the Gergesenes, there met him **two possessed with devils**, coming out of the tombs, exceeding fierce, so that no man might pass by that way.

Matthew 8:29

Freiburg Hebrew Manuscript

וְהִנֵּה הֵם צָעֲקוּ לֵאמֹר מָה לָנוּ וּלְךָ יֵשׁוּעַ הַבֵּן הָאֱלֹהִים אַתָּה בָּאתָ הֵנָּה לַהֲצִיקֵנוּ·

HTV: **"Behold!" they (the demons) shouted saying, "What are we to you - son of David - Yeshua Mashiach? Have you come here before the appointed time - to banish us?"**

> Note: All the demons knew Yeshua - and they knew he was coming for them. The demons knew of Judgement Day. Their days were numbered - but they hoped it would not be so soon.

KJV: And, behold, they cried out, saying, What have we to do with thee, Jesus, thou Son of God? art thou come hither to torment us before the time?

Chapter 8

Matthew 8:30

וַיְהִיָה לֹא רָחוֹק מֵהֶם עֵדֶר חֲזִירִים רַבִּים נִתְפַּרְנֵס

HTV: There was, not too distant from them, a large herd of many pigs who were feeding.

KJV: And there was a good way off from them an herd of many swine feeding.

Matthew 8:31

וְהַשֵּׁדִים יִשְׁאָלוּהוּ וַיֹּאמְרוּ אִם אַתָּה תְגָרֵשׁ אוֹתָנוּ מִכַּאן הַרְשֵׁה נָא שֶׁנָבוֹא בְּעֵדֶר חֲזִירִים

HTV: The demons pressed upon him saying, "If you banish us from here my Lord - allow us to enter into the herd of pigs."

KJV: So the devils besought him, saying, If thou cast us out, suffer us to go away into the herd of swine.

Matthew 8:32

וַיֹּאמֶר לָהֶם לְכוּ לָכֶם וְהֵמָּה יָצְאוּ וְנִכְנְסוּ בַּחֲזִירִים וְהִנֵּה כָּל הָעֵדֶר הָלַךְ נֶחְפַּז בְּרַעַשׁ גָּדוֹל בַּיָּם וּמֵתוּ בַמַּיִם

HTV: Yeshua Mashiach said to them, "GO!" And they went out and they entered every one of the herd - and the pigs rushed with a great loud noise into the sea and they died in the water.

KJV: And he said unto them, Go. And when they were come out, they went into the herd of swine: and, behold, the whole herd of swine ran violently down a steep place into the sea, and perished in the waters.

Matthew 8:33

Hebrew Gospels from Catalonia

133

The Hebrew Book of Matthew

והחזירים הפילו עצמם לים פתאום ומתו והרועים שהיו שומרים ראו
זה ברחו ובאו אל העיר מספרים מהמשוטן

HTV: The shepherds who were keeping them (the pigs) saw this - they ran away and came into the city - and told all these things - and what happened to the demon-possessed man.

> Note: Again, the HGC uses the word "satan" as a synonym for *demon*, which is common throughout the manuscript.

KJV: And they that kept them fled, and went their ways into the city, and told every thing, and what was befallen to the possessed of the devils.

Matthew 8:34

וְהִנֵּה כֹל הָעִיר יָצְאָה לִקְרַאת יֵשׁוּעַ וְאַחֲרֵי שֶׁרָאוּהוּ בִקְשׁוּ מִמֶּנּוּ
שֶׁיָּסוּר מֵאַרְצָם

HTV: The whole city came out to Yeshua Mashiach, and when they saw him, asked him to go away from their country.

KJV: And, behold, the whole city came out to meet Jesus: and when they saw him, they besought *him* that he would depart out of their coasts.

Matthew Chapter 9

Hebrew Text Version (HTV)

¹ And Yeshua got into a ship and crossed the sea and came unto his city (Capernaum).

² And behold, they brought and put *before* him a person who had lost control of his limbs - who was lying down on a bed. Yeshua saw their faith and said to the paralytic, "Faith, please, my son! Because your sins will be forgiven."

³ And behold, some of the scribes said between themselves, "This *man* blasphemes!"

⁴ And when Yeshua saw their thoughts - he said, "Why do you think evil in your hearts?"

⁵ "What is easier to say - Your sins are forgiven - or to say Get up and walk?"

⁶ "Indeed, so that you will know that - to the Son of Man authority *has been given* to forgive sins." And he said to the paralytic, "Get up, take your bed and go home."

⁷ Then he got up and went home.

⁸ But after people saw this, they feared and honored Elohim who gave power - such as this - to men.

⁹ After he crossed over, Yeshua saw a certain man, sitting by the tax booth, named Matthew. He said to him, "Come and follow me!" And he rose up and went after him.

¹⁰ And it came to pass, when he (Yeshua) sat with him (Matthew) in his house - Behold! - Tax collectors and sinners came and sat together with Yeshua at table, and also with his students.

¹¹ After the Pharisees saw *this* - they said to his students, "Why does your rabbi eat with tax collectors and with sinners?"

¹² When Yeshua heard this, he said, "The healer is not needed by the healthy - but by the sick."

¹³ "Go and learn what this means: 'I desired loving kindness and not sacrifice.' I did not come to call the righteous but sinners."

14 And then John (*the Baptist's*) disciples approached Yeshua the Messiah and said, "Why do we and the Pharisees fast so often - but your disciples do not fast?"

¹⁵ Yeshua said to them, "Do the sons of the groom mourn *while* he is still living among them? Truly the days will come when the groom will be taken from them - and then they will fast."

¹⁶ "There is no man to be found who will sew a new piece of clothing onto old clothing - because the piece will tear away from the old clothes and the tear at this spot will be even worse."

¹⁷ There is no one who puts new wine into old wineskins. And if so, behold the wineskins will be burst and the wine will be spilled, and the wineskins will be lost. But *if* they put new wine into new wineskins - both of them are preserved.

¹⁸ As he spoke to them about these things - behold - a chieftain came near to him and bowed down to him saying, "My Lord, come see, my daughter has just died. Please come and lay your hand and put it upon her, and she will revive."

¹⁹ Yeshua rose up - and also his disciples - and followed after him.

²⁰ Then behold, a woman - who had a flow of blood for twelve years - came close to him from behind and touched the hem of his clothing.

²¹ She had said to herself, in her distress, "If only I could touch his clothing - I will be saved *(from this malady)*."

²² Yeshua turned around, saw her and said to her, "Daughter, trust me - your faith has saved you." In that same hour, the woman was healed.

²³ When Yeshua came into the house of the chieftain and saw the *hired* mourners and the murmuring crowd,

²⁴ he (Yeshua) said to them, "Get out! The girl is not dead - she is sleeping." And they ridiculed him.

²⁵ When the crowd was thrown out, he (Yeshua) entered her room, took her hand and said to her, "Arise!" And the young girl arose.

²⁶ And the (*word*) hearing of this - went out into all the land.

²⁷ After Yeshua passed by them, two blind men came out after him and cried, "Have mercy on us, Son of David!"

²⁸ When he came into the house, the blind men approach him, and Yeshua said unto them, "Do you believe that I can do

this?" And they said to him, "Lord, truly we believe!"

²⁹ He touched their eyes and said, "Let it be unto you - according to your faith."

³⁰ And their eyes were opened. Yeshua commanded them saying gravely, "See that no man will know of this!"

³¹ However, they went out and made it known throughout the land.

³² And they went out and - behold, *others* brought to him a mute man with a demon in him.

³³ And when the demon was cast from him - behold - the mute spoke! The people were amazed, saying, "Never! Not in Israel - has this been seen!"

³⁴ In truth, the Pharisees said, "He casts out demons by the ruler of the demons! (Ha-Satan)"

³⁵ Yeshua went around to all the cities and villages teaching the people in every assembly and synagogue - the *Torah* (Midrash) - and the good news (Gospel) of the kingdom - healing all disease and all suffering.

³⁶ Yeshua saw the unwashed and had mercy on them - because they are abandoned and are scattered as sheep without a shepherd.

³⁷ He (Yeshua) said to his disciples, "Behold the harvest is vast but the workers are few."

³⁸ "Please pray to the Lord of the harvest - that He send workers into His harvest."

Matthew Chapter 9

HTV with translator notes and KJV comparison

Matthew 9:1

Freiburg Hebrew Manuscript

וַיַּעַל יֵשׁוּעַ בַּסְפִינָה וְעָבַר אֶת-הַיָּם וּבָא בָעִירוֹ

HTV: **And Yeshua got into a ship and crossed the sea and came unto his city (Capernaum).**

KJV: And he entered into a ship, and passed over, and came into his own city.

Matthew 9:2

וְהִנֵּה הִקְרִיבוּ לוֹ שׁוּם בַּעַל נְשִׁילַת אֲבָרִים הַשׁוֹכֵב בְּעֶרֶשׂ וַיַּרְא יֵשׁוּעַ אֶת הָאֱמוּנָתָם וַיֹּאמַר לְבַעַל נְשִׁילַת אֲבָרִים בְּטַח נָא בְנִי כִּי יִסָּלְחוּ לְךָ חֲטָאוֹתֶיךָ

HTV: **And behold, they brought and put *before* him a person who had lost control of his limbs - who was lying down on a bed. Yeshua saw their faith and said to the paralytic, "Faith, please, my son! Because your sins will be forgiven."**

KJV: And, behold, they brought to him a man sick of the palsy, lying on a bed: and Jesus seeing their faith said unto the sick of the palsy; Son, be of good cheer; thy sins be forgiven thee.

Matthew 9:3

וְהִנֵּה קְצָת מְסוֹפְרִים אָמְרוּ בֵּינוֹתֵיהֶם הַזֶּה מְחָרֵף

HTV: **And behold, some of the scribes said between themselves, "This *man* blasphemes!"**

KJV: And, behold, certain of the scribes said within themselves, This *man* blasphemeth.

Matthew 9:4

וּמִשֶּׁיֵּשׁוּעַ רָאָה אֶת-מַחֲשְׁבוֹתֵיהֶם הוּא אָמַר לָמָה אַתֶּם חוֹשְׁבִים רָעָה בְלִבּוֹתֵיכֶם

HTV: **And when Yeshua saw their thoughts - he said, "Why do you think evil in your hearts?"**

KJV: And Jesus knowing their thoughts said, Wherefore think ye evil in your hearts?

Matthew 9:5

מַה נָא יוֹתֵר קַל לֵאמֹר תְּסֻלַּחְנָה לְךָ חֲטָאוֹתֶיךָ אוֹ לֵאמֹר קוּמָה וְהַלֵּךְ

HTV: **"What is easier to say - Your sins are forgiven - or to say Get up and walk?"**

KJV: For whether is easier, to say, *Thy* sins be forgiven thee; or to say, Arise, and walk?

Matthew 9:6

אָמְנָם כְּדֵי שֶׁתֵּדְעוּ אֲשֶׁר לְבֶן אָדָם מֶמְשֶׁלֶת לִסְלֹחַ אֶת-חַטָּאוֹת וְאָז אָמַר לְבַעַל נְשִׁילַת אֲבָרִים קוּמָה וְטַל אֵת עֶרֶשׂ שֶׁלְּךָ וְהַלֵּךְ בְּבֵיתְךָ

HTV: **"Indeed, so that you will know that - to the Son of Man authority *has been given* to forgive sins." And he said to the paralytic, "Get up, take your bed and go home."**

KJV: But that ye may know that the Son of man hath power on earth to forgive sins, (then saith he to the sick of the palsy,) Arise, take up thy bed, and go unto thine house.

Matthew 9:7

אֲשֶׁר קָם וְהָלַךְ בְּבֵיתוֹ

HTV: **Then he got up and went home.**

KJV: And he arose, and departed to his house.

Matthew 9:8

אֲבָל אַחֲרֵי שֶׁכִּתִּים רָאוּ הַזֹּאת הֵמָה יָרְאוּ וְהָדְרוּ אֶת-אֱלֹהִים שֶׁנָּתַן מֶמְשֶׁלֶת כַּזֹּאת לָאֱנוֹשִׁים

HTV: **But after people saw this, they feared and honored Elohim who gave power - such as this - to men.**

KJV: But when the multitudes saw *it*, they marveled, and glorified God, which had given such power unto men.

Matthew 9:9

וּמִשֶּׁעָבַר יֵשׁוּעַ מִכָּאן רָאָה אֵיזֶה אָדָם הַיּוֹשֵׁב לְנִגֶּשׁ אֶת-הַמֶּכֶס שֶׁשְּׁמוֹ מַתִּי וַיֹּאמֶר לוֹ בֹּא נָא אַחֲרַי וַיָּקָם וַיָּבוֹא אַחֲרָיו

The Hebrew Book of Matthew

HTV: **After he crossed over, Yeshua saw a certain man, sitting by the tax booth, named Matthew. He said to him, "Come and follow me!" And he rose up and went after him.**

KJV: And as Jesus passed forth from thence, he saw a man, named Matthew, sitting at the receipt of custom: and he saith unto him, Follow me. And he arose, and followed him.

Matthew 9:10

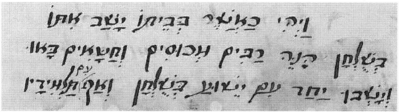
Freiburg Hebrew Manuscript

וַיְהִי כַּאֲשֶׁר בְּבֵיתוֹ יָשַׁב אִתּוֹ בְשֻׁלְחָן הִנֵּה רַבִּים מְכוּסִים וְחַטָּאִים בָּאוּ וְיָשְׁבוּ יַחַד

HTV: **And it came to pass, when he (Yeshua) sat with him (Matthew) in his house - Behold! - Tax collectors and sinners came and sat together with Yeshua at table, and also with his students.**

KJV: And it came to pass, as Jesus sat at meat in the house, behold, many publicans and sinners came and sat down with him and his disciples.

Matthew 9:11

אֲשֶׁר פְּרוּשִׁים הָיוּ רוֹאִים וְאָמְרוּ לְתַלְמִידָיו לָמָה נָא הָרַבִּי שֶׁלָּכֶם אוֹכֵל עִם מְכוּסִים וְעִם חַטָּאִים

HTV: **After the Pharisees saw** *this* **- they said to his students, "Why does your rabbi eat with tax collectors and with sinners?"**

KJV: And when the Pharisees saw *it*, they said unto his disciples, Why eateth your Master with publicans and sinners?

Chapter 9

Matthew 9:12

וְכַאֲשֶׁר יֵשׁוּעַ שָׁמַע זֹאת הוּא אָמַר אֵין הָרוֹפֵא צָרִיךְ לִבְרִיאִים כִּי אִם לְחוֹלִים

HTV: **When Yeshua heard this, he said, "The healer is not needed by the healthy - but by the sick."**

KJV: But when Jesus heard *that*, he said unto them, They that be whole need not a physician, but they that are sick.

Matthew 9:13

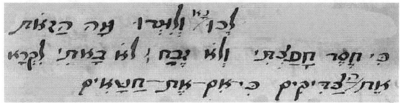
Freiburg Hebrew Manuscript

לְכוּ נָא וְלִמְדוּ מַה הַזֹּאת כִּי חֶסֶד חָפַצְתִּי וְלֹא זֶבַח לֹא בָאתִי לִקְרֹא אֶת-הַצַּדִּיקִים כִּי-אִם-אֶת-חַטָּאִים

HTV: **"Go and learn what this means: 'I desired loving kindness and not sacrifice.' I did not come to call the righteous but sinners."**

Note: Hosea 6:6 - For I desired steadfast love, and not sacrifice; and the knowledge of God more than burnt offerings.

KJV: But go ye and learn what *that* meaneth, I will have mercy, and not sacrifice: for I am not come to call the righteous, but sinners to repentance.

Matthew 9:14

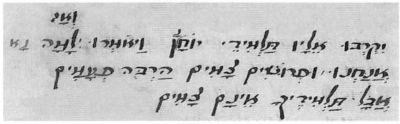
Freiburg Hebrew Manuscript

The Hebrew Book of Matthew

וְאָז יִקְרְבוּ אֵלָיו תַּלְמִידֵי יוֹחָנָן וַיֹּאמְרוּ לָמָה נָא אֲנַחְנוּ וּפְרוּשִׁים צָמִים הַרְבֵּה פְעָמִים אֲבָל תַּלְמִידֶיךָ אֵינָם צָמִים

HTV: And then John (*the Baptist's*) disciples approached Yeshua the Messiah and said, "Why do we and the Pharisees fast so often - but your disciples do not fast?"

> Note: In Matthew 21:9 in the Freiburg Hebrew manuscript - the people cry out to the Messiah, "Save us from the Romans!" Yeshua did not want his disciples to call him the Messiah, presumably because he did not come to lead a violent revolution and this is what would be expected of the *conquering-king* Messiah, so he played it down. Yeshua came as the *suffering-servant* Messiah. *Yeshua Mashiach* - Yeshua the Messiah, however, is common usage in the Hebrew Gospel from Catalonia (HGC). See Isaiah 52:13 and 53:12 for the scriptural description of the two different Messiah archetypes.

KJV: Then came to him the disciples of John, saying, Why do we and the Pharisees fast oft, but thy disciples fast not?

Matthew 9:15

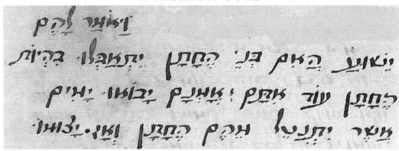
Freiburg Hebrew Manuscript

וַיֹּאמֶר לָהֶם יֵשׁוּעַ הַאִם בְּנֵי הֶחָתָן יִתְאַבְּלוּ בִּהְיוֹת הֶחָתָן עוֹד אִתָּם אָמְנָם יָבוֹאוּ יָמִים אֲשֶׁר יִנָּטֵל מֵהֶם הֶחָתָן וְאָז יָצוּמוּ·

HTV: Yeshua said to them, "Do the sons of the groom mourn *while* he is still living among them? Truly the days will come when the groom will be taken from them - and then they will fast."

KJV: And Jesus said unto them, Can the children of the bridechamber mourn, as long as the bridegroom is with them? but the days will come, when the bridegroom shall be taken from them, and then shall they fast.

Matthew 9:16

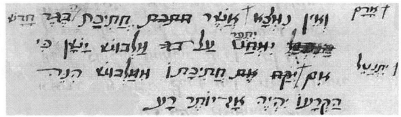

Freiburg Hebrew Manuscript

וְאֵין נִמְצָא אָדָם אֲשֶׁר חֲתִיכַת הַבֶּגֶד חָדָשׁ יִתְפֹּר עַל מַלְבּוּשׁ יָשָׁן כִּי אִם יִתְנַטֵּל חֲתִיכָתוֹ מִמַּלְבּוּשׁ הִנֵּה הַקְּרָעוֹ יִהְיֶה אָז יוֹתֵר רָע

HTV: **"There is no man to be found who will sew a new piece of clothing onto old clothing - because the piece will tear away from the old clothes and the tear at this spot will be even worse."**

KJV: No man putteth a piece of new cloth unto an old garment, for that which is put in to fill it up taketh from the garment, and the rent is made worse.

Matthew 9:17

Freiburg Hebrew Manuscript

וְאֵין שׁוֹלְחִים יַיִן חָדָשׁ בְּנֹאדִים יְשָׁנִים וְאִם כֵּן הִנֵּה הַנֹּאדִים יִבָּזְעוּ וְהַיַּיִן יִשָּׁפֵךְ וְהַנֹּאדִים יֹאבְרוּ כִּי אִם שׁוֹלְחִים אֶת-יַיִן חָדָשׁ בְּנֹאדִים חֲדָשִׁים וּשְׁנֵיהֶם יִשָּׁמְרוּ יַחְדָּיו

HTV: **There is no one who puts new wine into old wineskins. And if so, behold the wineskins will be burst and the wine will be spilled, and the wineskins will be lost. But *if* they put new wine into new wineskins - both of them are preserved.**

Note: Fermented liquids, like wine and beer, emit expanding gasses pressuring the container to the breaking point.

KJV: Neither do men put new wine into old bottles: else the bottles break, and the wine runneth out, and the bottles perish: but they put new wine into new bottles, and both are preserved.

Matthew 9:18

וּבְדַבְּרוֹ אֲלֵיהֶם אֶת-אֵלֶּה דְבָרִים הִנֵּה שׂוֹם שַׂר קָרֵב אֵלָיו וַיִּשְׁתַּחֲוֶה לוֹ וַיֹּאמַר לוֹ אֲדוֹנִי הִנֵּה בִתִּי כְבַר מֵתָה בָּא נָא וְשׂוֹם עָלֶיהָ אֶת-יָדְךָ וְתִחְיֶה

HTV: **As he spoke to them about these things - behold - a chieftain came near to him and bowed down to him saying, "My Lord, come see, my daughter has just died. Please come and lay your hand and put it upon her, and she will revive."**

KJV: While he spake these things unto them, behold, there came a certain ruler, and worshipped him, saying, My daughter is even now dead: but come and lay thy hand upon her, and she shall live.

Matthew 9:19

וַיָּקָם יֵשׁוּעַ וְנִמְשַׁךְ אַחֲרָיו וְגַם תַּלְמִידָיו

HTV: **Yeshua rose up - and also his disciples - and followed after him.**

KJV: And Jesus arose, and followed him, and *so did* his disciples.

Matthew 9:20

וְהִנֵּה אִיזוֹ אִשָּׁה שֶׁיָּזוֹב זוֹב הַדָּמָהּ שְׁנַיִם עָשָׂר שָׁנִים אֲשֶׁר תִּקְרַב אֵלָיו לְאָחוֹר וַתִּגַּע אֶת-שְׂפַת מַלְבּוּשׁוֹ

HTV: **Then behold, a woman - who had a flow of blood for twelve years - came close to him from behind and touched the hem of his clothing.**

KJV: And, behold, a woman, which was diseased with an issue of blood twelve years, came behind *him*, and touched the hem of his garment:

Chapter 9

Matthew 9:21

וַתֹּאמַר בְּנַפְשׁוֹ וְאִים לְבַד אֶגַּע אֶת-מַלְבּוּשׁוֹ אֲנִי אִוָּשֵׁעַ

HTV: She had said to herself, in her distress, "If only I could touch his clothing - I will be saved *(from this malady).*"

KJV: For she said within herself, If I may but touch his garment, I shall be whole.

Matthew 9:22

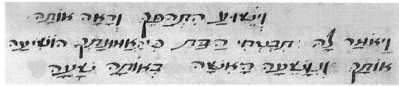
Freiburg Hebrew Manuscript

וְיֵשׁוּעַ הִתְהַפֵּךְ וְרָאָה אוֹתָהּ וְיֹאמַר לָהּ תִּבְטְחִי הַבַּת כִּי הָאֱמוּנָתֵךְ הוֹשִׁיעָה אוֹתָךְ וְנִוָּשְׁעָה הָאִשָּׁה בְּאוֹתָהּ שָׁעָה

HTV: Yeshua turned around, saw her and said to her, "Daughter, trust me - your faith has saved you." In that same hour, the woman was healed.

KJV: But Jesus turned him about, and when he saw her, he said, Daughter, be of good comfort; thy faith hath made thee whole. And the woman was made whole from that hour.

Matthew 9:23

וּמִשֶּׁיֵּשׁוּעַ בָּא בְּבֵית הַשָּׂר וְרָאָה אֶת-מְחַלְלִים וְאֶת-הֲמוֹן הַמְהַמֶּה

HTV: When Yeshua came into the house of the chieftain and saw the *hired* mourners and the murmuring crowd,

KJV: And when Jesus came into the ruler's house, and saw the minstrels and the people making a noise,

145

Matthew 9:24

Freiburg Hebrew Manuscript

וַיֹּאמֶר לָהֶם סוּרוּ מִכַּאן הַנַּעֲרָה אֵינָהּ מֵתָה כִּי אִם הִיא יְשֵׁנָה וְהֵמָּה יִלְעֲגוּהוּ

HTV: he (Yeshua) said to them, "Get out! The girl is not dead - she is sleeping." And they ridiculed him.

Note: Yeshua was distraught with the professional mourners, their instruments and the noisy wailing racket they were making. His remark was not addressed to the family.

KJV: He said unto them, Give place: for the maid is not dead, but sleepeth. And they laughed him to scorn.making

Matthew 9:25

וּמִשֶּׁהֲמוֹן יִהְיֶה נִגְרָשׁ לְחלְקָהּ אָז הוּא נִכְנַס וְאָחַז אֶת יָדָהּ וַיֹּאמֶר הַנַּעֲרָה קוּמִי וְקָמָה הַנַּעֲרָה

HTV: When the crowd was thrown out, he (Yeshua) entered her room, took her hand and said to her, "Arise!" And the young girl arose.

KJV: But when the people were put forth, he went in, and took her by the hand, and the maid arose.

Matthew 9:26

וַיֵּצֵא שֵׁמַע הַזֶּה בְּכֹל הָאָרֶץ

HTV: And the (*word*) hearing of this - went out into all the land.

KJV: And the fame hereof went abroad into all that land.

Matthew 9:27

וְאַחֲרֵי שֶׁיֵּשׁוּעַ עָבַר מִכַּאן נִמְשְׁכוּ אַחֲרָיו שְׁנַיִם עִוְרִים צוֹעֲקִים וְאוֹמְרִים חָנֵּנוּ הַבֵּן דָּוִד

Chapter 9

HTV: **After Yeshua passed by them, two blind men came out after him and cried, "Have mercy on us, Son of David!"**

KJV: And when Jesus departed thence, two blind men followed him, crying, and saying, *Thou* Son of David, have mercy on us.

Matthew 9:28

וְכַאֲשֶׁר בָּא בְּבֵית קָרְבוּ אֵלָיו הָעִוְרִים וַיֹּאמֶר יֵשׁוּעַ לָהֶם הַאִם אַתֶּם מַאֲמִינִים אֲשֶׁר אוּכַל לָכֶם לַעֲשׂוֹת הַזֹּאת וַיֹּאמְרוּ לוֹ בֶּאֱמֶת הָאֲדוֹנִי אֲנַחְנוּ מַאֲמִינִים

HTV: **When he came into the house, the blind men approach him, and Yeshua said unto them, "Do you believe that I can do this?" And they said to him, "Lord, truly we believe!"**

KJV: And when he was come into the house, the blind men came to him: and Jesus saith unto them, Believe ye that I am able to do this? They said unto him, Yea, Lord.

Matthew 9:29

וְנָגַע אֶת-עֵינֵיהֶם וַיֹּאמַר יְהִי לָכֶם לְפִי הָאֱמוּנַתְכֶם

HTV: **He touched their eyes and said, "Let it be unto you - according to your faith."**

KJV: Then touched he their eyes, saying, According to your faith be it unto you.

Matthew 9:30

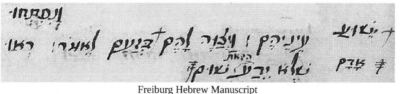
Freiburg Hebrew Manuscript

וְנִפְתְּחוּ עֵינֵיהֶם וַיְצַוֶּה לָהֶם יֵשׁוּעַ בְּזַעַם לֵאמֹר רְאוּ שֶׁלֹּא יֵדַע הַזֹּאת שׁוּם אָדָם

HTV: **And their eyes were opened. Yeshua commanded them saying gravely, "See that no man will know of this!"**

KJV: And their eyes were opened; and Jesus straitly charged them, saying, See *that* no man know *it*.

Matthew 9:31

אָמְנָם הֵמָה יָצְאוּ וּפִרְסָמוּהוּ בְּכֹל הָאָרֶץ

HTV: **However, they went out and made it known throughout the land.**

KJV: But they, when they were departed, spread abroad his fame in all that country.

Matthew 9:32

וּמִשֶּׁיָּצְאוּ הִנֵּה הִקְרִיבוּ לוֹ אָדָם אִלֵּם שֶׁבּוֹ שֵׁד

HTV: **And they went out and - behold, *others* brought to him a mute man with a demon in him.**

KJV: As they went out, behold, they brought to him a dumb man possessed with a devil.

Matthew 9:33

וְכַאֲשֶׁר גֵּרֵשׁ מִמֶּנּוּ אֶת הַשֵּׁד הִנֵּה דִּבֶּר הָאִלֵּם וַיִּתְמְהוּ הַכִּתִּיִּים לֵאמֹר לְעוֹלָם לֹא נִרְאָה כֵן בְּיִשְׂרָאֵל

HTV: **And when the demon was cast from him - behold - the mute spoke! The people were amazed, saying, "Never! Not in Israel - has this been seen!"**

KJV: And when the devil was cast out, the dumb spake: and the multitudes marvelled, saying, It was never so seen in Israel.

Matthew 9:34

אָמְנָם הַפְּרוּשִׁים אָמְרוּ הוּא גוֹרֵשׁ אֶת שֵׁדִים בְּקְצִין הַשֵּׁדִים

HTV: **In truth, the Pharisees said, "He casts out demons by the ruler of the demons! (Ha-Satan)"**

Chapter 9

KJV: But the Pharisees said, He casteth out devils through the prince of the devils.

Matthew 9:35

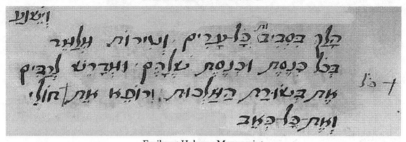

Freiburg Hebrew Manuscript

וְיֵשׁוּעַ הָלַךְ בִּסְבִיבוֹת כָּל עָרִים וְטִירוֹת מְלַמֵּד בְּכָל כְּנֶסֶת וּכְנֶסֶת שֶׁלָּהֶם וּמִדְרֶשׁ לָרַבִּים אֶת בְּשׂוּרַת הַמַּלְכוּת וְרוֹפֵא אֶת כָּל חוֹלִי וְאֶת-כָּל כְּאֵב

HTV: **Yeshua went around to all the cities and villages teaching the people in every assembly and synagogue - the *Torah* (Midrash)* - and the good news (Gospel) of the kingdom - healing all disease and all suffering.**

*Note: *Midrash* is a discussion of the meaning of Torah. Now, we would call it a Bible study.

KJV: And Jesus went about all the cities and villages, teaching in their synagogues, and preaching the gospel of the kingdom, and healing every sickness and every disease among the people.

Matthew 9:36

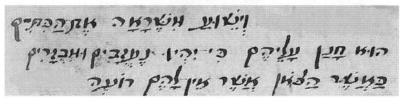

Freiburg Hebrew Manuscript

וְיֵשׁוּעַ מִשֶּׁרָאָה אֶת-הַכִּתִּים הוּא חָנַן עֲלֵיהֶם כִּי יִהְיוּ נֶעֱזָבִים וּמְבֻזָּרִים כַּאֲשֶׁר הַצֹּאן אֲשֶׁר אֵין לָהֶם רוֹעֶה

HTV: **Yeshua saw the unwashed and had mercy on them - because they are abandoned and are scattered as sheep without a shepherd.**

149

KJV: But when he saw the multitudes, he was moved with compassion on them, because they fainted, and were scattered abroad, as sheep having no shepherd.

Matthew 9:37

וַיֹּאמֶר לְתַלְמִידִים שֶׁלוֹ הִנֵּה קָצִיר גָּדוֹל אֲבָל מְעַטִּים פּוֹעֲלִים

HTV: **He (Yeshua) said to his disciples, "Behold the harvest is vast but the workers are few."**

KJV: Then saith he unto his disciples, The harvest truly *is* plenteous, but the labourers *are* few;

Matthew 9:38

שַׁאֲלוּ נָא אֶת-אֲדוֹן הַקָּצִיר שֶׁיִּשְׁלַח פּוֹעֲלִים בַּקְּצִירוֹ

HTV: **"Please pray to the Lord of the harvest - that He send workers into His harvest."**

KJV: Pray ye therefore the Lord of the harvest, that he will send forth labourers into his harvest.

Matthew Chapter 10

Hebrew Text Version (HTV)

¹ When he (Yeshua) called his twelve disciples to him. He gave them authority over unclean spirits - to cast them out - and heal every pain and every disease.

² These are the names of the twelve apostles, the first, Shimon (Simon) called Khefa (Peter), and Andrew his brother, Philip, and Bartholomew, Ya'akov (Jacob - James in English) son of Zebedee, and Yohanan (John) his brother…

³ Toma (Thomas), and Mati (Matthew) who was a tax collector, and Ya'akov (Jacob - James in English) *son* of Alphi (Alphaeus), and Thadi (Thaddaeus)…

⁴ Shimon the Canaanite and Yehuda (Judas) Ischariot - who betrayed him to death.

⁵ Yeshua sent these twelve, he commanded them saying, "Do not go the way of the Gentiles *nor* into the cities of the Samaritans."

⁶ "Rather, go to the lost sheep of the house of Israel."

⁷ "Go and preach to many saying - 'The kingdom of Heaven is at hand!' "

⁸ "Heal the sick, raise the dead, cleanse the lepers and cast out demons. Do not take wages. Freely you have received and freely you shall give."

⁹ "Do not gather up gold and silver - nor (store up) wealth in your purse."

¹⁰ "Do not take a bag for your journey, nor two shirts, nor shoes, nor a walking stick, for the worker is worthy of his food."

¹¹ "Whatever city and manor (house) that you come to, ask who is worthy - and stay there until you go."

¹² "When you come into a house - proceed to speak shalom (peace) over that house and all who dwelt in it."

¹³ "If that house is worthy, then your shalom (peace) will come into it - if it is not worthy - your peace will remain

The Hebrew Book of Matthew

(dwelling) within you."

¹⁴ "Whosoever will not take you in, and will not listen to your words; when you go out of that city or house - shake off the dust from your feet!"

¹⁵ "In truth, I say to you that it will be better for the land of Sodom and Gomorrah - in the day of judgment - than for this city!"

¹⁶ "Behold! I send you as sheep among wolves - Therefore be crafty as serpents and innocent as doves."

¹⁷ "Beware of *those* men who will deliver you unto their congregations and they will scourge you with whips."

¹⁸ "They will bring you before rulers and kings for my sake - as a testimony to the nations."

¹⁹ "When they deliver you, do not think how or what you will say - because it will be given to you in the same hour what to speak."

²⁰ "So that you are not speaking - but the Holy Spirit of your Father speaks through you."

²¹ "The brother will deliver up his brother *to die* - and the father, his son. The children will rise up against their parents and cause them to be killed!"

²² "And you will be hated by all men because of my name - but he who will persist until the end - that man will be saved!"

²³ "When they persecute you in one city, leave to another city. In truth I say to you - you shall not go into all the cities of Israel until the Son of Adam (Man) returns to his disciples."

²⁴ "The disciple is not greater than his teacher - nor the servant his master."

²⁵ "It will suffice for the disciple that he be like his teacher. And for the servant that he be like his master. But if they called the owner of the house 'Ba'al Zebub (Satan) - so all the children of his house likewise would be called [sons of Satan]."

²⁶ "You must not fear them - because there is nothing concealed which will not be revealed - and there is nothing hidden that will not be *made* known!"

²⁷ "Whatever I say to you in the darkness - you shall speak in the light - and whatever you hear whisper*ed** in your ears - declare *it* from the rooftops!"

²⁸ "You must not fear those who kill the body - for they

cannot kill the soul. But you should fear him who is able to destroy the soul and the body in Gehenna."

²⁹ "Are not two sparrows sold for a penny? One, no - not one of them - will fall to the ground apart from your Father's will."

³⁰ "Every hair on your head is numbered."

³¹ "Therefore, don't be afraid because you are more valued than many sparrows."

³² "Everyone that confesses me before the people - even more so - shall I *confess him* before my Father who is in heaven."

³³ "Whosoever will deny me before men - I will also deny him before my Father in heaven!"

³⁴ Furthermore, Yeshua Ha Mashiach said to his disciples, "Do not think that I came to send peace on the earth - I did not come to send peace but the sword!"

³⁵ "For I have come to cause contention - division between a man and his son - and between a daughter and her mother - and between a daughter-in-law and her mother-in-law."

³⁶"To *that* man those born of his house will be enemies!"

³⁷ "He who loves his father or his mother more than me - shall not be deserving of me - and he who loves his son or daughter more than me - the same shall not be worthy of me."

³⁸ "He who shall not take the *crucifixion* upon himself and follow after me - he shall not be worthy of me."

³⁹ "He who loses his life for my sake - the same shall find it!"

⁴⁰ "He who shall receive you (my disciple), the same shall receive me (Yeshua). And he who shall receive me - the same shall receive he who sent me (my Father)."

⁴¹ "He who shall receive a prophet in the name of the prophet, the same shall receive the prophet's reward - and he who shall receive a righteous man in the name of the righteous man, the same shall receive the righteous man's reward."

⁴² "All who shall give to drink - to the least of my disciples - one cup of cold water in the name of the disciple of truth (Yeshua) - I declare to you he shall not lose his reward."

Matthew Chapter 10

HTV with translator notes and KJV comparison

Matthew 10:1

וְכַאֲשֶׁר קָרָא אֶצְלוֹ אֶת-שְׁנֵים עָשָׂר תַּלְמִידָיו הוּא נָתַן לָהֶם מֶמְשֶׁלֶת עַל רוּחוֹת טְמֵאִים שֶׁיְּגָרְשׁוּם וְיִרְפְּאוּ כָל כְּאֵב וְכָל חוֹלִי

    HTV: **When he (Yeshua) called his twelve disciples to him. He gave them authority over unclean spirits - to cast them out - and heal every pain and every disease.**

    KJV: And when he had called unto *him* his twelve disciples, he gave them power *against* unclean spirits, to cast them out, and to heal all manner of sickness and all manner of disease.

Matthew 10:2

Freiburg Hebrew Manuscript

וְאֵלֶּה שְׁמוֹת שְׁנֵים עָשָׂר הַשְּׁלִיחִים הָרִאשׁוֹן שִׁמְעוֹן הַנִּקְרָא כֵּיפָא וְאַנְדְּרֵעַ אָחִיו פִּילְפּוֹס וּבַרְתַּלְמִי יַעֲקוֹב בֶּן זַבְדִּי וְיוֹחָנָן אָחִיו

    HTV: **These are the names of the twelve apostles, the first, Shimon (Simon) called Khefa (Peter), and Andrew his brother, Philip, and Bartholomew, Ya'akov (Jacob - James in English) son of Zebedee, and Yohanan (John) his brother,**

Chapter 10

Note: The Hebrew manuscripts put **Phillip and Bartholomew before James and John**. James and John come first in the Greek. The apostles are the same, but the order is different in the Hebrew manuscripts and the Greek manuscripts. This is a marker of the Hebrew Gospels.

Note: **Hebrew Order of the Apostles of Yeshua:** (in Freiburg Manuscript., STM, and HGC) Shimon (Simon) called Khefa (Peter), and Andrew his brother, **Philip, and Bartholomew, Ya'akov (Jacob - James in English) son of Zebedee, and Yohanan (John) his brother**, Toma (Thomas), and Mati (Matthew) who was a tax collector, and Ya'akov (Jacob - James in English) *son* of Alfi (Alphaeus), and Thadi (Thaddaeus), Shimon the Canaanite and Yehuda (Judas) Ischariot - who betrayed him to death.

Greek Order of the Apostles of Yeshua:
Simon who is called Peter, and Andrew his brother, **James the son of Zebedee, and John** his brother, **Phillip, and Bartholomew**, Thomas, and Matthew the tax collector, James the son of Alphaeus, and Judas Iscariot who betrayed him.

KJV: Now the names of the twelve apostles are these; The first, Simon, who is called Peter, and Andrew his brother; James *the son* of Zebedee, and John his brother;

Matthew 10:3

Freiburg Hebrew Manuscript

תּוֹמָה וּמַתִּי אֲשֶׁר יִהְיֶה נוֹגֵשׂ מֶכֶס וְיַעֲקוֹב אלפִי וְתַדִי

HTV: **Toma (Thomas), and Mati (Matthew) who was a tax collector, and Ya'akov (Jacob - James in English)** *son* **of Alphi (Alphaeus), and Thadi (Thaddaeus)**

Note: There were two apostles named Ya'akov (James) - one was James son of Zebedee and the other James son of Alphaeus - which is why their parentage is listed to distinguish them.

Note: This manuscript uses the short form of the names; **Mati** (short for Mattiyahu in Hebrew), **Alfi** (short for Alphaeus), and **Thadi** (short for Thaddaeus), The English equivalents would be Tom, Matt, Alfie, and Tod.

KJV: Philip, and Bartholomew; Thomas, and Matthew the publican; James *the son* of Alphaeus, and Lebbaeus, whose surname was Thaddaeus;

Matthew 10:4

Freiburg Hebrew Manuscript

שִׁמְעוֹן הַכְּנַעֲנִי וִיהוּדָה אִישְׁכַּרְיוּת אֲשֶׁר הָיָה מוֹסְרוֹ לְמִיתָה

HTV: Shimon the Canaanite and Yehuda (Judas) Ischariot - who betrayed him to death.

> Note: Again, there were two apostles named Simon - Simon Peter and Simon the Cananite, more often called Simon the Zealot in the Gospels. Yehuda becomes Judas, the Y is exchanged for J in English, and the S is the typical ending for Greek names - which causes significant confusion in Scripture when Zachariah suddenly becomes Zacharias, Elijah becomes Elias etcetera and so on. Even Yeshua is changed to the Greek S creating the name Jesus.

KJV: Simon the Canaanite, and Judas Iscariot, who also betrayed him.

Matthew 10:5

וַיִּשְׁלַח יֵשׁוּעַ הָאֵלֶה שְׁנַיִם עָשָׂר וַיְצַוֶּה לָהֶם לֵאמֹר אַל תֵּלְכוּ בְּדֶרֶךְ הַגּוֹיִם וְאַל תִּכָּנְסוּ בְּעָרֵי שַׁמְרוֹנִיִּים

HTV: Yeshua sent these twelve, he commanded them saying, "Do not go the way of the Gentiles *nor* into the cities of the Samaritans."

KJV: These twelve Jesus sent forth, and commanded them, saying, Go not into the way of the Gentiles, and into *any* city of the Samaritans enter ye not:

Matthew 10:6

כִּי אִם תֵּלְכוּ אֶל-הַצֹּאן שֶׁאָבְדוּ מִבֵּית יִשְׂרָאֵל

HTV: "Rather, go to the lost sheep of the house of Israel."

KJV: But go rather to the lost sheep of the house of Israel.

Matthew 10:7

לְכוּ נָא וְדָרְשׁוּ לָרַבִּים לֵאמֹר כִּי בָאָה מַלְכוּת הַשָּׁמַיִם

Chapter 10

HTV: **"Go and preach to many saying - 'The kingdom of Heaven is at hand!' "**

KJV: And as ye go, preach, saying, The kingdom of heaven is at hand.

Matthew 10:8
אֶת-חוֹלִים רְפָאוּ וְהָקִימוּ אֶת-הַמֵּתִים וְאֶת-צְרוּעִים טַהֲרוּ וְאֶת-הַשֵּׁדִים גָּרְשׁוּ בְחִנָּם לְקַחְתֶּם וּבְחִנָּם תִּנּוּ

HTV: **"Heal the sick, raise the dead, cleanse the lepers and cast out demons. Do not take wages. Freely you have received and freely you shall give."**

KJV: Heal the sick, cleanse the lepers, raise the dead, cast out devils: freely ye have received, freely give.

Matthew 10:9

[Freiburg Hebrew Manuscript image]

Freiburg Hebrew Manuscript

אַל תֵּקְנוּ לָכֶם לֹא הַזָּהָב וְלֹא הַכֶּסֶף וְלֹא יִהְיֶה לָכֶם כֶּסֶף בְּכִיסֵיכֶם

HTV: **"Do not gather up gold and silver - nor (store up) wealth in your purse."**

Note: The translation of this verse comes from the Shem Tov Manuscript. The KJV manuscript is rather vague.

KJV: Provide neither gold, nor silver, nor brass in your purses,

Matthew 10:10
וְלֹא תִקְחוּ תַרְמִיל לַדֶּרֶךְ וְלֹא שְׁתֵּי כֻתֳּנוֹת וְלֹא נְעָלִים וְלֹא מַקֵּל כִּי הַפּוֹעֵל הוּא רָאוּי לְקַחַת אֶת הַזַּנְתוֹ

HTV: **"Do not take a bag for your journey, nor two shirts, nor shoes, nor a walking stick, for the worker is worthy of his food."**

The Hebrew Book of Matthew

KJV: Nor scrip for *your* journey, neither two coats, neither shoes, nor yet staves: for the workman is worthy of his meat.

Matthew 10:11

Freiburg Hebrew Manuscript

וּבְכֹל עִיר וְטִירָה אֲשֶׁר תָּבוֹאוּ אַתֶּם תִשְׁאַלֹד מִי בָה רָאוּי וְשָׁם תֵּשְׁבוּ עַד אֲשֶׁר תֵּצְאוּ

HTV: "Whatever city and manor (house) that you come to, ask who is worthy - and stay there until you go."

KJV: And into whatsoever city or town ye shall enter, enquire who in it is worthy; and there abide till ye go thence.

Matthew 10:12

וּבָאִים בְּבַיִת תַקְדִימוּ לוֹ אֶת-הַשָׁלוֹם לֵאמֹר הַשָׁלוֹם לְבַיִת הַזֶה

HTV: "When you come into a house - proceed to speak shalom (peace) over that house and all who dwelt in it."

KJV: And when ye come into a house, salute it.

Matthew 10:13

וְאִם הַבַּיִת הַהוּא יִהְיֶה רָאוּי אָז יָבוֹא הַשָׁלוֹם שֶׁלָכֶם עָלָיו וְאִם לֹא יִהְיֶה רָאוּי הַשְׁלוֹמְכֶם יָשׁוּב אֲלֵיכֶם

HTV: "If that house is worthy, then your shalom (peace) will come into it - if it is not worthy - your peace will remain (dwelling) within you."

KJV: And if the house be worthy, let your peace come upon it: but if it be not worthy, let your peace return to you.

Matthew 10:14

Freiburg Hebrew Manuscript

וְכֹל שֶׁלֹא יִקַּח אֶתְכֶם וְלֹא יִשְׁמַע אֶת אִמְרֵיכֶם בְּצֵאת תֵּצְאוּ חוּצָה מֵאוֹתָהּ הָעִיר אוֹ הַבַּיִת בְּנַעֵר תְּנַעֲרוּ אֶת-עָפָר מַרְגְלֵיכֶם

HTV: "Whosoever will not take you in, and will not listen to your words; when you go out of that city or house - shake off the dust from your feet!"

KJV: And whosoever shall not receive you, nor hear your words, when ye depart out of that house or city, shake off the dust of your feet.

Matthew 10:15

בֶּאֱמֶת אֲנִי אוֹמֵר לָכֶם שֶׁיִּהְיֶה יוֹתֵר קַל לָאָרֶץ סְדוֹם וַעֲמוֹרָה בְּיוֹם הַמִשְׁפָּט מִלָּעִיר הַזֹּאת

HTV: "In truth, I say to you that it will be better for the land of Sodom and Gomorrah - in the day of judgment - than for this city!"

KJV: Verily I say unto you, It shall be more tolerable for the land of Sodom and Gomorrha in the day of judgment, than for that city.

Matthew 10:16

הִנֵּה אֲנִי שׁוֹלֵחַ אֶתְכֶם כְּמוֹ הַצֹּאן בְּתוֹךְ זְאֵבִים לְפִיכָךְ תִּהְיוּ מַשְׂכִּילִים כְּמוֹ הַנְּחָשִׁים וּפְתָאִים כְּמוֹ הַיּוֹנִים

HTV: "Behold! I send you as sheep among wolves - Therefore be crafty as serpents and innocent as doves."

KJV: Behold, I send you forth as sheep in the midst of wolves: be ye therefore wise as serpents, and harmless as doves.

Matthew 10:17

הִשָּׁתַמְּרוּ מֵאֲנוֹשִׁים כִּי יִמְסְרוּכֶם בְּעֵדוֹתֵיהֶם וּבַכְּנָס יוֹתִיהֶם וְיַכּוּכֶם בְּשֹׁטִים

HTV: **"Beware of** *those* **men who will deliver you unto their congregations and they will scourge you with whips."**

KJV: But beware of men: for they will deliver you up to the councils, and they will scourge you in their synagogues;

Matthew 10:18

Freiburg Hebrew Manuscript

וְיָבִיאוּ אֶתְכֶם אֶל-הַשִּׁלְטוֹנִים וְאֶל הַמְלָכִים בַּעֲבוּרִי לָהֶם לְעֵדוּת וּלְגוֹיִם

HTV: **"They will bring you before rulers and kings for my sake - as a testimony to the nations."**

KJV: And ye shall be brought before governors and kings for my sake, for a testimony against them and the Gentiles.

Matthew 10:19

וְכַאֲשֶׁר יִמְסְרוּכֶם אַל-תַּחֲשֹׁב אֵיכָה אוֹ מַה תִהְיוּ מְדַבְּרִים כִּי יִנָּתֵן לָכֶם בְּאוֹתָהּ שָׁעָה מַה שֶׁלָּכֶם לְדַבֵּר

HTV: **"When they deliver you, do not think how or what you will say - because it will be given to you in the same hour what to speak."**

KJV: But when they deliver you up, take no thought how or what ye shall speak: for it shall be given you in that same hour what ye shall speak.

Matthew 10:20

כִּי אֵינְכֶם מְדַבְּרִים כִּי אִם רוּחַ הָאֲבִיכֶם הוּא מְדַבֵּר בָּכֶם

HTV: **"So that you are not speaking - but the Holy Spirit of your Father speaks through you."**

KJV: For it is not ye that speak, but the Spirit of your Father which speaketh in you.

Chapter 10

Matthew 10:21

Freiburg Hebrew Manuscript

כִּי הָאָח יִמְסוֹר אֶת אָחִיו לְמִיתָה וְהָאָב אֶת-בְּנוֹ וְיָקוּמוּ הַבָּנִים הֶפֶךְ הָאֲבוֹתֵיהֶם וַיְמוֹתְתוּ אוֹתָם

HTV: "The brother will deliver up his brother *to die* - and the father, his son. The children will rise up against their parents and cause them to be killed!"

> Note: In the persecution of the first century, and later persecutions such as the Inquisition, family and friends were pressured, even tortured, to give up their own who had converted - to be killed!

KJV: And the brother shall deliver up the brother to death, and the father the child: and the children shall rise up against *their* parents, and cause them to be put to death.

Matthew 10:22

וְתִהְיוּ לְשִׂנְאָה לְכֹל אֱנוֹשִׁים בַּעֲבוּר שְׁמִי וַאֲשֶׁר יַתְמִיד עַד הַסּוֹף הַזֶּה יִוָּשֵׁעַ

HTV: "And you will be hated by all men because of my name - but he who will persist until the end - that man will be saved!"

KJV: And ye shall be hated of all *men* for my name's sake: but he that endureth to the end shall be saved.

Matthew 10:23

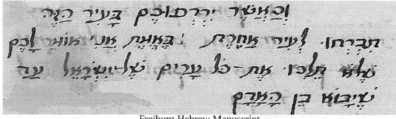
Freiburg Hebrew Manuscript

The Hebrew Book of Matthew

וְכַאֲשֶׁר יִרְדְּפוּכֶם בָּעִיר הַזֶּה תִּבְרְחוּ לְעִיר אַחֶרֶת בֶּאֱמֶת אֲנִי אוֹמֵר לָכֶם שֶׁלֹּא תֵלְכוּ אֶת-כָּל עָרִים שֶׁל יִשְׂרָאֵל עַד שֶׁיָּבוֹא בֶּן הָאָדָם

HTV: **"When they persecute you in one city, leave to another city. In truth I say to you - you shall not go into all the cities of Israel until the Son of Adam (Man) returns to his disciples."**

> Note: The Hebrew Gospels from Catalonia (HGC) say "**Son of Eloah**" in place of **Son of Adam** or **Man**. Yeshua is both human and divine. He is the man without sin, the descendant of Adam who must atone for Adam's (Man's) sin of disobedience. There is no other way. As Yehovah says (Lev 17:11), "The life of the flesh is in the blood and I Myself have given it unto you upon the altar to make an atonement for your souls. For it is the blood that makes an atonement for the soul."

KJV: But when they persecute you in this city, flee ye into another: for verily I say unto you, Ye shall not have gone over the cities of Israel, till the Son of man be come.

Matthew 10:24

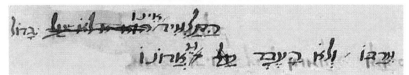

Freiburg Hebrew Manuscript

הַתַּלְמִיד אֵינוּ גָדוֹל מֵרַבּוֹ וְלֹא הָעֶבֶד מֵאֲדוֹנוֹ

HTV: **"The disciple is not greater than his teacher - nor the servant his master."**

KJV: The disciple is not above *his* master, nor the servant above his lord.

Matthew 10:25

סָפֵק לְתַלְמִיד שֶׁיִּהְיֶה דוֹמֶה לְרַבּוֹ וְלָעֶבֶד שֶׁיִּהְיֶה דוֹמֶה לַאֲדוֹנוֹ וְאִם אֶת-בַּעַל הַבַּיִת קָרְאוּ בַּעַל זְבוּב כָּל-שֶׁכֵּן אֶת-יְלִידֵי בֵיתוֹ

HTV: **"It will suffice for the disciple that he be like his teacher. And for the servant that he be like his master. But if they called the owner of the house 'Ba'al Zebub (Satan) - so all the children of his house likewise would be called [sons of Satan]."**

Chapter 10

KJV: It is enough for the disciple that he be as his master, and the servant as his lord. If they have called the master of the house Beelzebub, how much more *shall they call* them of his household?

Matthew 10:26
וְאַל תִּירְאוּם כִּי אֵין מְאוּמָה מְכֻסָּה אֲשֶׁר לֹא יִגָּלֶה וְאֵין נִסְתָּר שֶׁלֹּא יִוָּדַע

HTV: **"You must not fear them - because there is nothing concealed which will not be revealed - and there is nothing hidden that will not be *made* known!"**

KJV: Fear them not therefore: for there is nothing covered, that shall not be revealed; and hid, that shall not be known.

Matthew 10:27
אֲשֶׁר אֲנִי אוֹמֵר לָכֶם בַּחֲשָׁכִים אַתֶּם תֹּאמְרוּ בָאוֹר וַאֲשֶׁר אַתֶּם שׁוֹמְעִים בַּחֲשַׁאי בְּאָזְנֵיכֶם תַּגִּידוּ עַל-הַגַּגּוֹת

HTV: **"Whatever I say to you in the darkness - you shall speak in the light - and whatever you hear whisper*ed* in your ears - declare *it* from the rooftops!"**

KJV: What I tell you in darkness, *that* speak ye in light: and what ye hear in the ear, *that* preach ye upon the housetops.

Matthew 10:28

Freiburg Hebrew Manuscript

אַל תִּירָאוּם אֲשֶׁר הוֹרְגִים אֶת-הַגּוּף כִּי לֹא-יוּכְלוּ לַהֲרוֹג אֶת-הַנֶּפֶשׁ אֲבָל כָּל שֶׁכֵּן תִּירָאוּהוּ אֲשֶׁר יָכוֹל לְאַבֵּד אֶת-הַנֶּפֶשׁ וְאֶת-הַגּוּף בְּגֵיהִנָּם.

HTV: **"You must not fear those who kill the body - for they cannot kill the soul. But you should fear him who is able to destroy the soul and the body in Gehenna*."**

*Note: **Gei-Henom** in Hebrew means the **valley of Hinnom**. This was the area outside of Jerusalem where trash was burned. It became the place of sacrifice where infants were burned alive by putting them in the red-hot arms of a statue of Moloch. Drums and flutes and horns and tambourines and voices would be raised to drown out the shrieks of the babies being seared to death. This was done under Solomon and became the visual icon of hell to the Israelites.

KJV: And fear not them which kill the body, but are not able to kill the soul: but rather fear him which is able to destroy both soul and body in hell.

Matthew 10:29

הֲלֹא שְׁנֵי צִפּוֹרִים נִמְכָּרִים תַּחַת פְּרוּטָא אֶחָד וְלֹא אֶחָד מֵהֶם יִפּוֹל עַל אֶרֶץ זָלָתִי רְצוֹן הָאָבִיכֶם

HTV: **"Are not two sparrows sold for a penny? One, no - not one of them - will fall to the ground apart from your Father's will."**

KJV: Are not two sparrows sold for a farthing? and one of them shall not fall on the ground without your Father.

Matthew 10:30

כִּי כָל שַׂעֲרוֹת הָרֹאשְׁכֶם יֵשׁ מִסְפָּרוֹת

HTV: **"Every hair on your head is numbered."**

KJV: But the very hairs of your head are all numbered.

Matthew 10:31

לְפִיכָךְ אַל-תִּירְאוּ כִּי אַתֶּם טוֹבִים מִצִּפּוֹרִים רַבִּים

HTV: **"Therefore, don't be afraid because you are more valued than many sparrows."**

KJV: Fear ye not therefore, ye are of more value than many sparrows.

Matthew 10:32

כֹּל שֶׁיּוֹדֶה אוֹתִי לִפְנֵי הָאֲנוֹשִׁים אֲנִי אוֹדֵהוּ לִפְנֵי הָאָבִי אֲשֶׁר בַּשָּׁמַיִם

Chapter 10

HTV: **"Everyone that confesses me before the people - even more so - shall I *confess him* before my Father who is in heaven."**

KJV: Whosoever therefore shall confess me before men, him will I confess also before my Father which is in heaven.

Matthew 10:33

וַאֲשֶׁר יְכַחֲדֵנִי לִפְנֵי הָאֲנוֹשִׁים וְגַם אֲנִי אַכְחִידֵהוּ לִפְנֵי הָאָבִי שֶׁבַּשָּׁמַיִם

HTV: **"Whosoever will deny me before men - I will also deny him before my Father in heaven!"**

KJV: But whosoever shall deny me before men, him will I also deny before my Father which is in heaven.

Matthew 10:34

Freiburg Hebrew Manuscript

אַל-תַּחְשְׁבוּ שֶׁבָּאתִי לִשְׁלוֹחַ אֶת-הַשָּׁלוֹם בָּאָרֶץ לֹא בָאתִי לִשְׁלוֹחַ אֶת-שָׁלוֹם כִּי אִם אֶת-הָחֶרֶב

HTV: **Furthermore, Yeshua Ha Mashiach said to his disciples, "Do not think that I came to send peace on the earth - I did not come to send peace but the sword!"**

Note: This sounds like an earthly call to arms but it is not. The battle Yeshua brings is a supernatural battle against evil that is fought with the Sword of the Spirit - the Word of Yehovah!

KJV: Think not that I am come to send peace on earth: I came not to send peace, but a sword.

Matthew 10:35

כִּי בָאתִי לְהָעִיר מַחֲלוֹקֶת בֵּין אָדָם וּבְנוֹ וּבֵן בַּת-וְאִמָּה וּבֵין כַּלָּה וַחֲמוֹתָהּ

HTV: **"For I have come to cause contention - division between a man and his son - and between a daughter and her mother - and between a daughter-in-law and her mother-in-law."**

> Note: Many, but not all, will come to the truth Yeshua has brought. It may come to the father but not the son, to the daughter but not the mother, etcetera. There will be contention in the house.

KJV: For I am come to set a man at variance against his father, and the daughter against her mother, and the daughter in law against her mother in law.

Matthew 10:36

וּלְאָדָם יִהְיוּ יְלִידֵי בֵיתוֹ אוֹיְבִים

HTV: **"To *that* man those born of his house will be enemies!"**

> Note: Does this not play out still? Where the children of a righteous man fall away into sin and hate their father. Or the son may come to believe and be rejected by the father who does not. The supernatural battle Yeshua engages in will take place in the hearts and minds of our own.

KJV: And a man's foes *shall be* they of his own household.

Matthew 10:37

וַאֲשֶׁר יֶאֱהַב אֶת-אָבִיו אוֹ אֶת-אִמּוֹ יוֹתֵר מִמֶּנִּי הוּא אֵין יִהְיֶה רָאוּי לִי
וַאֲשֶׁר יֶאֱהַב אֶת-בְּנוֹ אוֹ אֶת-בִּתּוֹ יוֹתֵר מִמֶּנִּי הַהוּא אֵין יִהְיֶה לִי רָאוּי

HTV: **"He who loves his father or his mother more than me - shall not be deserving of me - and he who loves his son or daughter more than me - the same shall not be worthy of me."**

> Note: To put loyalty to family over truth is to deny truth. It will not save the family but it will condemn the denier - who rejects the Savior along with the truth.

KJV: He that loveth father or mother more than me is not worthy of me: and he that loveth son or daughter more than me is not worthy of me.

Matthew 10:38

Freiburg Hebrew Manuscript

וַאֲשֶׁר לֹא יִקַּח אֶת-צְלִיבָתוֹ עָלָיו וְנִמְשַׁךְ אַחֲרַי הוּא לֹא יִהְיֶה לִי רָאוּי

HTV: "He who shall not take the *crucifixion* upon himself and follow after me - he shall not be worthy of me."*

> *Note: This verse is a later edit to the text of the Gospels because the **cross** and the **crucifixion** were not added into the Christian creed until the fourth century by Constantine. In the earliest Greek texts it is called a "stauros" - a stake - everywhere it is used in Scripture. This is why this verse is missing in the Shem Tov Manuscript (STM) and the Hebrew Gospel from Catalonia (HGC) not as a denial of Yeshua's sacrifice but a reflection that the word **cross** was not yet used.
>
> Note: Neither is fear of death an excuse. We will all die. Fear of death is Satan's mighty weapon against us but Yeshua has conquered death. "He that believes in me, though he were dead - yet shall he live. Whosoever lives and believes in me shall never die!" (John 11:25-6)

KJV: And he that taketh not his cross, and followeth after me, is not worthy of me.

Matthew 10:39

וַאֲשֶׁר אָבַד אֶת-נַפְשׁוֹ בַּעֲבוּרִי הַהוּא יִמְצָא אוֹתָהּ

HTV: "He who loses his life for my sake - the same shall find it!"

KJV: He that findeth his life shall lose it: and he that loseth his life for my sake shall find it.

Matthew 10:40

וַאֲשֶׁר יִקַּח אֶתְכֶם הַהוּא אוֹתִי יִקַּח וַאֲשֶׁר אוֹתִי יִקַּח הַהוּא יִקַּח אֲשֶׁר שְׁלָחָנִי

HTV: "He who shall receive you (my disciple), the same shall receive me (Yeshua). And he who shall receive me - the same shall receive he who sent me (my Father)."

The Hebrew Book of Matthew

KJV: He that receiveth you receiveth me, and he that receiveth me receiveth him that sent me.

Matthew 10:41

וַאֲשֶׁר יִקַּח אֶת-נָבִיא בְּשֵׁם הַנָּבִיא הַהוּא יִקַּח שְׂכַר הַנָּבִיא וַאֲשֶׁר יִקַּח אֶת-צַדִּיק בְּשֵׁם הַצַּדִּיק הַהוּא יִקַּח אֶת-שְׂכַר הַצַּדִּיק

HTV: **"He who shall receive a prophet in the name of the prophet, the same shall receive the prophet's reward - and he who shall receive a righteous man in the name of the righteous man, the same shall receive the righteous man's reward."**

KJV: He that receiveth a prophet in the name of a prophet shall receive a prophet's reward; and he that receiveth a righteous man in the name of a righteous man shall receive a righteous man's reward.

Matthew 10:42

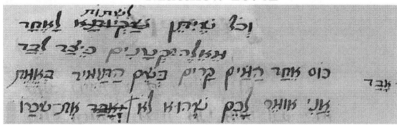
Freiburg Hebrew Manuscript

וְכֹל שֶׁיִּתֵּן לִשְׁתּוֹת לְאֶחָד מֵאֵלֶּה הַקְּטַנִּים כַּיָּצַד לְבַד כּוֹס אֶחָד הַמַּיִם קָרִים בְּשֵׁם הַתַּלְמִיד בֶּאֱמֶת אֲנִי אוֹמֵר לָכֶם שֶׁהוּא לֹא אָבַד אֶת-שְׂכָרוֹ

HTV: **"All who shall give to drink - to the least of my disciples - one cup of cold water in the name of the disciple of truth* (Yeshua) - I declare to you he shall not lose his reward."**

> Note: This is Yeshua's blessing as he sends his disciples out to preach. In the Hebrew it says THE disciple, not *A* disciple, so it is not about receiving one in the name of the disciple - but in the name of the Son, the disciple of truth.

KJV: And whosoever shall give to drink unto one of these little ones a cup of cold *water* only in the name of a disciple, verily I say unto you, he shall in no wise lose his reward.

Matthew Chapter 11
Hebrew Text Version (HTV)

¹ So it was - when Yeshua had finished instructing his twelve disciples - he *also* went forth in order to teach and preach to many *people* in their (*assigned*) cities.

² Afterwards, John - who had heard in the prison of the works of Yeshua - then, sent two of his disciples,

³ To ask of him, "Are you the one who is expected to come? Or should we await another?"

⁴ So Yeshua answered and told them, "Go and declare to John what you have heard - and what you have seen."

⁵ "Behold - the blind see, the lame walk, lepers are cleansed, the deaf hear - the dead rise up from the *grave* - and the good news (Gospel) is revealed to the needy!"

⁶ "Blessed is he who *avoids* the snare because *of* me."

⁷ As they (John's disciples) withdrew from him, Yeshua began saying to the crowds - because of John's words, "Behold! Now why did you go out to the desert to see John? - A reed shaken by the wind *of the Spirit*?"

⁸ "What then did you go out to see? If it was a man clothed in soft garments - Look, those who are dressed in soft garments - they are found in the palaces of kings."

⁹ "So what was it you went out to see - a prophet? I say to you he is more than a prophet."

¹⁰ "This is the one of which was written - 'Behold, *I* am sending my messenger and he will prepare the way before you.'"

¹¹ "Truly, I say to you that no one has risen - born of women - greater than John the Baptist . Nevertheless, *he* who is least in the kingdom of heaven is greater than he (*who is born of women*)."

¹² "From the days of John the Baptist until this day - the

The Hebrew Book of Matthew

kingdom of heaven is flashing forth in strength - and mighty men seize it."

[13] "Because all of the prophets - and the Torah - prophesied concerning John."

[14] "And if you want to receive it (the kingdom of heaven), this (John the Baptist) is *like unto* Elijah, who has been prepared to come."

[15] Whoever has ears to hear, he will hear."

[16] "Who does this generation resemble? It resembles children sitting in the market - who call out to their friends (*to play*):"

[17] And say, "Behold! We sang to you and you did not dance - and we mourned and you did not mourn."

[18] "Because John came and did not eat (meat) or drink (*wine*) - they say the devil is in him."

[19] And the Son of man came eating and drinking - and they say "Behold, *this* man *is* a glutton and a drunkard and loves tax collectors and sinners!" - *Therefore*, **foolish children** *are* **judging the wise.** *(STM)*

[20] Then (Yeshua) started to reproach the towns *where* many of his mighty deeds were carried out - because they did not repent.

[21] "Woe to you Chorazin, and woe to you Bethsaida - because if the mighty works done in you had been done in Tyre and Sidon they would repent in sackcloth and ashes."

[22] "Indeed I say to you - for Tyre and Sidon it will be easier - in the day of judgment - than it will be for your leaders."

[23] "And you, Capernaum - which we exalt up to heaven - will be thrown down to hell - since, if in Sodom were done the mighty deeds that were done in you - it would stand to this very day."

[24] "But I say to you - the land of the Sodomites will have it easier in the day of judgment - than will your leaders."

[25] At that time, Yeshua turned and said, "I thank you Father of heaven and earth - because you have hidden these things from the cunning and educated - but you have revealed them to the humble."

[26] "In truth, my Father - so it has been shown to be your will."

[27] "All things are delivered to me from my Father - and no one knows the Son but the Father - and *no one* knows the Father but the Son - and whomever the Son will choose to reveal Him."

[28] "Come now unto me, all who are burdened and are *heavy* laden - and I will sustain you!"

²⁹ "Take my yoke upon you - and learn from me - for I am meek and humble in heart - and you will find rest for your souls."
³⁰ "For my yoke - it is sweet - and my burden is light."

Matthew Chapter 11
HTV with translator notes and KJV comparison

Matthew 11:1

Freiburg Hebrew Manuscript

וַיְהִי מִשֶּׁיֵּשׁוּעַ כָּלָה לְצַוֹת לִשְׁנֵי עָשָׂר תַּלְמִידָיו הוּא הָלַךְ מִכָּאן כְּדֵי שֶׁיְלַמֵּד וְיִדְרוֹשׁ לָרַבִּים בְּעָרֵיהֶם

HTV: So it was - when Yeshua had finished instructing his twelve disciples - he *also* went forth in order to teach and preach to many *people* in their (*assigned*) cities.

> Note: Yeshua is sending his disciples out for the first time to preach, teach and heal on their own but still under his supervision. They are mostly from the same place (Galilee) so "their cities" are not where they dwelt but where they have been told to go, two by two (it says in Mark and Luke), to prepare the way for Yeshua coming and teaching after them. See notes in Luke 10:1 & 17 on the many other followers who increasingly accompanied Yeshua and his twelve disciples.

KJV: And it came to pass, when Jesus had made an end of commanding his twelve disciples, he departed thence to teach and to preach in their cities.

Matthew 11:2

וְיוֹחָנָן אַחֲרֵי שֶׁשָּׁמַע בְּבֵית אֲסִירִים אֶת-מַעֲשֵׂי יֵשׁוּעַ אָז-שָׁלַח שְׁנַיִם מִתַּלְמִידָיו

Matthew 11:3

לֵאמֹר לוֹ הַאִם אַתָּה הַהוּא שֶׁעָתִיד לָבוֹא אוֹ-נְחַכֶּה הָאַחֵר

HTV: **To ask of him, "Are you the one who is expected to come? Or should we await another?"**

KJV: And said unto him, Art thou he that should come, or do we look for another?

Matthew 11:4

וַיַּעַן יֵשׁוּעַ וַיֹּאמֶר לָהֶם לְכוּ וְהַגִּידוּ לְיוֹחָנָן אֲשֶׁר שְׁמַעְתֶּם וַאֲשֶׁר רְאִיתֶם

HTV: **So Yeshua answered and told them, "Go and declare to John what you have heard - and what you have seen."**

KJV: Jesus answered and said unto them, Go and shew John again those things which ye do hear and see:

Matthew 11:5

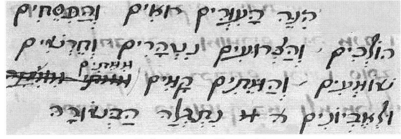

Freiburg Hebrew Manuscript

הִנֵּה הָעִוְרִים רוֹאִים וְהַפִּסְחִים הוֹלְכִים וְהַצָּרוּעִים נִטְהָרִים וְחֵדְשִׁים שׁוֹמְעִים וְהַמֵּתִים קָמִים מִמֵּתִים וּלְאֶבְיוֹנִים נִתְגַּלָּה הַבְּשׂוֹרָה

At top of page:

The Hebrew Book of Matthew

HTV: **Afterwards, John - who had heard in the prison of the works of Yeshua - then, sent two of his disciples,**

KJV: Now when John had heard in the prison the works of Christ, he sent two of his disciples,

Chapter 11

HTV: "Behold - the blind see, the lame walk, lepers are cleansed, the deaf hear - the dead rise up from the *grave* - and the good news (Gospel) is revealed to the needy!"

KJV: The blind receive their sight, and the lame walk, the lepers are cleansed, and the deaf hear, the dead are raised up, and the poor have the gospel preached to them.

Matthew 11:6

אַשְׁרֵי הַהוּא שֶׁלֹּא יִפּוֹל בְּמוֹקֵשׁ בַּעֲבוּרִי

HTV: "Blessed is he who *avoids* the snare because *of* me."

KJV: And blessed is *he*, whosoever shall not be offended in me.

Matthew 11:7

Freiburg Hebrew Manuscript

וּמִשֶּׁסָרוּ מִמֶּנּוּ הִנֵּה יֵשׁוּעַ הִתְחִיל לֵאמֹר אֶל הַכִּתִּים מִדִּבְרֵי יוֹחָנָן מָה-נָא-יְצָאתֶם לַמִּדְבָּר הַאִם לִרְאוֹת אֶת-קָנֶה אֲשֶׁר מֵרוּחַ נִתְנַדַּד

HTV: As they (John's disciples) withdrew from him, Yeshua began saying to the crowds - because of John's words, "Behold! Now why did you go out to the desert to see John? - A reed shaken by the wind *of the Spirit*?"

KJV: And as they departed, Jesus began to say unto the multitudes concerning John, What went ye out into the wilderness to see? A reed shaken with the wind?

Matthew 11:8

וּמָה יְצָאתֶם הַאִם לִרְאוֹת אָדָם הַנִּתְלַבֵּשׁ בְּמַלְבּוּשִׁים חֲלָקִים הִנֵּה אֲשֶׁר נִתְלַבְּשִׁים בְּמַלְבּוּשִׁים חֲלָקִים הֵמָּה נִמְצָאִים בְּבָתֵּי הַמְּלָכִים

HTV: **"What then did you go out to see? If it was a man clothed in soft garments - Look, those who are dressed in soft garments - they are found in the palaces of kings."**

KJV: But what went ye out for to see? A man clothed in soft raiment? behold, they that wear soft *clothing* are in kings' houses.

Matthew 11:9

וּמָה יְצָאתֶם הָאִם לִרְאוֹת הַנָּבִיא אֲנִי אוֹמֵר לָכֶם הוּא יֵשׁ יוֹתֵר מִנָּבִיא

HTV: **"So what was it you went out to see - a prophet? I say to you he is more than a prophet."**

KJV: But what went ye out for to see? A prophet? yea, I say unto you, and more than a prophet.

Matthew 11:10

הַזֶּה הַהוּא אֲשֶׁר מִמֶּנּוּ כָּתִיב הִנְנִי שׁוֹלֵחַ מַלְאָכִי וּפִנָּה דֶרֶךְ לְפָנֶיךָ

HTV: **"This is the one of which was written - 'Behold, *I* am sending my messenger and he will prepare the way before you.'"**

Note: Yeshua is referring to Malachi 3:1.

KJV: For this is *he*, of whom it is written, Behold, I send my messenger before thy face, which shall prepare thy way before thee.

Matthew 11:11

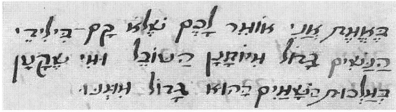

Freiburg Hebrew Manuscript

Chapter 11

בֶּאֱמֶת אֲנִי אוֹמֵר לָכֶם שֶׁלֹּא קָם בְּיְלִידֵי הַנָּשִׁים גָּדוֹל מִיוֹחָנָן הַטּוֹבֵל
וּמִי שֶׁקָּטָן בְּמַלְכוּת הַשָּׁמַיִם הַהוּא גָּדוֹל מִמֶּנּוּ

HTV: "Truly, I say to you that no one has risen - born of women - greater than John the Baptist. Nevertheless, *he* who is least in the kingdom of heaven is greater than he (*who is born of women*)."

> Note: Yeshua is trying to draw his disciples, and his followers, away from the earthly battle and into the spiritual realm. It is the heavenly battle that we are to fight. And those who have entered into the kingdom have received awareness and power from Yehovah that is more than that of any man who lives on earth.

KJV: Verily I say unto you, Among them that are born of women there hath not risen a greater than John the Baptist: notwithstanding he that is least in the kingdom of heaven is greater than he.

Matthew 11:12

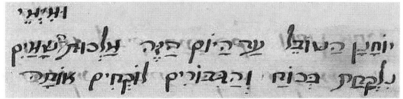
Freiburg Hebrew Manuscript

וּמִימֵי יוֹחָנָן הַטּוֹבֵל עַד הַיּוֹם הַזֶּה מַלְכוּת הַשָּׁמַיִם נִלְקַחַת בְּכֹחַ
וְהַגִּבּוֹרִים לוֹקְחִים אוֹתָהּ

HTV: "From the days of John the Baptist until this day - the kingdom of heaven is flashing forth in strength - and mighty men seize it."

> Note: The "it" that is "flashing forth" is the "Light of the World" - Yeshua (John 1:1). It happened in the time of John the Baptist, in the immediate past. John is only six months older than Yeshua. Something has just begun. What did John do? John baptized Yeshua, beginning his ministry - releasing the "Light of the World" (Yeshua) bursting forth from the kingdom of heaven. Those mighty men of God that He has prepared for this moment (the disciples) seized upon it with joy, not violence. This is reflected in the recurrence of this verse in Luke 16:16. **There is a huge difference here between the Hebrew and the Greek/English version of the KJV below!**

KJV: And from the days of John the Baptist until now the kingdom of heaven suffereth violence, and the violent take it by force.

Matthew 11:13

כִּי כֹל הַנְּבִיאִים וְהַתּוֹרָה נִבְּאוּ עַד יוֹחָנָן

HTV: **"Because all of the prophets - and the Torah - prophesied concerning John."**

Note: See Isaiah 22:22, Rev 3:7. The Hebrew uses the word **Torah** not law.

KJV: For all the prophets and the law prophesied until John.

Matthew 11:14

Freiburg Hebrew Manuscript

וְאִם תִּרְצוּ לְקַבֵּל הִנֵּה הַהוּא אֵלִיָּהוּ אֲשֶׁר עָתִיד לָבוֹא

HTV: **"And if you want to receive it (the kingdom of heaven), this (John the Baptist) is *like unto* Elijah, who has been prepared to come."**

Note: In the Hebrew tradition, at Passover, a place is set for Elijah with a chair and an empty cup. Elijah is the harbinger of the Messiah to come, "before the great and dreadful day of Yehovah!" (Malachi 4:5-6).

KJV: And if ye will receive *it*, this is Elias, which was for to come.

Matthew 11:15

אֲשֶׁר לוֹ אָזְנַיִם לִשְׁמוֹעַ הוּא יִשְׁמָע

HTV: **"Whoever has ears to hear, he will hear."**

Note: Those prepared to hear the truth.

KJV: He that hath ears to hear, let him hear.

Matthew 11:16

Freiburg Hebrew Manuscript

לְמִי נָא אֲדַמֶּה אֶת הַדּוֹר הַזֶּה הוּא דוֹמֶה לַתִּינוֹקִים הַיּוֹשְׁבִים בַּשּׁוּק אֲשֶׁר קוֹרְאִים לַחֲבֵרֵיהֶם

HTV: "**Who does this generation resemble? It resembles children sitting in the market - who call out to their friends (*to play*):**"

> Note: Yeshua is describing children at play who invent scenarios of war, weddings or festivals, or funerals and blow their toy flutes and dance, or wail, and all who come into their playground must conform to their childish games. They have no depth of understanding or spirit.
>
> This is a dramatic condemnation of the religious leaders of this generation. They are like children.

KJV: But whereunto shall I liken this generation? It is like unto children sitting in the markets, and calling unto their fellows,

Matthew 11:17

וְאוֹמְרִים הִנֵּה אֲנַחְנוּ שַׁרְנוּ לָכֶם וְלֹא רְקַדְתֶּם וְהָיִינוּ סוֹפְדִים וְלֹא סְפַדְתֶּם

HTV: **And say, "Behold! We sang to you and you did not dance - and we mourned and you did not mourn."**

KJV: And saying, We have piped unto you, and ye have not danced; we have mourned unto you, and ye have not lamented.

Matthew 11:18

כִּי יוֹחָנָן בָּא וְלֹא אָכַל וְלֹא שָׁתָה וְהֵמָה אוֹמְרִים שֶׁהַשֵּׁד בּוֹ

HTV: **"Because John came and did not eat (meat) or drink (*wine*) - they say the devil is in him."**

KJV: For John came neither eating nor drinking, and they say, He hath a devil.

Matthew 11:19

¹⁹ובן האדם בא לאכול ולשתות ואומר עליו שהוא זולל וסובא ואוהב לפריצים וחוטאים והסכלים שופטים לחכמים.

Shem Tov Manuscript
ובן האדם בא לאכול ולשתות ואומר עליו שהוא זולל וסובא ואוהב לפריצים וחוטאים והסכלים שופטים לחכמים.

HTV: **And the Son of man came eating and drinking - and they say "Behold,** *this* **man** *is* **a glutton and a drunkard and loves tax collectors and sinners!" -** *Therefore***, foolish children** *are* **judging the wise.** *(STM)*

> Note: Yeshua is completing his metaphor of the present generation and their leaders as foolish children. When Yehovah sends his anointed ones, they condemn and persecute them. The religious leaders of this generation are but children judging God's prophets. Clearly, the Greeks did not understand this - their translation below - of the concluding sentence is nonsense.

KJV: The Son of man came eating and drinking, and they say, Behold a man gluttonous, and a winebibber, a friend of publicans and sinners. **But wisdom is justified of her children.**

Matthew 11:20

וְאָז הִתְחִיל לְחָרֵף אֶת עָרִים שֶׁבָּהֶם נָעֲשׂוּ רַבּוֹת גְּבוּרוֹתָיו שֶׁלֹא שָׁבוּ בִּתְשׁוּבָה

HTV: **Then (Yeshua) started to reproach the towns** *where* **many of his mighty deeds were carried out - because they did not repent.**

KJV: Then began he to upbraid the cities wherein most of his mighty works were done, because they repented not:

Matthew 11:21

הוֹי לָךְ כּוֹרָזִין הוֹי לָךְ בֵּיתְצָיְדָה כִּי אִם בְּצוֹר וּבְצִידוֹן נָעֲשׂוּ הַגְּבוּרוֹת אֲשֶׁר נֶעֱשׂוּ בָךְ הִנֵּה לְפָנִים בְּדֶשֶׁן וּבִלְבוּשׁ שְׂעָרוֹת עִזִּים עָשׂוּ תְּשׁוּבָה

HTV: **"Woe to you Chorazin, and woe to you Bethsaida**

Chapter 11

- because if the mighty works done in you had been done in Tyre and Sidon they would repent in sackcloth and ashes."

KJV: Woe unto thee, Chorazin! woe unto thee, Bethsaida! for if the mighty works, which were done in you, had been done in Tyre and Sidon, they would have repented long ago in sackcloth and ashes.

Matthew 11:22

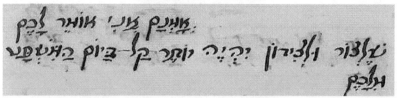

Freiburg Hebrew Manuscript

אָמְנָם אֲנִי אוֹמֵר לָכֶם שֶׁלְצוֹר וּלְצִידוֹן יִהְיֶה קַל בָּיוֹם הַמִּשְׁפָּט מִלָּכֶם

HTV: "Indeed I say to you - for Tyre and Sidon it will be easier - in the day of judgment - than it will be for your leaders."

KJV: But I say unto you, It shall be more tolerable for Tyre and Sidon at the day of judgment, than for you.

Matthew 11:23

וְאַתָּה כְּפַר נַחוּם אֲשֶׁר נִתְרוֹמֵם עַד הַשָּׁמַיִם הִנֵּה תָשְׁלַךְ עַד-שְׁאוֹל כִּי אִם בִּסְדוֹם נֶעֱשׂוּ הַגְּבוּרוֹת שֶׁנֶּעֱשׂוּ בְּךָ שֶׁמָּא עַד הַיּוֹם הַזֶּה תַעֲמוֹד

HTV: "And you, Capernaum - which we exalt up to heaven - will be thrown down to hell - since, if in Sodom were done the mighty deeds that were done in you - it would stand to this very day."

KJV: And thou, Capernaum, which art exalted unto heaven, shalt be brought down to hell: for if the mighty works, which have been done in thee, had been done in Sodom, it would have remained until this day.

Matthew 11:24

אָמְנָם אֲנִי אוֹמֵר לָכֶם שֶׁיִּהְיֶה יוֹתֵר קַל-לְאֶרֶץ סְדוֹמִיִּים בַּיוֹם הַמִּשְׁפָּט מִלָּכֶם

HTV: **"But I say to you - the land of the Sodomites will have it easier in the day of judgment - than will your leaders."**

KJV: But I say unto you, That it shall be more tolerable for the land of Sodom in the day of judgment, than for thee.

Matthew 11:25

Freiburg Hebrew Manuscript

בְּאוֹתוֹ זְמָן הֵשִׁיב יֵשׁוּעַ וַיֹּאמַר אֲנִי מוֹדֶה לְךָ הָאָב הַשָּׁמַיִם וְאֶרֶץ אֲשֶׁר הִסְתַּרְתָּ הָאֵלֶּה דְּבָרִים מֵהַחֲכָמִים וּמִמַּשְׂכִּילִים וְהִגְלִיתָ לִקְטַנִּים

HTV: **At that time, Yeshua turned and said, "I thank you Father of heaven and earth - because you have hidden these things from the cunning and educated - but you have revealed them to the humble."**

> Note: Yeshua has typified the religious leaders of this generation as 'foolish children playing at games' - now he is concluding his remarks by assessing them as cunning (pretending to be wise). Reminiscent of 2nd Timothy 3:7, these leaders are "ever learning but never able to come to the knowledge of truth." The humble, we know to be Yeshua's disciples, chosen by God.

KJV: At that time Jesus answered and said, I thank thee, O Father, Lord of heaven and earth, because thou hast hid these things from the wise and prudent, and hast revealed them unto babes.

Matthew 11:26

בֶּאֱמֶת הָאָבִי כֵּן נִרְאָה לְךָ לְרָצוֹן

HTV: **"In truth, my Father - so it has been shown to be your will."**

KJV: Even so, Father: for so it seemed good in thy sight.

Matthew 11:27

כֹּל דְּבָרִים נִמְסְרוּ לִי מֵאָבִי וְאֵין יוֹדֵעַ שׁוּם אֶת-הַבֵּן כִּי אִם הָאָב וְאֶת הָאָב אֵין יוֹדֵעַ שׁוּם כִּי אִם הַבֵּן וּלְמִי הַבֵּן יִרְצֶה לְהַגְלוֹת

HTV: "**All things are delivered to me from my Father - and no one knows the Son but the Father - and** *no one* **knows the Father but the Son - and whomever the Son will choose to reveal Him.**"

KJV: All things are delivered unto me of my Father: and no man knoweth the Son, but the Father; neither knoweth any man the Father, save the Son, and *he* to whomsoever the Son will reveal *him*.

Matthew 11:28

בֹּאוּ נָא אֵלַי כֹּל הַטּוֹרְחִים וַאֲשֶׁר נִתְעַמְּסִים וַאֲנִי אַסְעִידְכֶם

HTV: "**Come now unto me, all who are burdened and are** *heavy* **laden - and I will sustain you!**"

KJV: Come unto me, all ye that labor and are heavy laden, and I will give you rest.

Matthew 11:29

שְׂאוּ אֶת-עוֹלִי עֲלֵיכֶם וְלִמְדוּ מִמֶּנִּי כִּי אָנוֹכִי עָנָו וּשְׁפַל הַלֵּב וְתִמְצְאוּ מְנוּחָה לְנַפְשׁוֹתֵיכֶם

HTV: "**Take my yoke upon you - and learn from me - for I am meek and humble in heart - and you will find rest for your souls.**"

KJV: Take my yoke upon you, and learn of me; for I am meek and lowly in heart: and ye shall find rest unto your souls.

Matthew 11:30

כִּי הָעוֹלִי הוּא מָתוֹק וּמַשָּׂא שֶׁלִּי הוּא קַל

HTV: "**For my yoke - it is sweet - and my burden is light.**"

KJV: For my yoke *is* easy, and my burden is light.

Matthew Chapter 12

Hebrew Text Version (HTV)

¹ At that time, Yeshua passed through standing grain on a Sabbath. His disciples, being hungry, began to break off heads of grain - which they ate.

² When the Pharisees saw this, they said to him, "Look! Your disciples do that which is not right for them to do on the Sabbath!"

³ *Yeshua* said to them, "Have you not read what David did when he was starving - and those who were with him?"

⁴ "How he (David) entered into the house of Elohim (the *Tabernacle*) and he ate the bread of the Presence - which it is not proper for him to eat - nor for those with him - but only for the priests alone?"

⁵ "Or have you not read that the priests profane the Sabbath in the Temple - and yet they *are* without sin?"

⁶ "Truly I say to you that here *is* he who is greater *than* the Temple."

⁷ "But if you know that, 'I desired loving kindness - not sacrifice' You would never have condemned the innocent."

⁸ "For the Son of Man is also Lord of the Sabbath."

⁹ And it came to pass that Yeshua went into their (the Pharisees') synagogue.

¹⁰ Now behold, a certain man was there whose hand was withered. So they (Pharisees) asked Yeshua, saying - "Is it permitted to heal on the Sabbath?" This they did in order that they could denounce Yeshua.

¹¹ Then Yeshua said to them, "Who among you men, who has one sheep - if on the Sabbath it falls into a pit - will not grab it and pull it from there?"

¹² "How much more is a man *worth* than a sheep? Therefore - it is permitted to do good on the Sabbath!"

¹³ Then Yeshua said to the man, "Stretch forth your hand!"

And he stretched forth *his hand* and it was restored, like the other one!"

¹⁴ Nevertheless, the Pharisees went out and took counsel against Yeshua - how they would kill him.

¹⁵ Truly, when Yeshua knew this, he walked away from there - many followed after him, and he healed them all.

¹⁶ And Yeshua commanded them that *it* should not be revealed.

¹⁷ In order to fulfill what was spoken according to Isaiah the prophet who said -

¹⁸ "Behold, my Son - I will lift up! In him - My Chosen One (elect) - in whom my soul delights - through him I will give my *Holy* Spirit and he will bring forth judgment to the nations."

¹⁹ "He shall not fear - nor shall he run away - nor shall he cry out in the street - nor make a sound!"

²⁰ "A bruised reed - he shall not break, and a smoking wick - he shall not quench - until truth is brought forth at the Judgment!"

²¹ "And in his name - the nations will hope!"

²² One was brought unto Yeshua - who had in him a demon and was blind and dumb. Yeshua healed him - until he (the man) spoke and he saw! The *crowd* saw *all of this*.

²³ And all the people were astonished and said - "Is this not the son of David?"

²⁴ When the Pharisees heard this, they said, "This man does not cast out demons - except by the hand of Beelzebud - head of the demons!"

²⁵ Indeed Yeshua knew their thoughts, he said to them, "Behold! Every kingdom divided against itself will be destroyed - and every city or house divided against itself will not stand."

²⁶ "If Satan cast out Satan, he will be divided against himself - if so how will his kingdom stand?"

²⁷ "If I cast out demons by the hand of Beelzebub - by whom do your sons (the younger generation) cast them out - they will be your judges!"

²⁸ "However, if I cast out demons by the Spirit of Elohim - Behold! The Kingdom of Elohim has come to you."

²⁹ "How can anyone enter into the house of a strong man to loot his goods - unless he first binds the strong man - then loots

his house."

³⁰ "He who is not with me is against me - and he that does not gather (join) unto me is scattered."

³¹ "For this reason, I say to you that all sin and blasphemy will be forgiven to men. However, rebuking the Holy Spirit will not be forgiven."

³² "Whoever will speak a word against the Son of Adam (Man), it will be forgiven to him. However, whoever will speak a word against the Holy Spirit - it will not be forgiven to him - not in this world nor in the world to come."

³³ "Either make the tree good, and its fruit good - or make the tree evil, and its fruit evil - for the tree is known by its fruit."

³⁴ "Oh generation of serpents! How can you produce good things (or good words) while you are evil? For the mouth speaks out of the abundance of the heart."

³⁵ "A good man, from a good treasure - produces good things. An evil man, from an evil treasure - produces evil things."

³⁶ "Therefore I say to you - every word or thing - which man shall speak from his heart - he must give account of - on the day of judgment!"

³⁷ "From your *own* words you will be justified - or from the words of your *own* mouth you will be condemned."

³⁸ At that time, some of the scribes and the Pharisees replied to him (Yeshua), saying: "Rabbi, we wish to see some sign from you."

³⁹ Then he (Yeshua) answered them, saying: "An evil and adulterous generation asks for a sign - and no sign will be given - except for the sign of the prophet Jonah."

⁴⁰ "For as Jonah was in the belly of the great fish three days and three nights - so will the Son of Man be in the heart of the earth three days and three nights."

⁴¹ "The men of Nineveh will rise up in judgment against this generation. They will condemn it - because they repented at the call of Jonah. Behold! In this place is found one who is greater than Jonah!"

⁴² "The queen of Sheba shall rise up in judgment against this generation - and shall condemn it! For she came from the end of the earth to hear the wisdom of Solomon. Here is one greater than Solomon!"

⁴³ "When an unclean spirit *leaves* any man - behold! - it walks upon dry places demanding (seeking) rest - but it finds none."

⁴⁴ "Then he will say in his heart, 'I will return to my house from which I came.' - And when he comes and finds it purified and restored -

⁴⁵ "Behold, he will take *back* with him seven more of his fellow *spirits* - who are more evil than him - and they *will all* come *in*. And the last state of that person will be worse than the first. And so it will happen to this generation, which is very, very evil."

⁴⁶ While he was speaking to the crowds, behold, his mother and his brothers were standing outside asking to speak with him.

⁴⁷ And *someone* said to him, "Behold, your mother and your brothers are standing outside, asking to speak with you."

⁴⁸ Yeshua responded to the one who told him, saying, "Who is my mother? And who are my brothers?"

⁴⁹ And Yeshua stretched out his hand towards his disciples and said, "Behold my brothers and my mother."

⁵⁰ "Whoever does the will of my Father - who is in heaven - he is my brother, and my sister, and my mother!"

Matthew Chapter 12

HTV with translator notes and KJV comparison

Matthew 12:1

בְּאוֹתוֹ זְמָן עָבַר יֵשׁוּעַ בְּשַׁבָּת בְּתוֹךְ עַל הַזֶּרַע וְתַלְמִידִים שֶׁלוֹ
בִּהְיוֹתָם רְעֵבִים הִתְחִילוּ לִכְרוֹת אֶת שִׁבֳּלִים וְיֹאכְלוּ

HTV: **At that time, Yeshua passed through standing grain on a Sabbath. His disciples, being hungry, began to break off heads of grain - which they ate.**

KJV: At that time Jesus went on the sabbath day through the corn; and his disciples were an hungered, and began to pluck the ears of corn, and to eat.

Matthew 12:2

כַּאֲשֶׁר הַפְּרוּשִׁים רָאוּ הַזֹּאת אָמְרוּ לוֹ הִנֵּה הַתַּלְמִידֶיךָ עוֹשִׂים שֶׁלֹּא יִתָּכֵן לָהֶם לַעֲשׂוֹת בַּשַּׁבָּת

HTV: **When the Pharisees saw this, they said to him, "Look! Your disciples do that which is not right for them to do on the Sabbath!"**

KJV: But when the Pharisees saw *it*, they said unto him, Behold, thy disciples do that which is not lawful to do upon the sabbath day.

Matthew 12:3

Freiburg Hebrew Manuscript

וְהוּא אָמַר לָהֶם הַאִם לֹא קְרָאתֶם מַה שֶּׁדָּוִיד עָשָׂה כַּאֲשֶׁר יִרְעָב וַאֲשֶׁר יִהְיוּ אִתּוֹ

HTV: ***Yeshua* said to them, "Have you not read what David did when he was starving - and those who were with him?"**

*Note: See 1st Samuel 21:1-6, see also 1st Samuel 14:24-48 when Yehovah does not honor Saul's curse that his warriors not eat before battle.

KJV: But he said unto them, Have ye not read what David did, when he was an hungred, and they that were with him;

Matthew 12:4

Freiburg Hebrew Manuscript

Chapter 12

אֵיךְ הוּא נִכְנַס בְּבֵית הָאֱלֹהִים וַיֹּאכַל אֶת-לֶחֶם הַפָּנִים אֲשֶׁר לֹא-יִתָּכֵן לְאָכְלוֹ וְלֹא לַאֲשֶׁר אִתּוֹ כִּי-אִם-לְכֹּהֲנִים לְבַדָּם

HTV: "How he (David) entered into the house of Elohim (the *Tabernacle*) and he ate the bread of the Presence - which it is not proper for him to eat - nor for those with him - but only for the priests alone?"

> Note: See Numbers 18:8-10 for God's instructions on the shewbread. David and his men met the three criteria for eating the shewbread. As David and his men had washed, were ritually clean, and David had been chosen and anointed by Samuel at his father's (Jesse) house. They had abstained from women. One need not be a priest to take of the shewbread. Therefore the accusation was a "Takanot" one of the <u>commandments of men</u> - that Yeshua often disputed with the Rabbis. Yeshua is not endorsing their "only for the priests" commandment, but instead is alluding to Yehovah Himself anointing David and his men, in the Temple.

KJV: How he entered into the house of God, and did eat the shewbread, which was not lawful for him to eat, neither for them which were with him, but only for the priests?

Matthew 12:5

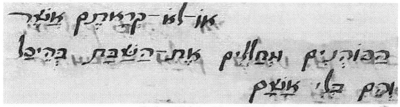
Freiburg Hebrew Manuscript

אוֹ לֹא קְרָאתֶם אֲשֶׁר הַכֹּהֲנִים מְחַלְלִים אֶת-הַשַּׁבָּת בַּהֵיכָל וְהֵם בְּלִי אָשָׁם

HTV: "Or have you not read that the priests profane the Sabbath in the Temple - and yet they *are* without sin?"

> Note: See Deuteronomy 5:12-15, "Observe the Sabbath day... and do no work." Again, Yeshua is not endorsing the priests' determination that "they are without sin" he is contradicting them. Apparently, the priests considered themselves above the law and did what they pleased on Sabbath. They sold animals for sacrifice and changed money on the Sabbath.

KJV: Or have ye not read in the law, how that on the sabbath days the priests in the temple profane the sabbath, and are blameless?

The Hebrew Book of Matthew

Matthew 12:6

אָמְנָם אֲנִי אוֹמֵר לָכֶם שֶׁשָּׁם הַהוּא אֲשֶׁר גָּדוֹל מֵהֵיכָל

HTV: "Truly I say to you that here *is* he who is greater *than* the Temple."

KJV: But I say unto you, That in this place is *one* greater than the temple.

Matthew 12:7

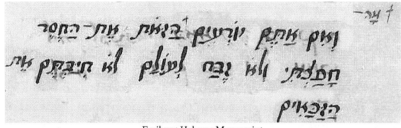
Freiburg Hebrew Manuscript

וְאִם אַתֶּם יוֹדְעִים מָה הַזֹּאת אֶת-הַחֶסֶד חָפַצְתִּי וְלֹא זֶבַח לְעוֹלָם לֹא חִיַּבְתֶּם אֶת הַזַּכָּאִים

HTV: "But if you know that, 'I desired loving kindness - not sacrifice' You would never have condemned the innocent."

Note: See Hosea 6:6 "For I desired mercy, and not sacrifice; and the knowledge of God more than burnt offerings" God is more concerned with loving-kindness than sacrifice, or punishment, of those who may have been, innocently, in error.

KJV: But if ye had known what *this* meaneth, I will have mercy, and not sacrifice, ye would not have condemned the guiltless.

Matthew: 12:8

כִּי הַבֶּן הָאָדָם הוּא גַם אָדוֹן הַשַּׁבָּת

HTV: "For the Son of Man is also Lord of the Sabbath."

KJV: For the Son of man is Lord even of the sabbath day.

Matthew 12:9

וְכַאֲשֶׁר הָלַךְ מִכַּאן הוּא בָא בַּכְּנֶסֶת שֶׁלָהֶם

HTV: And it came to pass that Yeshua went into their (the Pharisees') synagogue.

KJV: And when he was departed thence, he went into their synagogue:

Matthew 12:10

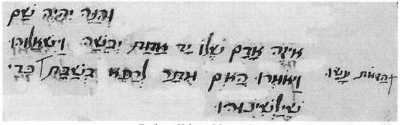

Freiburg Hebrew Manuscript

וְהִנֵּה יִהְיֶה שָׁם אִיֶּה אָדָם שֶׁלוֹ יָד יְבֵשָׁה וַיִּשְׁאָלוּהוּ וַאֲמְרוּ הָאִם מֻתָּר לִרְפֵּא בְּשַׁבָּת הַזֹּאת עָשׂוּ כְּדֵי שֶׁיִלְשִׁינוּהוּ

HTV: Now behold, a certain man was there whose hand was withered. So they (Pharisees) asked Yeshua, saying - "Is it permitted to heal on the Sabbath?" This they did in order that they could denounce Yeshua.

Note: This verse, and following, indicate the Pharisees knew Yeshua was a healer and were challenging him in order to denounce him for profaning the Sabbath.

KJV: And, behold, there was a man which had *his* hand withered. And they asked him, saying, Is it lawful to heal on the sabbath days? that they might accuse him.

Matthew 12:11

וְהוּא אָמַר לָהֶם מִי נָא יִהְיֶה מִמְּכֶם אָדָם אֲשֶׁר לוֹ צֹאן אֶחָד וְאִם בְּשַׁבָּת יִפּוֹל בְּשַׁחַת הֲלֹא יְחַזִּיקוּ וְיִמְשֹׁךְ מִכַּאן

HTV: Then Yeshua said to them, "Who among you men, who has one sheep - if on the Sabbath it falls into a pit - will not grab it and pull it from there?"

The Hebrew Book of Matthew

KJV: And he said unto them, What man shall there be among you, that shall have one sheep, and if it fall into a pit on the sabbath day, will he not lay hold on it, and lift

Matthew 12:12

כַּמָּה נָא הָאָדָם טוֹב-מִצֹּאן לְפִיכַךְ יִתָּכֵן לְהֵיטִיב בְּשַׁבָּת

HTV: **"How much more is a man *worth* than a sheep? Therefore - it is permitted to do good on the Sabbath!"**

KJV: How much then is a man better than a sheep? Wherefore it is lawful to do well on the sabbath days.

Matthew 12:13

וְאָז אָמַר לְאָדָם פְּרוֹשׂ נָא אֶת-יָדְךָ וַיִּפְרוֹשׂ וְהִיא נִתְרַפְּאָה כָּאַחֶרֶת

HTV: **Then Yeshua said to the man, "Stretch forth your hand!" And he stretched forth *his hand* and it was restored, like the other one!"**

KJV: Then saith he to the man, Stretch forth thine hand. And he stretched *it* forth; and it was restored whole, like as the other.

Matthew 12:14

Freiburg Hebrew Manuscript

אֲבָל הַפְּרוּשִׁים יָצְאוּ וְיָעֲצוּ כְּנֶגְדוֹ אֵיכָה יה יְמוֹתְתוּהוּ

HTV: **Nevertheless, the Pharisees went out and took counsel against Yeshua - how they would kill him.**

Note: The Freiberg is the only Hebrew manuscript that has the word "Yah" - perhaps an abbreviation - for" Yeshua" here.

KJV: Then the Pharisees went out, and held a council against him, how they might destroy him.

Matthew 12:15

אָמְנָם יֵשׁוּעַ יִהְיֶה יוֹדֵעַ הַזֹּאת וְהָלַךְ מִכַּאן וְרַבִּים יִרְדְּפוּ אַחֲרָיו וַיִּרְפָּא כֻלָּם

HTV: **Truly, when Yeshua knew this, he walked away from there - many followed after him, and he healed them all.**

KJV: But when Jesus knew *it*, he withdrew himself from thence: and great multitudes followed him, and he healed them all;

Matthew 12:16

Freiburg Hebrew Manuscript

וְהוּלְגִי אֱלֹשׁ סְהֵל הוֹצִיָו

HTV: **And Yeshua commanded them that *it* should not be revealed.**

Note: "*It*" being - he healed them - see Matthew 12:17 and note 2 on Matthew 12:18. This is a theme of the Gospels, Yeshua did not want to openly proclaim his messiahship because the people wanted, and expected, a "conquering-king" messiah to lead them against the Romans. See Isaiah 35:5-6 for the types of healing which were signs of the coming Messiah.

KJV: And charged them that they should not make him known:

Matthew 12:17

רְמֹאל איבָנָה וְהִיָעֲשַׂי יִפּ-לַע רְמַאֲנֶשׁ הֲמָ אלֲמַיֵּשׁ יָדְךָ

HTV: **In order to fulfill what was spoken according to Isaiah the prophet who said -**

KJV: That it might be fulfilled which was spoken by Esaias the prophet, saying,

Matthew 12:18

הֵן בֶּן אֶתְמָךְ בֹּו-בְחִירִי רָצְתָה נַפְשִׁי בֹו אֶתֵן רוּחִי עָלָיו מִשְׁפָּט לַגּוֹיִם יוֹצִיא

HGC Hebrew Gospel from Catalonia

HTV: "Behold, my Son - I will lift up! In him - My Chosen One (elect) - in whom my soul delights - through him I will give my *Holy* Spirit and he will bring forth judgment to the nations."

> Note: This verse refers to Isaiah 42:1. **The inclusion of "Son" in the Hebrew Gospel from Catalonia is a distinct difference** from the Greek Translation which says **"servant."**

KJV: Behold my servant, whom I have chosen; my beloved, in whom my soul is well pleased: I will put my spirit upon him, and he shall shew judgment to the Gentiles.

Matthew 12:19

לֹא יִצְעַק וְלֹא יִשָּׂא וְלֹא יַשְׁמִיעַ בַּחוּץ קוֹלוֹ

Freiburg Hebrew Manuscript

HTV: "He shall not fear - nor shall he run away - nor shall he cry out in the street - nor make a sound!"

> Note: This verse is from Isaiah 42:2 - these verses refer to the persecution of Yeshua. Otherwise, the Greek translation of this verse is meaningless.

KJV: He shall not strive, nor cry; neither shall any man hear his voice in the streets.

Matthew 12:20

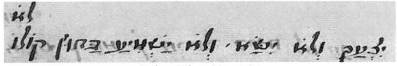

Freiburg Hebrew Manuscript

Chapter 12

קָנֶה רָצוּץ לֹא יִשְׁבּוֹר וּפִשְׁתָּה כֵהָה לֹא יְכַבֶּנָּה עַד לֶאֱמֶת יוֹצִיא אֶת הַמִשְׁפָּט

HTV: "A bruised reed - he shall not break, and a smoking wick - he shall not quench - until truth is brought forth at the Judgment!"

Note: This verse is from Isaiah 42:3. A candle is a symbol of the light of the truth. So the wick, the truth, shall not be extinguished until the Judgment comes to pass.

KJV: A bruised reed shall he not break, and smoking flax shall he not quench, till he send forth judgment unto victory.

Matthew 12:21

וּבִשְׁמוֹ גּוֹיִם יְיַחְלוּ

HTV: "And in his name - the nations will hope!"

Note: Isaiah 42:4.

KJV: And in his name shall the Gentiles trust.

Matthew 12:22

וְאָז הוּבָא אֶצְלוֹ שׁוּם אֲשֶׁר בּוֹ הַשֵּׁד וְעִוֵּר וְאִלֵּם וַיִּרְפָּא אוֹתוֹ עַד שֶׁהוּא יִהְיֶה מְדַבֵּר ורוּאֶה

HTV: **One was brought unto Yeshua - who had in him a demon and was blind and dumb. Yeshua healed him - until he (the man) spoke and he saw! The *crowd* saw *all of this*.**

KJV: Then was brought unto him one possessed with a devil, blind, and dumb: and he healed him, in so much that the blind and dumb both spake and saw.

Matthew 12:23

וְכֹל כִּתִּים יִשְׁתּוֹמְמוּ וְיֹאמְרוּ הֲלֹא הֲזֶה הַבֵּן דָּוִד

HTV: **And all the people were astonished and said - "Is this not the son of David?"**

193

KJV: And all the people were amazed, and said, Is not this the son of David?

Matthew 12:24

וּמִשְׁפְּרוּשִׁים שָׁמְעוּ הַזֹּאת אָז-אָמְרוּ הַזֶּה אֵינוֹ גוֹרֵשׁ אֶת-שֵׁדִים כִּי-אִם-בְּיַד הַבַּעַל זְבוּב הָרֹאשׁ שֵׁדִים

HTV: **When the Pharisees heard this, they said, "This man does not cast out demons - except by the hand of Beelzebud - head of the demons!"**

KJV: But when the Pharisees heard *it*, they said, This *fellow* doth not cast out devils, but by Beelzebub the prince of the devils.

Matthew 12:25

אָמְנָם יֵשׁוּעַ יוֹדֵעַ אֶת-מַחְשְׁבוֹתֵיהֶם אָמַר לָהֶם הִנֵּה כֹּל מַלְכוּת הַנִּתְחַלְקָה בְעַצְמָהּ הִיא תִּתְחָרֵב וְכֹל עִיר אוֹ בַּיִת הַנִּתְחַלֵּק בְּעַצְמוֹ לֹא יַעֲמוֹד

HTV: **Indeed, Yeshua knew their thoughts, he said to them, "Behold! Every kingdom divided against itself will be destroyed - and every city or house divided against itself will not stand."**

KJV: And Jesus knew their thoughts, and said unto them, Every kingdom divided against itself is brought to desolation; and every city or house divided against itself shall not stand:

Matthew 12:26

וְאִם הַשָׂטָן גּוֹרֵשׁ אֶת הַשָׂטָן הוּא נִמְצָא נִתְחַלֵּק בְּעַצְמוֹ וְאִם כֵּן-אֵיכָה נָא-תַעֲמוֹד מַלְכוּתוֹ

HTV: **"If Satan cast out Satan, he will be divided against himself - if so, how will his kingdom stand?"**

KJV: And if Satan cast out Satan, he is divided against himself; how shall then his kingdom stand?

Matthew 12:27

Freiburg Hebrew Manuscript

וְאִם אֲנִי גּוֹרֵשׁ אֶת-שֵׁדִים בְּיַד הַבַּעַל זְבוּב בְּאֵיזֶה נָא הַבְּנֵיכֶם
גּוֹרְשִׁים עָלְכֵן הֵמָה יִהְיוּ שׁוֹפְטֵיכֶם

HTV: "If I cast out demons by the hand of Beelzebub - by whom do your sons (the younger generation) cast them out - they will be your judges!"

> Note: In Matthew chapter 10, Yeshua has sent out his young disciples, and their followers, seventy in all - to heal, cast out demons and preach. This younger generation (figuratively the "sons" of the Pharisees) have already cast out demons in the name and authority of Yeshua. Certainly, this was known.
>
> So, Yeshua is challenging the Pharisees - are all their sons possessed of Satan? The younger generation see Yeshua as a prophet and miracle worker. See also Mark 9:38-40.

KJV: And if I by Beelzebub cast out devils, by whom do your children cast *them* out? Therefore they shall be your judges.

Matthew 12:28

וְאִם אֲנִי גּוֹרֵשׁ אֶת-שֵׁדִים בְּרוּחַ הָאֱלֹהִים הִנֵּה בָּאָה אֲלֵיכֶם מַלְכוּת
הָאֱלֹהִים

HTV: "However, if I cast out demons by the Spirit of Elohim - Behold! The Kingdom of Elohim has come to you."

KJV: But if I cast out devils by the Spirit of God, then the kingdom of God is come unto you.

Matthew 12:29

Freiburg Hebrew Manuscript

The Hebrew Book of Matthew

אוֹ-אֵיךְ-יוּכַל שׂוּם לְכָנֵס בְּבֵית הֶחָזָק לְבוֹזֵז אֶת-כָּלָיו אִם לֹא קֶדֶם יִקְשׁוֹר אֶת-הֶחָזָק הַהוּא אָז יְבוֹזֵז אֶת-בֵּיתוֹ

HTV: "How can anyone enter into the house of a strong man to loot his goods - unless he first binds the strong man - then loots his house."

> Note: In other words, Yeshua is saying that Satan must be bound first in order to heal someone that is afflicted by demons. Therefore, the Pharisees accusation is meaningless.

KJV: Or else how can one enter into a strong man's house, and spoil his goods, except he first bind the strong man? and then he will spoil his house.

Matthew 12:30

אֲשֶׁר לֹא עִמָּדִי הַהוּא יֵשׁ כְּנֶגְדִי וַאֲשֶׁר אֵין לוֹקֵט עִמִּי הַהוּא מְפַזֵּר

HTV: "He who is not with me is against me - and he that does not gather (join) unto me is scattered."

KJV: He that is not with me is against me; and he that gathereth not with me scattereth abroad.

Matthew 12:31

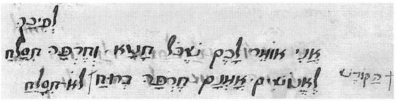
Freiburg Hebrew Manuscript

לְפִיכָךְ אֲנִי אוֹמֵר לָכֶם שֶׁכֹּל חֵטְא וְחֶרְפָּה תִּסָּלַח לָאֱנוֹשִׁים אָמְנָם חֶרְפָּה בְּרוּחַ הַקּוֹדֶשׁ לֹא תִסָּלַח

HTV: "For this reason, I say to you that all sin and blasphemy will be forgiven to men. However, rebuking the Holy Spirit will not be forgiven."

> Note: If one does not repent and accept the Holy Spirit then they are unforgiven. They are rebuking - rejecting - the Holy Spirit of Yehovah! If they repent and accept the Holy Spirit - all sin - even blasphemy can and will be forgiven. "Therefore, if any man be in Yeshua Ha Mashiach - he is a new creature, old things are passed away. Behold, all things are become new." 2 Corinthians 5:17.

KJV: Wherefore I say unto you, All manner of sin and blasphemy shall be forgiven unto men: but the blasphemy *against* the *Holy* Ghost shall not be forgiven unto men.

Matthew 12:32

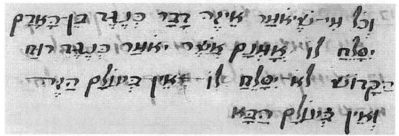

Freiburg Hebrew Manuscript

וְכֹל מִי שֶׁיֹּאמַר אֵיזֶה דָבָר כְּנֶגֶד בֶּן-הָאָדָם יִסָּלַח לוֹ אָמְנָם אֲשֶׁר יֹאמַר כְּנֶגֶד רוּחַ הַקֹּדוֹשׁ לֹא יִסָּלַח לוֹ אֵין בְּעוֹלָם הַזֶּה וְאֵין בְּעוֹלָם הַבָּא

HTV: **"Whoever will speak a word against the Son of Adam (Man), it will be forgiven to him. However, whoever will speak a word against the Holy Spirit - it will not be forgiven to him - not in this world nor in the world to come."**

> Note: To "speak a word against" Yeshua, Yehovah, or His Holy Spirit is to rebuke them. Since salvation is granted through the indwelling of the Holy Spirit - its rebuke is one's condemnation.

KJV: And whosoever speaketh a word against the Son of man, it shall be forgiven him: but whosoever speaketh against the Holy Ghost, it shall not be forgiven him, neither in this world, neither in the *world* to come.

Matthew 12:33

אוֹ עֲשׂוּ אִילָן טוֹב וּפִרְיוֹ טוֹב אוֹ עֲשׂוּ אִילָן רַע וּפִרְיוֹ רַע כִּי הָאִילָן יִנָּכֵר מִפִּרְיוֹ

HTV: **"Either make the tree good, and its fruit good - or make the tree evil, and its fruit evil - for the tree is known by its fruit."**

KJV: Either make the tree good, and his fruit good; or else make the tree corrupt, and his fruit corrupt: for the tree is known by *his* fruit.

The Hebrew Book of Matthew

Matthew 12:34

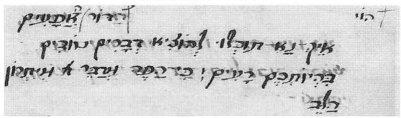

Freiburg Hebrew Manuscript

הוֹי הַדּוֹר הָאֲפָעִים אֵיךְ נָא תוּכְלוּ לְהוֹצִיא דְבָרִים טוֹבִים בִּהְיוֹתְכֶם רָעִים כִּי הַפֶּה מְדַבֵּר מִיִּתְרוֹן הַלֵּב

HTV: "Oh generation of serpents! How can you produce good things (or good words) while you are evil? For the mouth speaks out of the abundance of the heart."

Note: If your heart is evil then your words and deeds will also be evil.

KJV: O generation of vipers, how can ye, being evil, speak good things? for out of the abundance of the heart the mouth speaketh.

Matthew 12:35

הָאָדָם טוֹב מוֹצִיא מֵאוֹצָר טוֹב דְּבָרִים טוֹבִים וְהָאָדָם רָע מוֹצִיא מֵאוֹצָר רָע דְּבָרִים רָעִים

HTV: "A good man, from a good treasure - produces good things. An evil man, from an evil treasure - produces evil things."

KJV: A good man out of the good treasure of the heart bringeth forth good things: and an evil man out of the evil treasure bringeth forth evil things.

Matthew 12:36

אָמְנָם אֲנִי אוֹמֵר לָכֶם אֲשֶׁר אֲנוֹשִׁים יִתְּנוּ סִבָּה מִכֹּל דָּבָר וְדָבָר בָּטֵן בְּיוֹם הַמִּשְׁפָּט שֶׁיְּדַבְּרוּ

HTV: "Therefore I say to you - every word or thing - which man shall speak from his heart - he must give account of - on the day of judgment!"

Chapter 12

KJV: But I say unto you, That every idle word that men shall speak, they shall give account thereof in the day of judgment.

Matthew 12:37

מִדְבָרֶיךָ אַתָּה תִצְטַדֵּק וּמִדְבְרֵי פִּיךָ אַתָּה תִתְחַיֵּב

HTV: "From your *own* words you will be justified - or from the words of your *own* mouth you will be condemned."

KJV: For by thy words thou shalt be justified, and by thy words thou shalt be condemned.

Matthew 12:38

וְאָז קְצָתָם מְסוֹפְרִים וּפְרוֹשִׁים הֵשִׁיבוּ לוֹ לֵאמֹר רַבִּי אֲנַחְנוּ רוֹצִים לִרְאוֹת אֵיזוֹ אוֹת מִמְּךָ

HTV: At that time, some of the scribes and the Pharisees replied to him (Yeshua), saying: "Rabbi, we wish to see some sign from you."

KJV: Then certain of the scribes and of the Pharisees answered, saying, Master, we would see a sign from thee.

Matthew 12:39

אֲשֶׁר נָתַן לָהֶם מַעֲנֶה וַיֹּאמַר הַדּוֹר הָרַע וְהַמְנָאֵף שׁוֹאֵל אוֹת וְלֹא יִנָּתֵן לוֹ אוֹת כִּי אִם הָאוֹת שֶׁל יוֹנָה הַנָּבִיא

HTV: Then he (Yeshua) answered them, saying: "An evil and adulterous generation asks for a sign - and no sign will be given - except for the sign of the prophet Jonah."

KJV: But he answered and said unto them, An evil and adulterous generation seeketh after a sign; and there shall no sign be given to it, but the sign of the prophet Jonas:

The Hebrew Book of Matthew

Matthew 12:40

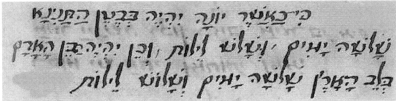
Freiburg Hebrew Manuscript

כִּי כַאֲשֶׁר יוֹנָה יִהְיֶה בְּבֶטֶן הַתַּנִינָא שְׁלֹשָׁה יָמִים וְשָׁלֹשׁ לֵילוֹת וְכֵן יִהְיֶה הַבֶּן הָאָדָם בְּלֵב הָאָרֶץ שְׁלֹשָׁה יָמִים וְשָׁלֹשׁ לֵילוֹת -

HTV: "For as Jonah was in the belly of the great fish three days and three nights - so will the Son of Man be in the heart of the earth three days and three nights."

> Note: In Jonah 1:17 the narrative says: "Yehovah created a great fish" The people of Nineveh worshipped a great fish god called Dagan. A great fish spitting out a prophet on their shores would have gotten their attention.

KJV: For as Jonas was three days and three nights in the whale's belly; so shall the Son of man be three days and three nights in the heart of the earth.

Matthew 12:41

אַנְשֵׁי נִינְוֵה יָקוּמוּ בַּמִּשְׁפָּט עִם הַדּוֹר הַזֶּה וַיְחַיְּיבוּהוּ כִּי הֵמָה עָשׂוּ תְשׁוּבָה לְהַקְרִיאַת יוֹנָה וְהִנֵּה בְּמָקוֹם הַזֶּה נִמְצָא אֲשֶׁר יוֹתֵר מִיוֹנָה

HTV: "The men of Nineveh will rise up in judgment against this generation. They will condemn it - because they repented at the call of Jonah. Behold! In this place is found one who is greater than Jonah!"

KJV: The men of Nineveh shall rise in judgment with this generation, and shall condemn it: because they repented at the preaching of Jonas; and, behold, a greater than Jonas is here.

Matthew 12:42

הַמַּלְכָּה שֶׁמְּדָרוֹם תָּקוּם בַּמִּשְׁפָּט עִם הַדּוֹר הַזֶּה וְתְחַיְּיבֵהוּ כִּי בָּאָה מִקְצֵה הָאָרֶץ לִשְׁמוֹעַ חָכְמַת שְׁלֹמֹה וְהִנֵּה שָׁם אֲשֶׁר יוֹתֵר מִשְּׁלֹמֹה

HTV: **"The queen of Sheba shall rise up in judgment against this generation - and shall condemn it! For she came from the end of the earth to hear the wisdom of Solomon. Here is one greater than Solomon!"**

KJV: The queen of the south shall rise up in the judgment with this generation, and shall condemn it: for she came from the uttermost parts of the earth to hear the wisdom of Solomon; and, behold, a greater than Solomon *is* here.

Matthew 12:43

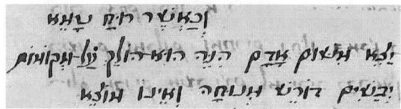
Freiburg Hebrew Manuscript

וְכַאֲשֶׁר רוּחַ טָמֵא יֵצֵא מִשּׁוּם אָדָם הִנֵּה הוּא הוֹלֵךְ עַל מְקוֹמוֹת יְבֵשִׁים דּוֹרֵשׁ מְנוּחָה וְאֵינוֹ מוֹצֵא

HTV: **"When an unclean spirit *leaves* any man - behold! - it walks upon dry places* demanding (seeking) rest - but it finds none."**

*Note: An unclean spirit is inherently empty of God's Spirit, the Holy Spirit. They are described as dry, empty husks which seems a quite appropriate metaphor.

KJV: When the unclean spirit is gone out of a man, he walketh through dry places, seeking rest, and findeth none.

Matthew 12:44

אָז יֹאמַר בְּלִבּוֹ אֲנִי אָשׁוּב לְבֵיתִי אֲשֶׁר מִמֶּנּוּ יָצָאתִי וְכַאֲשֶׁר יָבוֹא וְיִמְצָא אוֹתוֹ מְטֹהָר וּמְתֻקָּן

HTV: **"Then he will say in his heart, 'I will return to my house from which I came.' - And when he comes and finds it purified and restored -**

KJV: Then he saith, I will return into my house from whence I came out; and when he is come, he findeth *it* empty, swept, and garnished.

Matthew 12:45

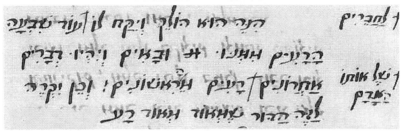

Freiburg Hebrew Manuscript

הִנֵּה הוּא הוֹלֵךְ וְיִקַּח לוֹ לַחֲבֵרִים עוֹד שִׁבְעָה הָרָעִים מִמֶּנּוּ וּבָאִים וְיִהְיוּ דְּבָרִים אַחֲרוֹנִים שֶׁל אוֹתוֹ הָאָדָם רָעִים מֵהָרִאשׁוֹנִים וְכֵן יִקְרֶה לַזֶּה הַדּוֹר שֶׁמְּאוֹד מְאוֹד רַע

HTV: **"Behold, he will take *back* with him seven more of his fellow *spirits* - who are more evil than him - and they *will all* come *in*. And the last state of that person will be worse than the first. And so it will happen to this generation, which is very, very evil."**

Note: With these metaphors, Yeshua completes his condemnation of the current generation and their leaders first mentioned in 12:41.

KJV: Then goeth he, and taketh with himself seven other spirits more wicked than himself, and they enter in and dwell there: and the last *state* of that man is worse than the first. Even so shall it be also unto this wicked generation.

Matthew 12:46

וְעוֹדֶנּוּ מְדַבֵּר אֶל הַכִּתִּים הִנֵּה אִמּוֹ וְאֶחָיו יִהְיוּ עוֹמְדִים חוּצָה מְבַקְשִׁים לְדַבֵּר אִתּוֹ

HTV: **While he was speaking to the crowds, behold, his mother and his brothers were standing outside asking to speak with him.**

KJV: While he yet talked to the people, behold, *his* mother and his brethren stood without, desiring to speak with him.

Matthew 12:47

וַיֹּאמֶר לוֹ שׁוּם הִנֵּה אִמְּךָ וְאַחִים שֶׁלְּךָ עוֹמְדִים חוּצָה אֲשֶׁר מְבַקְּשִׁים לְדַבֵּר אִתְּךָ

HTV: And *someone* said to him, "Behold, your mother and your brothers are standing outside, asking to speak with you."

KJV: Then one said unto him, Behold, thy mother and thy brethren stand without, desiring to speak with thee.

Matthew 12:48

וַיַּעַן לְמִי שֶׁאָמַר לוֹ לֵאמֹר אֵיהִיא אִמִּי וְאֵי אֵלּוּ אֶחָי

HTV: Yeshua responded to the one who told him, saying, "Who is my mother? And who are my brothers?"

> Note: In Mark 3:21-22 it says that Yeshua's relatives and/or friends and fellow townspeople said, "He is beside himself," or "out of his mind." The scribes coming from Jerusalem said he "casts out demons by Ba'alzebub... the Prince of demons." Some of this contention comes from his friends and family - astounded that Yeshua is God's Messiah with a great multitude following him - while the priests are trying to take him down by calling him a demon worshiper.

KJV: But he answered and said unto him that told him, Who is my mother? and who are my brethren?

Matthew 12:49

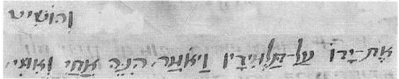
Freiburg Hebrew Manuscript

וְהוֹשִׁיט אֶת-יָדוֹ עַל תַּלְמִידָיו וַיֹּאמֶר הִנֵּה אֶחָי וְאִמִּי

HTV: And Yeshua stretched out his hand towards his disciples and said, "Behold my brothers and my mother."

> Note: Yeshua is re-directing attention - away from the distraction - to his disciples who have done miracles witnessed by many of the followers present at this gathering.

KJV: And he stretched forth his hand toward his disciples, and said, Behold my mother and my brethren!

Matthew 12:50

אֲשֶׁר יַעֲשֶׂה רְצוֹן הָאָבִי אֲשֶׁר בְּשָׁמַיִם הַהוּא יֵשׁ אָחִי וְאַחוֹתִי וְאִמִּי

HTV: **"Whoever does the will of my Father - who is in heaven - he is my brother, and my sister, and my mother!"**

KJV: For whosoever shall do the will of my Father which is in heaven, the same is my brother, and sister, and mother.

Matthew Chapter 13

Hebrew Text Version (HTV)

1 On that day - Yeshua left the house and sat by the seashore.

2 Many gathered near him to the point *that* Yeshua got into *a* ship and sat *down*. And all the crowd stood by the seashore.

3 Yeshua spoke many things to them in parables, saying, "Behold, the sower went out to sow."

4 "And behold, some of his seed(s) fell by the road, and the birds of the air came and ate them."

5 Some seeds fell among rocks where there was no depth of soil, and when they sprang up - they withered because there was not much soil there.

6 "After the sun rose, they were burned - because they had no root, they withered."

7 "And *other seeds* fell among the thorns - and the thorns grew *up* and choked them."

8 "These (seeds) fell in good earth and brought forth fruit - these a hundred(fold), and these sixty(fold), and these thirty(fold)."

Chapter 13

9 "Whosoever has ears to hear it, he will hear it."

10 And Yeshua's disciples came near and said to him, "Why do you speak to them in parables?"

11 Therefore, Yeshua answered them and said, "It was given to you to know the secrets of the kingdom of heaven - but it was not given to them."

12 "To whomever much has been given - let him give abundantly - and more will be given unto him. To whomever little has been given - and gives nothing - even that little, which he has, may be taken away.

13 "Therefore, I speak to them in parables because - those seeing do not see - and the hearers do not hear - and do not understand"

14 "That the prophecy of Isaiah was fulfilled in them, saying, 'You will hear, but you will not understand; and you will see, but you will not know.' "

15 "Because the heart of this people has become fat, and their ears have become dulled, and their eyes closed - so that they will not see with their eyes and hear with their ears - *lest* in their heart they would understand and repent, and I would heal them."

16 "Blessed are your eyes, because they see (*the truth*), and your ears because they hear (*the truth*)!"

17 "Truly I say to you that many prophets and righteous ones desired to see what you see and they did not see, and to hear what you hear and they did not hear."

18 "And now you have heard the parable of the sower."

19 "The Sower is the Son of Man. Everyone who hears the word of the kingdom (the word of God) and does not understand - Behold! Satan comes and uproots what was sown in his heart - this is that (seed) which was sown by the wayside."

20 "He who sows in rocky places - is he who hears the Word of the Master - and immediately receives it with joy!"

21 "Indeed, he has no root in him - except for a quickly passing renewal. When troubles and persecution take away the Word - he immediately stumbles into a snare."

22 "That seed which was sown *among* thorns and thistles - is the one who hears the Word of Yehovah but *is* preoccupied with this world and its deceitful riches - then will the Word of God be

choked and strangled out - producing no fruit."

23 "Whosoever sows in good ground is the one who hears the Word, and understands it, and brings forth fruit - some of them one hundred times, some sixty *times,* and some thirty *times what was sown!"*

24 Afterward, he put forth to them another trustworthy parable saying, "The kingdom of heaven is like a man who sows good seed in his field."

25 "While the man slept in this place - the enemy came and sowed thorns and thistles among the wheat - then went his way."

26 "When the grain grew and brought forth fruit - *then too* the thorns and thistles appeared."

27 "The servants of the master came to the house and asked him, 'Lord, did you not sow good seed in your field? So where did the thorns and thistles come from?' "

28 "He said to them, 'The enemy did this!' His servants said to him, 'If you want, we will go and uproot them.'"

29 "He said, 'No - so as not to tear the wheat out along with the thorns and thistles.'"

30 "Leave both alone to grow for now - until the time of the harvest. When harvest time comes, I will tell the reapers - first gather the thorns and thistles into bundles - then burn them - but gather the wheat into my granary."

31 Yeshua presented another parable before them, saying, "The kingdom of heaven is like the mustard seed which the man took and sowed in his field."

32 "It is smaller than all the other seeds - but then it will grow bigger than all the bushes - and will be a tree - so big that the birds of the sky will come and nest in its branches."

33 Yeshua brought forth yet another parable - saying, "The kingdom of heaven *is* leaven which a woman took and concealed in three measures of flour until it all grew *throughout.*"

34 Yeshua spoke all these matters to the crowds in parables, and he spoke nothing other than parables to them.

35 In order to fulfill what was said according to the prophet who says, "I will open my mouth in parables and I will pour out *the* secrets of eternity."

36 After Yeshua sent the crowds away from him - his

disciples drew near him. They said, "Explain to us the parable of the thorns and thistles in the field."

37 *To* which Yeshua responded - and said, "The sower of the good seed - he is the Son of Man."

38 "The field - it *is* the world - and the good seed - they *are* the righteous children of the kingdom (*of heaven*) - but the thorns are the *wicked* children of *the* evil *one*."

39 "The enemy who sowed them - he is Satan - and the harvest - it *is* the end of the world - and the reapers - they are the angels."

40 "Just as the thorns and thistles *are* gathered and burnt - so shall it be at the end of the world."

41 "The Son of Man will send his angels - and they will uproot from his kingdom - all *those who* are causing transgression (sin) - and those who are transgressors."

42 "They will be sent to the fiery furnace of hell (Gei-Hinnom); *and* there will be wailing and gnashing of teeth."

43 "Then the righteous will shine like the sun in the kingdom of my Father - Whoever has ears to hear, let them hear."

44 "Behold, the kingdom of heaven is like a man who finds a treasure hidden in the field - which if a man finds it - he goes with joy and sells everything *he owns* and buys that field."

45 "In addition - the kingdom of heaven is compared to a merchant who is seeking priceless pearls."

46 "When he found one pearl of great price - he went and sold all of his possessions and he bought it."

47 "Yet again, the kingdom of heaven is compared to a net cast into the sea - *which* gathers all kinds of fish."

48 "When it was full, they took it out and sat down at the sea shore. They gathered the good ones into their vessels - and threw out the bad ones."

49 "So shall it be at the end of the age - at that time the angels will come forth and will separate the wicked from the righteous."

50 "They (the angels) will cast them (the wicked) into the furnace of fire - there will be wailing and gnashing of teeth."

51 Yeshua said to them, "Have you understood all these things?" They said to him, "Yes Lord."

52 Then Yeshua said to them, "Therefore every scribe who teaches of the kingdom of heaven is like the master of a house - a

The Hebrew Book of Matthew

father who brings out of his treasure - *things both* new and old."

53 It came to pass, after Yeshua finished these (*parables*) he passed on from there.

54 Yeshua came unto his home country (Galilee) - he taught them in their synagogues - in such a way that they were astonished, and *they* said, "From where is this wisdom and *these* mighty works (*coming*)."

55 "Isn't he the son of the smith [Napach], and isn't his mother's name Myriam, and his brothers Jacob and Yosef and Simeon and Jude (or Yehuda)?"

56 "And his sisters, are they not all with us? Where did he get all these words *of wisdom*?"

57 And they were struggling *to believe* in him. And Yeshua said to them, "There is no prophet found without honor - except in his native land and in his home town."

58 And there he did not do many great wonders before them - because they did not believe in him.

Matthew Chapter 13

HTV with translator notes and KJV comparison

Matthew 13:1

בְּאוֹתוֹ הַיּוֹם יָצָא יֵשׁוּעַ מִבַּיִת וַיֵּשֶׁב אֵצֶל הַיָּם

Freiburg Hebrew Manuscript

HTV: **On that day - Yeshua left the house and sat by the seashore.**

KJV: The same day went Jesus out of the house, and sat by the sea side.

Matthew 13:2

וְנִקְבְּצוּ אֶצְלוֹ כִּתִּים רַבִּים עַד שֶׁנִּכְנַס בִּסְפִינָה וְיָשַׁב וְכֹל כַּת וְכַת יַעֲמוֹד בִּשְׂפַת הַיָם

HTV: **Many gathered near him to the point** *that* **Yeshua got into** *a* **ship and sat** *down*. **And all the crowd stood by the seashore.**

KJV: And great multitudes were gathered together unto him, so that he went into a ship, and sat; and the whole multitude stood on the shore.

Matthew 13:3

וַיְדַבֵּר לָהֶם רַבִּים בִּמְשָׁלִים לֵאמֹר הִנֵּה יָצָא הַזּוֹרֵעַ לִזְרוֹעַ

HTV: **Yeshua spoke many things to them in parables, saying, "Behold, the sower went out to sow."**

KJV: And he spake many things unto them in parables, saying, Behold, a sower went forth to sow;

Matthew 13:4

וּבְזָרְעוֹ הִנֵּה קְצָתָם נָפְלוּ אֵצֶל הַדֶּרֶךְ וּבָאוּ עוֹפוֹת הַשָּׁמַיִם וַאֲכָלוּם

HTV: **"And behold, some of his seed(s) fell by the road, and the birds of the air came and ate them."**

KJV: And when he sowed, some *seeds* fell by the way side, and the fowls came and devoured them up:

Matthew 13:5

וממנה נפלה באבן שאין שם עובי עפר ובצמחו נתייבש לפי שאין שם עפר לרוב.

Shem Tov Manuscript

וממנה נפלה באבן שאין שם עובי עפר ובצמחו נתייבש לפי שאין שם עפר לרוב.

HTV: **Some seeds fell among rocks where there was no depth of soil, and when they sprang up - they withered because there was not much soil there.**

KJV: Some fell upon stony places, where they had not much earth: and forthwith they sprung up, because they had no deepness of earth:

Matthew 13:6

וְאַחֲרֵי שֶׁהַשֶּׁמֶשׁ זָרַח הֵמָה נִשְׂרְפוּ וּמִפְּנֵי שֶׁלֹּא יִהְיֶה לָהֶם שׁוֹרֶשׁ יָבֵשׁוּ

HTV: **"After the sun rose, they were burned - because they had no root, they withered."**

KJV: And when the sun was up, they were scorched; and because they had no root, they withered away.

Matthew 13:7

וְאֵלֶּה נָפְלוּ בְקוֹצִים וְצָמְחוּ הַקּוֹצִים וְהֶחֱנִיקוּם

HTV: **"And *other seeds* fell among the thorns - and the thorns grew *up* and choked them."**

KJV: And some fell among thorns; and the thorns sprung up, and choked them:

Matthew 13:8

Freiburg Hebrew Manuscript

וְאֵלֶּה נָפְלוּ בְאָרֶץ טוֹבָה וְהוֹצִיאוּ פְּרִי הַזֶּה מֵאָה וְהַזֶּה שִׁשִּׁים וְהַזֶּה שְׁלֹשִׁים

HTV: **"These (seeds) fell in good earth and brought forth fruit - these a hundred(fold), and these sixty(fold), and these thirty(fold)."**

KJV: But other fell into good ground, and brought forth fruit, some an hundredfold, some sixtyfold, some thirtyfold.

Matthew 13:9

וַאֲשֶׁר לוֹ אָזְנַיִם לִשְׁמוֹעַ הַהוּא יִשְׁמַע

Chapter 13

HTV: **"Whosoever has ears to hear it, he will hear it."**

KJV: Who hath ears to hear, let him hear.

Matthew 13:10
וַיִּקְרְבוּ הַתַּלְמִידָיו וַיֹּאמְרוּ לוֹ לָמָה אַתָּה מְדַבֵּר לָהֶם בִּמְשָׁלִים

HTV: **And Yeshua's disciples came near and said to him, "Why do you speak to them in parables?"**

KJV: And the disciples came, and said unto him, Why speakest thou unto them in parables?

Matthew 13:11
וַיַּעַן לָהֶם וַיֹּאמַר כִּי לָכֶם נִתַּן לָדַעַת אֶת-סוֹדוֹת מַלְכוּת הַשָּׁמַיִם וְלָהֶם לֹא נִתַּן

HTV: **Therefore, Yeshua answered them and said, "It was given to you to know the secrets of the kingdom of heaven - but it was not given to them."**

KJV: He answered and said unto them, Because it is given unto you to know the mysteries of the kingdom of heaven, but to them it is not given.

Matthew 13:12

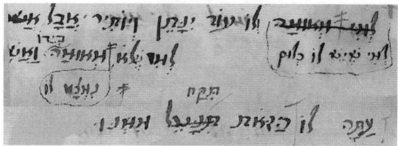

Freiburg Hebrew Manuscript

לְמִי שֶׁיֵּשׁ לוֹ כְּלוּם וְלוֹ עוֹד יִנָּתֵן וְיוֹתִיר - אֲבָל לְמִי שֶׁלֹּא נִמְצָא לוֹ מְאוּמָה בְּיָדוֹ וַאֲשֶׁר לוֹ עַתָּה הַזֹּאת תִּקַּח מִמֶּנּוּ

The Hebrew Book of Matthew

HTV: **"To whomever much has been given - let him give abundantly - and more will be given unto him. To whomever little has been given - and gives nothing - even that little, which he has, may be taken away.**

> Note: This is the theme of the parable of the talents (Mt 25:14-30), also see 2nd Cor 9:6-8 on giving abundantly. God has given blessings to all of us - what have we done to merit these blessings? Have we given, unto those in need, of our prosperity? Have we sown seeds of faith to others? To those who have given nothing of the little they have - they will receive nothing - in fact - the blessings God gave to them may even be taken away. Those who give of what they have will receive more blessings.

KJV: For whosoever hath, to him shall be given, and he shall have more abundance: but whosoever hath not, from him shall be taken away even that he hath.

Matthew 13:13

Freiburg Hebrew Manuscript

לְפִיכָךְ אֲנִי מְדַבֵּר לָהֶם בִּמְשָׁלִים כִּי הָרוֹאִים אֵינָם רוֹאִים וְהַשׁוֹמְעִים אֵינָם שׁוֹמְעִים וְאֵין מְבִינִים

HTV: **"Therefore, I speak to them in parables because - those seeing do not see - and the hearers do not hear - and do not understand"**

> Note: The value of parables is that they give concrete examples which make more sense than analytical discussion. Otherwise, many people hear, or see, but simply do not get it.

KJV: Therefore speak I to them in parables: because they seeing see not; and hearing they hear not, neither do they understand.

Matthew 13:14

Freiburg Hebrew Manuscript

Chapter 13

אֲשֶׁר בָּהֶם נִמְלְאָה הַנְּבוּאַת יְשַׁעְיָהוּ הָאוֹמֵר שָׁמוֹעַ תִּשְׁמְעוּ וְלֹא תָבִינוּ וְרָאוֹ תִרְאוּ וְאַל תֵּדָעוּ

HTV: "That the prophecy of Isaiah was fulfilled in them, saying, 'You will hear, but you will not understand; and you will see, but you will not know.'"

Note: See Isaiah 6:9 - He said, "Go and tell this people: '"Be ever hearing, but never understanding; be ever seeing, but never perceiving.'

KJV: And in them is fulfilled the prophecy of Esaias, which saith, By hearing ye shall hear, and shall not understand; and seeing ye shall see, and shall not perceive:

Matthew 13:15

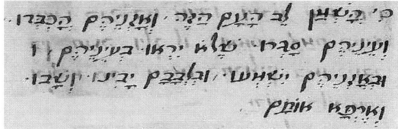

Freiburg Hebrew Manuscript

כִּי הַשְׁמֵן לֵב הָעָם הַזֶּה וְאָזְנֵיהֶם הַכְבֵּדוּ וְעֵינֵיהֶם סָגְרוּ שֶׁלֹּא יִרְאוּ בְעֵינֵיהֶם וּבְאָזְנֵיהֶם יִשְׁמָעוּ וּבִלְבָבָם יָבִינוּ וְשָׁבוּ וְאֶרְפָּא אוֹתָם

HTV: "Because the heart of this people has become fat, and their ears have become dulled, and their eyes closed - so that they will not see with their eyes and hear with their ears - *lest* in their heart they would understand and repent, and I would heal them."

Note: Clearly the people are resisting understanding what Yeshua is saying. They refuse to hear. They refuse to see. It reflects the often used phrase, or paraphrase, 'Those who have ears to hear (the truth), let them hear. Those who have eyes to see (the truth) let them see.'

KJV: For this people's heart is waxed gross, and *their* ears are dull of hearing, and their eyes they have closed; lest at any time they should see with *their* eyes, and hear with *their* ears, and should understand with *their* heart, and should be converted, and I should heal them.

The Hebrew Book of Matthew

Matthew 13:16

אַשְׁרֵי הָעֵינַיכֶם כִּי רוֹאִים וַאֲזְנֵיכֶם כִּי שׁוֹמְעִים

HTV: "Blessed are your eyes, because they see (*the truth*), and your ears because they hear (*the truth*)!"

KJV: But blessed *are* your eyes, for they see: and your ears, for they hear.

Matthew 13:17

בֶּאֱמֶת אֲנִי אוֹמֵר לָכֶם שֶׁרַבִּים נְבִיאִים וְצַדִּיקִים חָמְדוּ לִרְאוֹת אֲשֶׁר אַתֶּם רוֹאִים וְלֹא רָאוּ וְלִשְׁמוֹעַ אֲשֶׁר אַתֶּם שׁוֹמְעִים וְלֹא שָׁמָעוּ

HTV: "Truly I say to you that many prophets and righteous ones desired to see what you see and they did not see, and to hear what you hear and they did not hear."

KJV: For verily I say unto you, That many prophets and righteous *men* have desired to see *those things* which ye see, and have not seen *them*; and to hear *those things* which ye hear, and have not heard *them*.

Matthew 13:18

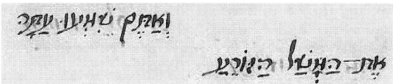

Freiburg Hebrew Manuscript

וְאַתֶּם שִׁמְעוּ עַתָּה אֶת-הַמָּשָׁל הַזּוֹרֵעַ

HTV: "And now you have heard the parable of the sower."

Note: This is a significant difference between the Hebrew and the Greek. The hearing of the parable of the sower has already taken place. What follows here is the interpretation.

KJV: Hear ye therefore the parable of the sower.

Matthew 13:19

הזורע הוא בן אדם והזרע שנפל בדרך כל השומע מלכות שמים ולא יבין. יבא השטן ויחתוף מלבו כל מה שנזרע בו. וזהו הזרע שנפל על הדרך.

Shem Tov Manuscript

הזורע הוא בן אדם והזרע שנפל בדרך כל השומע מלכות שמים ולא יבין. וזהו הזרע שנפל על הדרך.

HTV: "The Sower is the Son of Man. Everyone who hears the word of the kingdom (the word of God) and does not understand - Behold! Satan comes and uproots what was sown in his heart - this is that (seed) which was sown by the wayside."

> Note: This refers to those who encounter the Word in a somewhat casual manner - "by the wayside" so to speak. Whatever they have gotten from it is easily uprooted by Satan for it is not deeply held.

KJV: When any one heareth the word of the kingdom, and understandeth *it* not, then cometh the wicked *one*, and catcheth away that which was sown in his heart. This is he which received seed by the way side.

Matthew 13:20

וַאֲשֶׁר נִזְרַע בְּמָקוֹם בַּעַל אֲבָנִים הוּא אֲשֶׁר שׁוֹמֵעַ אֶת-הַדָּבָר וּמִיָּד יְקַבְּלוּ בְשִׂמְחָה

HTV: "He who sows in rocky places - is he who hears the Word of the Master - and immediately receives it with joy!"

KJV: But he that received the seed into stony places, the same is he that heareth the word, and anon with joy receiveth it;

Matthew 13:21

אָמְנָם לֹא בוֹ שׁוֹרֶשׁ אֲשֶׁר הוּא לְבַד זְמַנִּי וְאִם תִּתְחַדֵּשׁ צָרָה וּרְדִיפָה מִפְּנֵי הַדָּבָר הוּא מִיָּד יִפּוֹל בְּמוֹקֵשׁ

HTV: "Indeed, he has no root in him - except for a quickly passing renewal. When troubles and persecution take away the Word - he immediately stumbles into a snare."

The Hebrew Book of Matthew

KJV: Yet hath he not root in himself, but dureth for a while: for when tribulation or persecution ariseth because of the word, by and by he is offended.

Matthew 13:22

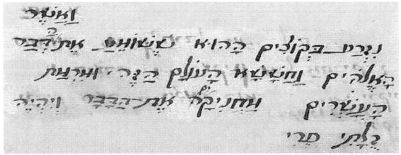

Freiburg Hebrew Manuscript

וַאֲשֶׁר נִזְרַע בְּקוֹצִים הָהוּא שֶׁשּׁוֹמֵעַ אֶת-הַדָּבָר הָאֱלֹהִים וַחֲשָׁשָׁא הָעוֹלָם הַזֶּה וּמִרְמַת הָעֲשָׁרִים מַחֲנִיקִים אֶת-הַדָּבָר וְיִהְיֶה זָלָתִי פְּרִי

HTV: "That seed which was sown *among* thorns and thistles - is the one who hears the Word of Yehovah but *is* preoccupied with this world and its deceitful riches - then will the Word of God be choked and strangled out - producing no fruit."

KJV: He also that received seed among the thorns is he that heareth the word; and the care of this world, and the deceitfulness of riches, choke the word, and he becometh unfruitful.

Matthew 13:23

וַאֲשֶׁר נִזְרַע בָּאֶרֶץ הַטּוֹבָה יֵשׁ הַזֶּה אֲשֶׁר שׁוֹמֵעַ אֶת-הַדָּבָר וּמֵבִין אוֹתוֹ וּמוֹצִיא פְּרִי אֲשֶׁר מֵהֶם הַזֶּה עוֹשֶׂה מֵאָה וְהַזֶּה שִׁישִׁים וְהַזֶּה שְׁלֹשִׁים

HTV: "Whosoever sows in good ground is the one who hears the Word, and understands it, and brings forth fruit - some of them one hundred times, some sixty *times*, and some thirty *times what was sown*!"

KJV: But he that received seed into the good ground is he that heareth the word, and understandeth *it*; which also beareth fruit, and bringeth forth, some an hundredfold, some sixty, some thirty.

Chapter 13

Matthew 13:24

וְאַחֲרֵי כֵן הוֹצִיא לָהֶם מָשָׁל אַחֵר לֵאמֹר הַמַּלְכוּת הַשָּׁמַיִם הִיא נִתְדָּמָה לְאָדָם אֲשֶׁר זָרַע זֶרַע טוֹב בְּשָׂדֵהוּ

HTV: **Afterward, he put forth to them another trustworthy parable saying, "The kingdom of heaven is like a man who sows good seed in his field."**

KJV: Another parable put he forth unto them, saying, The kingdom of heaven is likened unto a man which sowed good seed in his field:

Matthew 13:25

שֶׁאֲנוֹשִׁים יָשְׁנוּ הִנֵּה בָא הָאוֹיְבוֹ וַיִּזְרַע חָרוּל בֵּין הַחִטָּה וַיֵּלֶךְ לוֹ

HTV: **"While the man slept in this place - the enemy came and sowed thorns and thistles among the wheat - then went his way."**

KJV: But while men slept, his enemy came and sowed tares among the wheat, and went his way.

Matthew 13:26

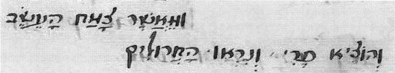
Freiburg Hebrew Manuscript

וּמֵאֲשֶׁר צָמַח הָעֵשֶׂב וְהוֹצִיא פְּרִי וְנִרְאוּ הַחֲרוּלִים

HTV: **"When the grain grew and brought forth fruit - *then too* the thorns and thistles appeared."**

KJV: But when the blade was sprung up, and brought forth fruit, then appeared the tares also.

Matthew 13:27

בָּאוּ עַבְדֵי הַבַּעַל בַּיִת וַיֹּאמְרִים לוֹ אֲדוֹנִי הֲלֹא אַתָּה זֶרַע טוֹב זָרַעְתָּ בְּשָׂדֶה שֶׁלְּךָ מֵאַיִן נָא הַחֲרוּלִים לוֹ

217

The Hebrew Book of Matthew

HTV: **"The servants of the master came to the house and asked him, 'Lord, did you not sow good seed in your field? So where did the thorns and thistles come from?'"**

KJV: So the servants of the householder came and said unto him, Sir, didst not thou sow good seed in thy field? from whence then hath it tares?

Matthew 13:28

וַיֹּאמֶר לָהֶם הָאָדָם הָאוֹיֵב עָשָׂה הַזֹּאת וַעֲבָדִים אָמְרוּ לוֹ אִם תִּרְצֶה אֲנַחְנוּ נֵלֵךְ וְנִלְקְטֵם

HTV: **"He said to them, 'The enemy did this!' His servants said to him, 'If you want, we will go and uproot them.'"**

KJV: He said unto them, An enemy hath done this. The servants said unto him, Wilt thou then that we go and gather them up?

Matthew 13:29

וַיֹּאמֶר לֹא פֶּן בְּלַקְטְכֶם אֶת-חֲרוּלִים תִּתְלֹשׁוּ יַחַד אִתָּם גַּם אֶת-הַחִטָּה

HTV: **"He said, 'No - so as not to tear the wheat out along with the thorns and thistles.'"**

KJV: But he said, Nay; lest while ye gather up the tares, ye root up also the wheat with them.

Matthew 13:30

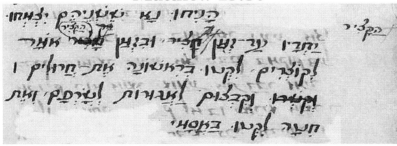

Freiburg Hebrew Manuscript

הַנִּיחוּ נָא שְׁשְׁנֵיהֶם יִצְמְחוּ יַחְדָּיו עַד זְמַן הַקָּצִיר וּבִזְמַן הַקָּצִיר אָמַר לַקּוֹצְרִים לִקְטוּ בָּרִאשׁוֹנָה אֶת-חֲרוּלִים וְקִבְּצוּם לַאֲגוּרוֹת לְשָׂרְפָם וְאֶת חִטָּה לִקְטוּ בַּאֲסָמִי

Chapter 13

HTV: **"Leave both alone to grow for now - until the time of the harvest. When harvest time comes, I will tell the reapers - first gather the thorns and thistles into bundles - then burn them - but gather the wheat into my granary."**

> Note: In the natural realm, the evil will grow up with the good - but at the judgement - the evil will be cast into the lake of fire. Then the righteous will be taken into heaven.

KJV: Let both grow together until the harvest: and in the time of harvest I will say to the reapers, Gather ye together first the tares, and bind them in bundles to burn them: but gather the wheat into my barn.

Matthew 13:31

וְעוֹד הוֹצִיא מָשָׁל אַחֵר לִפְנֵיהֶם לֵאמֹר מַלְכוּת הַשָּׁמַיִם הִיא נִתְדָמָה
לְגַרְעִין הַחַרְדָל אֲשֶׁר לָקַח הָאָדָם וַיִּזְרַע בְּשָׂדֵה שֶׁלוֹ

HTV: **Yeshua presented another parable before them, saying, "The kingdom of heaven is like the mustard seed which the man took and sowed in his field."**

KJV: Another parable put he forth unto them, saying, The kingdom of heaven is like to a grain of mustard seed, which a man took, and sowed in his field:

Matthew 13:32

שֶׁקָטָן מִכֹּל אֲחֵרִים זְרָעִים אֲשֶׁר מִשֶּׁיִצְמַח הוּא-גָדוֹל מִכֹּל יְרָקִים
וְיִהְיֶה אִילָן כֹּל כָּךְ גָדוֹל שֶׁיָבוֹאוּ עוֹפוֹת הַשָּׁמַיִם נִיקוֹנְנוּ בַעֲנָפָיו

HTV: **"It is smaller than all the other seeds - but then it will grow bigger than all the bushes - and will be a tree - so big that the birds of the sky will come and nest in its branches."**

KJV: Which indeed is the least of all seeds: but when it is grown, it is the greatest among herbs, and becometh a tree, so that the birds of the air come and lodge in the branches thereof.

Matthew 13:33

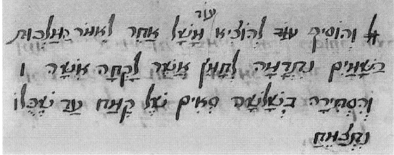

Freiburg Hebrew Manuscript

וְהוֹסִיף לְהוֹצִיא עוֹד מָשָׁל אַחֵר לֵאמֹר הַמַלְכוּת הַשָׁמַיִם נִתְדָּמָה לְחָמֵץ אֲשֶׁר לָקְחָה אִשָׁה וְהִסְתִּירָה בִּשְׁלֹשָׁה סְאִים שֶׁל קֶמַח עַד שֶׁכָּלוּ נִתְצַמֵחַ

HTV: Yeshua brought forth yet another parable - saying, "The kingdom of heaven *is* leaven which a woman took and concealed in three measures of flour until it all grew *throughout*."

Note: This parable is a clear metaphor used often by Yeshua. Leaven, whether of a good or evil nature, can take over the entire person. In this case the leaven is not of sin but it is the "kingdom of heaven" which being concealed in the heart of man, or woman, will transform them entirely.

KJV: Another parable spake he unto them; The kingdom of heaven is like unto leaven, which a woman took, and hid in three measures of meal, till the whole was leavened.

Matthew 13:34

כֹּל אֵלֶּה דְבָרִים דִבֶּר יֵשׁוּעַ לִכְתִּיִים בִּמְשָׁלִים וְזָלָתִי מְשָׁלִים לֹא דִבֶּר לָהֶם כְּלוּם

HTV: Yeshua spoke all these matters to the crowds in parables, and he spoke nothing other than parables to them.

KJV: All these things spake Jesus unto the multitude in parables; and without a parable spake he not unto them:

Matthew 13:35

שֶׁיִּמָלֵא מַה שֶׁנֶּאֱמַר עַל פִּי הַנָּבִיא הָאוֹמֵר אֶפְתְחָה בִּמְשָׁלִים פִּי אַבִּיעָה חִידוֹת מִנִּי קֶדֶם

HTV: **In order to fulfill what was said according to the prophet who says, "I will open my mouth in parables and I will pour out *the* secrets of eternity."**

> Note: See Psalm 78:2, "I will open with a parable. I will utter hidden things, things from of old."

KJV: That it might be fulfilled which was spoken by the prophet, saying, I will open my mouth in parables; I will utter things which have been kept secret from the foundation of the world.

Matthew 13:36

וְאַחֲרֵי שֶׁשָּׁלַח מִמֶּנּוּ אֶת-הַכִּתִּים וַיִּקְרְבוּ אֵצְלוֹ הַתַּלְמִידָיו וַיֹּאמְרוּ פָּרֶשׁ לָנוּ אֶת-מְשַׁל חָרוּלֵי הַשָּׂדֶה

HTV: **After Yeshua sent the crowds away from him - his disciples drew near him. They said, "Explain to us the parable of the thorns and thistles in the field."**

KJV: Then Jesus sent the multitude away, and went into the house: and his disciples came unto him, saying, Declare unto us the parable of the tares of the field.

Matthew 13:37

אֲשֶׁר עָנָה וְאָמַר הַזּוֹרֵעַ אֶת-זֶרַע הַטּוֹב הוּא הַבֶּן הָאָדָם

HTV: ***To* which Yeshua responded - and said, "The sower of the good seed - he is the Son of Man."**

KJV: He answered and said unto them, He that soweth the good seed is the Son of man;

Matthew 13:38

הַשָּׂדֶה הוּא הָעוֹלָם וְזֶרַע הַטּוֹב הֵם בְּנֵי הַמַּלְכוּת וַחֲרוּלִים הֵם בְּנֵי הָרָע

HTV: **"The field - it *is* the world - and the good seed - they *are* the righteous children of the kingdom (*of heaven*) - but the thorns are the *wicked* children of *the* evil *one*."**

KJV: The field is the world; the good seed are the children of the kingdom; but the tares are the children of the wicked *one*;

Matthew 13:39

וְהָאוֹיֵב אֲשֶׁר זְרָעָם הוּא הַשָּׂטָן וְהַקָּצִיר הוּא תַכְלִית הָעוֹלָם וְהַקּוֹצְרִים הֵם הַמַּלְאָכִים

HTV: "The enemy who sowed them - he is Satan - and the harvest - it *is* the end of the world - and the reapers - they are the angels."

KJV: The enemy that sowed them is the devil; the harvest is the end of the world; and the reapers are the angels.

Matthew 13:40

וּכְמוֹ הַחֲרוּלִים נִקְבָּצִים וְנִשְׂרָפִים וְכֵן בְּתַכְלִית הָעוֹלָם

HTV: "Just as the thorns and thistles *are* gathered and burnt - so shall it be at the end of the world."

KJV: As therefore the tares are gathered and burned in the fire; so shall it be in the end of this world.

Matthew 13:41

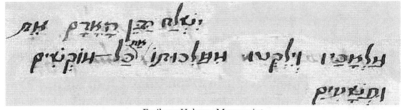

Freiburg Hebrew Manuscript

יִשְׁלַח הַבֵּן הָאָדָם אֶת מַלְאָכָיו וְיִלְקְטוּ מִמַּלְכוּתוֹ אֶת כָּל מוֹקְשִׁים וּפֹשְׁעִים

HTV: "The Son of Man will send his angels - and they will uproot from his kingdom - all *those who* are causing transgression (sin) - and those who are transgressors."

Note: Transgression of the Torah is sin. In this case, there are those who are directing (causing) sin and those who are carrying it out. (1st John 3:2) "Sin is transgression of Torah (lawlessnes)."

KJV: The Son of man shall send forth his angels, and they shall gather out of his kingdom all things that offend, and them which do iniquity;

Matthew 13:42

וְיִשְׁלְחוּם בְּתַנּוּר הָאֵשׁ שָׁם יִהְיֶה בְכִי וְחָרוּק הַשִּׁנָּיִם

HTV: "They will be sent to the fiery furnace of hell (Gei-Hinnom); *and* there will be wailing and gnashing of teeth."

KJV: And shall cast them into a furnace of fire: there shall be wailing and gnashing of teeth.

Matthew 13:43

וְאָז יִצְהֲרוּ הַצַּדִּיקִים בְּמַלְכוּת הָאָבִי כְּמוֹ הַשֶּׁמֶשׁ אֲשֶׁר לוֹ אָזְנַיִם לִשְׁמוֹעַ הָהוּא יִשְׁמַע

HTV: "Then the righteous will shine like the sun in the kingdom of my Father - Whoever has ears to hear, let them hear."

KJV: Then shall the righteous shine forth as the sun in the kingdom of their Father. Who hath ears to hear, let him hear.

Matthew 13:44

Freiburg Hebrew Manuscript

הִנֵּה הַמַּלְכוּת הַשָּׁמַיִם הִיא נִמְשֶׁלֶת לָאוֹצָר הַנִּסְתָּר בְּשָׂדֶה אֲשֶׁר אִם יִמְצָאֵהוּ אָדָם הוּא מַסְתִּירוֹ וְהוֹלֵךְ בְּשִׂמְחָה בַּעֲבוּרוֹ וּמוֹכֵר כֹּל שֶׁלּוֹ וְקוֹנֶה אֶת אוֹתוֹ הַשָּׂדֶה

HTV: "Behold, the kingdom of heaven is like a man who finds a treasure hidden in the field - which if a man finds it - he goes with joy and sells everything *he owns* and buys that field."

KJV: Again, the kingdom of heaven is like unto treasure hid in a field; the which when a man hath found, he hideth, and for joy thereof goeth and selleth all that he hath, and buyeth that field.

The Hebrew Book of Matthew

Matthew 13:45

וְעוֹד נִמְשָׁלָה הַמַּלְכוּת הַשָּׁמַיִם לְאָדָם הַסּוֹחֵר אֲשֶׁר דּוֹרֵשׁ פְּנִינִים טוֹבִים

HTV: "In addition - the kingdom of heaven is compared to a merchant who is seeking priceless pearls."

KJV: Again, the kingdom of heaven is like unto a merchant man, seeking goodly pearls:

Matthew 13:46

וּמִשֶּׁמָּצָא אֶחָד פָּנִין יָקָר הוּא הָלַךְ וַיִּמְכֹּר כֹּל מִקְנֶה שֶׁלּוֹ וַיִּקְנֵהוּ

HTV: "When he found one pearl of great price - he went and sold all of his possession*s* and he bought it."

KJV: Who, when he had found one pearl of great price, went and sold all that he had, and bought it.

Matthew 13:47

Freiburg Hebrew Manuscript

וְעוֹד נִמְשָׁלָה הַמַּלְכוּת הַשָּׁמַיִם לָרֶשֶׁת הַמּוּשְׁלָכָה בַיָּם הַקּוֹבֶצֶת מִכֹּל מִינֵי הַדָּגִים

HTV: "Yet again, the kingdom of heaven is compared to a net cast into the sea - *which* gathers all kinds of fish."

KJV: Again, the kingdom of heaven is like unto a net, that was cast into the sea, and gathered of every kind:

Matthew 13:48

וַאֲשֶׁר מִשֶּׁנִּמְלְאָה הוֹצִיאוּהוּ וְיָשְׁבוּ בִּשְׂפַת הַיָּם וְלָקְטוּ אֶת-הַטּוֹבִים בִּכְלֵיהֶם וְהָרָעִים הִשְׁלִיכוּ חוּצָה

HTV: **"When it was full, they took it out and sat down at the sea shore. They gathered the good ones into their vessels - and threw out the bad ones."**

KJV: Which, when it was full, they drew to shore, and sat down, and gathered the good into vessels, but cast the bad away.

Matthew 13:49

Freiburg Hebrew Manuscript

וּכְמוֹ כֵן יִהְיֶה בְּתַכְלִית הָעוֹלָם אָז יֵצְאוּ הַמַּלְאָכִים וְיַפְרִישׁוּ אֶת־הָרָעִים מִתּוֹךְ הַצַּדִּיקִים

HTV: **"So shall it be at the end of the age - at that time the angels will come forth and will separate the wicked from the righteous."**

KJV: So shall it be at the end of the world: the angels shall come forth, and sever the wicked from among the just,

Matthew 13:50

וְיִשְׁלְחוּם בַּתַּנּוּר הָאֵשׁ שָׁם יִהְיֶה בְּכִי וְחֲרוּק שִׁנַיִם

HTV: **"They (the angels) will cast them (the wicked) into the furnace of fire - there will be wailing and gnashing of teeth."**

KJV: And shall cast them into the furnace of fire: there shall be wailing and gnashing of teeth.

Matthew 13:51

וַיֹּאמֶר לָהֶם יֵשׁוּעַ הַאִם הֲבַנְתֶּם אֶת כָּל אֵלֶּה דְּבָרִים וַיֹּאמְרוּ לוֹ הֵן אֲדוֹנִי

HTV: **Yeshua said to them, "Have you understood all these things?" They said to him, "Yes Lord."**

KJV: Jesus saith unto them, Have ye understood all these things? They say unto him, Yea, Lord.

Matthew 13:52

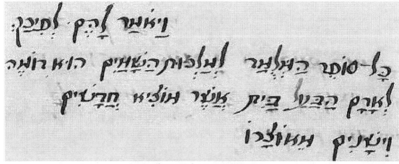

Freiburg Hebrew Manuscript

וַיֹּאמֶר לָהֶם לְפִיכָךְ כָּל סוֹפֵר הַמְלֻמַּד לְמַלְכוּת הַשָּׁמַיִם הוּא דוֹמֶה לְאָדָם הַבַּעַל בַּיִת אֲשֶׁר מוֹצִיא חֲדָשִׁים וִישָׁנִים מֵאוֹצָרוֹ

HTV: **Then Yeshua said to them, "Therefore every scribe who teaches of the kingdom of heaven is like the master of a house - a father who brings out of his treasure -** *things both* **new and old."**

> Note: The scribe is in the role of the Father bringing forth from His treasure - the Word of God - things known from antiquity as well as fresh revelation. In this case, the Old Testament and the New.

KJV: Then said he unto them, Therefore every scribe *which is* instructed unto the kingdom of heaven is like unto a man *that is* an householder, which bringeth forth out of his treasure *things* new and old.

Matthew 13:53

וַיְהִי אַחֲרֵי שֶׁכָּלָה יֵשׁוּעַ אֶת-מְשָׁלִים הָאֵלֶּה הוּא עָבַר מִכַּאן

HTV: **It came to pass, after Yeshua finished these (***parables***) he passed on from there.**

KJV: And it came to pass, *that* when Jesus had finished these parables, he departed thence.

Chapter 13

Matthew 13:54

וַיָּבוֹא בָאָרֶץ מוֹלַדְתּוֹ וַיְלַמְּדֵם בַּכְּנֵסִיּוֹתֵיהֶם וְזֹאת בְּדֶרֶךְ הַזֶּה שֶׁכֻּלָּם יִתְמְהוּ וַיֹּאמְרוּ מֵאַיִן לָזֶה הַחָכְמָה הַזֹּאת וּגְבוּרוֹת

HTV: Yeshua came unto his home country (Galilee) - he taught them in their synagogues - in such a way that they were astonished, and *they* said, "From where is this wisdom and *these* mighty works (*coming*)."

KJV: And when he was come into his own country, he taught them in their synagogue, insomuch that they were astonished, and said, Whence hath this *man* this wisdom, and *these* mighty works?

Matthew 13:55

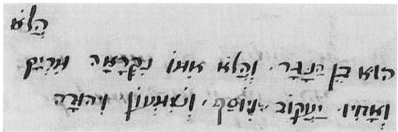

Freiburg Hebrew Manuscript

הֲלֹא הוּא בֶן הַנַּגָּר וַהֲלֹא אִמּוֹ נִקְרָאָה מִרְיָם וְאֶחָיו יַעֲקוֹב וְיוֹסֵף וְשִׁמְעוֹן וִיהוּדָה

HTV: "Isn't he the son of the smith [Napach], and isn't his mother's name Myriam, and his brothers Jacob and Yosef and Simeon and Jude (or Yehuda)?"

Note: The Hebrew Gospels (STM & HGC) have Yeshua's profession as NaPaCH, smith. The Greek Gospels have his profession as Technon, builder. The work of a builder involves all the building trades, carpentry, stone mason, and smith - you make your own nails and hinges, etc.

KJV: Is not this the carpenter's son? is not his mother called Mary? and his brethren, James, and Joses, and Simon, and Judas?

Matthew 13:56

וְאֲחָיוֹתָיו הֲלֹא כֻלָּם אֶצְלֵנוּ מֵאַיִן נָא לוֹ כֹּל אֵלֶּה דְּבָרִים

227

HTV: **"And his sisters, are they not all with us? Where did he get all these words *of wisdom*?"**

KJV: And his sisters, are they not all with us? Whence then hath this *man* all these things?

Matthew 13:57

וַיִּוָּקְשׁוּ בּוֹ וְיֵשׁוּעַ אָמַר לָהֶם אֵין נִמְצָא הַנָּבִיא בְּלִי הָדָר כִּי אִם בָּאָרֶץ מוֹלַדְתּוֹ וּבְבֵיתוֹ

HTV: **And they were struggling *to believe* in him. And Yeshua said to them, "There is no prophet found without honor - except in his native land and in his home town."**

KJV: And they were offended in him. But Jesus said unto them, A prophet is not without honour, save in his own country, and in his own house.

Matthew 13:58

וְלֹא עָשָׂה שָׁם רַבּוֹת גְּבוּרוֹת מִפְּנֵי שֶׁלֹּא הֶאֱמִינוּ בוֹ

HTV: **And there he did not do many great wonders before them - because they did not believe in him.**

KJV: And he did not many mighty works there because of their unbelief.

Matthew Chapter 14

Hebrew Text Version (HTV)

1 At that time, Herod the Tetrarch heard from one of *his* four agents that he had heard of Yeshua.

2 He said to his servants, "This is John the *Baptizer* - he has risen from the dead! For this reason *his* mighty acts *are* increased."

3 For Herod had arrested John and bound him - then he sent him to prison. The cause - Herod *had taken* Herodias, his brother's wife.

4 And John had said to *Herod*, "It is not lawful for you to have her."

5 Because of this, Herod wanted to kill him - but he feared the people, because - in their eyes - John was accounted a prophet.

6 On Herod's birthday, the daughter of Herodias (*Salome*) danced seductively center *stage* - which was pleasing in the sight of Herod!

7 Herod promised (*made an oath*) to give her whatever she asked of him.

8 However, she was instructed by her mother to say to him, "Give me the head of John the Baptist - in a bowl."

9 The king was grieved in his soul - but for the sake of the oath - *made before* those who sat with him dining - Herod ordered the head of Yohanan be given to her.

10 And Herod sent *people* to behead John in the prison.

11 And John's head was brought in a bowl - and it was given to the girl (Salome) - and she brought it to her mother (Herodias).

12 And John's disciples drew near and took hold of his body and buried it. *Then* they went and told Yeshua.

13 When Yeshua heard it - he *left* in *a* boat to the wilderness - And when the people heard - they *were drawn out* of the cities and *followed* after him on foot.

14 Yeshua went out and saw the large crowd - and he pitied them and healed their sick.

15 After the sun had set, Yeshua's disciples approached him, saying, "Behold, the hour is late - send the people to the town to buy food.

16 Yeshua said to *his disciples* - "there is no need for them to leave here. Give them *food* to eat."

17 And *his disciples* answered Yeshua - "They *can* not stay because we have only five loaves of bread and two fish."

18 To which Yeshua said, "Bring them here to me."

19 Yeshua ordered the people to sit upon the grass. He took the five loaves of bread and two fish and turned his eyes to heaven - he blessed it, and broke the bread, and gave it to his disciples - and his disciples gave it to the people.

20 All of them ate until they were completely satisfied - leaving remains of twelve baskets full of bread.

21 The number of people who had eaten was five thousand, including the women and children.

22 He sent away the crowds, then ascended the mountain by himself to pray. Afterward, it was evening - then he was there alone.

24 The ship was in the midst of the sea - tossed here and there by the waves - and the wind was against *them*!

25 In the fourth watch of the night - Yeshua came to them walking on the surface of the sea.

26 When they saw him - they were shocked - and said, "This is a great delusion!" And they cried out with fear and trembling!

27 Right away, Yeshua spoke saying, "Have faith! It is I, do not be afraid."

28 Peter (Kayfa) answered, and he said, "Lord, command that I come to you on the surface of the water."

29 And Yeshua said, "Come!" Peter got out of the ship and walked on the surface of the water to come toward Yeshua.

30 When he (Peter) saw the powerful wind - he was afraid and started to sink. He cried out saying, "Lord save me!"

31 Promptly, Yeshua stretched forth his hand and grasped him strongly, and said unto him, "Man of little faith - why did you doubt?"

32 And when Yeshua went up into the boat - the wind stopped blowing!

33 Those who were in the boat - bowed down and worshipped

him - and said, "Truly, you are the Son of God!"

34 And after they had crossed the sea (of Galilee) - they came into the land of Gennesaret.

35 When the men of that place recognized him - they sent around about to all the nearby places - and they brought him all their sick.

36 And they asked of him (Yeshua) that they *might* touch only the hem of his garments - and all *who* touched him were healed!

Matthew Chapter 14
HTV with translator notes and KJV comparison

Matthew 14:1

בְּאוֹתוֹ זְמָן שָׁמַע הֵרוֹדוּס שֶׁאֶחָד מֵאַרְבָּעָה הַקְצִינִים אֶת-שֶׁמַע יֵשׁוּעַ

HTV: At that time, Herod the Tetrarch heard from one of *his* four agents that he had heard of Yeshua.

Note: The Herods were famous for their vast secret police organization. They could rally a mob anytime they wished such as at the trial of Yeshua before Pontius Pilot. Also secret police agents were sent incognito into the Temple attempting to get Zachariah to give up Yohanan's location so Herod could have him killed. Zachariah refused and Herod's agents finally killed him. (in the *Gospel of James* chapters 22-24, also called the *Proto-Evangelion of James*).

KJV: At that time Herod the tetrarch heard of the fame of Jesus,

Matthew 14:2

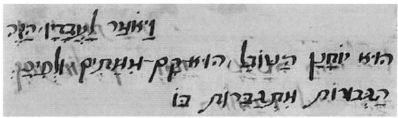

Freiburg Hebrew Manuscript

וַיֹּאמֶר לַעֲבָדָיו הִנֵּה הוּא יוֹחָנָן הַטּוֹבֵל הוּא קָם מִמֵּתִים וּלְפִיכָךְ הַגְּבוּרוֹת מִתְגַּבְּרוֹת בּוֹ

HTV: He said to his servants, "This is John the *Baptizer* - he has risen from the dead! For this reason *his* mighty acts *are* increased."

Note: John had already been killed by Herod. The following verses tell the story as a flashback. At this time, Herod Antipas was rapidly sliding into insanity. He was very paranoid and superstitious. Herod felt haunted by John.

KJV: And said unto his servants, This is John the Baptist; he is risen from the dead; and therefore mighty works do shew forth themselves in him.

Matthew 14:3

כִּי הֵרוֹדֵס הֶחֱזִיק אֶת-יוֹחָנָן וְהִקְשִׁירוּהוּ וַיִּשְׁלַח אוֹתוֹ בְּבֵית אֲסִירִים מִפְּנֵי הֵרוֹדְאַדִיס הָאִשֶׁת אָחִיו

HTV: For Herod had arrested John and bound him - then he sent him to prison. The cause - Herod *had taken* Herodias, his brother's wife.

KJV: For Herod had laid hold on John, and bound him, and put *him* in prison for Herodias' sake, his brother Philip's wife.

Matthew 14:4

כִּי יוֹחָנָן אָמַר לוֹ אַל רָאוּי לְךָ שֶׁתִּבְעַל אוֹתָהּ

HTV: And John had said to *Herod*, "It is not lawful for you to have her."

KJV: For John said unto him, It is not lawful for thee to have her.

Matthew 14:5

וְשָׁם בְּנַפְשׁוֹ לַהֲמִיתוֹ אֲבָל יִהְיֶה יָרֵא אֶת-הָעָם כִּי נֶחֱשָׁב בְּעֵינֵיהֶם כְּהַנָּבִיא

HTV: Because of this, Herod wanted to kill him - but he feared the people, because - in their eyes - John was accounted a prophet.

Chapter 14

KJV: And when he would have put him to death, he feared the multitude, because they counted him as a prophet.

Matthew 14:6

Freiburg Hebrew Manuscript

אָמְנָם בְּיוֹם הַלֵּידַת הֵרוֹדֵס תִּהְיֶה בַת הֵרוֹדְאַדֵס מְרַקֶּדֶת בָּאֶמְצַע אֲשֶׁר יִהְיֶה לְרָצוֹן בְּעֵינֵי הֵרוֹדֵס

HTV: On Herod's birthday, the daughter of Herodias (*Salome*) danced seductively center *stage* - which was pleasing in the sight of Herod!

KJV: But when Herod's birthday was kept, the daughter of Herodias danced before them, and pleased Herod.

Matthew 14:7

וְהִבְטִיחָה לָתֵת לָהּ־כָּל־מָה שֶׁתִּשְׁאַל מִמֶּנּוּ

HTV: Herod promised (*made an oath*) to give her whatever she asked of him.

KJV: Whereupon he promised with an oath to give her whatsoever she would ask.

Matthew 14:8

אַךְ הִיא הוּזְהֲרָה מֵאִמָּהּ לֵאמֹר לוֹ תֵּן לִי בִּקְעָרָה הַזֹּאת אֶת־רֹאשׁ יוֹחָנָן הַטּוֹבֵל

HTV: However, she was instructed by her mother to say to him, "Give me the head of John the Baptist - in a bowl."

KJV: And she, being before instructed of her mother, said, Give me here John Baptist's head in a charger.

233

The Hebrew Book of Matthew

Matthew 14:9

וְנִתְדָּאֵג הַמֶּלֶךְ בְּנַפְשׁוֹ בַּעֲבוּר הַשְּׁבוּעָה וְאַף אֲשֶׁר יִהְיוּ יוֹשְׁבִים אִתּוֹ בְּשֻׁלְחָן וַיְצַוֶּה לְהִנָּתֵן לָהּ

HTV: **The king was grieved in his soul - but for the sake of the oath -** *made before* **those who sat with him dining - Herod ordered the head of Yohanan be given to her.**

KJV: And the king was sorry: nevertheless for the oath's sake, and them which sat with him at meat, he commanded *it* to be given her.

Matthew 14:10

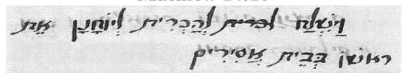
Freiburg Hebrew Manuscript

וַיִּשְׁלַח לְהַכְרִית לְיוֹחָנָן אֶת רֹאשׁוֹ בְּבֵית אֲסִירִים

HTV: **And Herod sent** *people* **to behead John in the prison.**

KJV: And he sent, and beheaded John in the prison.

Matthew 14:11

וְהוּבָא הָרֹאשׁוֹ בִּקְעָרָה וְנָתַן לְנַעֲרָה וְהִיא הֱבִיאָה אוֹתוֹ לְאִמָּהּ

HTV: **And John's head was brought in a bowl - and it was given to the girl (Salome) - and she brought it to her mother (Herodias).**

KJV: And his head was brought in a charger, and given to the damsel: and she brought *it* to her mother.

Matthew 14:12

וַיִּקְרְבוּ הַתַּלְמִידָיו וְנָטְלוּ אֶת גּוּפוֹ וַיִּקְבְּרוּהוּ וּבָאוּ וְהִגִּידוּ לְיֵשׁוּעַ

HTV: **And John's disciples drew near and took hold of his body and buried it.** *Then* **they went and told Yeshua.**

KJV: And his disciples came, and took up the body, and buried it, and went and told Jesus.

Matthew 14:13

וּמִשֶּׁשָׁמַע יֵשׁוּעַ הוּא סָר מִכַּאן בִּסְפִינָה לְמָקוֹם מַדְבָּרִי וְכַאֲשֶׁר הַכִּתִּים שָׁמְעוּ נִמְשְׁכוּ אַחֲרָיו רְגְלִיִים מֵעָרִים

HTV: **When Yeshua heard it - he *left* in *a* boat to the wilderness - And when the people heard - they *were drawn out* of the cities and *followed* after him on foot.**

KJV: When Jesus heard *of it*, he departed thence by ship into a desert place apart: and when the people had heard *thereof*, they followed him on foot out of the cities.

Matthew 14:14

וַיֵּצֵא וַיַּרְא אֶת־כַּת־הַגָּדוֹל וַיִּתְחַנֵּן עֲלֵיהֶם וַיְרַפֵּא אֶת־חוֹלֵיהֶם

HTV: **Yeshua went out and saw the large crowd - and he pitied them and healed their sick.**

KJV: And Jesus went forth, and saw a great multitude, and was moved with compassion toward them, and he healed their sick.

Matthew 14:15

וְאַחֲרֵי שֶׁנָּטָה הַשֶּׁמֶשׁ לַעֲרוֹב אָז יִקְרְבוּ אֵלָיו הַתַּלְמִידָיו לֵאמֹר הִנֵּה הַמָּקוֹם הַזֶּה מַדְבָּרִי וְשָׁעָה כְּבָר עָבְרָה הַשְׁלַח נָא אֶת־כִּתִּים שֶׁיֵּלְכוּ בַטִּירוֹת וְיִקְנוּ לָהֶם אוֹכֶל

HTV: **After the sun had set, Yeshua's disciples approached him, saying, "Behold, the hour is late - send the people to the town to buy food.**

KJV: And when it was evening, his disciples came to him, saying, This is a desert place, and the time is now past; send the multitude away, that they may go into the villages, and buy themselves victuals.

The Hebrew Book of Matthew

Matthew 14:16

וַיֹּאמֶר לָהֶם יֵשׁוּעַ אֵין צָרִיךְ שֶׁיֵּלְכוּ מִכַּאן אַתֶּם תֵּא הַאֲכִילוּם

HTV: **Yeshua said to *his disciples* - "there is no need for them to leave here. Give them *food* to eat."**

KJV: But Jesus said unto them, They need not depart; give ye them to eat.

Matthew 14:17

וַיַּעֲנוּ לוֹ אֵין לָנוּ שָׁם כִּי אִם חֲמִשָּׁה פִּתֵּי לֶחֶם וּשְׁנַיִם דָּגִים

HTV: **And *his disciples* answered Yeshua - "They *can* not stay because we have only five loaves of bread and two fish."**

KJV: And they say unto him, We have here but five loaves, and two fishes.

Matthew 14:18

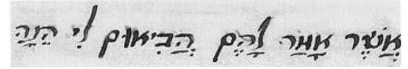

Freiburg Hebrew Manuscript

אֲשֶׁר אָמַר לָהֶם הֲבִיאוּם לִי הֵנָּה

HTV: **To which Yeshua said, "Bring them here to me."**

KJV: He said, Bring them hither to me.

Matthew 14:19

וְאַחֲרֵי שֶׁצִּוָּה אֶת-כַּת לָשֶׁבֶת עַל עֵשֶׂב אָז לָקַח אֶת חֲמִשָּׁה פִּתֵּי לֶחֶם וּשְׁנַיִם דָּגִים וְנָשָׂא אֶת-עֵינָיו לְשָׁמַיִם וַיְבָרֶךְ וַיִּפְרֹס וַיִּתֵּן אֶת-פִּתֵּי לֶחֶם לְתַלְמִידִים וְתַלְמִידִים נָתְנוּ לְכִתִּים

HTV: **Yeshua ordered the people to sit upon the grass. He took the five loaves of bread and two fish and turned his eyes to heaven - he blessed it, and broke the bread, and gave it to his disciples - and his disciples gave it to the people.**

KJV: And he commanded the multitude to sit down on the grass, and took the five loaves, and the two fishes, and looking up to heaven, he blessed, and brake, and gave the loaves to *his* disciples, and the disciples to the multitude.

Matthew 14:20

וַיֹּאכְלוּ כֻלָּם וַיִּשְׂבָּעוּ וַיִּטְלוּ מִשְׁאֵרִית שְׁנֵים עָשָׂר סַלִּים מְלֵאִים מִפִּתִּים

HTV: **All of them ate until they were completely satisfied - leaving remains of twelve baskets full of bread.**

KJV: And they did all eat, and were filled: and they took up of the fragments that remained twelve baskets full.

Matthew 14:21

וּמִסְפַּר הָאוֹכְלִים יִהְיֶה חֲמִשָּׁה אַלְפֵי אִישִׁים זָלָתִי הַנָּשִׁים וְתִינוֹקִים

HTV: **The number of people who had eaten was five thousand, including the women and children.**

KJV: And they that had eaten were about five thousand men, beside women and children.

Matthew 14:23

וּמִשֶּׁשִּׁלַּח אֶת־הַכַּת אָז עָלָה בָּהָר לְבַדּוֹ לְהִתְפַּלֵּל וְאַחֲרֵי שֶׁהָיָה עֶרֶב הִנֵּה הוּא יִהְיֶה לְבַדּוֹ שָׁם

HTV: **He sent away the crowds, then ascended the mountain by himself to pray. Afterward, it was evening - then he was there alone.**

KJV: And when he had sent the multitudes away, he went up into a mountain apart to pray: and when the evening was come, he was there alone.

Matthew 14:24

וּסְפִינָה תִּהְיֶה בְּתוֹךְ הַיָּם וְיִנָּדֵף הֵנָּה וְהֵנָּה מִגַּלִּים וְהָרוּחַ יִהְיֶה נְכוֹחִי

The Hebrew Book of Matthew

HTV: **The ship was in the midst of the sea - tossed here and there by the waves - and the wind was against *them*!**

KJV: But the ship was now in the midst of the sea, tossed with waves: for the wind was contrary.

Matthew 14:25

Freiburg Hebrew Manuscript

וּבְמִשְׁמֶרֶת רְבִיעִית הַלַּיְלָה בָּא אֲלֵיהֶם הוֹלֵךְ עַל פְּנֵי הַיָּם

HTV: **In the fourth watch of the night - Yeshua came to them walking on the surface of the sea.**

Note: The fourth watch was 3-6 am. Each watch was three hours. First watch of the night was 6-9 pm, second 9-12 pm, third 12-3 am, and fourth watch 3-6 am. They were called watches because typically one person watched/guarded during that period.

KJV: And in the fourth watch of the night Jesus went unto them, walking on the sea.

Matthew 14:26

וְכַאֲשֶׁר רָאוּהוּ נִשְׁתּוֹמְמוּ וַיֹּאמְרוּ הַזֹּאת מִרְמַת רָאוּת וַיִּצְעֲקוּ מֵרְעָדָה

HTV: **When they saw him - they were shocked - and said, "This is a great delusion!" And they cried out with fear and trembling!**

KJV: And when the disciples saw him walking on the sea, they were troubled, saying, It is a spirit; and they cried out for fear.

Matthew 14:27

וּמִיָּד דִּבֶּר יֵשׁוּעַ לֵאמֹר בִּטְחוּ נָא כִּי אָנֹכִי אַל תִּירָאוּ

HTV: **Right away, Yeshua spoke saying, "Have faith! It is I, do not be afraid."**

KJV: But straightway Jesus spake unto them, saying, Be of good cheer; it is I; be not afraid.

Matthew 14:28

וַיַּעַן כֵּיפָא וַיֹּאמַר אֲדוֹנִי אִם אַתָּה צַוֵּה נָא שֶׁאָבוֹא אֵלֶיךָ עַל־פְּנֵי הַמָּיִם

HTV: **Peter (Kayfa) answered, and he said, "Lord, command that I come to you on the surface of the water."**

KJV: And Peter answered him and said, Lord, if it be thou, bid me come unto thee on the water.

Matthew 14:29

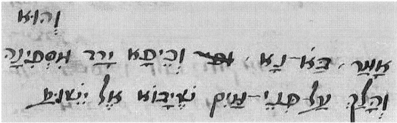
Freiburg Hebrew Manuscript

וְהוּא אָמַר בֹּא נָא וְכֵיפָא יָרַד מִסְּפִינָה וְהָלַךְ עַל פְּנֵי מַיִם שֶׁיָּבוֹא אֶל יֵשׁוּעַ

HTV: **And Yeshua said, "Come!" Peter got out of the ship and walked on the surface of the water to come toward Yeshua.**

KJV: And he said, Come. And when Peter was come down out of the ship, he walked on the water, to go to Jesus.

Matthew 14:30

וְכַאֲשֶׁר רָאָה רוּחַ חָזָק הוּא יִהְיֶה יָרֵא וּמִשֶּׁדִּתְחִיל לְהִטָּבֵל צָעַק וַיֹּאמֶר הָאֲדוֹנִי הוֹשִׁיעֵנִי

HTV: **When he (Peter) saw the powerful wind - he was afraid and started to sink. He cried out saying, "Lord save me!"**

KJV: But when he saw the wind boisterous, he was afraid; and beginning to sink, he cried, saying, Lord, save me.

The Hebrew Book of Matthew

Matthew 14:31

וּמִיָּד הוֹשִׁיט יֵשׁוּעַ אֶת־יָדוֹ וְהֶחֱזִיקוֹ וַיֹּאמַר לוֹ הַקְטַן אֱמוּנָה לָמָה נִסְתַּפַּקְתָּ

HTV: Promptly, Yeshua stretched forth his hand and grasped him strongly, and said unto him, "Man of little faith - why did you doubt?"

KJV: Immediately Jesus stretched forth *his* hand, and caught him, and said unto him, O thou of little faith, wherefore didst thou doubt?

Matthew 14:32

Freiburg Hebrew Manuscript

וְכַאֲשֶׁר עָלָה בַסְפִינָה אָז חָדַל הָרוּחַ לְנַשֵּׁב

HTV: And when Yeshua went up into the boat - the wind stopped blowing!

KJV: And when they were come into the ship, the wind ceased.

Matthew 14:33

אֲבָל אֲשֶׁר יִהְיוּ בַּסְפִינָה בָּאוּ וַיִּשְׁתַּחֲווּהוּ וַיֹּאמְרוּ לוֹ בֶּאֱמֶת אַתָּה הַבֵּן אֱלֹהִים

HTV: Those who were in the boat - bowed down and worshipped him - and said, "Truly, you are the Son of God!"

KJV: Then they that were in the ship came and worshipped him, saying, Of a truth thou art the Son of God.

Matthew 14:34

וְאַחֲרֵי שֶׁעָבְרוּ אֶת־הַיָּם בָּאוּ בְּאֶרֶץ גִּנּוֹסַר

HTV: And after they had crossed the sea (of Galilee) - they came into the land of Gennesaret.

KJV: And when they were gone over, they came into the land of Gennesaret.

Matthew 14:35

וּמִשֶּׁאָנְשֵׁי הָאוֹתוֹ מָקוֹם הִכִּירוּהוּ שָׁלְחוּ בְסָבִיב סָבִיב כֹּל הָאוֹתוֹ מְדִינָה וְהִקְרִיבוּ אֶצְלוֹ כֹּל חוֹלִים

HTV: **When the men of that place recognized him - they sent around about to all the nearby places - and they brought him all their sick.**

KJV: And when the men of that place had knowledge of him, they sent out into all that country round about, and brought unto him all that were diseased;

Matthew 14:36

וַיְבַקְשׁוּ מִמֶּנּוּ שֶׁלְבַד שׁוּלֵי מַלְבּוּשׁוֹ יִגְּעוּ וְכָלָם שֶׁנָּגְעוּ נִוְשָׁעוּ

HTV: **And they asked of him (Yeshua) that they *might* touch only the hem of his garments - and all *who* touched him were healed!**

KJV: And besought him that they might only touch the hem of his garment: and as many as touched were made perfectly whole.

Matthew Chapter 15

Hebrew Text Version (HTV)

[1] Then the scribes and Pharisees came to Yeshua from Jerusalem, saying,

[2] "Why do your students transgress the tradition of the elders* - since they do not wash their hands before they eat bread?"

[3] Yeshua answered them and said, "Why do you transgress the commandments of God for the sake of your traditions?"

[4] "For God said, 'Honor your father and your mother - but whoever curses his father and mother shall surely be put to death.'"

The Hebrew Book of Matthew

⁵ "But you profess that all *who* say to his father or to his mother, "All my possessions are <u>Qarban</u> (gifted to God) and will have the same benefit (*spiritual blessing*) for you."

⁶ "And *it* will not honor his father and his mother! You despise the commandment of God for the sake of your traditions."

⁷ "Woe, you hypocrites! Well did Isaiah prophesy of you, saying…"

⁸ " 'These people honor me with their lips - but their hearts are far from me.' " (Isaiah 29:13)

⁹ They honor me with no reason - because they teach as tradition the commandments *of* men.

¹⁰ And Yeshua called the people unto him and said to them, "Hear and understand!"

¹¹ comes out of the mouth that defiles the man!"

¹² Then his disciples approached, and said to him, you know that the Pharisees - after hearing these words - they will fall apart!

¹³ Yeshua answered and said, "Every plant - which your heavenly father did not plant - will be uprooted!"

¹⁴ Leave them alone because the blind (Pharisees) are leading the blind; and if a blind man leads another who is blind, both will fall into the pit.

¹⁵ Then Peter (Keyfa) said to Yeshua, "Please explain this parable to us?"

¹⁶ Then Yeshua said to him, "Are you still without understanding?"

¹⁷ "Do you not understand - that everything that enters into the mouth goes into the belly - and after will exit the way of waste."

¹⁸ "But whatever comes out from the mouth - comes from the heart - and *that is* what defiles the man."

¹⁹ "For out of the heart will go out evil thoughts - murder, adultery, theft, false witness and blasphemy."

²⁰ "Those are things which defile the man - truly, *however*, not washing hands ritually before taking food does not defile the man."

²¹ Yeshua left there and went into the region of Tyre and Sidon.

²² And there came - from out of that region - a Canaanite woman. She cried out and said to him, "Have mercy on me, my lord, son of David! Because my daughter is greatly tormented

by a demon!"

²³ Yeshua did not say a word to her. His disciples came and entreated him saying, "Let us leave her - she is screaming at us!"

²⁴ However, Yeshua responded and said, "I was not sent - except to the lost sheep of the House of Israel."

²⁵ Indeed, she drew near and bowed down to Yeshua - saying, "Please, I beg you my Lord, help me!"

²⁶ Yeshua answered and said, "It is not good to take the children's bread and cast *it* before dogs."

²⁷ Then she said, "Please, my lord - even the dogs eat the crumbs fallen from their master's table!"

²⁸ Then Yeshua responded and said to the woman, "Behold! Your faith is great! Let it be for you as you desire." - And her daughter was healed in *that* same hour.

²⁹ And when Yeshua passed over from there - he came unto the Sea of Galilee - and ascended a mountain and sat there.

³⁰ Many people approached Yeshua - who *brought* the mute, blind, lame, disabled, and others. They put them down *at* his feet - and Yeshua healed them!

³¹ The crowds were astonished to see the mute speak, and the lame walk, and the blind see! And they praised the Elohim (God) of Israel!

³² Yeshua called his disciples to him and said, "I have compassion for the multitudes. Now it is three days they *have been* with me - and they do not have anything to eat. I do not want them to fast so that they faint from hunger on the way."

³³ His disciples said to him, "From where will we *get* so much bread in the wilderness that will satisfy such a large multitude?"

³⁴ Yeshua said to them, "How many loaves of bread do you have?" And they said, "Seven, and a few fish."

³⁵ Yeshua directed the multitude to sit on the ground.

³⁶ Yeshua took the seven loaves of bread and the fish and blessed them. He broke *them* and gave *them* to his disciples, and his disciples gave *them* to the people.

³⁷ They all ate and were satisfied. From the remaining bread they took up seven baskets full.

³⁸ The number of those who ate was four thousand men, *including* women and children.

Matthew Chapter 15

HTV with translator notes and KJV comparison

Matthew 15:1

וְאָז בָּאוּ אֵלָיו סוֹפְרִים וּפְרוּשִׁים מִירוּשָׁלִַים וַיֹּאמְרוּ

HTV: **Then the scribes and Pharisees came to Yeshua from Jerusalem, saying,**

KJV: Then came to Jesus scribes and Pharisees, which were of Jerusalem, saying,

Matthew 15:2

Freiburg Hebrew Manuscript

לָמָה נָא הַתַּלְמִידֶיךָ עוֹבְרִים אֶת הַמַּסֹרֶת זְקֵנִים כִּי אֵינָם רוֹחֲצִים אֶת-יְדֵיהֶם אִם אוֹכְלִים אֶת-הַלֶּחֶם

HTV: **"Why do your students transgress the tradition of the elders* - since they do not wash their hands before they eat bread?"**

*Note: The phrase "traditions of the elders" is a catchphrase meaning the Oral Torah, tradition supposedly passed down since Sinai in the folk memory of the elders. Keep in mind, there is no law in Torah that one must wash their hands before eating. Good idea but not Torah. They are accusing Yeshua of transgressing the Oral Torah which the Pharisees consider as binding law. These " oral laws" - commandments of men - are called *taqanot*.

Chapter 15

KJV: Why do thy disciples transgress the tradition of the elders? for they wash not their hands when they eat bread.

Matthew 15:3

וְהוּא עָנָה לָהֶם וַיֹּאמַר לָמָה אַתֶּם עוֹבְרִים אֶת-מִצְוֹת הָאֱלֹהִים בַּעֲבוּר מְסוֹרַתְּכֶם

HTV: **Yeshua answered them and said, "Why do you transgress the commandments of God for the sake of your traditions?"**

KJV: But he answered and said unto them, Why do ye also transgress the commandment of God by your tradition?

Matthew 15:4

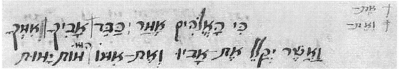
Freiburg Hebrew Manuscript

כִּי הָאֱלֹהִים אָמַר כַּבֵּד אֶת-אָבִיךָ וְאֶת-אִמֶּךָ וַאֲשֶׁר יְקַלֵּל אֶת-אָבִיו וְאֶת-אִמּוֹ הוּא מוֹת יָמוּת

HTV: **"For God said, 'Honor your father and your mother - but whoever curses his father and mother shall surely be put to death.*' "**

*Note: Exodus 21:15-17 " He who curses his father and mother shall surely be put to death."

KJV: For God commanded, saying, Honour thy father and mother: and, He that curseth father or mother, let him die the death.

Matthew 15:5

Freiburg Hebrew Manuscript

אֲבָל אַתֶּם אוֹמְרִים כֹּל שֶׁיֹּאמַר לְאָבִיו אוֹ לְאִמּוֹ כָּל-קָרְבָּן שֶׁיִּהְיֶה מִמֶּנִּי הוּא יוֹעִיל לְךָ

245

HTV: **"But you profess that all *who* say to his father or to his mother, "All my possessions are <u>Qarban</u>* (gifted to God) and will have the same benefit (*spiritual blessing*) for you."**

> *Note: But you say, "Whatever you would have received from me is *Corban*" (that is, a gift devoted to God) - therefore, he is no longer permitted to do anything for his father or mother. Thus, you nullify the word of God by the tradition you have handed down. (from Biblehub.com commentary)

KJV: But ye say, Whosoever shall say to *his* father or *his* mother, *It is* a gift, by whatsoever thou mightest be profited by me;

Matthew 15:6

וְלֹא יְכַבֵּד אֶת-אָבִיו וְאֶת-אִמּוֹ הִנֵּה אַתֶּם מְפִירִים אֶת מִצְוַת הָאֱלֹהִים בַּעֲבוּר הַמְסוֹרָתְכֶם

HTV: **"And *it* will not honor his father and his mother! You despise the commandment of God for the sake of your traditions."**

KJV: And honour not his father or his mother, *he shall be free*. Thus have ye made the commandment of God of none effect by your tradition.

Matthew 15:7

הוֹי הַחֲנֵפִים הֵיטֵב נִבָּא מִמְּכֶם יְשַׁעְיָהוּ לֵאמֹר

HTV: **"Woe, you hypocrites! Well did Isaiah prophesy of you, saying"**

KJV: *Ye* hypocrites, well did Esaias prophesy of you, saying,

Matthew 15:8

הָעָם הַזֶּה מְכַבֵּד אוֹתִי בִּשְׂפָתָיו וְלִבּוֹ רָחוּק מִמֶּנִּי

HTV: **" 'These people honor me with their lips - but their hearts are far from me.' "** (Isaiah 29:13)

Chapter 15

KJV: This people draweth nigh unto me with their mouth, and honoureth me with *their* lips; but their heart is far from me.

Matthew 15:9

הֵמָה בְּלִי סִבָּה מְכַבְּדִים אוֹתִי הַמְלַמְּדִים אֶת-מָסוֹרֶת וּמִצְוֹת הָאֱנוֹשִׁים

HTV: **They honor me with no reason - because they teach as tradition the commandments *of* men.**

KJV: But in vain they do worship me, teaching *for* doctrines the commandments of men.

Matthew 15:10

Freiburg Hebrew Manuscript

וַיִּקְרָא אֵלָיו אֶת-הַכִּתִּים וַאֹמַר לָהֶם שִׁמְעוּ וְהָבִינוּ

HTV: **And Yeshua called the people unto him and said to them, "Hear and understand!"**

KJV: And he called the multitude, and said unto them, Hear, and understand:

Matthew 15:11

לֹא שֶׁנִּכְנָס בְּפִי מַלְכְּךָ אֶת-הָאָדָם כִּי אִם מָה שֶׁיּוֹצֵא מִפִּי מַלְכְּךָ אֶת-הָאָדָם

HTV: **"It is not that *which* enters into the mouth that defiles the man - but that *which* comes out of the mouth that defiles the man!"**

KJV: Not that which goeth into the mouth defileth a man; but that which cometh out of the mouth, this defileth a man.

Matthew 15:12

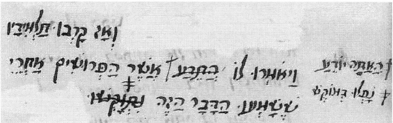

Freiburg Hebrew Manuscript

וְאָז קָרְבוּ תַלְמִידָיו וַיֹּאמְרוּ לוֹ הַאַתָּה יוֹדֵעַ אֲשֶׁר הַפְּרוּשִׁים אַחֲרֵי שֶׁשָּׁמְעוּ הַדָּבָר הַזֶּה נָפְלוּ בְמוֹקֵשׁ

HTV: **Then his disciples approached, and said to him, you know that the Pharisees - after hearing these words - they will fall apart!**

> Note: The word "nafloo" in Hebrew means to fall into a mine, a trap, a snare. It can mean fall apart. In this case that seems to be the appropriate meaning - having fallen into a trap they would be offended, even enraged and would seek vengeance.

KJV: Then came his disciples, and said unto him, Knowest thou that the Pharisees were offended, after they heard this saying?

Matthew 15:13

וַיַּעַן וַיֹּאמַר כֹּל נֶטַע אֲשֶׁר הָאָבִי הַשָּׁמֵימִי לֹא נָטַע הַהוּא יִנָּתֵשׁ

HTV: **Yeshua answered and said, "Every plant - which your heavenly father did not plant - will be uprooted!"**

KJV: But he answered and said, Every plant, which my heavenly Father hath not planted, shall be rooted up.

Matthew 15:14

הַנִּיחוּם כִּי הֵם עִוְרִים וּמַנְהִיגֵי הָעִוְרִים וְאִם הָעִוֵּר יַנְהִיג אֶת-הָעִוֵּר הִנֵּה שְׁנֵיהֶם יִפְּלוּ בְשַׁחַת

HTV: **Leave them alone because the blind (Pharisees) are leading the blind; and if a blind man leads another who is blind, both will fall into the pit.**

KJV: Let them alone: they be blind leaders of the blind. And if the blind lead the blind, both shall fall into the ditch.

Matthew 15:15

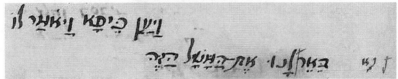
Freiburg Hebrew Manuscript

וַיַּעַן כֵּיפָא וַיֹּאמַר לוֹ בֵּאֶר נָא לָנוּ אֶת-הַמָּשָׁל הַזֶּה

HTV: **Then Peter (Keyfa) said to Yeshua, "Please explain this parable to us?"**

KJV: Then answered Peter and said unto him, Declare unto us this parable.

Matthew 15:16

אָמְנָם הוּא אָמַר לוֹ הַאִם עוֹדְכֶם בְּלִי בִינָה

HTV: **Then Yeshua said to him, "Are you still without understanding?"**

KJV: And Jesus said, Are ye also yet without understanding?

Matthew 15:17

הַאִם אֵינְכֶם מְבִינִים כִּי כֹל מַה שֶׁנִּכְנַס בְּפִי בָא בְתוֹךְ הַבֶּטֶן וְאַחַר כָּךְ יֵצֵא עַל דֶּרֶךְ פַּרְשְׁדוֹנָה

HTV: **"Do you not understand - that everything that enters into the mouth goes into the belly - and after will exit the way of waste."**

KJV: Do not ye yet understand, that whatsoever entereth in at the mouth goeth into the belly, and is cast out into the draught?

Matthew 15:18

אַךְ אֲשֶׁר יוֹצְאִים עַל דֶּרֶךְ הַפִּי הֵמָּה יוֹצְאִים מֵהַלֵּב וּמְלַכְלְכִים אֶת-הָאָדָם

The Hebrew Book of Matthew

HTV: **"But whatever comes out from the mouth - comes from the heart - and *that is* what defiles the man."**

KJV: But those things which proceed out of the mouth come forth from the heart; and they defile the man.

Matthew 15:19

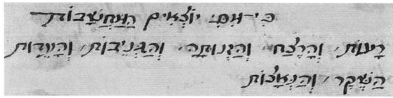
Freiburg Hebrew Manuscript

כִּי מִפִּי יוֹצְאִים הַמַּחֲשָׁבוֹת רָעוֹת וְהָרֶצַח וְהַזְנוּתָה וְהַגְּנֵיבוֹת וְהָעֵדוֹת הַשֶּׁקֶר וְהַנְאָצוֹת

HTV: **"For out of the heart will go out evil thoughts - murder, adultery, theft, false witness and blasphemy."**

Note: See Matthew 12:34, For the mouth speaks out of the abundance of the heart!"

KJV: For out of the heart proceed evil thoughts, murders, adulteries, fornications, thefts, false witness, blasphemies:

Matthew 15:20

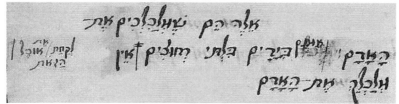
Freiburg Hebrew Manuscript

אֵלֶּה הֵם שֶׁמְּלַכְלְכִים אֶת-הָאָדָם אָמְנָם בְּיָדִים בִּלְתִי רְחוּצִים לָקַחַת אֶת-אוֹכֶל הַזֹּאת אֵין מְלַכְלֵךְ אֶת-הָאָדָם

HTV: **"Those are things which defile the man - truly, *however*, not washing hands ritually before taking food does not defile the man."**

Note: The Pharisees are demanding Yeshua and his disciples follow the Oral Torah of a prescribed ritual hand-washing ceremony before eating.

Yeshua is taking a very clear stand that these man-made ceremonies and taqanot (commandments of men) are not Torah.

KJV: These are *the things* which defile a man: but to eat with unwashen hands defileth not a man.

Matthew 15:21

וַיֵּצֵא יֵשׁוּעַ מִכַּאן וְהָלַךְ בִּמְחוֹזֵי צוֹר וְצִידוֹן

HTV: **Yeshua left there and went into the region of Tyre and Sidon.**

KJV: Then Jesus went thence, and departed into the coasts of Tyre and Sidon.

Matthew 15:22

וְהִנֵּה שׁוּם-אִשָּׁה כְּנַעֲנִית יָצְאָה מֵאוֹתָם גְּבוּלִים וַתִּצְעַק וַתֹּאמַר לוֹ חָנֵּנִי הָאֲדוֹנִי הַבֵּן דָּוִד כִּי בִתִּי מְאוֹד נִתְעַנָּה מֵהַשֵּׁד

HTV: **And there came - from out of that region - a Canaanite woman. She cried out and said to him, "Have mercy on me, my lord, son of David! Because my daughter is greatly tormented by a demon!"**

KJV: And, behold, a woman of Canaan came out of the same coasts, and cried unto him, saying, Have mercy on me, O Lord, *thou* Son of David; my daughter is grievously vexed with a devil.

Matthew 15:23

וְהוּא לֹא הֵשִׁיב לָהּ אֵיזֶה דָּבָר וַיִּקְרְבוּ הַתַּלְמִידִין וּשְׁאָלוּהוּ לֵאמֹר הֲנִיחָהּ כִּי הִיא צוֹעֶקֶת אַחֲרֵינוּ

HTV: **Yeshua did not say a word to her. His disciples came and entreated him saying, "Let us leave her - she is screaming at us!"**

KJV: But he answered her not a word. And his disciples came and besought him, saying, Send her away; for she crieth after us.

Matthew 15:24

Freiburg Hebrew Manuscript

אֲבָל הוּא עָנָה וַיֹּאמַר אֲנִי לֹא-נִשְׁלַחְתִּי כִּי-אִם-לְצֹאן הָאוֹבְדוֹת הַבֵּית יִשְׂרָאֵל

HTV: However, Yeshua responded and said, "I was not sent - except to the lost sheep of the House of Israel.*"

*Note: See Jeremiah 50:6, "My people have become lost sheep. Their shepherds have led them astray."

KJV: But he answered and said, I am not sent but unto the lost sheep of the house of Israel.

Matthew 15:25

אָמְנָם הִיא קָרְבָה וַתִּשְׁתַּחֲוֶה אוֹתוֹ לֵאמֹר אָנָא הָאֲדוֹנִי עָזְרֵנִי

HTV: Indeed, she drew near and bowed down to Yeshua - saying, "Please, I beg you my Lord, help me!"

KJV: Then came she and worshipped him, saying, Lord, help me.

Matthew 15:26

וַיַּעַן וַיֹּאמַר לֹא-טוֹב לָקַחַת הַלֶּחֶם הַבָּנִים וְלִשְׁלוֹחַ לִפְנֵי הַכְּלָבִים

HTV: Yeshua answered and said, "It is not good to take the children's bread and cast *it* before dogs."

KJV: But he answered and said, It is not meet to take the children's bread, and to cast *it* to dogs.

Matthew 15:27

וְהִיא אָמְרָה אָנָא הָאֲדוֹנִי כִּ- גַ- הַכְּלָבִים אוֹכְלִים מִפְּתִים הַנּוֹפְלִים מִשֻּׁלְחָן אֲדוֹנֵיהֶם

HTV: **Then she said, "Please, my lord - even the dogs eat the crumbs fallen from their master's table!"**

KJV: And she said, Truth, Lord: yet the dogs eat of the crumbs which fall from their masters' table.

Matthew 15:28

וְאָז עָנָה יֵשׁוּעַ וַיֹּאמַר לָהּ הָאִשָּׁה הִנֵּה אֱמוּנָתֵךְ הִיא גְדוֹלָה יְהִי לָךְ כְּמוֹ תִרְצֶה וְנִרְפְּאָה בִּתָּהּ בְּאוֹתָהּ שָׁעָה

HTV: **Then Yeshua responded and said to the woman, "Behold! Your faith is great! Let it be for you as you desire." - And her daughter was healed in *that* same hour.**

KJV: Then Jesus answered and said unto her, O woman, great *is* thy faith: be it unto thee even as thou wilt. And her daughter was made whole from that very hour.

Matthew 15:29

וְכַאֲשֶׁר יֵשׁוּעַ עָבַר מִכָּאן הוּא בָא אֵצֶל יָם גְּלִילָה וְעָלָה בָהָר וַיֵּשֶׁב שָׁם

HTV: **And when Yeshua passed over from there - he came unto the Sea of Galilee - and ascended a mountain and sat there.**

KJV: And Jesus departed from thence, and came nigh unto the sea of Galilee; and went up into a mountain, and sat down there.

Matthew 15:30

וַיִּקְרְבוּ אֵלָיו הֲכִתִּים רַבִּים אֲשֶׁר לָהֶם אִלְּמִים עִוְרִים פִּסְחִים חֲלָשִׁים וַאֲחֵרִים רַבִּים וְיַשְׁלִיכוּם אֶל רַגְלָיו וַיִּרְפֵּא אוֹתָם

HTV: **Many people approached Yeshua - who *brought* the mute, blind, lame, disabled, and others. They put them down *at* his feet - and Yeshua healed them!**

KJV: And great multitudes came unto him, having with them *those that were* lame, blind, dumb, maimed, and many others, and cast them down at Jesus' feet; and he healed them:

Matthew 15:31

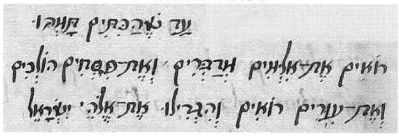

Freiburg Hebrew Manuscript

עַד שֶׁהַכִּתִּים תָּמְהוּ רוֹאִים אֶת-אִלְּמִים מְדַבְּרִים וְאֶת-פִּסְחִים הוֹלְכִים וְאֶת-עִוְּרִים רוֹאִים וְהִגְדִּילוּ אֶת-אֱלֹהֵי יִשְׂרָאֵל

HTV: **The crowds were astonished to see the mute speak, and the lame walk, and the blind see! And they praised the Elohim (God) of Israel!**

KJV: Insomuch that the multitude wondered, when they saw the dumb to speak, the maimed to be whole, the lame to walk, and the blind to see: and they glorified the God of Israel.

Matthew 15:32

וְיֵשׁוּעַ קָרָא אֶצְלוֹ אֶת-הַתַּלְמִידָיו וַיֹּאמֶר אֲנִי מְחוֹנֵן עַל הַכִּתִּים כִּי עַתָּה שְׁלוֹשָׁה יָמִים אֲשֶׁר הֵמָּה עוֹמְדִים אִתִּי וְאֵין לָהֶם מְאוּמָה לֶאֱכֹל וְאֵינִי רוֹצֶה לַהֲנִיחָם צָמִים כְּדֵי שֶׁלֹּא יַעַטְפוּ בָרָעָב בְּדֶרֶךְ

HTV: **Yeshua called his disciples to him and said, "I have compassion for the multitudes. Now it is three days they *have been* with me - and they do not have anything to eat. I do not want them to fast so that they faint from hunger on the way."**

KJV: Then Jesus called his disciples unto him, and said, I have compassion on the multitude, because they continue with me now three days, and have nothing to eat: and I will not send them away fasting, lest they faint in the way.

Matthew 15:33

וַיֹּאמֶר לוֹ תַלְמִידָיו מֵאַיִן נָא יִהְיֶה לָנוּ כַּמָּה לֶחֶם בַּמִּדְבָּר שֶׁנַּשְׂבִּיעַ כִּתִּים כָּךְ וְכָךְ גְּדוֹלִים

Chapter 15

HTV: **His disciples said to him, "From where will we *get* so much bread in the wilderness that will satisfy such a large multitude?"**

KJV: And his disciples say unto him, Whence should we have so much bread in the wilderness, as to fill so great a multitude?

Matthew 15:34

וַיֹּאמֶר לָהֶם יֵשׁוּעַ כָּמָה לָכֶם פִּתֵּי לֶחֶם אֲבָל הֵמָה אָמְרוּ שִׁבְעָה וּמְעַטִּים דָּגִים

HTV: **Yeshua said to them, "How many loaves of bread do you have?" And they said, "Seven, and a few fish."**

KJV: And Jesus saith unto them, How many loaves have ye? And they said, Seven, and a few little fishes.

Matthew 15:35

וַיְצַוֶּה אֶת-הַכִּתִּים לָשֶׁבֶת עַל אֶרֶץ

HTV: **Yeshua directed the multitude to sit on the ground.**

KJV: And he commanded the multitude to sit down on the ground.

Matthew 15:36

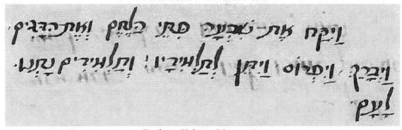

Freiburg Hebrew Manuscript

וַיִּקַּח אֶת-שִׁבְעָה פִּתֵּי הַלֶּחֶם וְאֶת-הַדָּגִים וַיְבָרֶךְ וַיִּפְרוֹס וַיִּתֵּן לְתַלְמִידָיו וְתַלְמִידִים נָתְנוּ לָעָם

255

HTV: **Yeshua took the seven loaves of bread and the fish and blessed them. He broke *them* and gave *them* to his disciples, and his disciples gave *them* to the people.**

KJV: And he took the seven loaves and the fishes, and gave thanks, and brake *them*, and gave to his disciples, and the disciples to the multitude.

Matthew 15:37

וְאָכְלוּ כֻלָם וַיִשְׂבָעוּ וּמִמָה שֶׁנוֹתָר מִפְּתִים הֵמָה נָטְלוּ שִׁבְעָה סַלִים מְלֵאִים

HTV: **They all ate and were satisfied. From the remaining bread they took up seven baskets full.**

KJV: And they did all eat, and were filled: and they took up of the broken *meat* that was left seven baskets full.

Matthew 15:38

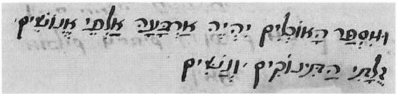
Freiburg Hebrew Manuscript

וּמִסְפַּר הָאוֹכְלִים יִהְיֶה אַרְבָּעָה אַלְפֵי אֲנוֹשִׁים זָלָתִי הַתִּינוֹקִים וְנָשִׁים

HTV: **The number of those who ate was four thousand men, *including* women and children.**

KJV: And they that did eat were four thousand men, beside women and children.

Matthew Chapter 16
Hebrew Text Version (HTV)

¹ The Pharisees and the Sadducees came to tempt Yeshua - imploring him to show them a sign from heaven.

² Yeshua answered and said to them, "Look, when it is evening you say, 'It will be clear *weather*, for the skies have become red.'"

³ "But in the morning, 'The day will be stormy - for the skies are painted red and darkening.' You hypocrites, you know how to read the face of the skies – but you are not able to *read* the signs of the times."

⁴ "This evil and adulterous generation demands a sign - and no sign shall be given to it - except the sign of Jonah the Prophet." Then Yeshua left them, and departed.

⁵ When Yeshua's disciples crossed over the sea - they forgot to take bread.

⁶ Yeshua said to them, "Take heed of the times when the Pharisees and Sadducees risk *their souls* because of their leaven."

⁷ So, they thought to themselves and said, "It is because we did not bring bread."

⁸ Yeshua knew this and said, "You of little faith! Why do you think to yourselves it is because you have no bread!"

⁹ How do you not understand? - Nor remember the five loaves of bread and five thousand people - and how many baskets you took up *afterwards*?"

¹⁰ "And the seven loaves of bread *among* four thousand people - and how many baskets you took up?"

¹¹ "Why do you not understand - that I am not speaking about bread? But I am saying to you - that you must beware of the leaven of the Sadducees and the Pharisees!"

¹² Then they realized - that Yeshua did not say they should be protected from the leaven of the bread - but from the teachings of the Pharisees and Sadducees.

The Hebrew Book of Matthew

¹³ Yeshua came to the borders of Caesarea Philippi - and he asked his disciples, saying "What do people say *of* the Son of Adam (Man)?"

¹⁴ They said unto Yeshua, "Some say he is John the Baptist, some say he is Elijah, and some he is Jeremiah, or one of the prophets."

¹⁵ Yeshua said to them, "In truth, who do you say I am?"

¹⁶ And Simon Peter answered, "You are the Messiah - the son of the living God!"

¹⁷ - for flesh and blood has not revealed it to you - but my Father who is in heaven."

¹⁸ "I say unto you - You are Peter (Keyfa = stone) and upon this stone I will build my House of Prayer - and the gates of Hell shall not prevail against it!"

¹⁹ "I will give unto you the keys of heaven. All that you shall forbid on earth shall be forbidden in heaven - and all that you permit on earth will be permitted in heaven."

²⁰ Then Yeshua commanded his disciples - they should not say to anyone that he is Yeshua the Messiah.

²¹ And from that day, Yeshua began to reveal to his disciples - that it is upon him to go to Jerusalem - to suffer much evil at the hand of the elders, and the scribes, and the chief priests - and to be killed - and to rise from death on the third day.

²² And Peter took him aside and began to rebuke him, and he said, "God forbid, please, God forbid! My Lord, God will not let this happen to you!"

²³ Yeshua *then* turned around and said to Peter "Get away from me, Satan! Because you are a snare to me - Because you do not understand the matters of Elohim - but "*those* of men."

²⁴ Then Yeshua said to his disciples, "Whosoever would come after me - must deny himself - take *up* his cross - and follow me."

²⁵ "Everyone who wishes to save his life - it will be lost for my sake. He who loses his life in this world for my sake - will save his soul for the life of the world to come."

²⁶ "What benefit is there for man - if he gains the whole world but loses his soul? What *value* could man exchange for his soul?"

²⁷ "For the Son of Man shall come in the glory of his Father together with his angels - and shall reward each and every one according to his deeds."

²⁸ Truly, I say to you, there are a few standing here who will not taste death until they see the Son of Man coming in his kingdom."

Matthew Chapter 16
HTV with translator notes and KJV comparison

Matthew 16:1

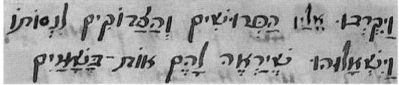

Freiburg Hebrew Manuscript

וַיִּקְרְבוּ אֵלָיו הַפְּרוּשִׁים וְהַצַּדּוֹקִים לְנַסּוֹתוֹ וַיִּשְׁאָלוּהוּ שֶׁיַּרְאֶה לָהֶם אוֹת בַּשָּׁמַיִם

HTV: **The Pharisees and the Sadducees came to tempt Yeshua - imploring him to show them a sign from heaven.**

KJV: The Pharisees also with the Sadducees came, and tempting desired him that he would shew them a sign from heaven.

Matthew 16:2

וַיַּעַן לָהֶם וַיֹּאמַר וְהִנֵּה כַּאֲשֶׁר יִהְיֶה עֶרֶב אַתֶּם אוֹמְרִים הִנֵּה יִהְיֶה הַזְּמַן טוֹהַר כִּי הַשָּׁמַיִם מַאֲדִימִים

HTV: **Yeshua answered and said to them, "Look, when it is evening you say, 'It will be clear *weather*, for the skies have become red.' "**

KJV: He answered and said unto them, When it is evening, ye say, *It will be* fair weather: for the sky is red.

Matthew 16:3

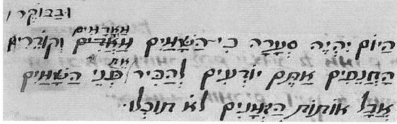

Freiburg Hebrew Manuscript

וּבַבּוֹקֶר הַיּוֹם יִהְיֶה סְעָרָה כִּי הַשָּׁמַיִם מַאֲדָמִים וְקוֹדְרִים הַחֲנֵפִים אַתֶּם יוֹדְעִים לְהַכִּיר אֶת פְּנֵי הַשָּׁמַיִם אֲבָל אוֹתוֹת הַזְּמַנִים לֹא תוּכְלוּ

HTV: "But in the morning, 'The day will be stormy - for the skies are painted red and darkening.' You hypocrites, you know how to read the face of the skies – but you are not able to *read* the signs of the times."

Note: This is a reference to reading the *Moedim* - the signs in the heavens prophesying things to come. These signs need to be heeded. See Psalms 19:1-2, Luke 21:11 and Luke 21:20 where the Messianics are warned to leave Jerusalem when the armies surround it.

KJV: And in the morning, *It will be foul* weather today: for the sky is red and lowring. O ye hypocrites, *ye* can *discern* the face of the sky; but can ye not discern the signs of the times?

Matthew 16:4

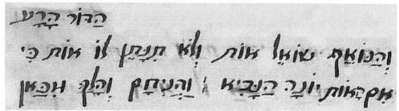

Freiburg Hebrew Manuscript

הַדּוֹר הָרָע וְהַנּוֹאֵף שׁוֹאֵל אוֹת וְלֹא תִנָּתֵן לוֹ אוֹת כִּי אִם הָאוֹת יוֹנָה הַנָּבִיא וַהֲנִיחָם וְהָלַךְ מִכָּאן

HTV: "This evil and adulterous generation demands a sign - and no sign shall be given to it - except the sign of Jonah the Prophet." Then Yeshua left them, and departed.

Note: Yeshua gave huge significance to the sign of Jonah. He mentions it three times during his recorded ministry. Jonah is the only prophet

Yeshua associates himself with by name (Matthew 12:41). It is the sole prophecy upon which Yeshua declared his authenticity may be judged.

KJV: A wicked and adulterous generation seeketh after a sign; and there shall no sign be given unto it, but the sign of the prophet Jonas. And he left them, and departed.

Matthew 16:5

וְכַאֲשֶׁר תַּלְמִידָיו עָבְרוּ אֶת-הַיָּם וְשָׁכְחוּ לָקַחַת אֶת לֶחֶם

HTV: **When Yeshua's disciples crossed over the sea - they forgot to take bread.**

KJV: And when his disciples were come to the other side, they had forgotten to take bread.

Matthew 16:6

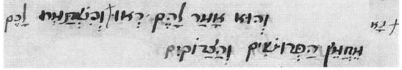
Freiburg Hebrew Manuscript

וְהוּא אָמַר לָהֶם רְאוּ נָא וְכִשְׁתַּמְרוּ לָכֶם מֵחָמֵץ הַפְּרוּשִׁים וְהַצַּדּוֹקִים

HTV: **Yeshua said to them, "Take heed of the times when the Pharisees and Sadducees risk *their souls* because of their leaven."**

Note: Here *Leaven* (chamets), refers to evil which once introduced takes over everything. The Pharisees are scheming with the Sadducees to destroy Yeshua because he is threatening to destroy the Temple system they profit from - it has become evil, corrupt and greedy to the point that the priests are willing to kill the Son of God to preserve it.

KJV: Then Jesus said unto them, Take heed and beware of the leaven of the Pharisees and of the Sadducees.

Matthew 16:7

וְהֵמָּה חָשְׁבוּ בְעַצְמָם וַיֹּאמְרוּ הִנֵּה לֹא לָקַחְנוּ לֶחֶם

HTV: **So, they thought to themselves and said, "It is because we did not bring bread."**

KJV: And they reasoned among themselves, saying, *It is* because we have taken no bread.

Matthew 16:8

וְיֵשׁוּעַ הַזֹּאת יָדַע וַיֹּאמַר הַקְטַנֵּי אֱמוּנָה מָה אַתֶּם חוֹשְׁבִים בְּקִרְבְּכֶם אֲשֶׁר אֵין לָכֶם לֶחֶם

HTV: **Yeshua knew this and said, "You of little faith! Why do you think to yourselves it is because you have no bread!"**

KJV: *Which* when Jesus perceived, he said unto them, O ye of little faith, why reason ye among yourselves, because ye have brought no bread?

Matthew 16:9

הַאִם אֵינְכֶם מְבִינִים וְאֵין מַזְכִּירִים אֶת־חֲמִשָּׁה פִּתֵּי לֶחֶם וְחֲמִשָּׁה אַלְפֵי אֲנוֹשִׁים וְכַמָּה סַלִּים נְטַלְתֶּם

HTV: **"How do you not understand? - Nor remember the five loaves of bread and five thousand people - and how many baskets you took up *afterwards*?"**

KJV: Do ye not yet understand, neither remember the five loaves of the five thousand, and how many baskets ye took up?

Matthew 16:10

וְאֵין הַשִּׁבְעָה פִּתֵּי לֶחֶם וְאַרְבָּעָה אַלְפֵי אֲנוֹשִׁים וְכַמָּה סַלִּים נְטַלְתֶּם

HTV: **"And the seven loaves of bread *among* four thousand people - and how many baskets you took up?"**

KJV: Neither the seven loaves of the four thousand, and how many baskets ye took up?

Matthew 16:11

לָמָה נָא אֵינְכֶם יוֹדְעִים שֶׁלֹא אָמַרְתִּי מִלְּחֶם כַּאֲשֶׁר אָמַרְתִּי שֶׁתִּשְׁתַּמְּרוּ מֵחֲמֵץ הַפְּרוּשִׁים וְצַדּוֹקִים

HTV: **"Why do you not understand - that I am not speaking about bread? But I am saying to you - that you must beware of the leaven of the Sadducees and the Pharisees!"**

KJV: How is it that ye do not understand that I spake *it* not to you concerning bread, that ye should beware of the leaven of the Pharisees and of the Sadducees?

Matthew 16:12

וְאָז הֵבִינוּ שֶׁלֹא אָמַר שֶׁיֵּשׁ לָהֶם לְהִשְׁתַּמֵּר מֵחֲמֵץ הַלֶּחֶם כִּי אִם מִלִּמּוּד פְּרוּשִׁים וְצַדּוֹקִים

HTV: **Then they realized - that Yeshua did not say they should be protected from the leaven of the bread - but from the teachings of the Pharisees and Sadducees.**

KJV: Then understood they how that he bade them not beware of the leaven of bread, but of the doctrine of the Pharisees and of the Sadducees.

Matthew 16:13

Freiburg Hebrew Manuscript

וְיָבוֹא יֵשׁוּעַ לִגְבוּלֵי הָאוֹתָהּ קָסָרִיעָה שֶׁמְּכַמָה פִלְפִּי וַיִּשְׁאַל אֶת-תַּלְמִידָיו לֵאמֹר אֵיזֶה אוֹמְרִים אֲנוֹשִׁים הֱיוֹת אֶת-בֶּן הָאָדָם

HTV: **Yeshua came to the borders of Caesarea Philippi - and he asked his disciples, saying "What do people say *of* the Son of Adam (Man)?"**

The Hebrew Book of Matthew

Note: In 1st Corinthians 15:21-22, Paul said, "For since by man (Adam) came death, by man (son of Adam) also came the resurrection. For as in Adam all die - even so in Christ (son of Adam) shall all be made alive." 15:45 "The first man, Adam, was made a living soul - the last Adam was made a quickening spirit." 15:47 "The first man (Adam) is of the earth - the second man (son of Adam - son of Man) is the Lord from heaven."

The **"Son of Adam"** is poorly understood because **Adam** also means **Man. Adam brought death into the world - it is to the Son of Adam - the Son of Man without sin, to sacrifice himself to remove that original sin. See Leviticus 17:11 where Yehovah says, "The life of the flesh is in the blood: and I myself have given it to you upon the altar to make an atonement for your souls - for it is the blood that makes an atonement for the soul."**

KJV: When Jesus came into the coasts of Caesarea Philippi, he asked his disciples, saying, Whom do men say that I the Son of man am?

Matthew 16:14
אֲבָל הֵמָה אָמְרוּ לוֹ קְצָתָם אוֹמְרִים שֶׁהוּא יוֹחָנָן הַטּוֹבֵל וּקְצָתָם שֶׁהוּא אֵלִיָּהוּ וּקְצָתָם שֶׁהוּא יִרְמְיָהוּ אוֹ אֶחָד מֵהַנְּבִיאִים

HTV: **They said unto Yeshua, "Some say he is John the Baptist, some say he is Elijah, and some he is Jeremiah, or one of the prophets."**

KJV: And they said, Some *say that thou art* John the Baptist: some, Elias; and others, Jeremias, or one of the prophets.

Matthew 16:15
וַיֹּאמֶר לָהֶם יֵשׁוּעַ אָמְנָם אֵיזֶה הֱיוֹתִי אַתֶּם אוֹמְרִים

HTV: **Yeshua said to them, "In truth, who do you say I am?"**

KJV: He saith unto them, But whom say ye that I am?

Matthew 16:16
וַיַּעַן שִׁמְעוֹן כֵּיפָה אַתָּה הַמָּשִׁיחַ הַבֵּן הָאֱלֹהִים חָי

HTV: **And Simon Peter answered, "You are the Messiah - the son of the living God!"**

Chapter 16

KJV: And Simon Peter answered and said, Thou art the Christ, the Son of the living God.

Matthew 16:17

וַיַּעַן יֵשׁוּעַ וַיֹּאמַר לוֹ אַשְׁרֶיךָ שִׁמְעוֹן בַּר יוֹנָה כִּי הַבָּשָׂר וְהַדָּם לֹא הִגְלָה לְךָ הַזֹּאת כִּי אִם הָאָבִי אֲשֶׁר בַּשָּׁמַיִם

HTV: Yeshua answered and said unto him, "Blessed are you Simon son of Jonah - for flesh and blood has not revealed it to you - but my Father who is in heaven."

KJV: And Jesus answered and said unto him, Blessed art thou, Simon Barjona: for flesh and blood hath not revealed *it* unto thee, but my Father which is in heaven.

Matthew 16:18

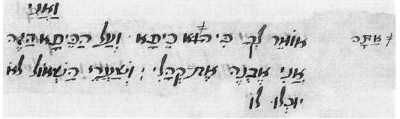
Freiburg Hebrew Manuscript

וַאֲנִי אוֹמֵר לְךָ כִּי אַתָּה כֵיפָא וְעַל הַכֵּיפָא הַזֶּה אֲנִי אֶבְנֶה אֶת-קְהָלִי וְשַׁעֲרֵי הַשְׁאוֹל לֹא יוּכְלוּ לוֹ

HTV: "I say unto you - You are Peter (Keyfa = stone) and upon this stone I will build my House of Prayer - and the gates of Hell shall not prevail against it!"

> Note: The word "keyfa" means stone or rock. So Yeshua is using a play on words, using the name of Peter, *Keyfa* (stone) in Hebrew, *Petros* (stone) in Greek from which his name Peter is derived. This is perinamosia, using the same root word twice in one sentence with two different meanings. "You are **Keyfa** - and upon this **Keyfa** I will build my House of Prayer!"

KJV: And I say also unto thee, That thou art Peter, and upon this rock I will build my church; and the gates of hell shall not prevail against it.

265

Matthew 16:19

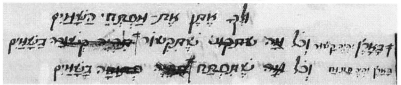

Freiburg Hebrew Manuscript

וּלְךָ אֶתֵּן אֶת-מַפְתְּחֵי הַשָּׁמַיִם וְכֹל שֶׁתִּקְשׁוֹר בָּאָרֶץ יִהְיֶה קָשׁוּר בַּשָּׁמַיִם וְכֹל שֶׁתִּפְתַּח בָּאָרֶץ יִהְיֶה פָּתוּחַ בַּשָּׁמַיִם

HTV: "I will give unto you the keys of heaven. All that you shall forbid on earth shall be forbidden in heaven - and all that you permit on earth will be permitted in heaven."

Note: The Hebrew verb pair "**bind or loosen**" in a spiritual context means to **forbid** or **permit**.

KJV: And I will give unto thee the keys of the kingdom of heaven: and whatsoever thou shalt bind on earth shall be bound in heaven: and whatsoever thou shalt loose on earth shall be loosed in heaven.

Matthew 16:20

וְאָז צִוָּה לְתַלְמִידָיו שֶׁלֹּא יֹאמְרוּ לְשׁוּם אֲשֶׁר הוּא יֵשׁוּעַ הַמָּשִׁיחַ

HTV: Then Yeshua commanded his disciples - they should not say to anyone that he is Yeshua the Messiah.

KJV: Then charged he his disciples that they should tell no man that he was Jesus the Christ.

Matthew 16:21

וּמִכַּאן הִתְחִיל לְגַלּוֹת שֶׁמֻּטָּל עָלָיו לָהֵלֵךְ לִירוּשָׁלַיִם וְלִסְבּוֹל רַבּוֹת רָעוֹת עַל יַד הַזְּקֵנִים וְסוֹפְרִים וְרָאשֵׁי הַכּוֹהֲנִים וּלְהֵרָג וּבַיּוֹם הַשְּׁלִישִׁי לָקוּם מִמֵּתִים

HTV: And from that day, Yeshua began to reveal to his disciples - that it is upon him to go to Jerusalem - to suffer much evil at the hand of the elders, and the scribes, and the chief priests - and to be killed - and to rise from death on the third day.

Chapter 16

KJV: From that time forth began Jesus to shew unto his disciples, how that he must go unto Jerusalem, and suffer many things of the elders and chief priests and scribes, and be killed, and be raised again the third day.

Matthew 16:22

וַיִּקָּחֵהוּ כֵיפָא לְבַדּוֹ וְהִתְחִיל לִגְעָרוֹ וַיֹּאמַר חָלִילָה נָּא חָלִילָה הָאֲדֹנִי אַל תְּבוֹאֲךָ הַזֹּאת

HTV: **And Peter took him aside and began to rebuke him, and he said, "God forbid, please, God forbid! My Lord, God will not let this happen to you!"**

KJV: Then Peter took him, and began to rebuke him, saying, Be it far from thee, Lord: this shall not be unto thee.

Matthew 16:23

אֲשֶׁר הִתְהַפֵּךְ וַיֹּאמֶר לְכֵיפָא סָר מִמֶּנִּי הַשָּׂטָן כִּי אַתָּה לִי לְמוֹקֵשׁ כִּי אֵינְךָ מֵבִין הַדְּבָרִים אֲשֶׁר לֵאלֹהִים כִּי אִם אֲשֶׁר לֶאֱנוֹשִׁים

HTV: **Yeshua *then* turned around and said to Peter "Get away from me, Satan! Because you are a snare to me - Because you do not understand the matters of Elohim - but *"those* of men."**

KJV: But he turned, and said unto Peter, Get thee behind me, Satan: thou art an offence unto me: for thou savourest not the things that be of God, but those that be of men.

Matthew 16:24

וְאָז אָמַר יֵשׁוּעַ לְתַלְמִידָיו אִם מִי יִרְצֶה לִרְדּוֹף אַחֲרֵי הַהוּא יְכַפֵּר אֶת-עַצְמוֹ וְיִטּוֹל אֶת-צְלִיבָתוֹ וְיִרְדְּפֵנִי

HTV: **Then Yeshua said to his disciples, "Whosoever would come after me - must deny himself - take *up* his cross - and follow me."**

KJV: Then said Jesus unto his disciples, If any man will come after me, let him deny himself, and take up his cross, and follow me.

The Hebrew Book of Matthew

Matthew 16:25

כל הרוצה להושיע נפשו יאבד אותה בעדי והמאבד את חייו
בעה"ז בשבילי יושיע נפשו לחיי העה"ב.

Shem Tov Manuscript (STM)

כל הרוצה להושיע נפשו יאבד אותה בעדי והמאבד את חייו
בעהייז בשבילי יושיע נפשו לחיי העהייב.

HTV: "Everyone who wishes to save his life - it will be lost for my sake. He who loses his life in this world for my sake - will save his soul for the life of the world to come."

KJV: For whosoever will save his life shall lose it: and whosoever will lose his life for my sake shall find it.

Matthew 16:26

אֵיזוֹ תוֹעֶלֶת יִצָמָא הָאָדָם אִם יָרְוִיַח אֶת-כֹּל הָעוֹלָם וְבֵין כַּךְ יַפִּיל
אֶת-נַפְשׁוֹ בְנֶזֶק אוֹ אֵיזֶה חִילוּף יִתֵּן הָאָדָם תַּחַת נַפְשׁוֹ

HTV: "What benefit is there for man - if he gains the whole world but loses his soul? What *value* could man exchange for his soul?"

KJV: For what is a man profited, if he shall gain the whole world, and lose his own soul? or what shall a man give in exchange for his soul?

Matthew 16:27

כִּי הַבֵּן הָאָדָם עָתִיד לָבוֹא בִּכְבוֹד אָבִיו יַחַד עִם מַלְאָכָיו וְאָז יִגְמוֹל
לְכֹל אֶחָד וְאֶחָד לְפִי הַמַעֲשָׂיו

HTV: "For the Son of Man shall come in the glory of his Father together with his angels - and shall reward each and every one according to his deeds."

KJV: For the Son of man shall come in the glory of his Father with his angels; and then he shall reward every man according to his works.

Matthew 16:28

בֶּאֱמֶת אֲנִי אוֹמֵר לָכֶם יֵשׁ קְצָת מֵעוֹמְדִים שָׁם אֲשֶׁר לֹא יִטְעֲמוּ אֶת
הַמָוֶת עַד שֶׁיִרְאוּ אֶת-הַבֵּן הָאָדָם לָבוֹא בְמַלְכוּתוֹ

HTV: "Truly, I say to you, there are a few standing here who will not taste death until they see the Son of Man coming in his kingdom."

KJV: Verily I say unto you, There be some standing here, which shall not taste of death, till they see the Son of man coming in his kingdom.

Matthew Chapter 17

Hebrew Text Version (HTV)

¹ After six days, Yeshua took Peter, James, and John his brother - and made them to ascend up to the mountain, just them alone.

² And Yeshua's image was transfigured before them - his face shone as the sun - and his clothing glowed as white as snow!

³ Moses and Elijah appeared and while they were speaking to Yeshua - (STM) They (Moses & Elijah) were revealed to them (the disciples) and they told Yeshua all which would happen to him in Jerusalem. Peter and his companions were asleep. Asleep but not asleep - Awake but not awake. They saw Yeshua's form and the two men with him.

⁴ Then Peter spoke, and said to Yeshua, "My Lord behold! It is good for us to be here and if you desire it - let us make three tabernacles - one for you, one for Moses, and one for Elijah."

⁵ And when he had spoken - a bright cloud overshadowed them - a voice came from the midst of the cloud, and said, "This is my beloved son. In him, I am well pleased - Hear and obey him!"

⁶ When the disciples heard these words - they fell on their faces and they were very much afraid!

⁷ Yeshua came near and touched them - and said to them, "Stand up and do not fear!"

⁸ And after that - they lifted up their eyes - they saw no one except Yeshua.

⁹ And when they came down from the mountain, Yeshua commanded them, saying, "Tell no one this vision until the Son of Man rises from death."

¹⁰ His disciples asked him and said, "Why do the sages say - it is necessary that Elijah comes first?"

¹¹ And Yeshua answered them and said, "Indeed! Elijah *is* come first to fulfill all things."

¹² "Indeed I say to you that Elijah has already come and they did not know him, but did to him whatever they wanted. *Likewise*, the Son of Man will suffer tragedies at their hand."

¹³ Then his disciples understood that Yeshua spoke to them of John the Baptist.

¹⁴ When Yeshua came to the people - there, a man approached him and fell to his knees saying,

¹⁵ He said: "Have mercy on me, Lord, and pity my son because he is terrified of an evil spirit and is very sick - He grinds his teeth, *foams* at his mouth, falls from his place onto the ground, and falls sometimes into the fire and sometimes into water."

¹⁶ "I brought him to your disciples but they were not able to heal him."

17 And Yeshua answered, "Woe! *You* perverse and unbelieving generation! How long shall I be with you? And how long shall I suffer you? Bring him to me."

¹⁸ Yeshua rebuked the demon and he went out of him - the youth was healed in that hour.

¹⁹ The disciples approached Yeshua upset to ask him, "Why were we not able to cast him (the demon) out?"

²⁰ Yeshua said to them, "You who do not believe! In truth, I say to you - if you have faith the size of a mustard seed and say to this mountain - move from here to there - it shall be moved! And no thing (no power) shall be withheld from you!"

²¹ "Indeed, it is true that this type (of demon) will not be cast out except with prayer and fasting."

²² As they walked through Galilee - Yeshua told them, "The Son of Man shall be betrayed into the hands of men!"

²³ And they shall kill him (Son of Man) - and on the third day - he will rise from *the* dead. And they were very grieved!

²⁴ And when Yeshua came into Capernaum - the tax collectors

came to collect the tax - they approached Peter, and said to him, "Your rabbi did not pay the tribute?"

²⁵ And he (Peter) said, "It is true." When he (Peter) came into the house, Yeshua anticipated him and said, "What do you think, Simon (Peter) - from whom do the kings of the earth take the tax and the tribute - from their sons or from others?"

²⁶ And he (Peter) answered, "From others." - Yeshua said to him, "Therefore *their* sons are exempt!"

²⁷ But lest it become an issue for them - He said to Peter - Take yourself down to the sea and cast a fishing hook and fish with it. In the mouth of the first one you catch you will find a silver coin. That you will give for us (for the tribute).

Matthew Chapter 17
HTV with translator notes and KJV comparison

Matthew 17:1

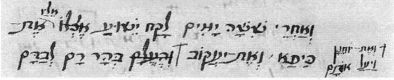

Freiburg Hebrew Manuscript

וְאַחֲרֵי שִׁשָּׁה יָמִים לָקַח יֵשׁוּעַ אֵלָיו אֶת-כֵּיפָא וְאֶת-יַעֲקוֹב וְאֶת-יוֹחָנָן וַיַּעַל אוֹתָם בָּהָר רַק לְבַדָּם

HTV: After six days, Yeshua took Peter, James, and John his brother - and made them to ascend up to the mountain, just them alone.

Note: It appears that Yeshua spiritually transported them into a vision of the mountain where Moses and Elijah appeared to them. Both of these other prophets took their marching orders from Yehovah on Mount Sinai. Is Mount Sinai the Mountain of Transformation? Matthew 17:9 Yeshua describes this incredible experience as a vision.

KJV: And after six days Jesus taketh Peter, James, and John his brother, and bringeth them up into an high mountain apart,

The Hebrew Book of Matthew

Matthew 17:2

וְנֶחֱלַף כְּפִי צוּרָתוֹ בְּעֵינֵיהֶם וְזָהֲרוּ הַפָּנָיו כְּמוֹ הַשֶּׁמֶשׁ וּמַלְבוֹשָׁיו נַעֲשׂוּ לְבָנִים כְּשֶׁלֶג

HTV: **And Yeshua's image was transfigured before them - his face shone as the sun - and his clothing glowed as white as snow!**

KJV: And was transfigured before them: and his face did shine as the sun, and his raiment was white as the light.

Matthew 17:3

אליהם משה ואליהו מדברים עמו והגידו ליש"ו כל מה שיקראהו בירושלם. ופייט'רוס וחביריו היו נרדמים. נים ולא נים תיר ולא תיר. ראו גופו ושני אנשים עמו.

Shem Tov Manuscript

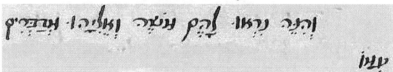

Freiburg Hebrew Manuscript

וְהִנֵּה נִרְאוּ לָהֶם מֹשֶׁה וְאֵלִיָּהוּ מְדַבְּרִים עִמּוֹ

HTV: **Moses and Elijah appeared and while they were speaking to Yeshua - (STM) *They (Moses & Elijah) were revealed to them (the disciples) and <u>they told Yeshua all which would happen to him in Jerusalem. Peter and his companions were asleep. Asleep but not asleep - Awake but not awake. They saw Yeshua's form and the two men with him.</u>**

> *Note: The Greek text has only the first sentence. The Hebrew Gospel (STM) has the rest which is a crucial addition to the narrative of the Mountain of Transfiguration.

KJV: And, behold, there appeared unto them Moses and Elias talking with him.

Matthew 17:4

וַיַּעַן כֵּיפָא וַיֹּאמֶר אֶל יֵשׁוּעַ וְהָאֲדוֹנִי הִנֵּה טוֹב לָנוּ לִהְיוֹת שָׁם וְאִם תִּרְצֶה נַעֲשֶׂה שָׁם שְׁלֹשָׁה אֹהָלִים לְךָ אֶחָד לְמֹשֶׁה אֶחָד וּלְאֵלִיָּהוּ אֶחָד

Chapter 17

HTV: **Then Peter spoke, and said to Yeshua, "My Lord behold! It is good for us to be here and if you desire it - let us make three tabernacles - one for you, one for Moses, and one for Elijah."**

KJV: Then answered Peter, and said unto Jesus, Lord, it is good for us to be here: if thou wilt, let us make here three tabernacles; one for thee, and one for Moses, and one for Elias.

Matthew 17:5

וּבְדַבְּרוֹ הִנֵּה עָנָן בָּהִיר יִהְיֶה סוֹכֵךְ עֲלֵיהֶם וְקוֹל נִתְוַלְדָת מִשָּׁמַיִם וְאוֹמֶרֶת הִנֵּה הַזֶּה בְנִי הֶחָבִיב אֲשֶׁר בּוֹ חָפַצְתִּי שְׁמָעוּהוּ

HTV: **And when he had spoken - a bright cloud overshadowed them - a voice came from the midst of the cloud, and said, "This is my beloved son. In him, I am well pleased - Hear and obey him!"**

KJV: While he yet spake, behold, a bright cloud overshadowed them: and behold a voice out of the cloud, which said, This is my beloved Son, in whom I am well pleased; hear ye him.

Matthew 17:6

וְכַאֲשֶׁר הַתַּלְמִידִים שָׁמְעוּ הָאֵלֶּה דְבָרִים הֵם נָפְלוּ עַל פְּנֵיהֶם וַיִּרְאוּ מְאֹד

HTV: **When the disciples heard these words - they fell on their faces and they were very much afraid!**

KJV: And when the disciples heard *it*, they fell on their face, and were sore afraid.

Matthew 17:7

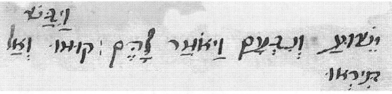

Freiburg Hebrew Manuscript

The Hebrew Book of Matthew

וַיִּגַּשׁ יֵשׁוּעַ וְנִגְעָם וַיֹּאמַר לָהֶם קוּמוּ וְאַל תִּירָאוּ

HTV: Yeshua came near and touched them - and said to them, "Stand up and do not fear!"

KJV: And Jesus came and touched them, and said, Arise, and be not afraid.

Matthew 17:8

וְאַחֲרֵי שֶׁנָשְׂאוּ אֶת-עֵינֵיהֶם לֹא רָאוּ שׁוּם כִּי-אִם לְבַד אֶת יֵשׁוּעַ

HTV: And after that - they lifted up their eyes - they saw no one except Yeshua.

KJV: And when they had lifted up their eyes, they saw no man, save Jesus only.

Matthew 17:9

וּמִשֶׁיָּרְדוּ מֵהָר צִוָּה לָהֶם יֵשׁוּעַ לֵאמוֹר אַל תֹּאמְרוּ לְשׁוּם אֶת-חֲזוֹן
הַזֶּה עַד שֶׁבֶּן הָאָדָם יָקוּם מִמֵּתִים

HTV: And when they came down from the mountain, Yeshua commanded them, saying, "Tell no one this vision until the Son of Man rises from death."

KJV: And as they came down from the mountain, Jesus charged them, saying, Tell the vision to no man, until the Son of man be risen again from the dead.

Matthew 17:10

Freiburg Hebrew Manuscript

וַיִּשְׁאֲלוּ אוֹתוֹ הַתַּלְמִידָיו וַיֹּאמְרוּ מָה נָא שֶׁאוֹמְרִים הַסוֹפְרִים שֶׁצָּרִיךְ
שֶׁאֵלִיָּהוּ קוֹדֶם יָבוֹא

Chapter 17

HTV: **His disciples asked him and said, "Why do the sages say - it is necessary that Elijah comes first?"**

> Note: See Malachi 4:5-6, "Behold I will send you Elijah before the coming of the great and dreadful day of Yehovah!" Isaiah 40:3, "The voice of one crying in the wilderness."
>
> In John 1:23, when John the Baptist was questioned as to what he would say of himself, "I am the voice of one crying in the wilderness, make straight the way of Yehovah!" All Hebrews believed Elijah would announce the Messiah - Yeshua said John was Elijah.

KJV: And his disciples asked him, saying, Why then say the scribes that Elias must first come?

Matthew 17:11

וַיַּעַן לָהֶם וַיֹּאמַר אֵלִיָּהוּ עָתִיד לָבוֹא וִיקַיֵּים אֶת כֹּל דְּבָרִים

HTV: **And Yeshua answered them and said, "Indeed! Elijah *is* come first to fulfill all things."**

KJV: And Jesus answered and said unto them, Elias truly shall first come, and restore all things.

Matthew 17:12

אָמְנָם אֲנִי אוֹמֵר לָכֶם שֶׁאֵלִיָּהוּ כְּבָר בָּא וְלֹא יְדָעוּהוּ אֲבָל עָשׂוּ בוֹ כָּל שֶׁיִּרְצוּ וְכֵן אַךְ הַבֵּן הָאָדָם יִסְבּוֹל עַל יְדָם הַצָּרוֹת

HTV: **"Indeed I say to you that Elijah has already come and they did not know him, but did to him whatever they wanted. *Likewise*, the Son of Man will suffer tragedies at their hand."**

KJV: But I say unto you, That Elias is come already, and they knew him not, but have done unto him whatsoever they listed. Likewise shall also the Son of man suffer of them.

Matthew 17:13

וְאָז הֵבִינוּ תַלְמִידָיו אֲשֶׁר דִּבֵּר לָהֶם מִיוֹחָנָן הַטּוֹבֵל

HTV: **Then his disciples understood that Yeshua spoke to them of John the Baptist.**

The Hebrew Book of Matthew

KJV: Then the disciples understood that he spake unto them of John the Baptist.

Matthew 17:14

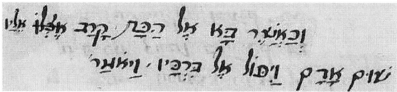
Freiburg Hebrew Manuscript

וְכַאֲשֶׁר בָּא אֶל הַכַּת קָרַב אֵלָיו שׁוּם אָדָם וַיִּפֹּל אֶל בִּרְכָּיו וַיֹּאמַר

HTV: **When Yeshua came to the people - there, a man approached him and fell to his knees saying,**

> Note: In Luke 9:37 it says, "on the next day when they were come down from the mountain, many people met them."

KJV: And when they were come to the multitude, there came to him a *certain* man, kneeling down to him, and saying,

Matthew 17:15

הָאֲדוֹנִי חוֹנֵן נָא עַל בְּנִי כִּי הוּא מְשֻׁוגָּע וּמְאֹד נִתְעַצֵּב כִּי נוֹפֵל הַרְבֵּה פְּעָמִים בָּאֵשׁ וְהַרְבֵּה פְּעָמִים בְּמַיִם

HTV: **He said: "Have mercy on me, Lord, and pity my son because he is terrified of an evil spirit and is very sick - He grinds his teeth, *foams* at his mouth, falls from his place onto the ground, and falls sometimes into the fire and sometimes into water."**

KJV: Lord, have mercy on my son: for he is lunatick, and sore vexed: for ofttimes he falleth into the fire, and oft into the water.

Matthew 17:16

וַהֲבֵאתִיהוּ אֶל הַתַּלְמִידֶיךָ וְלֹא יָכְלוּ לְרַפֵּא אוֹתוֹ

HTV: **"I brought him to your disciples but they were not able to heal him."**

KJV: And I brought him to thy disciples, and they could not cure him.

Matthew 17:17

וַיַּעַן יֵשׁוּעַ הוֹי הַדּוֹר בִּלְתִּי מַאֲמִין עַד מָתַי אֶהְיֶה אֶצְלְכֶם וְעַד מָתַי אֶסְבּוֹל אֶתְכֶם הַקְרִיבוּהוּ אֵלַי

HTV: And Yeshua answered, "Woe! *You* perverse and unbelieving generation! How long shall I be with you? And how long shall I suffer you? Bring him to me."

KJV: Then Jesus answered and said, O faithless and perverse generation, how long shall I be with you? how long shall I suffer you? bring him hither to me.

Matthew 17:18

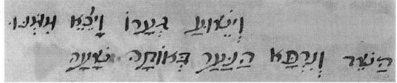

Freiburg Hebrew Manuscript

הָעַשׂ הַתּוֹאָב רַעֲנָה אָפְרָנוֹ דְּשֶׁה וּגְמִמּ אִצֵּי וְרַעֵג עַוֹּשִׂין

HTV: Yeshua rebuked the demon and he went out of him - the youth was healed in that hour.

KJV: And Jesus rebuked the devil; and he departed out of him: and the child was cured from that very hour.

Matthew 17:19

וַיִּקְרְבוּ הַתַּלְמִידִים אֶל יֵשׁוּעַ בַּחֲשַׁאי וַיֹּאמְרוּ לָמָה נָא אֲנַחְנוּ לֹא נוּכַל לְגָרְשׁוֹ

HTV: The disciples approached Yeshua upset to ask him, "Why were we not able to cast him (the demon) out?"

KJV: Then came the disciples to Jesus apart, and said, Why could not we cast him out?

Matthew 17:20

וַיֹּאמֶר לָהֶם יֵשׁוּעַ מִפְּנֵי שֶׁאֵינְכֶם מַאֲמִינִים בֶּאֱמֶת אֲנִי אוֹמֵר לָכֶם אִם תִּהְיֶה לָכֶם אֱמוּנָה כִּכְמוּת הַגַּרְעִין חַרְדֵּל וְתֹאמְרוּ לָהָר הַזֶּה הִתְנַטֵּל מִשָּׁם לְשָׁם וְיִתְנַטֵּל וְלֹא יִהְיֶה לָכֶם כְּלוּם נִמְנַע

The Hebrew Book of Matthew

HTV: **Yeshua said to them, "You who do not believe! In truth, I say to you - if you have faith the size of a mustard seed and say to this mountain - move from here to there - it shall be moved! And no thing (no power) shall be withheld from you!"**

KJV: And Jesus said unto them, Because of your unbelief: for verily I say unto you, If ye have faith as a grain of mustard seed, ye shall say unto this mountain, Remove hence to yonder place; and it shall remove; and nothing shall be impossible unto you.

Matthew 17:21

אָמְנָם הַסּוּג הַזֶּה לֹא יְגֹרֵשׁ כִּי אִם בַּתְּפִלָּה וְצוֹם

HTV: **"Indeed, it is true that this type (of demon) will not be cast out except with prayer and fasting."**

KJV: Howbeit this kind goeth not out but by prayer and fasting.

Matthew 17:22

בְּהָלְכָם בְּגָלִילָה אָמַר לָהֶם יֵשׁוּעַ בֶּן הָאָדָם יִמָּסֵר בְּיַד אֱנוֹשִׁים

HTV: **As they walked through Galilee - Yeshua told them, "The Son of Man shall be betrayed into the hands of men!"**

KJV: And while they abode in Galilee, Jesus said unto them, The Son of man shall be betrayed into the hands of men:

Matthew 17:23

וַיְהָרְגוּהוּ וּבַיּוֹם הַשְּׁלִישִׁי יָקוּם מִמֵּתִים וְנִתְקַדְּרוּ מְאֹד

HTV: **And they shall kill him (Son of Man) - and on the third day - he will rise from *the* dead. And they were very grieved!**

KJV: And they shall kill him, and the third day he shall be raised again. And they were exceeding sorry.

Chapter 17

Matthew 17:24

וּמִשֶּׁבָּא בִכְפַר-נָחוּם אָז קָרְבוּ הַנּוֹגְשִׂים אֶת-דַּרְכְּמוֹן הַמַּס אֶל כֵּיפָא וַיֹּאמְרוּ לוֹ הֲרַבּוֹנְכֶם הַאִם אֵינוֹ מְשַׁלֵּם אֶת-דַּרְכְּמוֹן הַמַּס

HTV: And when Yeshua came into Capernaum - the tax collectors came to collect the tax - they approached Peter, and said to him, "Your rabbi did not pay the tribute?"

KJV: And when they were come to Capernaum, they that received tribute *money* came to Peter, and said, Doth not your master pay tribute?

Matthew 17:25

וַיֹּאמֶר יְהֵן וְכַאֲשֶׁר בָּא בַּבַּיִת הִנֵּה קִדֵּם לוֹ יֵשׁוּעַ וַיֹּאמַר מָה נִרְאֶה לְךָ שִׁמְעוֹן מִמִּי נָא לוֹקְחִים הַמַּלְכֵי הָאָרֶץ אֶת-הַמַּס וְאֶת-הַכַּרְגָא מִבְּנֵיהֶם אוֹ מֵאֲחֵרִים

HTV: And he (Peter) said, "It is true." When he (Peter) came into the house, Yeshua anticipated him and said, "What do you think, Simon (Peter) - from whom do the kings of the earth take the tax and the tribute - from their sons or from others?"

KJV: He saith, Yes. And when he was come into the house, Jesus prevented him, saying, What thinkest thou, Simon? of whom do the kings of the earth take custom or tribute? of their own children, or of strangers?

Matthew 17:26

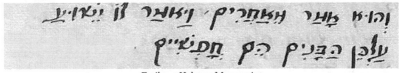
Freiburg Hebrew Manuscript

וְהוּא אָמַר מֵאֲחֵרִים וַיֹּאמֶר לוֹ יֵשׁוּעַ עַל-כֵּן הַבָּנִים הֵם חָפְשִׁיִּים

HTV: And he (Peter) answered, "From others." - Yeshua said to him, "Therefore *their* sons are exempt!"

Note: Yeshua seems to be saying that the sons of kings receive tribute - but the sons of God receive wealth from Yehovah. To emphasize this he makes a silver coin miraculously appear.

279

See Deuteronomy 8:18, "Remember Yehovah your God, for it is He that gives you power to get wealth, that He may establish His covenant... and it shall be if you do not forget your Yehovah."

KJV: Peter saith unto him, Of strangers. Jesus saith unto him, Then are the children free.

Matthew 17:27

אַךְ שֶׁלֹּא נִהְיֶה לָהֶם לְמוֹקֵשׁ לֵךְ-לְךָ אֶל הַיָּם וְהַשְׁלִיךְ אֶת-הַחַכָּה וְאֶת-הַדָּג אֲשֶׁר יַעֲלֶה בָרִאשׁוֹנָה קַח אוֹתוֹ וּמִשֶּׁיִּפָּתַח פִּיהוּ תִּמְצָא לָטֵר אֲשֶׁר תִּקַּח וְתִתֵּן לָהֶם בַּעֲדִי וּבַעֲדֶךָ

HTV: **But lest it become an issue for them - He said to Peter - Take yourself down to the sea and cast a fishing hook and fish with it. In the mouth of the first one you catch you will find a silver coin. That you will give for us (for the tribute).**

KJV: Notwithstanding, lest we should offend them, go thou to the sea, and cast an hook, and take up the fish that first cometh up; and when thou hast opened his mouth, thou shalt find a piece of money: that take, and give unto them for me and thee.

Matthew Chapter 18

Hebrew Text Version (HTV)

¹ At that time, the disciples approached Yeshua and they said, "Who do you think to be the greatest in the kingdom of heaven?"

² And Yeshua called to one young boy and stood him among them (the disciples).

³ And Yeshua said, "Truly, I say to you, unless you repent and become like this boy - you will not enter the kingdom of heaven!"

4 "All that will humble themselves like this boy - will be the greater in the kingdom of heaven."

5 "And whoever will receive one child like this - in my name

Chapter 18

- he receives me."

6 "And whoever will be a snare for one of these children - that believe in me - it would be better that a millstone be hung around his neck and he be thrown into the depth of the sea!"

7 "Woe to the world for the presence of the snare! Snares will come of necessity - but truly - Woe to the man through whose hand comes the snare!"

8 "But if your hand or foot shall become a snare to you - then cast it from you! Because it is much better for you to go through life without a hand *or* foot - than to have two hands and two feet and *be* cast into eternal fire!"

9 "But if your eye shall become a snare to you - gouge it out - and throw it away from you! Because it is better for you that you come to everlasting life than - for the sake of two eyes - be cast into the fire."

10 "Take heed that you do not scorn any of these little ones - because I say - in heaven their angels see continually the face of my Father - who is in heaven."

11 "For the Son of Man came to save that which was lost."

12 "What do you think - If a man has a hundred sheep, and one of them goes astray? Does he not leave the ninety-nine in the mountains - and go seek for the one gone astray?"

13 "If he should find it - truly, I say to you - much more shall he rejoice over it - than over the ninety-nine which did not go astray."

14 "Likewise, it is not the will of your Father - who is in heaven - that the least of these should perish."

15 "If your brother should sin against you - go and rebuke him privately. If he will listen to you - *then* you have regained your brother."

16 "If he will not listen to you - take with you one or two *others* - so that by the mouth of two or three witnesses all things will stand *confirmed*."

17 "If he will not listen to them either - *then* tell it to the congregation. If he will not listen to the congregation - then let him be to you as a gentile or tax collector."

18 "Truly I tell you (my disciples), all that you forbid on earth, *is* forbidden in heaven - and all you permit on earth *is* permitted in heaven."

¹⁹ "Furthermore, I tell you, if two of you agree upon peace on earth among yourselves about a matter - it will be for you whatever you ask for it to be - from my Father in heaven."

²⁰ "Where two or three are gathered in my name, there I will be with them."

²¹ Then Peter approached Yeshua to ask, "My Lord, how many times shall my brother sin against me and I forgive him? Must it be up to seven times?"

²² Yeshua said to him, "I do not say to you - up to seven times - but seven times seventy!"

²³ "The kingdom of heaven is like a man who was king and wanted to reckon with his servants."

²⁴ "When he began to calculate - he came to one who owed him ten thousand talents."

²⁵ "When he (the debtor) had nothing in his hand to pay - his master commanded they sell him, his wife, children and all that is his - in order to pay."

²⁶ "And that servant fell on his face and begged him, saying, "Have mercy with me - and I will repay you everything!"

²⁷ "And his Lord had mercy on him - forgave all the debt - and let him go!"

²⁸ "That *same* servant went out and found one of his fellow servants - who owed him a hundred mites (pennies) - He took him by the throat and strangled him, saying - 'Pay what you owe!' "

²⁹ "And that servant fell before him and begged him saying, "Have mercy on me - and I will repay you everything!' "

³⁰ "However, he did not pardon him - but cast him into prison - until he should repay the debt."

³¹ The servants of the king saw that which he did.

They were very angry! - They went and told their Lord."

³² "After that the king summoned him - and said unto him, 'Evil servant!' - I pardoned all your debt because you implored me."

³³ "Should you not also have pardoned the servant - as I have pardoned you?"

³⁴ "And the Lord (King) was angry and delivered him to the torturers until he should repay him all the debt!"

³⁵ "So likewise shall my heavenly Father do to you - if each of you - do not forgive your brother - with all your heart!"

Matthew Chapter 18
HTV with translator notes and KJV comparison

Matthew 18:1

Freiburg Hebrew Manuscript

בְּאוֹתָהּ הַשָּׁעָה נָגְשׁוּ תַלְמִידִים לְיֵשׁוּעַ וַיֹּאמְרוּ אֶת מִי אַתָּה חוֹשֵׁב הֱיוֹת יוֹתֵר גָּדוֹל בְּמַלְכוּת הַשָּׁמַיִם

HTV: **At that time, the disciples approached Yeshua and they said, "Who do you think to be the greatest in the kingdom of heaven?"**

KJV: At the same time came the disciples unto Jesus, saying, Who is the greatest in the kingdom of heaven?

Matthew 18:2

וַיִּקְרָא יֵשׁוּעַ אֵלָיו שׁוּם תִּינוֹק וְהֶעֱמִידֵהוּ בְּתוֹכָם

HTV: **And Yeshua called to one young boy and stood him among them (the disciples).**

KJV: And Jesus called a little child unto him, and set him in the midst of them,

Matthew 18:3

וַיֹּאמֶר בֶּאֱמֶת אֲנִי אוֹמֵר לָכֶם לוּלֵי תָשׁוּבוּ וְתֵעָשׂוּ דוֹמִים לַתִּינוֹקִים לֹא תָבוֹאוּ בְּמַלְכוּת הַשָּׁמַיִם

HTV: **And Yeshua said, "Truly, I say to you, unless you repent and become like this boy - you will not enter the kingdom of heaven!"**

KJV: And said, Verily I say unto you, Except ye be converted, and become as little children, ye shall not enter into the kingdom of heaven.

Matthew 18:4

וְכָל שֶׁיַּשְׁפִּיל עַצְמוֹ כְּתִינוֹק הַזֶּה הוּא יִהְיֶה הַיּוֹתֵר גָּדוֹל בְּמַלְכוּת הַשָּׁמַיִם

HTV: **"All that will humble themselves like this boy - will be the greater in the kingdom of heaven."**

KJV: Whosoever therefore shall humble himself as this little child, the same is greatest in the kingdom of heaven.

Matthew 18:5

Freiburg Hebrew Manuscript

וַאֲשֶׁר יְקַבֵּל אֶחָד תִּינוֹק כָּזֶה בִּשְׁמִי הַהוּא מְקַבֵּל אוֹתִי

HTV: **"And whoever will receive one child like this - in my name - he receives me."**

KJV: And whoso shall receive one such little child in my name receiveth me.

Matthew 18:6

וַאֲשֶׁר יִהְיֶה לְאֶחָד מֵאֵלֶּה תִּינוֹקִים לְמוֹקֵשׁ הַמַּאֲמִינִים בִּי הִנֵּה יִהְיֶה לוֹ טוֹב שֶׁאֶבֶן הָרֵחַיִם תִּתָּלֶה עַל צַוָּארוֹ וְיֻשְׁלַךְ בְּעוֹמֶק הַיָּם

HTV: **"And whoever will be a snare for one of these children - that believe in me - it would be better that a millstone be hung around his neck and he be thrown into the depth of the sea!"**

KJV: But whoso shall offend one of these little ones which believe in me, it were better for him that a millstone were hanged about his neck, and *that* he were drowned in the depth of the sea.

Chapter 18

Matthew 18:7

Freiburg Hebrew Manuscript

הוֹי לָעוֹלָם מִפְּנֵי הַמּוֹקֵשׁ כִּי צָרִיךְ שֶׁיָּבוֹאוּ מֻקְשִׁים אֲמָנָם הוֹי לְאוֹתוֹ הָאָדָם אֲשֶׁר עַל יָדוֹ יָבוֹא מוֹקֵשׁ

HTV: "Woe to the world for the presence of the snare! Snares will come of necessity - but truly - Woe to the man through whose hand comes the snare!"

KJV: Woe unto the world because of offences! for it must needs be that offences come; but woe to that man by whom the offence cometh!

Matthew 18:8

וְאִם יָדְךָ אוֹ רַגְלְךָ תִּהְיֶה לְךָ לְמוֹקֵשׁ חֲתָכָהּ וְהַשְׁלֵךְ מִמְּךָ כִּי יוֹתֵר טוֹב לְךָ בִּלְתִּי יָד וּבִלְתִּי רֶגֶל לָבוֹא לַחַיִּים מִשֶּׁתִּהְיֶינָה לְךָ שְׁתֵּי יָדַיִם וּשְׁתֵּי רַגְלַיִם וְהַשְׁלֵחַ בָּאֵשׁ עוֹלָמִי

HTV: "But if your hand or foot shall become a snare to you- then cast it from you! Because it is much better for you to go through life without a hand *or* foot - than to have two hands and two feet and *be* cast into eternal fire!"

KJV: Wherefore if thy hand or thy foot offend thee, cut them off, and cast *them* from thee: it is better for thee to enter into life halt or maimed, rather than having two hands or two feet to be cast into everlasting fire.

Matthew 18:9

וְאִם עֵינְךָ תִּהְיֶה לְךָ לְמוֹקֵשׁ נָקְרָהּ וְהַשְׁלִיךְ מִמְּךָ כִּי לְךָ יוֹתֵר טוֹב שֶׁתִּהְיֶה לְךָ עַיִן אַחַת וְתָבוֹא לַחַיִּים עוֹלָמִים מִשְּׁתֵּי עֵינֶיךָ וְהַשְׁלֵחַ לְגֵיהִנֹּם הָאֵשׁ

HTV: "But if your eye shall become a snare to

The Hebrew Book of Matthew

you - gouge it out - and throw it away from you! Because it is better for you that you come to everlasting life than - for the sake of two eyes - be cast into the fire."

KJV: And if thine eye offend thee, pluck it out, and cast *it* from thee: it is better for thee to enter into life with one eye, rather than having two eyes to be cast into hell fire.

Matthew 18:10

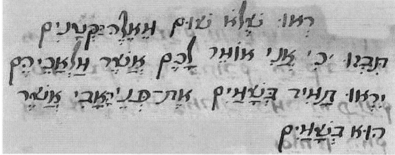

Freiburg Hebrew Manuscript

רְאוּ שֶׁלֹּא שׁוּם מֵאֵלֶּה הַקְּטַנִּים תִּבְזוּ כִּי אֲנִי אוֹמֵר לָכֶם אֲשֶׁר מַלְאָכֵיהֶם יִרְאוּ תָמִיד בְּשָׁמַיִם אֶת-פְּנֵי הָאָבִי אֲשֶׁר הוּא בְשָׁמַיִם

HTV: **"Take heed that you do not scorn any of these little ones - because I say - in heaven their angels see continually the face of my Father - who is in heaven."**

KJV: Take heed that ye despise not one of these little ones; for I say unto you, That in heaven their angels do always behold the face of my Father which is in heaven.

Matthew 18:11

כִּי בֶן הָאָדָם בָּא לְהוֹשִׁיעַ מָה שֶׁאָבַד

HTV: **"For the Son of Man came to save that which was lost."**

KJV: For the Son of man is come to save that which was lost.

Matthew 18:12

מַה נִּרְאֶה לָכֶם אִם תִּהְיֶינָה לְשׂוּם אָדָם מֵאָה צֹאן וְתִתְעֶה אַחַת מֵהֶן הֲלֹא הוּא יַנִּיחַ אֶת-תִּשְׁעִים וְתִשְׁעָה בֶּהָרִים וְיֵלֵךְ לְבַקֵּשׁ אֲשֶׁר תִּהְיֶה תּוֹעָה

HTV: "What do you think - If a man has a hundred sheep, and one of them goes astray? Does he not leave the ninety-nine in the mountains - and go seek for the one gone astray?"

KJV: How think ye? if a man have an hundred sheep, and one of them be gone astray, doth he not leave the ninety and nine, and goeth into the mountains, and seeketh that which is gone astray?

Matthew 18:13

וְאִם יִקְרֶה שֶׁיִּמְצָא אוֹתָהּ בֶּאֱמֶת אֲנִי אוֹמֵר לָכֶם שֶׁיּוֹתֵר יִשְׂמַח עָלֶיהָ מֵעַל תִּשְׁעִים וְתִשְׁעָה אֲשֶׁר לֹא תָעוּ

HTV: "If he should find it - truly, I say to you - much more shall he rejoice over it - than over the ninety-nine which did not go astray."

KJV: And if so be that he find it, verily I say unto you, he rejoiceth more of that *sheep*, than of the ninety and nine which went not astray.

Matthew 18:14

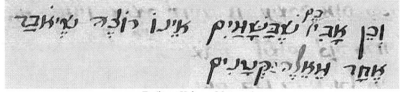
Freiburg Hebrew Manuscript

וְכֵן אֲבִיכֶם שֶׁבַּשָּׁמַיִם אֵינוֹ רוֹצֶה שֶׁיֹּאבַד אֶחָד מֵאֵלֶּה הַקְּטַנִּים

HTV: "Likewise, it is not the will of your Father - who is in heaven - that the least of these should perish."

KJV: Even so it is not the will of your Father which is in heaven, that one of these little ones should perish.

Matthew 18:15

וְאִם אָחִיךָ יֶחֱטָא לְךָ לֵךְ וְהוֹכִיחוֹ בֵּינוֹ וּבֵינְךָ לְבַד וְאִם יִשְׁמַע אוֹתְךָ אַתָּה הִרְוַחְתָּ אֶת-אָחִיךָ

HTV: "If your brother should sin against you - go and rebuke him privately. If he will listen to you - *then* **you have regained your brother."**

KJV: Moreover if thy brother shall trespass against thee, go and tell him his fault between thee and him alone: if he shall hear thee, thou hast gained thy brother.

Matthew 18:16

וְאִם לֹא יִשְׁמַע אוֹתְךָ קַח אִתְּךָ עוֹד אֶחָד אוֹ שְׁנַיִם כְּדֵי שֶׁבְּפִי הַשְּׁנַיִם אוֹ הַשְּׁלֹשָׁה עֵדִים יַעֲמוֹד כֹּל הַדָּבָר

HTV: "If he will not listen to you - take with you one or two *others* **- so that by the mouth of two or three witnesses all things will stand** *confirmed***."**

KJV: But if he will not hear *thee, then* take with thee one or two more, that in the mouth of two or three witnesses every word may be established.

Matthew 18:17

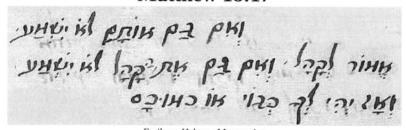
Freiburg Hebrew Manuscript

וְאִם גַּם אוֹתָם לֹא יִשְׁמַע אֱמוֹר לַקָּהָל וְאִם גַּם אֶת הַקָּהָל לֹא יִשְׁמַע וְאָז יְהִי לְךָ כְּגוֹי אוֹ כמוכס

HTV: "If he will not listen to them either - *then* **tell it to the congregation. If he will not listen to the congregation - then let him be to you as a gentile or tax collector."**

Chapter 18

Note: Jews did not associate with tax collectors since they took their money on behalf of the hated Romans, nor did they associate with gentiles to avoid their pagan beliefs and practices.

In short, if a brother will not resolve issues with you God's way then he is no longer a brother.

KJV: And if he shall neglect to hear them, tell *it* unto the church: but if he neglect to hear the church, let him be unto thee as an heathen man and a publican.

Matthew 18:18

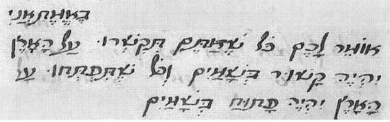

Freiburg Hebrew Manuscript

בֶּאֱמֶת אֲנִי אוֹמֵר לָכֶם כֹּל שֶׁאַתֶּם תִּקְשְׁרוּ עַל הָאָרֶץ יִהְיֶה קָשׁוּר בְּשָׁמַיִם וְכֹל שֶׁתִּפְתְּחוּ עַל הָאָרֶץ יִהְיֶה פָּתוּחַ בְּשָׁמַיִם

HTV: **"Truly I tell you (my disciples), all that you forbid on earth, *is* forbidden in heaven - and all you permit on earth *is* permitted in heaven."**

Note: John 14:17, "The Spirit of Truth... dwells with you and shall be in you." See also Psalm 119:89 on the permanence of God's commandments, Jer 31:33 "Torah written in your heart." **This is a power given only to the disciples who have the Spirit of Truth within them**.

They would therefore know and never contradict God's will. The misinterpretation of this verse has resulted in assuming the authority of God for ungodly pogroms, crusades, and inquisitions.

KJV: Verily I say unto you, Whatsoever ye shall bind on earth shall be bound in heaven: and whatsoever ye shall loose on earth shall be loosed in heaven.

Matthew 18:19

וְעוֹד אֲנִי אוֹמֵר לָכֶם אִם שְׁנַיִם מִכֶּם יַסְכִּימוּ בָּאָרֶץ בֵּינֵיהֶם עַל הַדָּבָר יִהְיֶה שֶׁיִּהְיֶה אֲשֶׁר יִשְׁאֲלוּ יִהְיֶה לָהֶם מֵאָבִי שֶׁבַּשָּׁמַיִם

HTV: **"Furthermore, I tell you, if two of you agree upon peace on earth among yourselves about a matter - it will be for you whatever you ask for it to be - from my Father in heaven."**

KJV: Again I say unto you, That if two of you shall agree on earth as touching any thing that they shall ask, it shall be done for them of my Father which is in heaven.

Matthew 18:20

Freiburg Hebrew Manuscript

בְּמָקוֹם שֶׁשְׁנַיִם אוֹ שְׁלֹשָׁה יִהְיוּ נִקְבָּצִים בִּשְׁמִי שָׁם אֶהְיֶה בְּתוֹכָם

HTV: **"Where two or three are gathered in my name, there I will be with them."**

> Note: "My Name" - certainly refers to that of Yeshua, the Son of God, who has been given all authority upon heaven and earth, see Matthew 28:18. But also to the name of our Father.

KJV: For where two or three are gathered together in my name, there am I in the midst of them.

Matthew 18:21

אָז קָרַב כֵּיפָא אֶל יֵשׁוּעַ וַיֹּאמַר הָאֲדוֹנִי כַּמָה נָא פְּעָמִים יֶחֱטָא הָאָחִי בִי וְאֶסְלַח לוֹ הַאִם עַד שִׁבְעָה פְּעָמִים

HTV: **Then Peter approached Yeshua to ask, "My Lord, how many times shall my brother sin against me and I forgive him? Must it be up to seven times?"**

KJV: Then came Peter to him, and said, Lord, how oft shall my brother sin against me, and I forgive him? till seven times?

Matthew 18:22

וַיֹּאמֶר לוֹ יֵשׁוּעַ אֵינִי אוֹמֵר לְךָ עַד שִׁבְעָה פְּעָמִים כִּי אִם שִׁבְעָתַיִם וְשִׁבְעָה

HTV: **Yeshua said to him, "I do not say to you - up to seven times - but seven times seventy!"**

KJV: Jesus saith unto him, I say not unto thee, Until seven times: but, Until seventy times seven.

Matthew 18:23

Freiburg Hebrew Manuscript

לְפִיכָךְ מַלְכוּת הַשָּׁמַיִם נִמְשְׁלָה לְאָדָם הַמֶּלֶךְ אֲשֶׁר רָצָה לְחַשֵּׁב עִם עֲבָדָיו

HTV: **"The kingdom of heaven is like a man who was king and wanted to reckon with his servants."**

KJV: Therefore is the kingdom of heaven likened unto a certain king, which would take account of his servants.

Matthew 18:24

וְכַאֲשֶׁר הִתְחִיל לְחַשֵּׁב בָּא אֶחָד אֵלָיו אֲשֶׁר יְחַיֵּיב לוֹ עֲשָׂרָה אַלְפֵי כִּכָּר

HTV: **"When he began to calculate - he came to one who owed him ten thousand talents."**

KJV: And when he had begun to reckon, one was brought unto him, which owed him ten thousand talents.

Matthew 18:25

וְכַאֲשֶׁר יָדוֹ אֵינָה מַשֶּׂגֶת לְשַׁלֵּם צִוָּה אֲדוֹנוֹ שֶׁיִּמְכּוֹר אֶת-אִשְׁתּוֹ וְאֶת בָּנָיו וְכֹל אֲשֶׁר לוֹ וַיְשַׁלֵּם

HTV: **"When he (the debtor) had nothing in his hand to pay - his master commanded they sell him, his wife, children and all that is his - in order to pay."**

The Hebrew Book of Matthew

KJV: But forasmuch as he had not to pay, his lord commanded him to be sold, and his wife, and children, and all that he had, and payment to be made.

Matthew 18:26

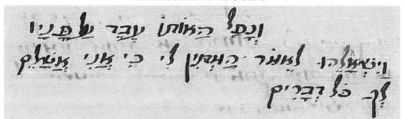

Freiburg Hebrew Manuscript

וְנָפַל הָאוֹתוֹ עֶבֶד עַל פָּנָיו וַיִּשְׁאַלֵהוּ לֵאמֹר הַמְתִּין לִי כִּי אֲנִי אֲשַׁלֵּם לְךָ כֹּל דְּבָרִים

HTV: "And that servant fell on his face and begged him, saying, "Have mercy with me - and I will repay you everything!"

KJV: The servant therefore fell down, and worshipped him, saying, Lord, have patience with me, and I will pay thee all.

Matthew 18:27

וַחֲנָנוּ אֲדוֹנוֹ וַעֲזָבוֹ וַיִּסְלַח לוֹ כֹּל חוֹבָה

HTV: "And his Lord had mercy on him - forgave all the debt - and let him go!"

KJV: Then the lord of that servant was moved with compassion, and loosed him, and forgave him the debt.

Matthew 18:28

וַיֵּצֵא הָעֶבֶד הַהוּא וַיִּמְצָא אֶחָד מֵעוֹבְדִים עִמּוֹ אֲשֶׁר יְחַיֵּיב לוֹ מֵאָה זוּזִים וְהֶחֱזִיקוֹ וַחֲנָקוֹ לֵאמֹר שַׁלֵּם שֶׁאַתָּה מְחַיֵּיב

HTV: "That *same* servant went out and found one of his fellow servants - who owed him a hundred mites (pennies) - He took him by the throat and strangled him, saying - 'Pay what you owe!' "

KJV: But the same servant went out, and found one of his fellow servants, which owed him an hundred pence: and he laid hands on him, and took *him* by the throat, saying, Pay me that thou owest.

Matthew 18:29

וַיִּפֹּל הָאוֹתוֹ עֶבֶד לְפָנָיו וַיִּשְׁאָלֵהוּ וַיֹּאמַר הַמְתִּין נָא וַאֲנִי אֲשַׁלֵּם לְךָ כֹּל דְּבָרִים

HTV: "And that servant fell before him and begged him saying, "Have mercy on me - and I will repay you everything!' "

KJV: And his fellow servant fell down at his feet, and besought him, saying, Have patience with me, and I will pay thee all.

Matthew 18:30

וְהוּא לֹא רָצָה כִּי אִם הָלַךְ וְהִשְׁלִיכוֹ בְּבֵית אֲסִירִים עַד שֶׁיְּשַׁלֵּם לוֹ אֶת-חוֹבָה

HTV: "However, he did not pardon him - but cast him into prison - until he should repay the debt."

KJV: And he would not: but went and cast him into prison, till he should pay the debt.

Matthew 18:31

Freiburg Hebrew Manuscript

וְהָעוֹבְדִים עִמּוֹ רָאוּ כֹּל מָה שֶׁיִּהְיֶה וְנִתְקַדְּרוּ מְאוֹד וַיָּבוֹאוּ וְהִגִּידוּ לַאֲדוֹנָם מָה שֶׁהָיָה

HTV: **The servants of the king saw that which he did. They were very angry! - They went and told their Lord."**

KJV: So when his fellow servants saw what was done, they were very sorry, and came and told unto their lord all that was done.

Matthew 18:32

וְאָז קְרָאוֹ הָאֲדוֹנוֹ וַיֹּאמַר לוֹ הָעֶבֶד רָע הִנֵּה סָלַחְתִּי לְךָ כֹּל חוֹבָה כִּי שְׁאַלְתָּנִי

HTV: "After that the king summoned him - and said unto him, 'Evil servant!' - I pardoned all your debt because you implored me."

KJV: Then his lord, after that he had called him, said unto him, O thou wicked servant, I forgave thee all that debt, because thou desiredst me:

Matthew 18:33

הֲלֹא יִהְיֶה רָאוּי שֶׁתְּחַנֵּן עַל הָעוֹבֵד אִתְּךָ כְּמוֹ גַם אֲנִי חָנַנְתִּי עָלֶיךָ

HTV: "Should you not also have pardoned the servant - as I have pardoned you?"

KJV: Shouldest not thou also have had compassion on thy fellow servant, even as I had pity on thee?

Matthew 18:34

וַיִּחַר הָאֲדוֹנוֹ וַיִּסְרֵהוּ לְשׁוֹטְרִים הַמְעַנִּים עַד שֶׁיְּשַׁלֵּם לוֹ כֹּל חוֹבָה

HTV: "And the Lord (King) was angry and delivered him to the torturers until he should repay him all the debt!"

KJV: And his lord was wroth, and delivered him to the tormentors, till he should pay all that was due unto him.

Matthew 18:35

וּכְמוֹ כֵן יַעֲשֶׂה לָכֶם גַּם הָאָבִי הַשְּׁמֵימִי אִם לֹא תִסְלְחוּ כֹּל אֶחָד וְאֶחָד לְאָחִיו מִכֹּל לִבְּכֶם

HTV: "So likewise shall my heavenly Father do to you - if each of you - do not forgive your brother - with all your heart!"

KJV: So likewise shall my heavenly Father do also unto you, if ye from your hearts forgive not every one his brother their trespasses.

Matthew Chapter 19

Hebrew Text Version (HTV)

¹ And it came to pass after Yeshua had finished all these words - he went from Galilee and came to the border of Judea across the Jordan.

² Multitudes followed Yeshua there and he healed them.

³ The Pharisees approached Yeshua and tempted him saying, "Is it a man's prerogative to divorce his wife for any reason whatsoever?"

⁴ To which Yeshua answered and said to them, "Have you not read how He who made Man - in the beginning - made them male and female?"

⁵ Yeshua said, "For this reason, a man shall leave his father and mother - and shall join to his wife - and they will be one flesh."

⁶ "Therefore, they are now not two - but one flesh - and that which God has joined, let no man separate."

⁷ They said to him, "If so, why did Moses command *us* to give a wife a writ of divorce and to send her away?"

⁸ And Yeshua said to them, "Moses - because of the hardness of your hearts - consented for you to send your wives away from your home. In truth, from the beginning this was not to be so."

⁹ "But I say to you, anyone who sends his wife from his home - except for adultery - and takes another, he will also commit adultery."

¹⁰ Then his disciples said to him, "If this matter be so *between* a man and his wife - is it not good for a man to take a wife?"

¹¹ To which Yeshua responded to them, "Not everyone will receive these words - except those to whom they are intended."

¹² "For there are eunuchs who were born eunuchs from their mother's womb. And there are eunuchs who are eunuchs by the hand of men. Also, there are eunuchs who *subdue their desires*

for the sake of the kingdom of heaven. He who can receive *this word* - let him receive *it!*"

¹³ Then little children were brought to him Yeshua

so that he would place his hands on them and pray for them. Instead, his disciples would drive them away.

¹⁴ Yeshua said to them, "Let the children be - and do not prevent them from coming to me - Truly I say to you that no one will enter the kingdom of heaven except *they shall become* like these."

¹⁵ After Yeshua had placed his hands upon them - he went from there.

¹⁶ Behold, a man approached and said to Yeshua, "My good Rabbi, what good *deed* can I do that I may obtain eternal life?"

¹⁷ And Yeshua said to him, "Why do you call me good? There is only one who is good - that one is God. If you want to come to eternal life - keep the commandments."

¹⁸ And he said to him, "Which ones?" And Yeshua said, "Do not murder, do not commit adultery, do not steal, do not witness falsely."

¹⁹ "Honor your father and mother. Love your neighbor as yourself."

²⁰ And the young man said to Yeshua, "All these things I have kept from my youth. What do I still lack?"

²¹ Yeshua said to him, "If you want to be complete, go and sell everything you own, and give *it* to the poor - and you will have treasure in heaven. Then come and follow after me."

²² When the young man heard this - he went away from him mourning - because he was very rich.

²³ Yeshua said to his disciples, "Truly, I say to you - The rich shall *only* by hardships enter the kingdom of heaven."

²⁴ "Again, I say to you - it is easier for a *camel* to go through the eye of a needle than for a rich man to enter the kingdom of heaven."

²⁵ When the disciples heard these words, they were very astonished, saying - "If so, who can be saved?"

²⁶ Yeshua looked at them saying, "With men these things are impossible - but with God all things are possible."

²⁷ Peter (Keyfa) answered and said unto him, "Behold! We have left everything and followed after you - what reward will we have?"

²⁸ Yeshua said to them, "In truth I say to you, that you - in the Day of Judgement - when the Son of Man shall sit upon the

throne of his glory - you shall also sit upon twelve thrones - to judge the twelve tribes of Israel."

²⁹ "Everyone who leaves house and home, brothers, sisters, or father and mother, or wife and sons, or lands - for my name's sake - he, in turn, will receive a hundredfold and obtain eternal life!"

³⁰ "But many who are first shall be last - and those who are last shall be first!"

Matthew Chapter 19
HTV with translator notes and KJV comparison

Matthew 19:1

Freiburg Hebrew Manuscript

וַיְהִי אַחֲרֵי שֶׁיֵּשׁוּעַ כָּלָה כֹּל אֵלֶּה הָאֲמָרִים הוּא הָלַךְ מִגָּלִילָה וּבָא בִּגְבוּלֵי יְהוּדָה עֵבֶר יַרְדֵּן

HTV: And it came to pass after Yeshua had finished all these words - he went from Galilee and came to the border of Judea across the Jordan.

KJV: And it came to pass, that when Jesus had finished these sayings, he departed from Galilee, and came into the coasts of Judaea beyond Jordan;

Matthew 19:2

וְנִמְשְׁכוּ אַחֲרָיו כִּתִּים רַבִּים וַיְרַפֵּא אוֹתָם שָׁם

HTV: Multitudes followed Yeshua there and he healed them.

The Hebrew Book of Matthew

KJV: And great multitudes followed him; and he healed them there.

Matthew 19:3

וַיִּקְרְבוּ אֵלָיו פְּרוּשִׁים וַיְנַסּוּהוּ לֵאמֹר הַאִם הָאָם שַׁיָּיךְ לְאָדָם לְהָנִיחַ מִמֶּנּוּ אֶת-אִשְׁתּוֹ מִכֹּל סִבָּה תִּהְיֶה אֲשֶׁר תִּהְיֶה

HTV: **The Pharisees approached Yeshua and tempted him saying, "Is it a man's prerogative to divorce his wife for any reason whatsoever?"**

KJV: The Pharisees also came unto him, tempting him, and saying unto him, Is it lawful for a man to put away his wife for every cause?

Matthew 19:4

אֲשֶׁר עָנָה וַיֹּאמַר לָהֶם הַאָם לֹא קְרָאתֶם כֵּיצַד מִי שֶׁעָשָׂה אֶת-הָאָדָם בְּרִאשׁוֹנָה עָשָׂה אוֹתָם זָכָר וּנְקֵבָה

HTV: **To which Yeshua answered and said to them, "Have you not read how He who made Man - in the beginning - made them male and female?"**

KJV: And he answered and said unto them, Have ye not read, that he which made *them* at the beginning made them male and female,

Matthew 19:5

וַיֹּאמַר עַל כֵּן יַעֲזוֹב אִישׁ אֶת-אָבִיו וְאֶת-אִמּוֹ וְדָבַק בְּאִשְׁתּוֹ וְהָיוּ לְבָשָׂר אֶחָד

HTV: **Yeshua said, "For this reason, a man shall leave his father and mother - and shall join to his wife - and they will be one flesh."**

KJV: And said, For this cause shall a man leave father and mother, and shall cleave to his wife: and they twain shall be one flesh?

Matthew 19:6

לְפִיכָךְ הֵמָה עַתָּה אֵין שְׁנַיִם כִּי אִם בָּשָׂר אֶחָד וַאֲשֶׁר אֱלֹהִים חִבֵּר הָאָדָם אַל יַפְרִיד

HTV: **"Therefore, they are now not two - but one flesh - and that which God has joined, let no man separate."**

KJV: Wherefore they are no more twain, but one flesh. What therefore God hath joined together, let not man put asunder.

Matthew 19:7

וַיֹּאמְרוּ לוֹ וְאִם כֵּן לָמָה מֹשֶׁה צִוָּה לָתֵת סֵפֶר כְּרִיתוּת וּלְשַׁלַּח אֵשֶׁת מִבֵּיתוֹ

HTV: **They said to him, "If so, why did Moses command *us* to give a wife a writ of divorce and to send her away?"**

KJV: They say unto him, Why did Moses then command to give a writing of divorcement, and to put her away?

Matthew 19:8

וַיֹּאמֶר לָהֶם הִנֵּה מֹשֶׁה מִפְּנֵי קְשׁוּת לְבַבְכֶם הִרְשָׁה לָכֶם לְשַׁלַּח אֶת-אִשּׁוֹתֵיכֶם מִבָּתֵּיכֶם אָמְנָם מֵרֵאשִׁית לֹא יִהְיֶה כֵן

HTV: **And Yeshua said to them, "Moses - because of the hardness of your hearts - consented for you to send your wives away from your home. In truth, from the beginning this was not to be so."**

KJV: He saith unto them, Moses because of the hardness of your hearts suffered you to put away your wives: but from the beginning it was not so.

Matthew 19:9

אֲבָל אֲנִי אוֹמֵר לָכֶם שֶׁכֹּל אֲשֶׁר יְשַׁלַּח אֶת-אִשְׁתּוֹ מִבֵּיתוֹ בִּלְתִּי בַעֲבוּר הַנַּאֲפוּפִים וְיִקַּח אַחֶרֶת הוּא יִנְאוֹף וְגַם הַלּוֹקֵחַ אֶת-הַמְשֻׁלַּחַת הוּא יִנְאָף

HTV: **"But I say to you, anyone who sends his wife from his home - except for adultery - and takes another, he will also commit adultery."**

KJV: And I say unto you, Whosoever shall put away his wife, except *it be* for fornication, and shall marry another, committeth adultery: and whoso marrieth her which is put away doth commit adultery.

The Hebrew Book of Matthew

Matthew 19:10

Freiburg Hebrew Manuscript

וַיֹּאמְרוּ לוֹ תַּלְמִידָיו וְאִם הַדָּבָר כֵּן לְאָדָם עִם אִשְׁתּוֹ לֹא טוֹב שֶׁיִּקַּח הָאָדָם אֵשֶׁת

HTV: Then his disciples said to him, "If this matter be so *between* a man and his wife - is it not good for a man to take a wife?"

Note: See also 1st Corinthians 7:8-32, where Paul continues the debate upon remaining celibate.

KJV: His disciples say unto him, If the case of the man be so with *his* wife, it is not good to marry.

Matthew 19:11

אֲשֶׁר אָמַר לָהֶם לֹא כֻלָּם מְקַבְּלִים אֶת-הַדָּבָר הַזֶּה כִּי אִם לַאֲשֶׁר נִתָּן

HTV: To which Yeshua responded to them, "Not everyone will receive these words - except those to whom they are intended."

KJV: But he said unto them, All *men* cannot receive this saying, save *they* to whom it is given.

Matthew 19:12

Freiburg Hebrew Manuscript

כִּי נִמְצָאִים סָרִיסִים אֲשֶׁר כֵּן נְתוֹלְדוּ מִבֶּטֶן אִמָּם גַּם נִמְצָאִים סָרִיסִים אֲשֶׁר נֶעֱשׂוּ סָרִיסִים עַל יַד אֲנוֹשִׁים וְנִמְצָאִים גַּם סָרִיסִים אֲשֶׁר כָּרְתוּ לְעַצְמָם אֶת-בֵּיצִים מִפְּנֵי מַלְכוּת הַשָּׁמַיִם אֲשֶׁר יָכוֹל לְקַבֵּל הוּא יְקַבֵּל

HTV: "For there are eunuchs who were born eunuchs from their mother's womb. And there are eunuchs who are eunuchs by the hand of men. Also, there are eunuchs who *subdue their desires* for the sake of the kingdom of heaven. He who can receive *this word* - let him receive *it!*"

Note: See 1st Corinthians 7:7, Paul the Apostle says, "I would that all men were as I myself (single)." Therefore, a believer could serve the Lord without a spouse and without distraction.

The Hebrew text actually says "cut off their testicles" instead of "subdue their desires" - but it is important to highlight - this is a metaphor, not an instruction to castrate oneself.

KJV: For there are some eunuchs, which were so born from *their* mother's womb: and there are some eunuchs, which were made eunuchs of men: and there be eunuchs, which have made themselves eunuchs for the kingdom of heaven's sake. He that is able to receive *it*, let him receive *it*.

Matthew 19:13

וְאָז הוּבְאוּ אֵלָיו תִּינוֹקִים כְּדֵי שֶׁיִּסְמוֹךְ עֲלֵיהֶם אֶת-יָדָיו וְיִתְפַּלֵּל אִמְנָם הַתַּלְמִידָיו יִגְעָרוּם

HTV: Then little children were brought to him Yeshua so that he would place his hands on them and pray for them. Instead, his disciples would drive them away.

KJV: Then were there brought unto him little children, that he should put *his* hands on them, and pray: and the disciples rebuked them.

Matthew 19:14

וְיֵשׁוּעַ אָמַר לָהֶם הַנִּיחוּ אֶת-תִּינוֹקִים וְאַל תִּמְנָעוּם לָבוֹא אֵלַי כִּי לָהֶם מַלְכוּת הַשָּׁמַיִם

HTV: Yeshua said to them, "Let the children be - and do not prevent them from coming to me - Truly I say to

you that no one will enter the kingdom of heaven except *they shall become* like these."

KJV: But Jesus said, Suffer little children, and forbid them not, to come unto me: for of such is the kingdom of heaven.

Matthew 19:15

וְאַחֲרֵי שֶׁסָּמַךְ עֲלֵיהֶם אֶת-יָדָיו הוּא הָלַךְ מִשָּׁם

HTV: **After Yeshua had placed his hands upon them - he went from there.**

KJV: And he laid *his* hands on them, and departed thence.

Matthew 19:16

Freiburg Hebrew Manuscript

וְהִנֵּה נִגַּשׁ אֶחָד וַיֹּאמַר לוֹ רַבִּי הַטּוֹב מָה נָא אֶעֱשֶׂה טוֹב שֶׁאֶמְצָא אֶת-חַיִּים עוֹלָמִיִּים

HTV: **Behold, a man approached and said to Yeshua, "My good Rabbi, what good *deed* can I do that I may obtain eternal life?"**

> Note: The word "deed" is often translated as "thing." In Hebrew, it comes from the root word "mitzvot" or commandment, which is exactly how Yeshua throws the question back to him. The Pharisees believed salvation comes from studying and obeying the commandments of the Torah.

KJV: And, behold, one came and said unto him, Good Master, what good thing shall I do, that I may have eternal life?

Matthew 19:17

Freiburg Hebrew Manuscript

Chapter 19

וַיֹּאמֶר לוֹ מָה אַתָּה קוֹרֵא אוֹתִי טוֹב כִּי לְבַד אֶחָד אֲשֶׁר טוֹב כֵּיצַד הָאֱלֹהִים וְאִם תִּרְצֶה לָבוֹא לְחַיִּים שְׁמוֹר אֶת הַמִּצְוֹת

HTV: **And Yeshua said to him, "Why do you call me good? There is only one who is good - that one is God. If you want to come to eternal life - keep the commandments."**

> Note: Roman 3:18, "there is none who does good - no, not one!" It seems Yeshua is leading the Torah-observant young man into recognizing something beyond the mitzvot (commandments).

KJV: And he said unto him, Why callest thou me good? *there is* none good but one, *that is,* God: but if thou wilt enter into life, keep the commandments.

Matthew 19:18

וַיֹּאמֶר לוֹ אֵי אֵלּוּ וַיֵּשׁוּעַ אָמַר לֹא תִרְצַח לֹא תִנְאָף לֹא תִגְנוֹב לֹא תַעֲנֶה בְרֵעֲךָ עֵד שָׁקֶר

HTV: **And he said to him, "Which ones?" And Yeshua said, "Do not murder, do not commit adultery, do not steal, do not witness falsely."**

KJV: He saith unto him, Which? Jesus said, Thou shalt do no murder, Thou shalt not commit adultery, Thou shalt not steal, Thou shalt not bear false witness,

Matthew 19:19

כַּבֵּד אֶת־אָבִיךָ וְאֶת־אִמֶּךָ תֶּאֱהַב אֶת־עֲמִיתְךָ כְּעַצְמְךָ

HTV: **"Honor your father and mother. Love your neighbor as yourself."**

KJV: Honour thy father and *thy* mother: and, Thou shalt love thy neighbour as thyself.

Matthew 19:20

וַיֹּאמֶר לוֹ הַנַּעַר כֹּל אֵלֶּה דְּבָרִים שָׁמַרְתִּי מִנְּעוּרַי מָה נָא אֲנִי עוֹד חָסֵר

The Hebrew Book of Matthew

HTV: **And the young man said to Yeshua, "All these things I have kept from my youth. What do I still lack?"**

KJV: The young man saith unto him, All these things have I kept from my youth up: what lack I yet?

Matthew 19:21

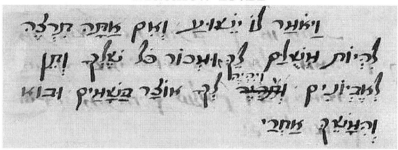

Freiburg Hebrew Manuscript

וַיֹּאמֶר לוֹ יֵשׁוּעַ וְאִם אַתָּה תִּרְצֶה לִהְיוֹת מְשֻׁלָּם לֵךְ וּמְכוֹר כֹּל שֶׁלְּךָ וְתֵן לָאֶבְיוֹנִים וְיִהְיֶה לְךָ אוֹצָר בַּשָּׁמַיִם וּבוֹא וְהַמָּשֵׁךְ אַחֲרַי

HTV: **Yeshua said to him, "If you want to be complete, go and sell everything you own, and give *it* to the poor - and you will have treasure in heaven. Then come and follow after me."**

Note: Yeshua is asking of the young man to take a step in faith - to be led by the Spirit.

KJV: Jesus said unto him, If thou wilt be perfect, go *and* sell that thou hast, and give to the poor, and thou shalt have treasure in heaven: and come *and* follow me.

Matthew 19:22

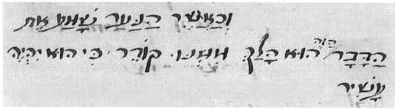

Freiburg Hebrew Manuscript

וְכַאֲשֶׁר הַנַּעַר שָׁמַע אֶת הַדָּבָר הַזֶּה הוּא הָלַךְ מִמֶּנּוּ קוֹדֵר כִּי הוּא יִהְיֶה עָשִׁיר

HTV: **When the young man heard this - he went away from him mourning - because he was very rich.**

> Note: In Matthew 6:24 Yeshua says, "No one can serve two masters - either he will hate the one and love the other - or tolerate one and despise the other. One cannot serve God and Mammon."

KJV: But when the young man heard that saying, he went away sorrowful: for he had great possessions.

Matthew 19:23

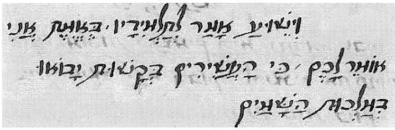

Freiburg Hebrew Manuscript

וְיֵשׁוּעַ אָמַר לְתַלְמִידָיו בֶּאֱמֶת אֲנִי אוֹמֵר לָכֶם כִּי הָעֲשִׁירִים בְּקָשׁוּת יָבוֹאוּ בְּמַלְכוּת הַשָּׁמַיִם

HTV: **Yeshua said to his disciples, "Truly, I say to you - The rich shall *only* by hardships enter the kingdom of heaven."**

> Note: The rich, by virtue of their wealth, often have trouble letting go of material concerns as we mentioned in Matthew 6:24 above, see also Luke 18:25.

KJV: Then said Jesus unto his disciples, Verily I say unto you, That a rich man shall hardly enter into the kingdom of heaven.

Matthew 19:24

וְעוֹד אֲנִי אוֹמֵר לָכֶם כִּי יוֹתֵר קַל לְגָמָל שֶׁיַּעֲבוֹר בְּנֶקֶב מַחַט מִשֶּׁעָשִׁיר יָבוֹא בְּמַלְכוּת הַשָּׁמַיִם

HTV: **"Again, I say to you - it is easier for a *camel* to go through the eye of a needle than for a rich man to enter the kingdom of heaven."**

KJV: And again I say unto you, It is easier for a camel to go through the eye of a needle, than for a rich man to enter into the kingdom of God.

Matthew 19:25

וְכַאֲשֶׁר שָׁמְעוּ אֵלֶּה דְבָרִים הַתַּלְמִידִים מְאוֹד הִשְׁתּוֹמְמוּ לֵאמֹר וְאִם כֵּן מִי נָא יוּכַל לְהִוָּשֵׁעַ

HTV: **When the disciples heard these words, they were very astonished, saying - "If so, who can be saved?"**

KJV: When his disciples heard *it*, they were exceedingly amazed, saying, Who then can be saved?

Matthew 19:26

וְהִבִּיטָם יֵשׁוּעַ וַיֹּאמֶר לָהֶם אֵצֶל אֲנוֹשִׁים יֵשׁ הַדָּבָר הַזֶּה אִי אֶפְשָׁר אָמְנָם אֵצֶל אֱלֹהִים כֹּל דְּבָרִים אֶפְשָׁרִיִּים

HTV: **Yeshua looked at them saying, "With men these things are impossible - but with God all things are possible."**

KJV: But Jesus beheld *them*, and said unto them, With men this is impossible; but with God all things are possible.

Matthew 19:27

וַיַּעַן כֵּיפָא וַיֹּאמֶר לוֹ הִנֵּה אֲנַחְנוּ עָזַבְנוּ כֹּל דְּבָרִים וְרָדַפְנוּ אַחֲרֶיךָ וְאֵיזֶה שָׂכָר יִהְיֶה לָנוּ

HTV: **Peter (Keyfa) answered and said unto him, "Behold! We have left everything and followed after you - what reward will we have?"**

KJV: Then answered Peter and said unto him, Behold, we have forsaken all, and followed thee; what shall we have therefore?

Matthew 19:28

וַיֹּאמֶר יֵשׁוּעַ לָהֶם בֶּאֱמֶת אֲנִי אוֹמֵר לָכֶם אֲשֶׁר אַתֶּם שֶׁתִּמָּשְׁכוּ אַחֲרֵי בַּבְּרִיאָה שֵׁנִית כַּאֲשֶׁר יֵשֵׁב בֶּן הָאָדָם בְּמוֹשַׁב כְּבוֹדוֹ תֵשְׁבוּ גַּם אַתֶּם עַל מוֹשָׁבִים שְׁנֵים עָשָׂר שׁוֹפְטִים אֶת-שְׁנֵים עָשָׂר שְׁבָטִים שֶׁל יִשְׂרָאֵל

Chapter 20

HTV: **Yeshua said to them, "In truth I say to you, that you - in the Day of Judgement - when the Son of Man shall sit upon the throne of his glory - you shall also sit upon twelve thrones - to judge the twelve tribes of Israel."**

KJV: And Jesus said unto them, Verily I say unto you, That ye which have followed me, in the regeneration when the Son of man shall sit in the throne of his glory, ye also shall sit upon twelve thrones, judging the twelve tribes of Israel.

Matthew 19:29

Freiburg Hebrew Manuscript

וְכֹל אֲשֶׁר יַעֲזוֹב אֶת-בַּיִת אֶת-אָחִים אֶת-אֲחָיוֹת אוֹ אֶת-הָאָב אוֹ אֶת-הָאֵם אוֹ אֶת-אֵשֶׁת אוֹ אֶת בָּנִים אוֹ אֶת שָׂדִים בַּעֲבוּר שְׁמִי הַהוּא תַּחַת הָאֵלֶּה מֵאָה יִקַּח וְיִמְצָא אֶת-חַיִּים עוֹלָמִיים

HTV: **"Everyone who leaves house and home, brothers, sisters, or father and mother, or wife and sons, or lands - for my name's sake - he, in turn, will receive a hundredfold and obtain eternal life!"**

> Note: Yeshua is promising a hundredfold in eternal life, not necessarily in this earthly life.

KJV: And every one that hath forsaken houses, or brethren, or sisters, or father, or mother, or wife, or children, or lands, for my name's sake, shall receive an hundredfold, and shall inherit everlasting life.

Matthew 19:30

וְרַבִּים הָרִאשׁוֹנִים יִהְיוּ אַחֲרוֹנִים וְהָאַחֲרוֹנִים יִהְיוּ רִאשׁוֹנִים

HTV: **"But many who are first shall be last - and those who are last shall be first!"**

KJV: But many *that are* first shall be last; and the last *shall be* first.

Matthew Chapter 20
Hebrew Text Version (HTV)

¹ After this, Yeshua said to his disciples, "Behold, the kingdom of heaven is like the master of a house who went out in the morning to hire workers in his vineyard."

² "He agreed to give them one silver coin a day - Then he sent them into his vineyard."

³ "And he went out in the third hour of the day and saw others standing idle at the gate of the marketplace."

⁴ "And he said to them, 'You go also into my vineyard and whatever is right I will give to you.' And they went."

⁵ "Again, he went forth in the sixth hour and in the ninth hour and did as before."

⁶ "And in the eleventh hour, he went forth and found others standing there. And he said to them, 'Why are you standing idle?'"

⁷ "To which they said, 'Because no overseer has hired us.' He said to them, 'Come also into my vineyard.'"

⁸ "And when sunset came - the master of the vineyard said to his overseer, 'Call the workers to give them their wage. Begin with the last ones - and end with the first ones.'"

⁹ "Those (workers) who came in the eleventh hour - each and every one received one day's pay - a silver coin."

¹⁰ "And when the first ones came - they thought they should receive more than all of the others - but each and every one received a single silver coin - a day's pay."

¹¹ "When they were to receive *their wages*, they complained among themselves against the master of the house,"

¹² Saying, "Look! These last ones worked just one hour and you gave the same to them as you gave to us - who bore the heat of the day."

¹³ "And he said to (*that* one of) them, 'Oh beloved! I am not mistreating you! You agreed with me in exchange for one day's pay.'"

¹⁴ "Take what is yours and go - because I want these last ones to *receive* the same as you."

¹⁵ "Is it not to me to do with what is mine - according to my desire? Does your eye *see* evil when I do good?" (present evil before you when I do good?)

¹⁶ "So the last shall be first, and the first, last. For many are called - but few are chosen."

¹⁷ Then Yeshua went up to Jerusalem, and he took his twelve disciples aside, and said to them,

¹⁸ "Behold, we are going up to Jerusalem and the Son of Adam (Man) will be delivered unto the chief priests and scribes - and they will condemn him to death!"

¹⁹ "And they will send him (Yeshua the Son of Man) to the Gentiles to be mocked, and to be beaten with whips, and to be crucified. And on the third day, he shall rise up from death."

²⁰ And then, the mother (Salome) of the sons of Zebedee approached him (Yeshua) with her sons - and she bowed to him and asked something from him.

²¹ Who (Yeshua) said to her, "What are you wanting?" And she said, "Please declare that these two sons of mine will sit, one to your right and the other to your left, in your kingdom."

²² Yeshua answered, "You do not know what you are asking. Are you able to endure the suffering and death that I myself will endure?" And they said to him, "Yes, we are able."

²³ He said to them, "Truly, you will drink from my cup, but to sit on my right hand and on my left, this is not in my power to give you, because that is prepared by my Father."

²⁴ When the *other* ten heard this thing, they were angry and filled with wrath at the two brothers.

²⁵ But Yeshua called them to him and said, "You know that

the rulers of the Gentiles seek dominion over all in order to exercise great power over them."

²⁶ "Indeed, it will not be so among you - because

if anyone among you wants to be great - you shall become a servant."

²⁷ "Whosoever wants to be first among you - he shall be your servant."

²⁸ Just as the Son of Adam (Man) does not come to be served by others - but rather to serve - and give his life to save many.

²⁹ When they had gone out from Jericho - a great crowd followed him.

³⁰ Behold - Two blind men who sat by the roadside heard that Yeshua *was* passing by - *so* they cried out saying, "My Lord, son of David, have mercy on us!"

³¹ Indeed the crowd was rebuking them - "Be silent!" But they continued crying out even louder, saying, "My Lord, son of David, have mercy upon us!"

³² Yeshua stopped. He called them and said, "What then do you want me to do for you?"

³³ They said to him, "My Lord - Open our eyes!"

³⁴ Yeshua had mercy on them and he touched their eyes and immediately - they could see! - And they followed him.

Matthew Chapter 20

HTV with translator notes and KJV comparison

Matthew 20:1

Freiburg Hebrew Manuscript

הִנֵּה הַמַּלְכוּת הַשָּׁמַיִם הִיא נִתְדָמָה לְבַעַל הַבַּיִת אֲשֶׁר יָצָא בַּבּוֹקֶר לְהַשְׂכִּיר אֶת-פּוֹעֲלִים בְּכַרְמוֹ

Chapter 20

HTV: After this, Yeshua said to his disciples, "Behold, the kingdom of heaven is like the master of a house who went out in the morning to hire workers in his vineyard."

Note: It is important to remember that the numbering of chapters and verses did not occur until the 12th century AD. So the continuation of parables begun in chapter 19 continues here. That is probably why the first part of this verse "**After this Yeshua said to his disciples**" is dropped from the later versions as it does not make sense at the beginning of a chapter. It is in the STM Hebrew Matthew. This is a proof the source of this manuscript was prior to the 12th century.

KJV: For the kingdom of heaven is like unto a man *that is* an householder, which went out early in the morning to hire labourers into his vineyard.

Matthew 20:2

וּמִשֶּׁהִתְוַנָה אִתָּם לָתֵת לָהֶם בְּיוֹם זוּז אֶחָד הִנֵּה שְׁלָחָם בְּכַרְמוֹ

HTV: "He agreed to give them one silver coin a day - Then he sent them into his vineyard."

KJV: And when he had agreed with the labourers for a penny a day, he sent them into his vineyard.

Matthew 20:3

וַיֵּצֵא בְּשָׁעָה שְׁלִישִׁית וַיִּרְאֶה אֲחֵרִים עוֹמְדִים בַּטְלָנִים

HTV: "And he went out in the third hour of the day and saw others standing idle at the gate of the marketplace."

KJV: And he went out about the third hour, and saw others standing idle in the marketplace,

Matthew 20:4

וַיֹּאמֶר לָהֶם לְכוּ גַם אַתֶּם בְּכַרְמִי וַאֲשֶׁר יִהְיֶה יָשָׁר אֲנִי אֶתֵּן לָכֶם וְהֵמָה הָלְכוּ

HTV: "And he said to them, 'You go also into my vineyard and whatever is right I will give to you.' And they went."

KJV: And said unto them; Go ye also into the vineyard, and whatsoever is right I will give you. And they went their way.

311

Matthew 20:5

Freiburg Hebrew Manuscript

וְעוֹד יָצָא בְּשָׁעָה תְּשִׁיעִית וְעָשָׂה כָּמוֹ לִפְנֵי זֶה

HTV: "Again, he went forth in the sixth hour and in the ninth hour and did as before."

Note: The text is counting by the hours of daylight. From sunrise to noon is the sixth hour of daylight, thus 3 in the afternoon is the ninth hour of daylight.

KJV: Again he went out about the sixth and ninth hour, and did likewise.

Matthew 20:6

וּבְשָׁעָה אַחַת עֶשְׂרֵה יָצָא וַיִּמְצָא אַחֵרִי עוֹמְדִים וַיֹּאמַר לָהֶם מָה אַתֶּם עוֹמְדִים שָׁם בַּטְלָנִים

HTV: "And in the eleventh hour, he went forth and found others standing there. And he said to them, 'Why are you standing idle?'"

KJV: About the eleventh hour he went out, and found others standing idle, and saith unto them, Why stand ye here all the day idle?

Matthew 20:7

אֲשֶׁר אָמְרוּ לוֹ כִּי אֵין אָדָם שׁוּם הִשְׂכִּירָנִי וַיֹּאמַר לָהֶם לְכוּ גַּם אַתֶּם בְּכַרְמִי

HTV: "To which they said, 'Because no overseer has hired us.' He said to them, 'Come also into my vineyard.'"

KJV: They say unto him, Because no man hath hired us. He saith unto them, Go ye also into the vineyard; and whatsoever is right, *that* shall ye receive.

Matthew 20:8

וּמִשֶּׁהַשֶּׁמֶשׁ נָטָה לַעֲרוֹב אָמַר הָאָדוֹן הַכֶּרֶם לְמֻשָּׁק שֶׁלּוֹ קְרָא אֶת-הַפּוֹעֲלִים וְתֵן לָהֶם אֶת-הַשָּׂכָר מַתְחִיל מֵאַחֲרוֹנִים עַד הָרִאשׁוֹנִים

Chapter 20

HTV: "And when sunset came - the master of the vineyard said to his overseer, 'Call the workers to give them their wage. Begin with the last ones - and end with the first ones.' "

KJV: So when even was come, the lord of the vineyard saith unto his steward, Call the labourers, and give them *their* hire, beginning from the last unto the first.

Matthew 20:9

Freiburg Hebrew Manuscript

וְכַאֲשֶׁר נִגְּשׁוּ אֲשֶׁר בָּאוּ בְשָׁעָה אַחַת עֲשִׂרֵה לָקְחוּ כָל אֶחָד וְאֶחָד זוּז אֶחָד

HTV: "Those (workers) who came in the eleventh hour - each and every one received one day's pay - a silver coin."

Note: The Hebrew word /zuz/ or /zuzim/ refers to "one day's pay" or a single silver coin.

KJV: And when they came that *were hired* about the eleventh hour, they received every man a penny.

Matthew 20:10

וּבָאוּ הָרִאשׁוֹנִים שֶׁחָשְׁבוּ אֲשֶׁר יִקְחוּ יוֹתֵר אָמְנָם כֹּל אֶחָד וְאֶחָד לָקְחוּ לְבַד זוּז אֶחָד

HTV: "And when the first ones came - they thought they should receive more than all of the others - but each and every one received a single silver coin - a day's pay."

KJV: But when the first came, they supposed that they should have received more; and they likewise received every man a penny.

The Hebrew Book of Matthew

Matthew 20:11

וְכַאֲשֶׁר לָקְחוּ הָיוּ מִתְלוֹנְנִים כְּנֶגֶד בַּעַל הַבַּיִת

HTV: "When they were to receive *their wages*, they complained among themselves against the master of the house,"

KJV: When they had received *it*, they murmured against the goodman of the house,

Matthew 20:12

לֵאמֹר הִנֵּה הָאֵלֶה אַחֲרוֹנִים פָּעֲלוּ לְבַד שָׁעָה אַחַת וְעָשִׂית אוֹתָם לָנוּ דוֹמִים אֲשֶׁר נָשָׂאנוּ אֶת־הַמַּשָּׂא שֶׁל הַיּוֹם וְהַשָּׁרָב

HTV: Saying, "Look! These last ones worked just one hour and you gave the same to them as you gave to us - who bore the heat of the day."

KJV: Saying, These last have wrought *but* one hour, and thou hast made them equal unto us, which have borne the burden and heat of the day.

Matthew 20:13

וַיַּעַן לְאֶחָד מֵהֶם וַיֹּאמֶר לוֹ הוֹי אָהוּב אֵינִי עוֹשֵׁק אוֹתְךָ הֲלֹא אַתָּה הִתְנֵיתָ אִתִּי תַּחַת זוּז לְיוֹם

HTV: "And he said to (*that* one of) them, 'Oh beloved! I am not mistreating you! You agreed with me in exchange for one day's pay.'"

KJV: But he answered one of them, and said, Friend, I do thee no wrong: didst not thou agree with me for a penny?

Matthew 20:14

טוֹל מַה שֶּׁלְּךָ וְלֵךְ לְךָ כִּי אֲנִי רוֹצֶה לָזֶה הָאַחֲרוֹנִי תֵּת כְּמוֹ לְךָ

HTV: "Take what is yours and go - because I want these last ones to *receive* the same as you."

KJV: Take *that* thine *is*, and go thy way: I will give unto this last, even as unto thee.

Matthew 20:15

Freiburg Hebrew Manuscript

הַאִם לֹא שַׁיָּיךְ לִי לַעֲשׂוֹת בְּמָה שֶׁלִּי לְפִי רְצוֹנִי הַאִם מִפְּנֵי שְׁעֵינְךָ רַע וַאֲנִי טוֹב

HTV: "Is it not to me to do with what is mine - according to my desire? Does your eye *see* evil when I do good?" (present evil before you when I do good?)

Note: Yeshua is speaking of salvation, not wages. To those who believe late in life is given the same salvation as those who believed from the first.

KJV: Is it not lawful for me to do what I will with mine own? Is thine eye evil, because I am good?

Matthew 20:16

וְכֵן יִהְיוּ הָאַחֲרוֹנִים רִאשׁוֹנִים וְהָרִאשׁוֹנִים אַחֲרוֹנִים כִּי רַבִּים יֵשׁ קְרוּאִים וּמְעַטִּים בְּחוּרִים

HTV: "So the last shall be first, and the first, last. For many are called - but few are chosen."

KJV: So the last shall be first, and the first last: for many be called, but few chosen.

Matthew 20:17

וַיַּעַל יֵשׁוּעַ לִירוּשָׁלַיִם וַיִּקַּח אִתּוֹ אֶת־שְׁנֵים עָשָׂר תַּלְמִידָיו לְבַדָּם וַיֹּאמַר לָהֶם

HTV: **Then Yeshua went up to Jerusalem, and he took his twelve disciples aside, and said to them,**

KJV: Jesus going up to Jerusalem took the twelve disciples apart in the way, and said unto them,

The Hebrew Book of Matthew

Matthew 20:18

הִנֵּה אֲנַחְנוּ עוֹלִים לִירוּשָׁלַיִם וּבֶן הָאָדָם יִמָּסֵר לְרָאשֵׁי הַכּוֹהֲנִים וּלְסוֹפְרִים וַיְחַיְּיבוּהוּ לְמִיתָה

HTV: "Behold, we are going up to Jerusalem and the Son of Adam (Man) will be delivered unto the chief priests and scribes - and they will condemn him to death!"

KJV: Behold, we go up to Jerusalem; and the Son of man shall be betrayed unto the chief priests and unto the scribes, and they shall condemn him to death,

Matthew 20:19

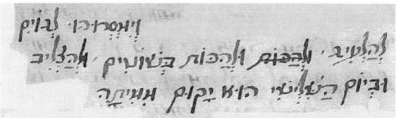

Freiburg Hebrew Manuscript

וְיִמְסְרוּהוּ לְגוֹיִם לְהַלְעִיג וּלְהַכּוֹת בְּשׁוֹטִים וּלְהַצְלִיב וּבְיוֹם הַשְּׁלִישִׁי הוּא יָקוּם מִמִּיתָה

HTV: "And they will send him (Yeshua the Son of Man) to the Gentiles to be mocked, and to be beaten with whips, and to be crucified. And on the third day, he shall rise up from death."

> Note: According to Bart Ehrman, renowned Bible scholar, the earliest Greek texts said "three days and three nights" but it was changed to "the third day" by later Greek scribes to fit the *"Good Friday to Easter Sunday - Lord's Day"* narrative promoted by the Gentile Church.

KJV: shall deliver him to the Gentiles to mock, and to scourge, and to crucify *him*: and the third day he shall rise again.

Matthew 20:20

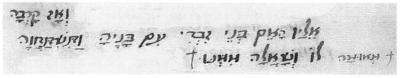

Freiburg Hebrew Manuscript

וְאָז קָרְבָה אֵלָיו הָאֵם בְּנֵי זִבְדִי עִם בָּנֶיהָ וַתִּשְׁתַּחֲוֶה לוֹ וְשָׁאֲלָה מִמֶּנּוּ מְאוּמָה

HTV: And then, the mother (Salome) of the sons of Zebedee approached him (Yeshua) with her sons - and she bowed to him and asked something from him.

> Note: Salome was the daughter of Cleophas (often called Alphaeus) who was the brother of Joseph, Yeshua's father. Cleophas had three sons: James the lesser and Jude Thaddeus who became Apostles of Yeshua, and Simeon (all Yeshua's cousins) who led the Church after James, Yeshua's brother, died. Salome married Zebedee and gave birth to James the Greater and John (sons of Zebedee called Sons of Thunder), who also became Apostles of Yeshua. Four Apostles were members of Yeshua's family. After Simeon, Yeshua's younger brother Jude took over the Messianic Movement. His sons and grandsons also led the church, that would be James and Zocher and finally Judah Kuriakos, the last Jewish Christian Bishop of Jerusalem.

KJV: Then came to him the mother of Zebedee's children with her sons, worshipping *him*, and desiring a certain thing of him.

Matthew 20:21

אֲשֶׁר אָמַר לָהּ מָה אַתְּ רוֹצָה וַתֹּאמַר לוֹ אֱמוֹר נָא שְׁאֵלָה שְׁנֵי בָנַי יֵשְׁבוּ אֶחָד לִימִינְךָ וְהָאַחֵר לִשְׂמֹאלְךָ בְּמַלְכוּתֶךָ

HTV: Who (Yeshua) said to her, "What are you wanting?" And she said, "Please declare that these two sons of mine will sit, one to your right and the other to your left, in your kingdom."

KJV: He said unto her, What wilt thou? She saith unto him, Grant that these my two sons may sit, the one on thy right hand, and the other on the left, in thy kingdom.

Matthew 20:22

²²ויען להם יש"ו לא תדעון מה תבקשון. התוכל לסבול היסורין והמיתה שאני עתיד לסבול? ויאמרו נוכל.

Shem Tov Manuscript

HTV: Yeshua answered, "You do not know what you are asking. Are you able to endure the suffering and

The Hebrew Book of Matthew

death that I myself will endure?" And they said to him, "Yes, we are able."

> Note: Salome is petitioniing that her sons James and John mount the throne with Yeshua. Yeshua is responding that it is not about mounting the throne but rather mounting the cross.

KJV: But Jesus answered and said, Ye know not what ye ask. Are ye able to drink of the cup that I shall drink of, and to be baptized with the baptism that I am baptized with? They say unto him, We are able.

Matthew 20:23

וַיֹּאמֶר לָכֶם אֱמֶת הוּא אֲשֶׁר תִּשְׁתּוּ אֶת־הַכּוֹסִי אֲבָל לָשֶׁבֶת לִימִינִי וְלִשְׂמוֹלִי הַזֹּאת לֹא בְיָדִי לָתֵת לָכֶם כִּי אִם לַאֲשֶׁר מְתֻקָּן מֵהָאָבִי

HTV: **He said to them, "Truly, you will drink from my cup, but to sit on my right hand and on my left, this is not in my power to give you, because that is prepared by my Father."**

KJV: He saith unto them, Ye shall drink indeed of my cup, and be baptized with the baptism that I am baptized with: but to sit on my right hand, and on my left, is not mine to give, but *it shall be given to them* for whom it is prepared of my Father.

Matthew 20:24

וּמִשֶּׁהָעָשָׂר שָׁמְעוּ אֶת־דָּבָר הַזֶּה הֵמָה קָצְפוּ עַל שְׁנַיִם אָחִים קָצֶף

HTV: **When the *other* ten heard this thing, they were angry and filled with wrath at the two brothers.**

KJV: when the ten heard *it*, they were moved with indignation against the two brethren.

Matthew 20:25

Freiburg Hebrew Manuscript

וַיֵּשׁוּעַ קְרָאָם אֵלָיו וַיֹּאמַר אַתֶּם יוֹדְעִים אֲשֶׁר קְצִינֵי הַגּוֹיִם מוֹשְׁלִים
עֲלֵיהֶם וְהַגְדוֹלִים בָּהֶם מוֹצִיאִים עֲלֵיהֶם אֶת־מֶמְשַׁלְתָּם

HTV: But Yeshua called them to him and said, "You know that the rulers of the Gentiles seek dominion over all in order to exercise great power over them."

Note: Yeshua is saying that the Gentiles rule over the Hebrew kings and all others in order to revel in their own power and ego. Those who follow Yeshua will serve the power of God.

KJV: But Jesus called them *unto him*, and said, Ye know that the princes of the Gentiles exercise dominion over them, and they that are great exercise authority upon them.

Matthew 20:26

אָמְנָם לֹא יִהְיֶה כֵן בֵּינֵיכֶם כִּי אִם כֹּל שֶׁיִּרְצֶה בֵינֵיכֶם לִהְיוֹת הַגָּדוֹל
הַהוּא יְהִי מְשָׁרֵת

HTV: "Indeed, it will not be so among you - because if anyone among you wants to be great - you shall become a servant."

KJV: But it shall not be so among you: but whosoever will be great among you, let him be your minister;

Matthew 20:27

וַאֲשֶׁר יִרְצֶה בֵינֵיכֶם לִהְיוֹת הָרִאשׁוֹן הַהוּא יְהִי עַבְדְּכֶם

HTV: "Whosoever wants to be first among you - he shall be your servant."

KJV: whosoever will be chief among you, let him be your servant:

Matthew 20:28

כְּמוֹ אַף בֶּן הָאָדָם לֹא בָא שֶׁאֲחֵרִים יְשָׁדְתוּ לוֹ כִּי אִם שֶׁהוּא יְשָׁרֵת
וְיִתֵּן אֶת־נַפְשׁוֹ לְהוֹשִׁיעַ רַבִּים

HTV: Just as the Son of Adam (Man) does not come to be served by others - but rather to serve - and give his life to save many.

The Hebrew Book of Matthew

KJV: Even as the Son of man came not to be ministered unto, but to minister, and to give his life a ransom for many.

Matthew 20:29

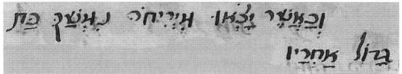

Freiburg Hebrew Manuscript

וְכַאֲשֶׁר יָצְאוּ מִיְרִיחֹה נִמְשַׁךְ כַּת גָדוֹל אַחֲרָיו

HTV: **When they had gone out from Jericho - a great crowd followed him.**

KJV: And as they departed from Jericho, a great multitude followed him.

Matthew 20:30

וְהִנֵּה שְׁנַיִם עִוְרִים הַיוֹשְׁבִים אֵצֶל הַדֶּרֶךְ שָׁמְעוּ שֶׁיֵּשׁוּעַ עוֹבֵר הֵמָה צָעֲקוּ לֵאמֹר הָאֲדוֹנִי חָנֵּנוּ הַבֵּן דָּוִד

HTV: **Behold - Two blind men who sat by the roadside heard that Yeshua** was **passing by -** so **they cried out saying, "My Lord, son of David, have mercy on us!"**

KJV: And, behold, two blind men sitting by the way side, when they heard that Jesus passed by, cried out, saying, Have mercy on us, O Lord, *thou* Son of David.

Matthew 20:31

אֱמְנָם הַכַּת יִהְיֶה גוֹעֲרִם שֶׁיִּשְׁתְּקוּ אֲבָל הֵמָה עוֹד יוֹתֵר וְיוֹתֵר יִהְיוּ צוֹעֲקִים לֵאמֹר הָאֲדוֹנִי חָנֵּנוּ הַבֵּן דָּוִד

HTV: **Indeed the crowd was rebuking them - "Be silent!" But they continued crying out even louder, saying, "My Lord, son of David, have mercy upon us!"**

KJV: And the multitude rebuked them, because they should hold their peace: but they cried the more, saying, Have mercy on us, O Lord, *thou* Son of David.

Matthew 20:32

וְעָמַד יֵשׁוּעַ וַיִּקְרָאָם וַיֹּאמַר לָהֶם מָה נָא אַתֶּם רוֹצִים שֶׁאַעֲשֶׂה לָכֶם

HTV: **Yeshua stopped. He called them and said, "What then do you want me to do for you?"**

KJV: And Jesus stood still, and called them, and said, What will ye that I shall do unto you?

Matthew 20:33

אֲשֶׁר אָמְרוּ לוֹ הָאֲדוֹנִי שֶׁיִּפָּתְחוּ עֵינֵינוּ

HTV: **They said to him, "My Lord - Open our eyes!"**

KJV: They say unto him, Lord, that our eyes may be opened.

Matthew 20:34

Freiburg Hebrew Manuscript

וְחוֹנֵן יֵשׁוּעַ עָלֵיהֶם וְנָגַע אֶת-עֵינֵיהֶם וּמִיָּד רָאוּ וְנִמְשְׁכוּ אַחֲרָיו

HTV: **Yeshua had mercy on them and he touched their eyes and immediately - they could see! - And they followed him.**

KJV: So Jesus had compassion *on them,* and touched their eyes: and immediately their eyes received sight, and they followed him.

The Hebrew Book of Matthew

Matthew Chapter 21

Hebrew Text Version (HTV)

¹ Afterward, they drew near to Jerusalem and came to Bethphage by the Mount of Olives, behold, Yeshua sent two disciples...

² Yeshua said to them, "Go to the village that is next to you, and immediately you will find a she-ass bound and her foal with her - untie it and bring it to me."

³ "If whosoever says anything to you - tell him that the Lord needs it - and he will give it to you at once."

⁴ All this was done to fulfill what was said by the prophet, saying:

⁵ They said to the daughter of Zion, "Behold, your king comes to you humbly and riding upon a donkey - with a foal of the donkey."

⁶ And the disciples went and did according to what Yeshua commanded them.

⁷ And they brought Yeshua the donkey and its foal - the son of the donkey - and they put their cloaks on them, and they placed him on top.

⁸ And a large multitude cast their garments upon the road - and some cut down *palm* branches and spread them upon the way.

⁹ And those before and after him were shouting, "Save *us*, please, son of David! Blessed is the one who comes in the name of *the* Lord! Save *us* from the Romans!"

¹⁰ And when Yeshua entered Jerusalem, behold, the whole city was divided, saying, "Who is this?"

¹¹ The crowds said, "In fact, this is Yeshua the prophet - from Nazareth of Galilee!"

¹² Yeshua came into the Temple of God - and drove out all the buyers and sellers from the Temple. He overturned the tables of the moneychangers - and threw out the seats of the merchants of doves.

Chapter 21

¹³ And he said to them, "Behold, it is written - My house is a house of prayer, it will be called *such* for all nations - but you have made it a den of murderers."

¹⁴ And the blind and lame came to him in the Temple and he healed them.

¹⁵ And when the chief priests and scribes saw the miracles Yeshua did, and the young boys shouting in the temple, saying, "Save us, Son of David!" - They (the priests) were enraged.

¹⁶ And they said to him, "Do you hear what these *youths* are saying?" And Yeshua said to them, "Have you not read how - 'from the mouth of babes and sucklings you have perfected praise?'"

¹⁷ And when Yeshua left them, he went out of the city to Bethany and lodged for the night. And there he was explaining to them the kingdom of God.

¹⁸ And Yeshua saw a fig tree near the road and came to it and found nothing but leaves. And he said to it, "No fruit will ever blossom from you!" And that fig tree dried up at once.

²⁰ After his students saw this, they were astonished, saying, "How quickly did it dry out?"

²¹ And Yeshua answered and said, "Truly I say to you, if you have faith and do not doubt - then you will not only do *as* the fig tree - but all that is worthy of *God's* trust - If you say to this mountain, 'Be taken away and be sent into the sea!' - behold, it will be so."

²² And whatever you ask in your prayer - if you believe - you will *surely* receive it.

²³ And when Yeshua came into the Temple, the chief priests and the elders of the people came to him while teaching, and said, "By what authority do you do these things, and who gave you this authority?"

²⁴ Yeshua answered and said to them, "Look, I will ask one thing of you. And if you tell me, I will also tell you by what authority I do these things."

²⁵ "The baptism of John - was it from heaven or from men?" Indeed, they conspired among themselves and said, "If we say 'From heaven', then he will say to us 'And if so - why did you not believe him?'"

²⁶ "And if we say 'From men', we fear the crowd - because

they all considered John to be a prophet."

²⁷ And they answered Yeshua and said, "We do not know." He then said to them, "Then, I will not tell you by which authority I do these things."

²⁸ "How does it seem to you? A certain man had two sons. He approached the first one and said to him, 'Go, my son - to work in my vineyard today.' "

²⁹ "He answered him and said, 'I do not want to!' But after this - he changed his mind - repented and went."

³⁰ "And he (the man) also approached the other *son* and said the same thing to him. However, *the son* answered and said, 'Here I am, Lord, I am going' - but he did not go!"

³¹ "Who of these two did the will of the father?" They said to him, "The first *son*." Yeshua said to them, "In truth, I say to you that tax collectors and prostitutes will precede you into the kingdom of Elohim."

³² "Yochanan came to you in the way of righteousness and you did not believe him - but the righteous, and *even* the publicans, believed him. And when you saw this - you did not repent afterwards - that you might have cause to believe." To the one (among you) who has ears to hear (the truth) - let him hear it in disgrace."

³³ "Listen to another parable. Behold, a man - the master of the house - who planted a vineyard, and strengthened it with a fence, and dug a wine cellar in it, and built a tower in it - then entrusted it to the workers - then went to a far country."

³⁴ "And when harvest time came - he sent his servants to the workers to collect his fruit."

³⁵ "But the workers seized his servants. One they killed - One they beat – and the other(s) they stoned!"

³⁶ "And he continued to send numerous other servants after the first - and they did the same to them also."

³⁷ "And in the end - he sent his son to them saying, 'They will respect my son!' "

³⁸ "And the workers, when they saw the son, said to themselves, "This is the heir. Come now, let us kill him, and to us will be his inheritance!"

³⁹ "Those who took him, cast him outside the vineyard - and

killed him!"

⁴⁰ "When the lord of the vineyard comes - what will he do to those workers?"

⁴¹ And they said to him, "Behold, they are evil *to the core* of their being! He will utterly destroy them - then entrust his vineyard to other workers who will give him the fruit *of the harvest* in its time."

⁴² Yeshua said to them, "Have you not read in the scriptures, 'The stone which the builders rejected - has become the cornerstone - *as intended* by Yehovah! It is marvelous in our eyes!' "

⁴³ "Therefore, I say to you that the kingdom of God will be taken from you - and will be given to a people who will produce its fruit!"

⁴⁴ "Whoever falls on this stone will be broken - but whoever it falls upon will be shattered."

⁴⁵ And when the chief priests and Pharisees heard his parables - they knew that Yeshua was speaking of them!

⁴⁶ They sought to seize Yeshua, but they feared the crowd - because he was like a prophet to them.

Matthew Chapter 21
HTV with translator notes and KJV comparison

Matthew 21:1

וְאַחֲרֵי שֶׁקָּרְבוּ לִירוּשָׁלַיִם וַיָּבוֹאוּ לְבֵית־פַּאגֵי אֶל הַר זֵיתִים הִנֵּה יֵשׁוּעַ שָׁלַח שְׁנַיִם תַּלְמִידִים

HTV: **Afterward, they drew near to Jerusalem and came to Bethphage by the Mount of Olives, behold, Yeshua sent two disciples.**

KJV: And when they drew nigh unto Jerusalem, and were come to Bethphage, unto the mount of Olives, then sent Jesus two disciples,

The Hebrew Book of Matthew

Matthew 21:2

וַיֹּאמֶר לָהֶם הַלְכוּ אֶל הַטִּירָה אֲשֶׁר לְמוּלְכֶם וּמִיָּד תִּמְצְאוּ אֶת-אָתוֹן הַקְּשׁוּרָה וְעַיִר בֶּן אֲתוֹנוֹת אִתָּהּ פִּתְחוּ וְהַגִּישׁוּ לִי

HTV: Yeshua said to them, "Go to the village that is next to you, and immediately you will find a she-ass bound and her foal with her - untie it and bring it to me."

KJV: Saying unto them, Go into the village over against you, and straightway ye shall find an ass tied, and a colt with her: loose *them*, and bring *them* unto me.

Matthew 21:3

וְאִם מִי יֹאמַר לָכֶם מְאוּמָה אָז תֹּאמְרוּ לוֹ כִּי הָאָדוֹן צָרִיךְ לָהּ וּמִיָּד יַנִּיחַ לָכֶם

HTV: "If whosoever says anything to you - tell him that the Lord needs it - and he will give it to you at once."

KJV: And if any *man* say ought unto you, ye shall say, The Lord hath need of them; and straightway he will send them.

Matthew 21:4

וְהַזֹּאת נֶעֶשְׂתָה שֶׁיִּמָּלֵא אֲשֶׁר נֶאֱמַר עַל פִּי הַנָּבִיא הָאוֹמֵר

HTV: All this was done to fulfill what was said by the prophet, saying:

KJV: All this was done, that it might be fulfilled which was spoken by the prophet, saying,

Matthew 21:5

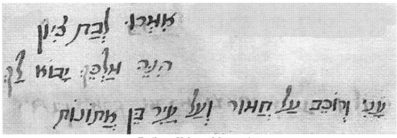

Freiburg Hebrew Manuscript

אָמְרוּ לְבַת צִיּוֹן הִנֵּה מַלְכֵּךְ יָבוֹא לָךְ עָנִי וְרוֹכֵב עַל חֲמוֹר וְעַל עַיִר בֶּן אֲתוֹנוֹת

HTV: **They said to the daughter of Zion, "Behold, your king comes to you humbly and riding upon a donkey - with a foal of the donkey."**

> Note: Zechariah 9:9, "Rejoice greatly, Daughter of Zion! Shout, Daughter of Jerusalem! See, your king comes to you righteous and victorious, humbly and riding on a donkey, with a colt - the foal of a donkey."

KJV: Tell ye the daughter of Sion, Behold, thy King cometh unto thee, meek, and sitting upon an ass, and a colt the foal of an ass.

Matthew 21:6

וְתַלְמִידִים הָלְכוּ וְעָשׂוּ לְפִי מָה שֶׁיֵּשׁוּעַ צִוָּה לָהֶם

HTV: **And the disciples went and did according to what Yeshua commanded them.**

KJV: And the disciples went, and did as Jesus commanded them,

Matthew 21:7

וְהִגִּישׁוּ לוֹ אֶת-אָתוֹן וְעַיִר בֶּן אֲתוֹנוֹת וְשָׂמוּ עֲלֵיהֶם אֶת-מַלְבּוּשֵׁיהֶם וְאוֹתוֹ הִרְכִּיבוּ מִלְמַעְלָה

HTV: **And they brought Yeshua the donkey and its foal - the son of the donkey - and they put their cloaks on them, and they placed him on top.**

KJV: And brought the ass, and the colt, and put on them their clothes, and they set *him* thereon.

Matthew 21:8

וְכַת-גָּדוֹל הִצִּיעוּ אֶת-מַלְבּוּשֵׁיהֶם בַּדֶּרֶךְ וּקְצָתָם כָּרְתוּ עֲנָפִים מֵאִילָנוֹת וְהִצִּיעוּם בַּדֶּרֶךְ

HTV: **And a large multitude cast their garments upon the road - and some cut down *palm* branches and spread them upon the way.**

The Hebrew Book of Matthew

KJV: And a very great multitude spread their garments in the way; others cut down branches from the trees, and strewed *them* in the way.

Matthew 21:9

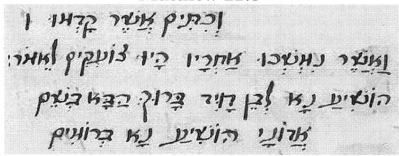

Freiburg Hebrew Manuscript

וְכִתִּים אֹשֶׁר קָדְמוּ וַאֲשֶׁר נִמְשְׁכוּ אַחֲרָיו הָיוּ צוֹעֲקִים לֵאמֹר הוֹשִׁיעַ נָא לְבֶן דָּוִד בָּרוּךְ הַבָּא הַשֵּׁם אֲדוֹנִי הוֹשִׁיעַ נָא בְרוֹמִים

HTV: **And those before and after him were shouting, "Save *us*, please, son of David! Blessed is the one who comes in the name of *the* Lord! Save *us* from the Romans!"**

> Note: The main reason the Jews did not embrace Yeshua the Messiah was that they wanted a conquering-king Messiah like King David (to kick out the Romans), not a suffering-servant Messiah like Joseph (or Yeshua).
>
> The **Roman** Church was not interested in including this part of the verse. This is also the reason Yeshua was reticent to declare himself the Messiah. He would have an army armed with pitchforks - demanding he lead them against the Romans.

KJV: And the multitudes that went before, and that followed, cried, saying, Hosanna to the Son of David: Blessed *is* he that cometh in the name of the Lord; Hosanna in the highest.

Matthew 21:10

וְכַאֲשֶׁר נִכְנַס בִּירוּשָׁלַיִם הִנֵּה נִתְמוֹטֵט כֹּל הָעִיר לֵאמֹר מִי נָא הַזֶּה

HTV: **And when Yeshua entered Jerusalem, behold, the whole city was divided, saying, "Who is this?"**

KJV: And when he was come into Jerusalem, all the city was moved, saying, Who is this?

Matthew 21:11

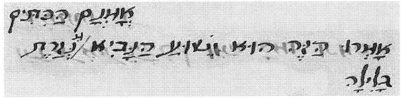

Freiburg Hebrew Manuscript

אָמְנָם הַכִּתִּים אָמְרוּ הֲזֶה הוּא יֵשׁוּעַ הַנָּבִיא מִנְּזֶרֶת גָּלִילָה

HTV: **The crowds said, "In fact, this is Yeshua the prophet - from Nazareth of Galilee!"**

KJV: And the multitude said, This is Jesus the prophet of Nazareth of Galilee.

Matthew 21:12

וּבָא יֵשׁוּעַ בְּהֵיכַל אֱלֹהִים וַיְגָרֶשׁ כֹּל מוֹכְרִים וְקוֹנִים בַּהֵיכָל וְאֶת-שֻׁלְחָנוֹת הַשֻּׁלְחָנִיִּים וְאֶת-כִּסְאוֹת הַמּוֹכְרִים יוֹנִים הוּא הָפַךְ

HTV: **Yeshua came into the Temple of Elohim - and drove out all the buyers and sellers from the Temple. He overturned the tables of the moneychangers - and threw out the seats of the merchants of doves.**

KJV: And Jesus went into the temple of God, and cast out all them that sold and bought in the temple, and overthrew the tables of the moneychangers, and the seats of them that sold doves,

Matthew 21:13

Freiburg Hebrew Manuscript

וַיֹּאמֶר לָהֶם הִנֵּה כָתִיב הַבַּיְתִי הוּא בֵית תְּפִלָּה יִקָּרֵא לְכֹל הָעַמִּים
וְאַתֶּם עֲשִׂיתֶם אוֹתוֹ מְעָרַת הָרוֹצְחִים

HTV: **And he said to them, "Behold, it is written - My house is a house of prayer, it will be called *such* for all nations - but you have made it a den of murderers."**

> Note: Isaiah 56:7, "My house shall be called the house of prayer for all nations." It would make sense that the merchants who were cheating the righteous would be called a "den of thieves." However, the priests who ran the Temple had been executing anyone who challenged their power. It was so bad the Romans had taken away their power of capital punishment. That is why Herod had to get Pontius Pilate, the Roman Governor, to condemn Yeshua to death.

KJV: And said unto them, It is written, My house shall be called the house of prayer; but ye have made it a den of thieves.

Matthew 21:14

וַיִּגְּשׁוּ אֵלָיו עִוְרִים וּפִסְחִים בְּהֵיכָל וּרְפָאָם

HTV: **And the blind and lame came to him in the Temple and he healed them.**

KJV: And the blind and the lame came to him in the temple; and he healed them.

Matthew 21:15

וְרָאשִׁים שֶׁל כּוֹהֲנִים וְהַסּוֹפְרִים רָאוּ אֶת הַנִּפְלָאוֹת אֲשֶׁר עָשָׂה
וּנְעָרִים הַצּוֹעֲקִים בְּהֵיכָל וְאוֹמְרִים הוֹשִׁיעָ נָא לְבֶן דָּוִד וַיִּחַר אַפָּם

HTV: **And when the chief priests and scribes saw the miracles Yeshua did, and the young boys shouting in the temple, saying, "Save us, Son of David!" - They (the priests) were enraged.**

KJV: And when the chief priests and scribes saw the wonderful things that he did, and the children crying in the temple, and saying, Hosanna to the Son of David; they were sore displeased,

Matthew 21:16

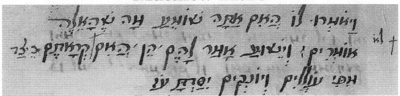

Freiburg Hebrew Manuscript

וַיֹּאמְרוּ לוֹ הַאִם אַתָּה שׁוֹמֵעַ מָה שֶׁהָאֵלֶּה אוֹמְרִים וְיֵשׁוּעַ אָמַר לָהֶם
הֲן הַאִם לֹא קְרָאתֶם כֵּיצַד מִפִּי עוֹלְלִים וְיוֹנְקִים יִסַּדְתָּ עֹז

HTV: And they said to him, "Do you hear what these *youths* are saying?" And Yeshua said to them, "Have you not read how - 'from the mouth of babes and sucklings you have perfected praise?"

> Note: Psalm 8:2, "Out of the mouth of babes and sucklings you have ordained strength (or perfected praise), because of your enemies, that you might still the enemy." Praise paralyzes Satan. Yeshua is giving notice to the high priests who - he makes clear elsewhere (Matt 18) - are evil. A generational change is coming. Within 40 years the Temple will be destroyed.

KJV: And said unto him, Hearest thou what these say? And Jesus saith unto them, Yea; have ye never read, Out of the mouth of babes and sucklings thou hast perfected praise?

Matthew 21:17

וּמִשֶּׁעֲזָבָם הוּא יָצָא מֵעִיר לְבֵית-עַנְיָה וְלָן שָׁם בְּלַיְלָה

HTV: And when Yeshua left them, he went out of the city to Bethany and lodged for the night. And there he was explaining to them the kingdom of God.

KJV: And he left them, and went out of the city into Bethany; and he lodged there.

Matthew 21:19

וַיַּרְא אֶת תְּאֵנָה אֵצֶל הַדֶּרֶךְ וַיָּבוֹא אֵלֶיהָ וְלֹא מָצָא בָהּ כְּלוּם כִּי אִם
לְבַד עָלִים וַיֹּאמַר לָהּ לְעוֹלָם לֹא יִפְרַח מִמֵּךְ פֶּרִי וְיָבְשָׁה הָאוֹתָהּ
תְּאֵנָה מִיָּד

The Hebrew Book of Matthew

HTV: **And Yeshua saw a fig tree near the road and came to it and found nothing but leaves. And he said to it, "No fruit will ever blossom from you!" And that fig tree dried up at once.**

Note: Yeshua had just condemned the Temple system and the priests as being evil and corrupt. They are finished in the eyes of God and will never bear fruit. They are cursed. They will wither.

KJV: And when he saw a fig tree in the way, he came to it, and found nothing thereon, but leaves only, and said unto it, Let no fruit grow on thee henceforward forever. And presently the fig tree withered away.

Matthew 21:20

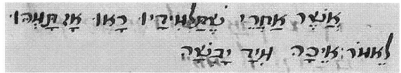

Freiburg Hebrew Manuscript

אֲשֶׁר אַחֲרֵי שֶׁתַּלְמִידָיו רָאוּ אָז תָּמְהוּ לֵאמֹר אֵיכָה מִיָּד יָבָשָׁה

HTV: **After his students saw this, they were astonished, saying, "How quickly did it dry out?"**

Note: Yeshua's disciples seem more fixed upon how the miracle was brought about rather than the meaning of the miracle.

KJV: And when the disciples saw *it*, they marvelled, saying, How soon is the fig tree withered away!

Matthew 21:21

וַיַּעַן יֵשׁוּעַ וַיֹּאמַר בֶּאֱמֶת אֲנִי אוֹמֵר לָכֶם אִם תִּהְיֶה לָכֶם אֱמוּנָה וְלֹא תִסְתַּפְּקוּ אָז לֹא לְבַד תַּעֲשׂוּ מַה שֶׁמִּתְאֲנָה אֲבָל כֹּל שֶׁכֵּן אִם תֹּאמְרוּ לְהַר הַזֶּה הִנָּטֵל וְהָשְׁלַךְ בַּיָּם הִנֵּה הַזֹּאת תִּהְיֶה

HTV: **And Yeshua answered and said, "Truly I say to you, if you have faith and do not doubt - then you will not only do *as* the fig tree - but all that is worthy of *God's* trust - If you say to this mountain, 'Be taken away and be sent into the sea!' - behold, it will be so."**

Chapter 21

KJV: Jesus answered and said unto them, Verily I say unto you, If ye have faith, and doubt not, ye shall not only do this *which is done* to the fig tree, but also if ye shall say unto this mountain, Be thou removed, and be thou cast into the sea; it shall be done.

Matthew 21:22

וְחִקְתְ סַתֶּא סִינִימְאַמ סִכֶּתְלַפְתֵּב וּלְאִשְׁתוֹשׁ הֲמָ לכֹן

HTV: **And whatever you ask in your prayer - if you believe - you will *surely* receive it.**

KJV: And all things, whatsoever ye shall ask in prayer, believing, ye shall receive.

Matthew 21:23

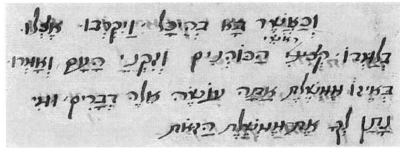
Freiburg Hebrew Manuscript

וְכַאֲשֶׁר בָּא בְהֵיכָל וַיִּקְרְבוּ אֶצְלוֹ בְּלַמְדוֹ רָאשֵׁי הַכּוֹהֲנִים וְזִקְנֵי הָעָם וְאָמְרוּ בְּאֵיזוֹ מֶמְשֶׁלֶת אַתָּה עוֹשֶׂה אֵלֶּה דְּבָרִים וּמִי נָתַן לְךָ אֶת-מֶמְשֶׁלֶת הַזֹּאת

HTV: **And when Yeshua came into the Temple, the chief priests and the elders of the people came to him while teaching, and said, "By what authority do you do these things, and who gave you this authority?"**

> Note: It is not certain whether the priests were objecting to Yeshua teaching in the Temple or whether they had heard of his miracles and healings and were asking by whose authority he did them. In any case, the priests were challenging Yeshua's authority to minister to the people.

KJV: And when he was come into the temple, the chief priests and the elders of the people came unto him as he was teaching, and said, By what authority doest thou these things? and who gave thee this authority?

The Hebrew Book of Matthew

Matthew 21:24

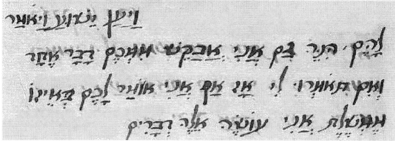

Freiburg Hebrew Manuscript

וַיַּעַן יֵשׁוּעַ וַיֹּאמַר לָהֶם הִנֵּה גַם אֲנִי אֲבַקֵּשׁ מִמְּכֶם דָּבָר אֶחָד וְאִם תֹּאמְרוּ לִי אָז אַף אֲנִי אוֹמֵר לָכֶם בְּאֵיזוֹ מֶמְשֶׁלֶת אֲנִי עוֹשֶׂה אֵלֶּה דְּבָרִים

HTV: **Yeshua answered and said to them, "Look, I will ask one thing of you. And if you tell me, I will also tell you by what authority I do these things."**

KJV: And Jesus answered and said unto them, I also will ask you one thing, which if ye tell me, I in like wise will tell you by what authority I do these things.

Matthew 21:25

Freiburg Hebrew Manuscript

הַטְבִילַת יוֹחָנָן מֵאַיִן תִּהְיֶה אִי מִשָּׁמַיִם אוֹ מֵאֲנוֹשִׁים אָמְנָם הֵמָּה חָשְׁבוּ בְעַצְמָם וְאָמְרוּ אִם נֹאמַר מִשָּׁמַיִם אָז יֹאמַר לָנוּ וְאִם כֵּן לָמָּה לֹא הֶאֱמַנְתֶּם לוֹ

HTV: **"The baptism of John - was it from heaven or from men?" Indeed, they conspired among themselves and said, "If we say 'From heaven', then he will say to us 'And if so - why did you not believe him?'"**

Note: See Isaiah 40:3, where John said, "*I am* a voice of one calling In the wilderness 'prepare the way for Yehovah - make straight in the desert a highway for our God.' "

So, if John's baptism or anointment was from God, as he said, to prepare the way for Yeshua, why aren't they listening?

KJV: The baptism of John, whence was it? from heaven, or of men? And they reasoned with themselves, saying, If we shall say, From heaven; he will say unto us, Why did ye not then believe him?

Matthew 21:26

וְאִם נֹאמַר מֵאֲנוֹשִׁים אֲנַחְנוּ יְרֵאִים אֶת-הַכַּת כִּי כֻלָּם חָשְׁבוּ אֶת-יוֹחָנָן הֱיוֹת דּוֹמֶה לְנָבִיא

HTV: **"And if we say 'From men', we fear the crowd - because they all considered John to be a prophet."**

KJV: But if we shall say, Of men; we fear the people; for all hold John as a prophet.

Matthew 21:27

וְעָנוּ לְיֵשׁוּעַ וְאָמְרוּ אֲנַחְנוּ אֵין יוֹדְעִים וְגַם הוּא אָמַר לָהֶם הִנֵּה אַף אֲנִי לֹא אֹמַר לָכֶם בְּאֵיזוֹ מֶמְשֶׁלֶת אֲנִי עוֹשֶׂה אֵלֶּה דְבָרִים

HTV: **And they answered Yeshua and said, "We do not know." He then said to them, "Then, I will not tell you by which authority I do these things."**

KJV: And they answered Jesus, and said, We cannot tell. And he said unto them, Neither tell I you by what authority I do these things.

Matthew 21:28

מָה נִרְאֶה לָכֶם הִנֵּה יִהְיוּ לְשׁוּם אָדָם שְׁנַיִם בָּנִים וַיִּגַּשׁ לְהָרִאשׁוֹן וַיֹּאמֶר לוֹ לֵךְ לְךָ בְּנִי שֶׁתִּפְעוֹל הַיּוֹם בְּכַרְמִי

HTV: **"How does it seem to you? A certain man had two sons. He approached the first one and said to him, 'Go, my son - to work in my vineyard today.'"**

KJV: But what think ye? A *certain* man had two sons; and he came to the first, and said, Son, go work today in my vineyard.

The Hebrew Book of Matthew

Matthew 21:29

וְהוּא עָנָה לוֹ וַיֹּאמַר אֵינִי רוֹצֶה וְאַחַר כָּךְ שָׁב לְעַצְמוֹ בִּתְשׁוּבָה וַיֵּלֶךְ

HTV: "He answered him and said, 'I do not want to!' But after this - he changed his mind - repented and went."

KJV: He answered and said, I will not: but afterward he repented, and went.

Matthew 21:30

וַיִּקְרַב גַּם לְאַחֵר וַיֹּאמַר לוֹ כְּמוֹ כֵן אֲבָל הוּא עָנָה וַיֹּאמַר הִנְנִי הָאֲדוֹנִי הוֹלֵךְ וְלֹא הָלַךְ

HTV: "And he (the man) also approached the other *son* and said the same thing to him. However, *the son* answered and said, 'Here I am, Lord, I am going' - but he did not go!"

KJV: And he came to the second, and said likewise. And he answered and said, I *go*, sir: and went not.

Matthew 21:31

מִי נָא מֵאֵלֶּה שְׁנַיִם עָשָׂה אֶת-רְצוֹן הָאָב וַיֹּאמְרוּ לוֹ הָרִאשׁוֹן וַיֹּאמַר יֵשׁוּעַ לָהֶם בֶּאֱמֶת אֲנִי אוֹמֵר לָכֶם שֶׁמּוֹכְסִים וְזוֹנוֹת תָּקַדְּמוּ אֶתְכֶם בְּמַלְכוּת הָאֱלֹהִים

HTV: "Who of these two did the will of the father?" They said to him, "The first *son*." Yeshua said to them, "In truth, I say to you that tax collectors and prostitutes will precede you into the kingdom of Elohim."

KJV: Whether of them twain did the will of *his* father? They say unto him, The first. Jesus saith unto them, Verily I say unto you, That the publicans and the harlots go into the kingdom of God before you.

Matthew 21:32

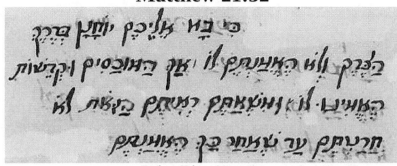

Freiburg Hebrew Manuscript

כִּי בָא אֲלֵיכֶם יוֹחָנָן בְּדֶרֶךְ הַצֶּדֶק וְלֹא הֶאֱמַנְתֶּם לוֹ אַךְ הַמּוֹכְסִים וּקְדֵשׁוֹת הֶאֱמִינוּ לוֹ וּמִשֶּׁאַתֶּם רְאִיתֶם הַזֹּאת לֹא חֲרַטְתֶּם עַד שֶׁאַחַר כָּךְ הֶאֱמַנְתֶּם

HTV: "Yochanan came to you in the way of righteousness and you did not believe him - but the righteous, and *even* the publicans, believed him. And when you saw this - you did not repent afterwards - that you might have cause to believe." To the one (among you) who has ears to hear (the truth) - let him hear it in disgrace."

Note: In other words, Yeshua is saying to those priests who can hear the truth - You know I am right but you cannot say it - and that is a disgrace to you!

KJV: For John came unto you in the way of righteousness, and ye believed him not: but the publicans and the harlots believed him: and ye, when ye had seen *it*, repented not afterward, that ye might believe him.

Matthew 21:33

שִׁמְעוּ נָא מָשָׁל אַחֵר הִנֵּה יִהְיֶה אָדָם בַּעַל הַבַּיִת אֲשֶׁר נָטַע אֶת כֶּרֶם וַיְעַזֵּק אוֹתוֹ בְּגֶדֶר וְחָצֵב בּוֹ יֶקֶב וּבָנוּי מִגְדָּל בְּתוֹכוֹ וְהִצִּיגוֹ לְאִכָּרִים וְהָלַךְ לְאֶרֶץ רְחוֹקָה

HTV: "Listen to another parable. Behold, a man - the master of the house - who planted a vineyard, and strengthened it with a fence, and dug a wine cellar in it, and built a tower in it - then entrusted it to the workers - then went to a far country."

KJV: Hear another parable: There was a certain householder, which planted a vineyard, and hedged it round about, and digged

The Hebrew Book of Matthew

a winepress in it, and built a tower, and let it out to husbandmen, and went into a far country:

Matthew 21:34

וְכַאֲשֶׁר זְמַן הַפְּרִי בָא שָׁלַח אֶת-עֲבָדָיו לְאִכָּרִים לָקַחַת אֶת-פֵּירוֹת שֶׁלּוֹ

HTV: "And when harvest time came - he sent his servants to the workers to collect his fruit."

KJV: And when the time of the fruit drew near, he sent his servants to the husbandmen, that they might receive the fruits of it.

Matthew 21:35

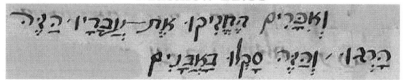
Freiburg Hebrew Manuscript

וְאִכָּרִים הֶחֱזִיקוּ אֶת-עֲבָדָיו הַזֶּה הָרְגוּ וְהַזֶּה סָקְלוּ בָּאֲבָנִים

HTV: "But the workers seized his servants. One they killed - One they beat – and the other(s) they stoned!"

Note: This may well be a parallel to Psalm 80:8-19, which speaks of the Son of Man coming.

KJV: And the husbandmen took his servants, and beat one, and killed another, and stoned another.

Matthew 21:36

וְהוֹסִיף לִשְׁלֹחַ עֲבָדִים אֲחֵרִים רַבִּים מֵרִאשׁוֹנִים עָשׂוּ גַם לָהֶם כְּמוֹכֵן

HTV: "And he continued to send numerous other servants after the first - and they did the same to them also."

KJV: Again, he sent other servants more than the first: and they did unto them likewise.

Matthew 21:37

וּבָאַחֲרוֹנָה שָׁלַח אֲלֵיהֶם אֶת-בְּנוֹ לֵאמֹר יִירְאוּ אֶת-בְּנִי

HTV: **"And in the end - he sent his son to them saying, 'They will respect my son!'"**

KJV: But last of all he sent unto them his son, saying, They will reverence my son.

Matthew 21:38

וְאִכָּרִים כַּאֲשֶׁר רָאוּ אֶת-הַבֵּן הִנֵּה אָמְרוּ בְעַצְמָם הַזֶּה הוּא הַיּוֹרֵשׁ בֹּאוּ נָא שֶׁנַּהַרְגוֹ אוֹתוֹ וְתִהְיֶה לָנוּ הַנַּחֲלָתוֹ

HTV: **"And the workers, when they saw the son, said to themselves, "This is the heir. Come now, let us kill him, and to us will be his inheritance!"**

KJV: But when the husbandmen saw the son, they said among themselves, This is the heir; come, let us kill him, and let us seize on his inheritance.

Matthew 21:39

וּמִשֶּׁהֶחֱזִיקוּהוּ גֵּרְשׁוּהוּ לְחוּצָה הַכֶּרֶם וְהָרְגוּ אוֹתוֹ

HTV: **"Those who took him, cast him outside the vineyard - and killed him!"**

KJV: And they caught him, and cast *him* out of the vineyard, and slew *him*.

Matthew 21:40

וְכַאֲשֶׁר הָאָדוֹן הַכֶּרֶם יָבוֹא מַה נָּא יַעֲשֶׂה לְאוֹתָם אִכָּרִים

HTV: **"When the lord of the vineyard comes - what will he do to those workers?"**

KJV: When the lord therefore of the vineyard cometh, what will he do unto those husbandmen?

Matthew 21:41

וַיֹּאמְרוּ לוֹ הִנֵּה בִּהְיוֹתָם רָעִים אַבֵּד יְאַבֵּד אוֹתָם וְכַרְמוֹ יַצִּיג לַאֲחֵרִים אִכָּרִים שֶׁיִּתְּנוּ לוֹ פְּרִי בִּזְמַנּוֹ

HTV: **And they said to him, "Behold, they are evil** *to the core* **of their being! He will utterly destroy them - then entrust his vineyard to other workers who will give him the fruit** *of the harvest* **in its time."**

KJV: They say unto him, He will miserably destroy those wicked men, and will let out *his* vineyard unto other husbandmen, which shall render him the fruits in their seasons.

Matthew 21:42

וַיֹּאמֶר יֵשׁוּעַ לָהֶם הַאִם לֹא קְרָאתֶם בִּכְתוּבִים אֶבֶן אֲשֶׁר מָאֲסוּ הַבּוֹנִים הָיְתָה לְרֹאשׁ פִּנָּה מֵאֵת יְהֹוָה הָיְתָה הַזֹּאת הִיא נִפְלָאת בְּעֵינֵינוּ

HTV: **Yeshua said to them, "Have you not read in the scriptures, 'The stone which the builders rejected - has become the cornerstone -** *as intended* **by Yehovah! It is marvelous in our eyes!'"**

Note: Yeshua is referring to Psalm 118:22-23

KJV: Jesus saith unto them, Did ye never read in the scriptures, The stone which the builders rejected, the same is become the head of the corner: this is the Lord's doing, and it is marvelous in our eyes?

Matthew 21:43

לְפִיכָךְ אֲנִי אוֹמֵר לָכֶם כִּי מַלְכוּת הָאֱלֹהִים תִּנָּטֵל מִמְּכֶם וְתִנָּתֵן לְעַם אֲשֶׁר יַעֲשֶׂה פִּרְיוֹ

HTV: **"Therefore, I say to you that the kingdom of Elohim will be taken from you - and will be given to a people who will produce its fruit!"**

KJV: Therefore say I unto you, The kingdom of God shall be taken from you, and given to a nation bringing forth the fruits thereof.

Matthew 21:44

וּמִי שֶׁיִּפּוֹל עַל אֶבֶן הַזֹּאת יִשָּׁבֵר וְעַל אֲשֶׁר נָפַל תְּשַׁבְּרוֹ

HTV: **"Whoever falls on this stone will be broken - but whoever it falls upon will be shattered."**

KJV: And whosoever shall fall on this stone shall be broken: but on whomsoever it shall fall, it will grind him to powder.

Matthew 21:45

וְכַאֲשֶׁר שָׁמְעוּ רָאשֵׁי הַכּוֹהֲנִים וּפְרוּשִׁים אֶת מְשָׁלָיו הֵם יָדְעוּ שֶׁמְדַבֵּר מֵהֶם

HTV: And when the chief priests and Pharisees heard his parables - they knew that Yeshua was speaking of them!

KJV: And when the chief priests and Pharisees had heard his parables, they perceived that he spake of them.

Matthew 21:46

וַיְבַקְשׁוּ לְהַחֲזִיקוֹ אַךְ יָרְאוּ אֶת-הַכִּתִּים כִּי יִהְיֶה לָהֶם כְּהַנָּבִיא

HTV: They sought to seize Yeshua, but they feared the crowd - because he was like a prophet to them.

KJV: But when they sought to lay hands on him, they feared the multitude, because they took him for a prophet.

Matthew Chapter 22

Hebrew Text Version (HTV)

¹ Yeshua continued to speak to them in parables, and he said,

² "The kingdom of heaven is like a king who made a wedding for his son."

³ "He sent his servants to summon the invited guests to the wedding - but they did not want to come."

⁴ "Again, he sent other servants, saying to them to tell the invited guests - 'See, I have prepared a banquet of fatted calves

and geese. They are carved and all things we have made ready. Come! Come to the wedding celebrations!' "

⁵ "And they were scornful, and refused, and turned away - this one to his field - and that one to his trade."

⁶ "And the others seized his servants - and after abusing them - they stoned them *to death*!"

⁷ "When the king heard, he was angry and his nostrils flared at them. He sent his armies and destroyed those murderers! Then he burned their house with fire."

⁸ "Then he said to his servants, 'The wedding is ready, but the ones who were invited are not worthy.' "

⁹ "Therefore, go into the roadways - bring all who you can find there - and invite them to the wedding!"

¹⁰ "His servants went out to the roadways and gathered everyone they found - the bad ones and the good ones - and they filled the wedding table with guests."

¹¹ "The king came to see the guests at the table - and there he saw one man who was without the proper wedding clothes."

¹² "He said to him, 'Dear friend, how can it be that you entered here without the proper wedding clothes?' And the man was silent."

¹³ "Then the king said to his servants, 'Bind him by his feet and hands - take him away - and throw him into the outer darkness! There shall be weeping and gnashing of teeth.'"

¹⁴ "For many are called but few are chosen!"

¹⁵ Then the Pharisees proceeded to take counsel together - to trap Yeshua with his *own* words.

¹⁶ They sent to him their disciples *along* with the Herodians, to say, "Rabbi, we know that you are a stern teacher - who teaches the way of God and truth. You do not respect the status of any person. You are fearful of no one."

¹⁷ "Therefore, tell us how it seems to you. Is it right to give tribute to Caesar - or not?"

¹⁸ Yeshua - knowing their deceit said, "Why do you tempt me - you hypocrites!"

¹⁹ "Show me the coin of tribute." They gave him a silver coin.

²⁰ Yeshua said to them, "Whose image is this - or the writing around it?"

Chapter 22

²¹ And they said, "Caesar's." So he said to them, "Give unto Caesar that which belongs to Caesar - and to God that which belongs to God."

²² After hearing *his words* - they were astonished and they left him alone and departed from him.

²³ On that same day, the Sadducees - who say there is no resurrection of the dead - approached and asked Yeshua,

²⁴ Saying, "Rabbi, behold, Moses said, 'If one will die with no son - his brother will take his wife to himself *to marry* - and for the wife he will raise up his brother's seed.'"

²⁵ "Indeed there were seven brothers near us - the first of whom took a wife. He died - with no seed - and his brother married his wife."

²⁶ "And likewise after that, the second, and the third - up to the seventh *brother*."

²⁷ "Every one of them died - and last of all - the woman also."

²⁸ "To whom shall she be married - in the resurrection of the dead - because every one of them were married to her?"

²⁹ Yeshua answered and said to them, "You are lost - not knowing the Scriptures - nor the might of Elohim."

³⁰ "Because in the resurrection of the dead they neither marry nor are given in marriage - but they shall be like the angels of Elohim in heaven."

³¹ "Have you not read what was spoken by Elohim - about the resurrection of the dead? As He says,"

³² "I am the Elohim of Abraham, the Elohim of Isaac, and the Elohim of Jacob." "He is not the Elohim of the dead - but of the living!"

³³ "When the crowds heard *this* - they marveled at his wisdom!"

³⁴ When the Pharisees heard that Yeshua had silenced the Sadducees - they counselled together.

³⁵ One of them, who was a teacher of Torah, asked Yeshua - challenging him - and said,

36 "Rabbi - which is the greatest commandment in the Torah?"

³⁷ Yeshua said unto him, "Love Yehovah your Elohim with all your heart, and with all your soul, and with all your strength!"

³⁸ "This is the first and greatest commandment!"

³⁹ "The second is like unto this - you shall love your neighbor

as yourself."

⁴⁰ "On these two commandments depend the whole of Torah and the prophets."

⁴¹ After the Pharisees were gathered together - Yeshua asked them

⁴² "What do you think of the Messiah? Whose son is he?" - They said unto him, "*The son* of David."

⁴³ Yeshua said unto them, "If so, how does David - by the Holy Spirit - call him Lord, saying…"

⁴⁴ "Yehovah said to my Lord - 'Sit at my right hand until I make your enemies your footstool.' "

⁴⁵ "Therefore - if David called him Lord - how then is he his son?"

⁴⁶ None of them were able to answer Yeshua a word - and from then on - no one dared to ask him anything more.

Matthew Chapter 22

HTV with translator notes and KJV comparison

Matthew 22:1

וַיַּעַן יֵשׁוּעַ וְהוֹסִיף לְדַבֵּר לָהֶם בִּמְשָׁלִים וַיֹּאמַר

HTV: Yeshua continued to speak to them in parables, and he said,

KJV: And Jesus answered and spake unto them again by parables, and said,

Matthew 22:2

<small>Freiburg Hebrew Manuscript</small>

הַמַּלְכוּת הַשָּׁמַיִם הִיא נִמְשָׁלָה לְאָדָם הַמֶּלֶךְ אֲשֶׁר עָשָׂה חֲתֻנּוֹת עִם בְּנוֹ

Chapter 22

HTV: "The kingdom of heaven is like a king who made a wedding for his son."

Note: The king is Yehovah and His son Yeshua Ha Mashiach. The wedding is for the bride of Yeshua - his followers - whether they be Jews or Gentiles. The parable explains why there must be more believers than the Jews alone - many will reject him, both Jews and Gentiles. "Salvation is from the Jews" but not solely for them - Yehovah intended it for all. (John 4:22)

KJV: The kingdom of heaven is like unto a certain king, which made a marriage for his son,

Matthew 22:3

וַיִּשְׁלַח אֶת-עֲבָדָיו לִקְרוֹא אֶת-קְרוּאִים לַחֲתֻנוֹת וְהֵמָה לֹא רָצוּ לָבוֹא

HTV: "He sent his servants to summon the invited guests to the wedding - but they did not want to come."

KJV: And sent forth his servants to call them that were bidden to the wedding: and they would not come.

Matthew 22:4

וְהוֹסִיף לִשְׁלַח עֲבָדִים אֲחֵרִים וַיֹּאמַר אִמְרוּ לִקְרוּאִים הִנֵּה כוֹנַנְתִּי אֶת אֲרוּחָתִי שְׁוָרַי וּבַרְבּוּרַי הֵם שְׁחוּטִים וְכֹל דְּבָרִים כּוֹנֲנוּ בּוֹאוּ נָא לַחֲתֻנוֹת

HTV: "Again, he sent other servants, saying to them to tell the invited guests - 'See, I have prepared a banquet of fatted calves and geese. They are carved and all things we have made ready. Come! Come to the wedding celebrations!' "

KJV: Again, he sent forth other servants, saying, Tell them which are bidden, Behold, I have prepared my dinner: my oxen and *my* fatlings *are* killed, and all things *are* ready: come unto the marriage.

Matthew 22:5

וְהֵמָה הִתְרַשְּׁלוּ וּמָאֲסוּ וְהָלְכוּ הַזֶּה בְּכַפְרָא שֶׁלּוֹ וְהַזֶּה לִסְחָרוּתוֹ

HTV: **"And they were scornful, and refused, and turned away - this one to his field - and that one to his trade."**

KJV: But they made light of *it*, and went their ways, one to his farm, another to his merchandise:

Matthew 22:6

וּשְׁאָרִים הֶחֱזִיקוּ אֶת-עֲבָדָיו וְאַחֲרֵי שֶׁהָם שֶׁגְדָפוּם אָז הֲרָגוּם

HTV: **"And the others seized his servants - and after abusing them - they stoned them *to death*!"**

KJV: And the remnant took his servants, and entreated *them* spitefully, and slew *them*.

Matthew 22:7

וְכַאֲשֶׁר הַמֶּלֶךְ שָׁמַע
חָרָה אַפּוֹ בָם וַיִּשְׁלַח אֶת-צְבָאוֹתָיו וְהִשְׁמִיד
הָאוֹתָם רוֹצְחִים וְאֶת-עִירָם שָׂרַף בָּאֵשׁ

Freiburg Hebrew Manuscript

וְכַאֲשֶׁר הַמֶּלֶךְ שָׁמַע חָרָה אַפּוֹ בָם וַיִּשְׁלַח אֶת-צְבָאוֹתָיו וְהִשְׁמִיד הָאוֹתָם רוֹצְחִים וְאֶת-עִירָם שָׂרַף בָּאֵשׁ

HTV: **"When the king heard, he was angry and his nostrils flared at them. He sent his armies and destroyed those murderers! Then he burned their house with fire."**

> Note: This parable is akin to the previous one in Matthew 21:43, "Therefore, I say to you that the kingdom of God will be taken from you - and given to a people who will produce its fruit!" This could mean a household, city, or religious system governed by a Temple (house of prayer) but the operant distinction is individual, those who embrace his son versus those who do not. Therefore, it is not a condemnation of whole people groups whether Hebrew or Gentile.

KJV: But when the king heard *thereof*, he was wroth: and he sent forth his armies, and destroyed those murderers, and burned up their city.

Matthew 22:8

וְאָז אָמַר לַעֲבָדָיו חֲתֻנּוֹת כּוֹנָנוּ אֲבָל אֲשֶׁר יִהְיוּ קְרוּאִים לֹא יִהְיוּ רְאוּיִם

HTV: "Then he said to his servants, 'The wedding is ready, but the ones who were invited are not worthy.' "

KJV: Then saith he to his servants, The wedding is ready, but they which were bidden were not worthy.

Matthew 22:9

עַל כֵּן לְכוּ לְאֻמּוֹת דְּרָכִים וְכֹל שֶׁתִּמְצָאוּ קִרְאוּ לַחֲתֻנּוֹת

HTV: "Therefore, go into the roadways - bring all who you can find there - and invite them to the wedding!"

KJV: Go ye therefore into the highways, and as many as ye shall find, bid to the marriage.

Matthew 22:1

וַעֲבָדָיו יָצְאוּ לַדְּרָכִים וַיְקַבְּצוּ כֻלָּם שֶׁמָּצְאוּ הָרָעִים וְהַטּוֹבִים וְנִמְלְאוּ הֶחֲתֻנּוֹת בְּיוֹשְׁבִים לְשֻׁלְחָן

HTV: "His servants went out to the roadways and gathered everyone they found - the bad ones and the good ones - and they filled the wedding table with guests."

KJV: So those servants went out into the highways, and gathered together all as many as they found, both bad and good: and the wedding was furnished with guests.

Matthew 22:11

וְהַמֶּלֶךְ בָּא לִרְאוֹת אֶת יוֹשְׁבִים לְשֻׁלְחָן וַיַּרְא שָׁם שׁוּם אָדָם שֶׁאֵין יִהְיֶה נִתְלַבֵּשׁ בְּמַלְבּוּשׁ חֲתֻנּוֹת

HTV: "The king came to see the guests at the table - and there he saw one man who was without the proper wedding clothes."

The Hebrew Book of Matthew

KJV: And when the king came in to see the guests, he saw there a man which had not on a wedding garment:

Matthew 22:12

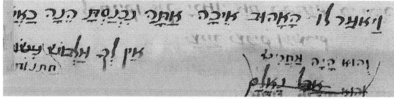
Freiburg Hebrew Manuscript

וַיֹּאמֶר לוֹ הָאָהוּב אֵיכָה אַתָּה נִכְנַסְתָּ הֵנָה כַּאֲשֶׁר אֵין לְךָ מַלְבּוּשׁ חֲתָנוֹת וְהוּא הָיָה מַחֲרִישׁ

HTV: **"He said to him, 'Dear friend, how can it be that you entered here without the proper wedding clothes?' And the man was silent."**

Note: Yeshua is speaking of the Anti-Christ. A wolf dressed in sheep's clothing (Matthew 7:15-20). One who is posing as a godly person but is, in fact, there to "steal, kill and destroy." John 2:18 states the Anti-Christ is not a single person - there will be many.

KJV: And he saith unto him, Friend, how camest thou in hither not having a wedding garment? And he was speechless.

Matthew 22:13

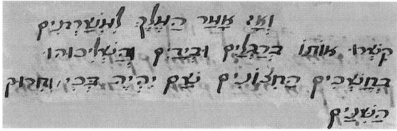
Freiburg Hebrew Manuscript

וְאָז אָמַר הַמֶּלֶךְ לִמְשָׁרְתִים קִשְׁרוּ אוֹתוֹ בְּרַגְלַיִם וּבְיָדַיִם וְהַשְׁלִיכוּהוּ בַּחֲשָׁכִים הַחִיצוֹנִים שָׁם יִהְיֶה בְּכִי וְחֵרוּק הַשִּׁנַּיִם

HTV: **"Then the king said to his servants, 'Bind him by his feet and hands - take him away - and throw him into the outer darkness! There shall be weeping and gnashing of teeth.'"**

Chapter 22

Note: The Anti-Christ who poses as a believer but is truly there to destroy is destined for divine punishment.

KJV: Then said the king to the servants, Bind him hand and foot, and take him away, and cast *him* into outer darkness; there shall be weeping and gnashing of teeth.

Matthew 22:14

כִּי רַבִּים קְרוּאִים וּמְעַטִים בְּחוּרִים

HTV: **"For many are called but few are chosen!"**

KJV: For many are called, but few *are* chosen.

Matthew 22:15

וְאָז הָלְכוּ לָהֶם פְּרוּשִׁים וְנוֹסְדוּ יַחַד לָקַחַת עֵצָה לְהוֹקִישׁוֹ בִּדְבָרָיו

HTV: **Then the Pharisees proceeded to take counsel together - to trap Yeshua with his *own* words.**

KJV: Then went the Pharisees, and took counsel how they might entangle him in *his* talk.

Matthew 22:16

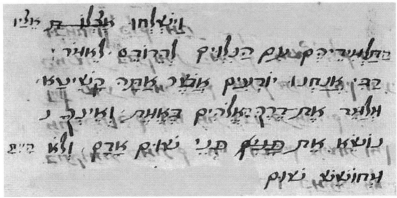

Freiburg Hebrew Manuscript

וַיִּשְׁלְחוּ אֵלָיו הַתַּלְמִידֵיהֶם עִם הַגָּלְוִים לְהֵרוֹדֵס לֵאמֹר רַבִּי אֲנַחְנוּ יוֹדְעִים אֲשֶׁר אַתָּה קָשִׁיטָא מְלַמֵּד אֶת-דֶּרֶךְ הָאֱלֹהִים בֶּאֱמֶת וְאֵינְךָ נוֹשֵׂא אֶת פְּנֵי שׁוּם אָדָם וְלֹא הָיִיתָ מְחוֹשֵׁשׁ שׁוּם

349

The Hebrew Book of Matthew

HTV: **They sent to him their disciples *along* with the Herodians, to say, "Rabbi, we know that you are a stern teacher - who teaches the way of God and truth. You do not respect the status of any person. You are fearful of no one."**

Note: The Pharisees have sent their students so they could deny any involvement. They also engaged the Herodian priests as witnesses. Herod and his priests were in control of the Temple and the Sanhedrin. As vassals of the Romans, they held the power. Their trap was to get Yeshua to speak out against the Romans.

The Herodians would take this to the Romans, their overlords, and have Yeshua destroyed for treason. See Luke 20:20-25 for more explicit details of the plot.

KJV: And they sent out unto him their disciples with the Herodians, saying, Master, we know that thou art true, and teachest the way of God in truth, neither carest thou for any *man*: for thou regardest not the person of men.

Matthew 22:17

לְפִיכָךְ אֱמוֹר לָנוּ מָה נִרְאֶה לְךָ הַאִם נָכוֹן לָתֵת לְקֵיסַר אֶת-הַמַּס אוֹ לֹא

HTV: **"Therefore, tell us how it seems to you. Is it right to give tribute to Caesar - or not?"**

KJV: Tell us therefore, What thinkest thou? Is it lawful to give tribute unto Caesar, or not?

Matthew 22:18

וּמִשֶׁיֵּשׁוּעַ יָדַע אֶת-פִּשְׁעָם אָמַר לָמָה אַתֶּם מְנַסִּים אוֹתִי אַתֶּם הַחֲנֵפִים

HTV: **Yeshua - knowing their deceit said, "Why do you tempt me - you hypocrites!"**

KJV: But Jesus perceived their wickedness, and said, Why tempt ye me, *ye* hypocrites?

Matthew 22:19

הַרְאוּ לִי אֶת-מַטְבֵּעַ הַמַּס וְהֵמָה הִקְרִיבוּ לוֹ זוּז

Chapter 22

HTV: **"Show me the coin of tribute." They gave him a silver coin.**

KJV: Shew me the tribute money. And they brought unto him a penny.

Matthew 22:20

וַיֹּאמֶר יֵשׁוּעַ לָהֶם לְמִי דְמוּת הַזֹּאת אוֹ הַכָּתָב בִּסְבִיבָתוֹ

HTV: **Yeshua said to them, "Whose image is this - or the writing around it?"**

KJV: And he saith unto them, Whose *is* this image and superscription?

Matthew 22:21

וְאָמְרוּ לוֹ לְקֵיסָר אָז אָמַר לָהֶם תְּנוּ לְקֵיסָר מָה שֶׁלְּקֵיסָר וּלְאֱלֹהִים מָה שֶׁלֵּאלֹהִים

HTV: **And they said, "Caesar's." So he said to them, "Give unto Caesar that which belongs to Caesar - and to God that which belongs to God."**

KJV: They say unto him, Caesar's. Then saith he unto them, Render therefore unto Caesar the things which are Caesar's; and unto God the things that are God's.

Matthew 22:22

וְאַחֲרֵי *שֶׁשָּׁמְעוּ* הֵם תָּמְהוּ וַהֲנִיחוּהוּ וְסָרוּ מִמֶּנּוּ

HTV: **After hearing *his words* - they were astonished and they left him alone and departed from him.**

KJV: When they had heard *these* words, they marvelled, and left him, and went their way.

Matthew 22:23

בְּאוֹתוֹ הַיּוֹם קָרְבוּ צָדוֹקִים אֲשֶׁר אוֹמְרִים שֶׁאֵין תְּקוּמַת הַמֵּתִים וַיִּשְׁאָלוּהוּ

351

HTV: **On that same day, the Sadducees - who say there is no resurrection of the dead - approached and asked Yeshua,**

KJV: The same day came to him the Sadducees, which say that there is no resurrection, and asked him,

Matthew 22:24

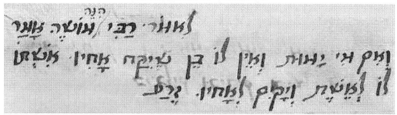
Freiburg Hebrew Manuscript

לֵאמֹר רַבִּי הִנֵּה מוֹשֶׁה אָמַר וְאִם מִי יָמוּת וְאֵין לוֹ בֵן שֶׁיִּקַּח אָחִיו אִשְׁתּוֹ לוֹ לְאִשָּׁה וְיָקִים לְאָחִיו זֶרַע

HTV: **Saying, "Rabbi, behold, Moses said, 'If one will die with no son - his brother will take his wife to himself *to marry* - and for the wife he will raise up his brother's seed.'"**

Note: See Deuteronomy 25:5, the family must give the widow a child of the same seed as the deceased husband - to take care of her in her old age.

In the account of Judah, it is the father who gives Tamar a child. For Ruth it is Boaz, the cousin, (Ruth 2:1) who marries her and gives her a child. Thus, the widow and child remain as a part of the family for support and nurture.

KJV: Saying, Master, Moses said, If a man die, having no children, his brother shall marry his wife, and raise up seed unto his brother.

Matthew 22:25

אָמְנָם יִהְיוּ אֶצְלֵנוּ שִׁבְעָה אָחִים אֲשֶׁר מֵהֶם הָרִאשׁוֹן מִשֶּׁלָּקַח לוֹ אֵשֶׁת הוּא מֵת וְאֵין לוֹ זֶרַע

HTV: **"Indeed there were seven brothers near us - the first of whom took a wife. He died - with no seed - and his brother married his wife."**

KJV: Now there were with us seven brethren: and the first, when he had married a wife, deceased, and, having no issue, left his wife unto his brother:

Matthew 22:26

וּכְמוֹ כֵן הַשֵּׁנִי וְהַשְּׁלִישִׁי עַד הַשְּׁבִיעִי

HTV: **"And likewise after that, the second, and the third - up to the seventh *brother*."**

KJV: Likewise the second also, and the third, unto the seventh.

Matthew 22:27

וּבָאַחֲרוֹן כֻּלָּם מֵתָה גַם הָאִשָּׁה

HTV: **"Every one of them died - and last of all - the woman also."**

KJV: And last of all the woman died also.

Matthew 22:28

וּלְמִי מִשִּׁבְעָה תִּהְיֶה הָאִשֶּׁת בִּתְקוּמַת הַמֵּתִים כִּי כֻלָּם יְבָעֲלוּהָ

HTV: **"To whom shall she be married - in the resurrection of the dead - because every one of them were married to her?"**

KJV: Therefore in the resurrection whose wife shall she be of the seven? for they all had her.

Matthew 22:29

וַיַּעַן יֵשׁוּעַ וַיֹּאמֶר לָהֶם אַתֶּם תּוֹעִים אֵין יוֹדְעִים אֶת-כְּתוּבִים וְלֹא אֶת-גְּבוּרַת הָאֱלֹהִים

HTV: **Yeshua answered and said to them, "You are lost - not knowing the Scriptures - nor the might of Elohim."**

The Hebrew Book of Matthew

KJV: Jesus answered and said unto them, Ye do err, not knowing the scriptures, nor the power of God.

Matthew 22:30

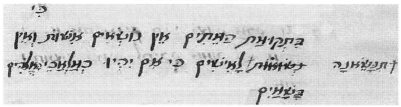

Freiburg Hebrew Manuscript

כִּי בִּתְקוּמַת הַמֵּתִים אֵין נוֹשְׂאִים אִשּׁוֹת וְאֵין תִּנָּשֵׂאנָה לָאִישִׁים כִּי אִם יִהְיוּ כְּמַלְאֲכֵי הָאֱלֹהִים בַּשָּׁמַיִם

HTV: **"Because in the resurrection of the dead they neither marry nor are given in marriage - but they shall be like the angels of Elohim in heaven."**

Note: Only one who had authority in heaven could make this statement as it is not from ancient Scripture. Spiritual bodies do not reproduce. No wonder the people were amazed.

KJV: For in the resurrection they neither marry, nor are given in marriage, but are as the angels of God in heaven.

Matthew 22:31

הַאִם לֹא קְרָאתֶם מָה שֶׁנֶּאֱמַר מִפִּי הָאֱלֹהִים עַל תְּקוּמַת הַמֵּתִים כַּאֲשֶׁר אוֹמֵר

HTV: **"Have you not read what was spoken by Elohim - about the resurrection of the dead? As He says,"**

KJV: But as touching the resurrection of the dead, have ye not read that which was spoken unto you by God, saying,

Matthew 22:32

Freiburg Hebrew Manuscript

Chapter 22

אָנוֹכִי אֱלֹהֵי אַבְרָהָם אֱלֹהֵי יִצְחָק וֵאלֹהֵי יַעֲקֹב הוּא לֹא אֱלֹהֵי הַמֵּתִים כִּי אִם אֱלֹהֵי הַחַיִּים

HTV: **"I am the Elohim of Abraham, the Elohim of Isaac, and the Elohim of Jacob." "He is not the Elohim of the dead - but of the living!"**

Note: Yeshua is contesting the Sadducees - who do not believe in the resurrection of the dead - by stating Elohim is the God of Abraham, Isaac, and Jacob - who are deceased but raised to eternal life - if not then Elohim would no longer be their God - as they would no longer exist.

KJV: I am the God of Abraham, and the God of Isaac, and the God of Jacob? God is not the God of the dead, but of the living.

Matthew 22:33

אֲשֶׁר מִשֶּׁהַכִּתִּים שָׁמְעוּ הֵמָּה תָּמְהוּ עַל לִימּוּדוֹ

HTV: **"When the crowds heard *this* - they marveled at his wisdom!"**

KJV: And when the multitude heard *this*, they were astonished at his doctrine.

Matthew 22:34

וְכַאֲשֶׁר הַפְּרוּשִׁים שָׁמְעוּ אֲשֶׁר הִשְׁתִּיק אֶת-צַדּוֹקִים הֵמָּה נוֹסְדוּ יַחַד

HTV: **When the Pharisees heard that Yeshua had silenced the Sadducees - they counselled together.**

KJV: But when the Pharisees had heard that he had put the Sadducees to silence, they were gathered together.

Matthew 22:35

וַיִּשְׁאֲלוּ אֶחָד מֵהֶם שֶׁיִּהְיֶה מוֹרֶה הַתּוֹרָה מְנַסֶּה אוֹתוֹ וַיֹּאמַר

HTV: **One of them, who was a teacher of Torah, asked Yeshua - challenging him - and said,**

KJV: Then one of them, *which was* a lawyer, asked *him* a question, tempting him, and saying,

The Hebrew Book of Matthew

Matthew 22:36

רַבִּי אֵיזוֹ מִצְוָה מַגְדּוֹלָה בַּתּוֹרָה

HTV: "Rabbi - which is the greatest commandment in the Torah?"

KJV: Master, which *is* the great commandment in the law?

Matthew 22:37

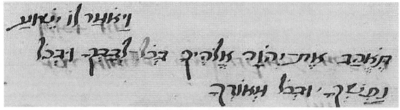
Freiburg Hebrew Manuscript

וַיֹּאמֶר לוֹ יֵשׁוּעַ תֶּאֱהַב אֶת-יְהֹוָה אֱלֹהֶיךָ בְּכֹל לְבָבְךָ וּבְכֹל נַפְשְׁךָ וּבְכֹל מְאוֹדְךָ

HTV: "Yeshua said unto him, "Love Yehovah your Elohim with all your heart, and with all your soul, and with all your strength!"

Note: This is from the *Shema* in Deuteronomy 6:5, Mark 12:28-29, also cited in other verses.

KJV: Jesus said unto him, Thou shalt love the Lord thy God with all thy heart, and with all thy soul, and with all thy mind.

Matthew 22:38

הַזֹּאת מִצְוָה הַגְּדוֹלָה וְרִאשׁוֹנָה

HTV: "This is the first and greatest commandment!"

KJV: This is the first and great commandment.

Matthew 22:39

הַשֵּׁנִית הִיא נִתְדָמָה לַזֹּאת כֵּיצַד תֶּאֱהַב אֶת-עֲמִיתְךָ כְּעַצְמְךָ

HTV: "The second is like unto this - you shall love your neighbor as yourself."

KJV: And the second *is* like unto it, Thou shalt love thy neighbour as thyself.

Matthew 22:40
בְּזֹאת שְׁתַּיִם מִצְוֹת תְּלוּיָה כָּל הַתּוֹרָה וּנְבִיאִים

HTV: **"On these two commandments depend the whole of Torah and the prophets."**

KJV: On these two commandments hang all the law and the prophets.

Matthew 22:41
וְאַחֲרֵי שֶׁהַפְּרוּשִׁים נִקְבְּצוּ יִשְׁאָלָם יֵשׁוּעַ

HTV: **After the Pharisees were gathered together - Yeshua asked them.**

KJV: While the Pharisees were gathered together, Jesus asked them,

Matthew 22:42
לֵאמֹר מָה נִרְאֶה לָכֶם מִמָּשִׁיחַ לְמִי הוּא בֵן אֲשֶׁר אָמְרוּ לוֹ לְדָוִד

HTV: **"What do you think of the Messiah? Whose son is he?" - They said unto him, "*The son* of David."**

KJV: Saying, What think ye of Christ? whose son is he? They say unto him, *The Son* of David.

Matthew 22:43
וַיֹּאמֶר לָהֶם וְאִם כֵּן אֵיךְ דָּוִד קוֹרֵא אוֹתוֹ בְּרוּחַ אָדוֹן לֵאמֹר

HTV: **Yeshua said unto them, "If so, how does David - by the Holy Spirit - call him Lord, saying."**

KJV: He saith unto them, How then doth David in spirit call him Lord, saying,

The Hebrew Book of Matthew

Matthew 22:44

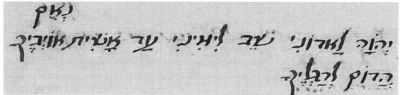
Freiburg Hebrew Manuscript

נְאֻם יְהֹוָה לַאדֹנִי שֵׁב לִימִינִי עַד אָשִׁית אֹיְבֶיךָ הֲדֹם לְרַגְלֶיךָ

HTV: "Yehovah said to my Lord - 'Sit at my right hand until I make your enemies your footstool.' "

Note: See Psalm 110:1 where it is clear that it is David who is making this statement.

KJV: The LORD said unto my Lord, Sit thou on my right hand, till I make thine enemies thy footstool?

Matthew 22:45

לְפִיכָךְ אִם דָּוִד קוֹרֵא אוֹתוֹ אָדוֹן אֵיכָה נָא הוּא בְנוֹ

HTV: "Therefore - if David called him Lord - how then is he his son?"

KJV: If David then call him Lord, how is he his son?

Matthew 22:4

וְלֹא יוּכַל לוֹ אִי זֶה מֵהֶם לַעֲנוֹת דָּבָר וְלֹא הֵעִיז עוֹד שׁוּם פָּנָיו לִשְׁאוֹל אוֹתוֹ

HTV: None of them were able to answer Yeshua a word - and from then on - no one dared to ask him anything more.

KJV: And no man was able to answer him a word, neither durst any man from that day forth ask him any more *questions*.

Matthew Chapter 23

Hebrew Text Version (HTV)

¹ Then Yeshua spoke to the crowd and to his disciples:

² "It is said the scribes and the Pharisees sat (*themselves*) on the seat of Moses."

³ "All that he (Moses) taught you to keep - guard *it*, do *it*, and make *it* happen! The (Sadducees and Pharisees) tell you to observe their commands - but do not follow them - because, according to their deeds - they do not observe them."

⁴ "They (scribes & Pharisees) conspire to bind you with heavy burdens - which are difficult to bear - and put *them* on the shoulders of the people - but they are not willing to lift even one finger to move them."

⁵ "They do all their deeds in order for them to be seen by men - so they widen their phylacteries - and the tassels on the edge of their clothing they enlarge and lengthen."

⁶ "They love the best seats at evening banquets - and the best seats in the assemblies"

⁷ "and *they love* being bowed to with greetings of peace (Shalom) in the markets - and to be called great (Rabbi) by the people."

⁸ "However, do not call yourselves *'rabbi'* (great) because there is only one who is Rabbi (greater) than you all - Indeed, *all* of you are brothers."

⁹ "Do not call yourselves *'father'* - on this earth - for you have only one Father who is in heaven."

¹⁰ "And don't be called Rabbi's (great ones) because there is to you only one great one - Yeshua the Messiah!"

¹¹ "He who is greatest among you - shall be your servant."

¹² Whoever shall exalt himself shall be humbled - and whoever shall humble himself shall be exalted."

¹³ "Woe to you scribes and Pharisees - hypocrites! For you shut off the kingdom of heaven from men - You do not enter

there yourselves - nor allow others to come in."

¹⁴ "Woe to you scribes and Pharisees - hypocrites!
You who consume the homes of widows - then pray lengthy prayers! - For this reason you shall receive damnation!"

¹⁵ "Woe to you scribes and Pharisees - hypocrites! You travel over land and sea to make one proselyte - and when he is found you make him double the son of Hell (Gehinnom) than you are."

¹⁶ "Woe to you leaders of the blind who say - 'All who swear by the Temple - this is nothing! Only *one* who swears by the gold of the Temple - will be obliged.' "

¹⁷ "You blind fools! What is greater - the gold - or the Temple which sanctifies the gold?"

¹⁸ "All who swear by the altar are not obliged. However, whosoever swears to make a gift on the altar - that one will be obliged!"

¹⁹ "O you Blind ones! Which is greater - the gift - or the altar that sanctifies the gift?"

²⁰ "Accordingly, whoever swears by the altar - also swears by all that is on the altar."

²¹ "And all who swear by the Temple - also swear by the One who dwells within it."

²² "He who swears by heaven - swears by the throne of Elohim and He who sits upon it!"

²³ "Woe you scribes and Pharisees - hypocrites! You tithe mint, rue, and cumin - but you forsake the weightier matters of the Torah - which *are* judgment, grace, and faith - These must be done! - And you must not leave them *undone!*"

²⁴ "You blind leaders - who strain at a flea - but swallow a camel!"

²⁵ "Woe to you scribes and Pharisees - hypocrites! For you cleanse the outside of a *vessel* (cup or bowl) - but on the inside you are full of extortion and impurity!"

²⁶ "Woe to the blind Pharisee! Purify beforehand - that which is inside the cup and bowl - so that which is outside will be purified."

²⁷ "Woe unto you scribes and Pharisees - hypocrites!

for you are likened unto sepulchres - which look white and beautiful outside - but inside they are full of the bones of the dead and all impurity."

²⁸ "And so also are you - because on the outside you are seen by men as righteous - however, within, you are full of hypocrisy and wickedness."

²⁹ "Woe unto you scribes and Pharisees - hypocrites! For you build sepulchres of the prophets - and repair the sepulchers of the righteous."

³⁰ "You say, if we had been in the days of our fathers - we would not be as them - spilling blood - the blood of the prophets."

³¹ "Therefore, you testify against yourselves - that you are the sons of those who killed the prophets!"

³² "And you fulfill the measure of your fathers!"

³³ "Behold you serpents - seed of vipers - I pray you flee from the judgement of hell (Gei-Hinnom)!"

³⁴ "Therefore I say - Behold! I sent you prophets and sages and scribes - and some you killed *or* crucified! - And some you have whipped in your synagogues and chased from city to city!"

³⁵ "Therefore, all the righteous blood which has been spilled on earth is upon you - from the blood of righteous Abel, to the blood of Zachariah - the blessed son - whom you killed between the sanctuary and the altar."

³⁶ "In truth I say to you, all these words shall come upon this generation."

³⁷ "O Jerusalem, Jerusalem - you who are killing the prophets - and stoning those who are sent to you. How many times did I desire to gather your children - as the hen gathers her chicks under her wings - but you were not willing!"

³⁸ "Behold, your house will be left desolate!"

³⁹ "Behold, I tell you that you will not see me again - until you say, 'Blessed is he that comes in the name of Yehovah!' "

Matthew Chapter 23

HTV with translator notes and KJV comparison

Matthew 23:1

אָז דִּבֶּר יֵשׁוּעַ אֶל כִּתִּים וְאֶל תַּלְמִידָיו

HTV: Then Yeshua spoke to the crowd and to his disciples:

Note: Yeshua was at the Temple, debating with the Pharisees, as continued from chapter 22.

KJV: Then spake Jesus to the multitude, and to his disciples,

Matthew 23:2

Freiburg Hebrew Manuscript

לֵאמוֹר עַל מוֹשַׁב מֹשֶׁה יָשְׁבוּ הַסּוֹפְרִים וְהַפְּרוּשִׁים

HTV: "It is said the scribes and the Pharisees sat (*themselves*) on the seat of Moses."

Note: It is clear this refers to the scribes and Pharisees taking the authority of Moses in interpreting their words as commands to the people. There is a Moses' seat in the synagogue. It is before the altar. This has been adopted into the Roman Church who proclaim *ex cathera* - *from the seat* of Moses - meaning they have the authority God gave to Moses directly on Sinai.

KJV: Saying, The scribes and the Pharisees sit in Moses' seat:

Matthew 23:3

Freiburg Hebrew Manuscript

כָּל מַה שֶׁיֹּאמְרוּ לָכֶם לִשְׁמוֹר שִׁמְרוּ וְלַעֲשׂוֹת וַעֲשׂוּ אָמְנָם לְפִי
מַעֲשֵׂיהֶם אַל תַּעֲשׂוּ כִּי הֵם אוֹמְרִים וְלֹא עוֹשִׂים

HTV: "All that he (Moses) taught you to keep - guard *it*, do *it*, and make *it* happen! The (Sadducees & Pharisees) tell you to observe their commands - but do not follow them - because, according to their deeds - they do not observe them."

Note: The Hebrew word (takanot) does not refer to the commandments of God but to the' commandments of men,' in this case the scribes and Pharisees - who do not even keep the commandments they proclaim to the people..

KJV: All therefore whatsoever they bid you observe, that observe and do; but do not ye after their works: for they say, and do not.

Matthew 23:4

כִּי קוֹשְׁרִים מַשָּׂאוֹת כְּבֵדוֹת אֲשֶׁר קָשׁוֹת לָשֵׂאת וְשָׂמִים עַל שְׁכֶם
אֲנָשִׁים אֲשֶׁר הֵם אֵין מוֹטִים וְלֹא בְּאֶצְבַּע אֶחָד

HTV: "They (scribes & Pharisees) conspire to bind you with heavy burdens - which are difficult to bear - and put *them* on the shoulders of the people - but they are not willing to lift even one finger to move them."

KJV: For they bind heavy burdens and grievous to be borne, and lay *them* on men's shoulders; but they *themselves* will not move them with one of their fingers.

Matthew 23:5

וְעוֹשִׂים כֹּל מַעֲשֵׂיהֶם שֶׁיֵּרָאוּ מֵאֲנָשִׁים כִּי מַרְחִיבִים אֶת-טוֹטָפוֹת
וּמַגְדִּילִים אֶת-שׁוּלֵי מַלְבּוּשֵׁיהֶם

HTV: "They do all their deeds in order for them to be seen by men - so they widen their phylacteries - and the tassels on the edge of their clothing they enlarge and lengthen."

Note: *Phylacteries* are boxes tied to the forehead and upper arms that contain prayers.

KJV: But all their works they do for to be seen of men: they make broad their phylacteries, and enlarge the borders of their garments,

The Hebrew Book of Matthew

Matthew 23:6

כִּי אוֹהֲבִים אֶת-מְסִיבוֹת הָרִאשׁוֹנוֹת בָּאֲרוּחוֹת הָעֶרֶב וְאֶת-רִאשׁוֹנוֹת כִּסְאוֹת בִּכְנֵסִיּוֹת

HTV: "They love the best seats at evening banquets - and the best seats in the assemblies"

KJV: And love the uppermost rooms at feasts, and the chief seats in the synagogues,

Matthew 23:7

Freiburg Hebrew Manuscript

וּקְדִימוּת שָׁלוֹם בְּשׁוּקִים וְיִקְרֵא רַבִּי מֵאֲנוֹשִׁים

HTV: "and *they love* being bowed to with greetings of peace (Shalom) in the markets - and to be called great (Rabbi) by the people."

> Note: The word Rabbi means "great" in Hebrew, so teachers are being referred to as *great ones*. Yeshua in the following verse uses the literal meaning of "great" - no one is Great but the Father.

KJV: And greetings in the markets, and to be called of men, Rabbi, Rabbi.

Matthew 23:8

אֲבָל אַתֶּם אַל תִּקָּרְאוּ רַבִּי כִּי לְבַד אֶחָד שֶׁרַבִּי לָכֶם אָמְנָם אַתֶּם יֵשׁ אָחִים אִישׁ לְרֵעֵהוּ

HTV: "However, do not call yourselves 'rabbi' (great) because there is only one who is Rabbi (greater) than you all - Indeed, *all* of you are brothers."

KJV: But be not ye called Rabbi: for one is your Master, *even* Christ; and all ye are brethren.

Matthew 23:9

וְאַל תִּקְרְאוּ לָכֶם אָב עַל הָאָרֶץ כִּי לָכֶם לְבַד אָב אֶחָד שֶׁהוּא בַּשָּׁמַיִם

Chapter 23

HTV: **"Do not call yourselves *'father'* - on this earth - for you have only one Father who is in heaven."**

KJV: And call no *man* your father upon the earth: for one is your Father, which is in heaven.

Matthew 23:10

וְאַל תִּקָּרְאוּ רַבּוֹת כִּי יֵשׁ לָכֶם לְבַד רַבִּי אֶחָד כֵּיצַד הַמָּשִׁיחַ

HTV: **"And don't be called Rabbi's (great ones) because there is to you only one great one - Yeshua the Messiah!"**

KJV: Neither be ye called masters: for one is your Master, *even* Christ.

Matthew 23:11

אֲשֶׁר בֵּינֵיכֶם הַגָּדוֹל הוּא יְהִי מְשָׁרֶתְכֶם

HTV: **"He who is greatest among you - shall be your servant."**

KJV: But he that is greatest among you shall be your servant.

Matthew 23:12

מִי שֶׁיְּרוֹמֵם עַצְמוֹ הַהוּא יִשָּׁפֵל וּמִי שֶׁיַּשְׁפִּיל עַצְמוֹ הַהוּא יָרוּם

HTV: **"Whoever shall exalt himself shall be humbled - and whoever shall humble himself shall be exalted."**

KJV: And whosoever shall exalt himself shall be abased; and he that shall humble himself shall be exalted.

Matthew 23:13

הוֹי לָכֶם הַסּוֹפְרִים וּפְרוּשִׁים הַחֲנֵפִים כִּי אַתֶּם סוֹגְרִים אֶת-מַלְכוּת הַשָּׁמַיִם לִפְנֵי אֱנוֹשִׁים וְאֵינְכֶם נִכְנָסִים וְאֵינְכֶם מְנִיחִים שֶׁאֲחֵרִים יָבוֹאוּ בָהּ

HTV: **"Woe to you scribes and Pharisees - hypocrites! For you shut off the kingdom of heaven from men - You do not enter there yourselves - nor allow others to come in."**

The Hebrew Book of Matthew

KJV: But woe unto you, scribes and Pharisees, hypocrites! for ye shut up the kingdom of heaven against men: for ye neither go in *yourselves*, neither suffer ye them that are entering to go in.

Matthew 23:14

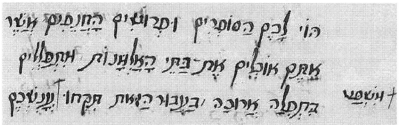

Freiburg Hebrew Manuscript

הוֹי לָכֶם הַסוֹפְרִים וּפְרוּשִׁים הַחֲנֵפִים אֲשֶׁר אַתֶּם אוֹכְלִים אֶת־בָּתֵּי הָאַלְמָנוֹת מִתְפַּלְלִים בִּתְפִלָּה אֲרוּכָה בַּעֲבוּר הַזֹּאת תִּקְחוּ מִשְׁפַּט עָנְשְׁכֶם

HTV: "**Woe to you scribes and Pharisees - hypocrites! You who consume the homes of widows - then pray lengthy prayers! - For this reason you shall receive damnation!**"

<small>Note: Yeshua is referring to the practice of '*Corban*' - an oath or will leaving all of one's property to the Temple of God even before you die. It allows one to claim poverty in the face of fiscal responsibilities such as taking care of parents. In this case, the man making the oath of Corban is deceased and the Priests are taking the house from his widow because it has been promised to the Temple of God. See also Matthew 15:6. Clearly, Yeshua hated this practice.</small>

KJV: Woe unto you, scribes and Pharisees, hypocrites! for ye devour widows' houses, and for a pretence make long prayer: therefore ye shall receive the greater damnation.

Matthew 23:15

הוֹי לָכֶם הַסוֹפְרִים וּפְרוּשִׁים הַחֲנֵפִים כִּי אַתֶּם סוֹבְבִים אֶת־הַיָּם וְאֶת־הַיַּבָּשָׁה עַד שֶׁתַּעֲשׂוּ אֶחָד גִּיּוֹרָא וּמִי שֶׁהוּא נַעֲשָׂה אַתֶּם עוֹשִׂים אוֹתוֹ בֶּן גֵּיהִנָּם כִּפְלַיִם בְּעֶרֶךְ אֲלֵיכֶם

HTV: "**Woe to you scribes and Pharisees - hypocrites! You travel over land and sea to make one proselyte - and when he** is found you make him double the son of Hell (Gehinnom) than you are."

KJV: Woe unto you, scribes and Pharisees, hypocrites! for ye compass sea and land to make one proselyte, and when he is made, ye make him twofold more the child of hell than yourselves.

Matthew 23:16

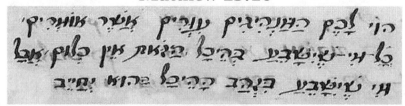

Freiburg Hebrew Manuscript.

הוֹי לָכֶם הַמַּנְהִיגִים עִוְרִים אֲשֶׁר אוֹמְרִים כָּל מִי שֶׁיִּשָּׁבַע בְּהֵיכָל הַזֹּאת אֵין כְּלוּם אֲבָל מִי שֶׁיִּשָּׁבַע בִּזְהַב הַהֵיכָל הַהוּא יְחַיֵּב

HTV: **"Woe to you leaders of the blind who say - 'All who swear by the Temple - this is nothing! Only *one* who swears by the gold of the Temple - will be obliged.' "**

Note: The use of the word בְּיָחִי/בְּיֵּחַי appears to be a word play. The Pharisees are inferring Yehovah is only **obliged** to answer your prayers if you put some gold on the altar for the Temple (priests). Judging from Yeshua's following comment - that is the meaning he is condemning.

KJV: Woe unto you, *ye* blind guides, which say, Whosoever shall swear by the temple, it is nothing; but whosoever shall swear by the gold of the temple, he is a debtor!

Matthew 23:17

הַכְּסִילִים וְעִוְרִים מָה נָא יוֹתֵר גָּדוֹל הַזָּהָב אוֹ הַהֵיכָל מַקְדִּישׁ אֶת זָהָב

HTV: **"You blind fools! What is greater - the gold - or the Temple which sanctifies the gold?"**

Note: See Matthew 5:22, for the discussion of the use of the word "fool(s)" and its many synonyms in other translations. The danger of hellfire is not upon the word itself but one who makes a false witness. In this case, that would be the priests claiming a gift of gold is needed for Yehovah to answer their prayers.

The Hebrew Book of Matthew

KJV: *Ye* fools and blind: for whether is greater, the gold, or the temple that sanctifieth the gold?

Matthew 23:18

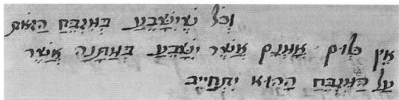

Freiburg Hebrew Manuscript

וְכֹל שֶׁיִּשָּׁבַע בְּמִזְבֵּחַ הַזֹּאת אֵין כְּלוּם אָמְנָם אֲשֶׁר יִשָּׁבַע בְּמַתָּנָה אֲשֶׁר עַל הַמִּזְבֵּחַ הַהוּא יִתְחַיֵּיב

HTV: **"All who swear by the altar are not obliged. However, whosoever swears to make a gift on the altar - that one will be obliged!"**

Note: This is a repetition of verse 16 - it is a rhetorical repetition - used for emphasis. Swearing by the gold of the Temple obliges you to pay the priests. Penitents who pray for grace and swear oaths to change their lives and return to Yehovah - that is meaningless! Only gold will do if you want Yehovah to respond to your prayers. The Greek text missed the meaning entirely.

KJV: And, Whosoever shall swear by the altar, it is nothing; but whosoever sweareth by the gift that is upon it, he is guilty.

Matthew 23:19

הָעִוְרִים אֵיזוֹ גְדוֹלָה הַמַּתָּנָה אוֹ הַמִּזְבֵּחַ אֲשֶׁר מַקְדִּישׁ אֶת-הַמַּתָּנָה

HTV: **"O you Blind ones! Which is greater - the gift - or the altar that sanctifies the gift?"**

KJV: *Ye* fools and blind: for whether *is greater*, the gift, or the altar that sanctifieth the gift?

Matthew 23:20

לְפִיכָךְ אֲשֶׁר נִשְׁבַּע בְּמִזְבֵּחַ הַהוּא נִשְׁבָּע בְּאוֹתוֹ וּבְכָלָּם אֲשֶׁר עָלָיו

HTV: **"Accordingly, whoever swears by the altar - also swears by all that is on the altar."**

KJV: Whoso therefore shall swear by the altar, sweareth by it, and by all things thereon.

Matthew 23:21

וְכֹל שֶׁיִּשָּׁבַע בְּהֵיכָל הַהוּא נִשְׁבָּע בְּאוֹתוֹ וּבְמִי שֶׁיּוֹשֵׁב בּוֹ

HTV: **"And all who swear by the Temple - also swear by the One who dwells within it."**

KJV: And whoso shall swear by the temple, sweareth by it, and by him that dwelleth therein.

Matthew 23:22

וַאֲשֶׁר נִשְׁבָּע בַּשָּׁמַיִם הַהוּא נִשְׁבָּע בְּכִסֵּא הָאֱלֹהִים וּבְאוֹתוֹ אֲשֶׁר יוֹשֵׁב עָלָיו

HTV: **"He who swears by heaven - swears by the throne of Elohim and He who sits upon it!"**

KJV: And he that shall swear by heaven, sweareth by the throne of God, and by him that sitteth thereon.

Matthew 23:23

Freiburg Hebrew Manuscript

הוֹי לָכֶם הַסּוֹפְרִים וּפְרוּשִׁים הַחֲנֵפִים אֲשֶׁר אַתֶּם מַעֲשִׂירִים אֶת־מִנְתָּא פִּיגָם וּכְמוֹנָא וְעוֹזְבִים אֲשֶׁר יוֹתֵר כְּבֵדִים בַּתּוֹרָה כֵּיצַד אֶת־הַמִּשְׁפָּט הַחֶסֶד וְהָאֱמוּנָה הָאֵלֶּה יְהוּ צָרִיךְ לַעֲשׂוֹת וְאוֹתָם לֹא לַעֲזוֹב

HTV: **"Woe you scribes and Pharisees - hypocrites! You tithe mint, rue, and cumin - but you forsake the weightier matters of the Torah - which *are* judgment, grace, and faith - These must be done! - And you must not leave them *undone!*"**

Note: The scribes and Pharisees' tithes of herbs and spices are trivial, lightweight offerings - the weighter offerings they should be making are righteous judgment, leading the people to grace and faith. These are not optional for righteous priests. They must be done! But they are not!

> The trivial tithes offered are literally being weighed against the weightier matters that are not being done.

KJV: Woe unto you, scribes and Pharisees, hypocrites! for ye pay tithe of mint and anise and cummin, and have omitted the weightier *matters* of the law, judgment, mercy, and faith: these ought ye to have done, and not to leave the other undone.

Matthew 23:24

הַמַּנְהִיגִים עִוְרִים אַתֶּם מְזַקְקִים אֶת פַּרְטָעָן וּבוֹלְעִים אֶת-הַגָּמָל

HTV: **"You blind leaders - who strain at a flea - but swallow a camel!"**

KJV: *Ye* blind guides, which strain at a gnat, and swallow a camel.

Matthew 23:25

הוֹי לָכֶם הַסּוֹפְרִים וּפְרוּשִׁים הַחֲנֵפִים כִּי אַתֶּם מְטֹהָרִים מָה שֶׁחוּצָה לַכּוֹס וְלַקְּעָרָה וּבְקִרְבְּכֶם אַתֶּם מְלֵאִים בַּגְזֵלָה וּבְטֻמְאָה

HTV: **"Woe to you scribes and Pharisees - hypocrites! For you cleanse the outside of a *vessel* (cup or bowl) - but on the inside you are full of extortion and impurity!"**

KJV: Woe unto you, scribes and Pharisees, hypocrites! for ye make clean the outside of the cup and of the platter, but within they are full of extortion and excess.

Matthew 23:26

הוֹי הַפָּרוּשׁ הָעִוֵּר טַהֵר נָא קוֹדֶם אֲשֶׁר בְּתוֹכוֹ הַכּוֹס וּקְעָרָה כְּדֵי שֶׁיִּטָהֵר מָה שֶׁחוּצָה

HTV: **"Woe to the blind Pharisee! Purify beforehand - that which is inside the cup and bowl - so that which is outside will be purified."**

KJV: *Thou* blind Pharisee, cleanse first that *which* is within the cup and platter, that the outside of them may be clean also.

Matthew 23:27

הוֹי לָכֶם הַסּוֹפְרִים וּפְרוּשִׁים הַחֲנֵפִים כִּי אַתֶּם נִתְדַּמִּים לִקְבָרִים

Chapter 23

הַמְּלֻבָּנִים אֲשֶׁר חוּצָה נִרְאִים יָפִים לָאֲנוּשִׁים וּבְקִרְבָּם הֵם מְלֵאִים בַּעֲצָמוֹת הַמֵּתִים וּבְכֹל טֻמְאוֹת

HTV: **"Woe unto you scribes and Pharisees - hypocrites! for you are likened unto sepulchres - which look white and beautiful outside - but inside they are full of the bones of the dead and all impurity."**

KJV: Woe unto you, scribes and Pharisees, hypocrites! for ye are like unto whited sepulchres, which indeed appear beautiful outward, but are within full of dead *men's* bones, and of all uncleanness.

Matthew 23:28

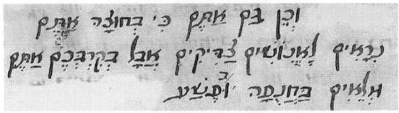

Freiburg Hebrew Manuscript

וְכֵן גַּם אַתֶּם כִּי בְחוּצָה אַתֶּם נִרְאִים לָאֲנוּשִׁים צַדִּיקִים אֲבָל בְּקִרְבְּכֶם אַתֶּם מְלֵאִים בַּחֲנֻפָה וּבְפֶשַׁע

HTV: **"And so also are you - because on the outside you are seen by men as righteous - however, within, you are full of hypocrisy and wickedness."**

KJV: Even so ye also outwardly appear righteous unto men, but within ye are full of hypocrisy and iniquity.

Matthew 23:29

הוֹי לָכֶם סוֹפְרִים וּפְרוּשִׁים הַחֲנֵפִים כִּי אַתֶּם בּוֹנִים קִבְרֵי הַנְּבִיאִים וּמְתַקְּנִים אֶת-קִבְרֵי הַצַּדִּיקִים

HTV: **"Woe unto you scribes and Pharisees - hypocrites! For you build sepulchres of the prophets - and repair the sepulchers of the righteous."**

KJV: Woe unto you, scribes and Pharisees, hypocrites! because ye build the tombs of the prophets, and garnish the sepulchres of the righteous,

The Hebrew Book of Matthew

Matthew 23:30

וְאַתֶּם אוֹמְרִים אִם הָיִינוּ בִּימֵי אֲבוֹתֵינוּ לֹא הָיִינוּ לָהֶם חֲבֵרִים בִּשְׁפִיכַת הַדָּם הַנְּבִיאִים

HTV: **"You say, if we had been in the days of our fathers - we would not be as them - spilling blood - the blood of the prophets."**

KJV: And say, If we had been in the days of our fathers, we would not have been partakers with them in the blood of the prophets.

Matthew 23:31

לְפִיכָךְ אַתֶּם מְעִידִים עֲלֵיכֶם אֲשֶׁר אַתֶּם בְּנֵיהֶם אֲשֶׁר הָרְגוּ אֶת-הַנְּבִיאִים

HTV: **"Therefore, you testify against yourselves - that you are the sons of those who killed the prophets!"**

KJV: Wherefore ye be witnesses unto yourselves, that ye are the children of them which killed the prophets.

Matthew 23:32

וְאַתֶּם מְלֵאִים אֶת-מִדַּת אֲבוֹתֵיכֶם

HTV: **"And you fulfill the measure of your fathers!"**

KJV: Fill ye up then the measure of your fathers.

Matthew 23:33

Freiburg Hebrew Manuscript

הוֹי הַנְּחָשִׁים וְהַדּוֹר אֲפָעִים אֵיכָה נָא תִבְרְחוּ מִמִּשְׁפַּט גֵּיהִנָּם

HTV: **"Behold you serpents - seed of vipers - I pray you flee from the judgement of hell (Gei-Hinnom)!"**

Chapter 23

Note: The Gei-Hinnom was the place of sacrificing infants to Molech by burning them alive in the red hot arms of a statue to Molech called the Topeth. It was so horrifying that it became the Israelites' vision of judgement and damnation to eternal torment - what we call "hell." Solomon permitted this to assuage his foreign wife or wives who were pagan Molech/Ba'al worshippers.

KJV: *Ye* serpents, *ye* generation of vipers, how can ye escape the damnation of hell?

Matthew 23:34

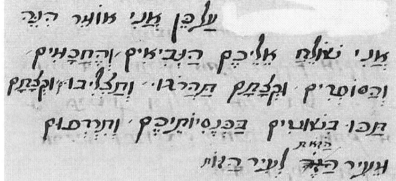

Freiburg Hebrew Manuscript

עַל כֵּן אֲנִי אוֹמֵר הִנֵּה אֲנִי שׁוֹלֵחַ אֲלֵיכֶם הַנְּבִיאִים וְהַחֲכָמִים וְהַסּוֹפְרִים וּקְצָתָם תַּהַרְגוּ וְתַצְלִיבוּים וּקְצָתָם תַּכּוּ בְּשׁוֹטִים בַּכְּנֵסִיּוֹתֵיכֶם וְתִרְדְּפוּם מֵעִיר הַזֹּאת לְעִיר הַזֹּאת

HTV: **"Therefore I say - Behold! I sent you prophets and sages and scribes - and some you killed *or* crucified! - And some you have whipped in your synagogues and chased from city to city!"**

Note: The entire chapter 23 is a profound condemnation of the Pharisees and Sadducces (called scribes). Most of it is written in the present or past describing the killing of all the prophets sent to them from the beginning of time (see Matthew 23:35). Yeshua is also referring to the Apostles he is sending out into the world as the result of his ministry.

KJV: Wherefore, behold, I send unto you prophets, and wise men, and scribes: and *some* of them ye shall kill and crucify; and *some* of them shall ye scourge in your synagogues, and persecute *them* from city to city:

The Hebrew Book of Matthew

Matthew 23:35

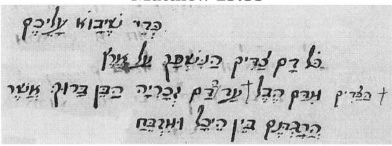

Freiburg Hebrew Manuscript

כְּדֵי שֶׁיָבוֹא עֲלֵיכֶם כֹּל דָם צַדִיק הַנִשְׁפָּךְ עַל אֶרֶץ מִדָם הֶבֶל הַצַדִיק עַד הַדָם זְכָרְיָה הַבֵּן בָּרוּךְ אֲשֶׁר הֲרַגְתֶם בֵּין הֵיכָל וּמִזְבֵּחַ

HTV: "Therefore, all the righteous blood which has been spilled on earth is upon you - from the blood of righteous Abel, to the blood of Zachariah - the blessed son - whom you killed between the sanctuary and the altar."

> Note: The KJV and other translations use "Zachariah, son of Berechiah." But not in the gospel of Luke 11:51, it says only "the blood of Zachariah." There is no "son of Berechiah." This is an addition to the gospel of Matthew. This entire chapter is a scorching condemnation of the Pharisees and Sadducces. If we include only those up to the time of Zechariah the prophet, son of Berechiah, then this incredible condemation by Yeshua of the priests only applies to those 600 years ago in the time of Berechiah.
>
> **The scribal addition of "son of Berechiah" which I believe was purposeful - would cancel the clear meaning of Yeshua's words!** The Gospel of James (Proto-Evangelion of James) tells the story of Herod's secret police killing Zachariah, John the Baptist's father, between the sanctuary and the altar. Yeshua's damning condemnation was for the past, the present, and the future!

KJV: That upon you may come all the righteous blood shed upon the earth, from the blood of righteous Abel unto the blood of Zacharias son of Barachias, whom ye slew between the temple and the altar.

Matthew 23:36

בֶּאֱמֶת אֲנִי אוֹמֵר לָכֶם כֹּל אֵלֶה דְבָרִים יָבוֹאוּ עַל הַדוֹר הַזֶה

HTV: "In truth I say to you, all these words shall come upon this generation."

> Note: The "words" Yeshua is talking about can mean "things, matters, issues." The blood of the prophets is upon this generation - It is not a

Chapter 23

forgotten issue of the past. The sons are the measure of their fathers in these sins. The current generation will commit the same sins.

KJV: Verily I say unto you, All these things shall come upon this generation.

Matthew 23:37

יְרוּשָׁלַיִם יְרוּשָׁלַיִם אֲשֶׁר הוֹרֶגֶת אֶת-הַנְּבִיאִים וְסוֹקֶלֶת בָּאֲבָנִים אֶת-אֵלֶּה אֲשֶׁר נִשְׁלְחוּ אֵלֶיךְ כַּמָּה נָא פְעָמִים רָצִיתִי לִקְבּוֹץ אֶת-בָּנֶיךְ כְּמוֹ הַתַּרְנְגוֹלֶת אֶת-אֶפְרוֹחֶיהָ עַל כְּנָפֶיהָ וְלֹא רָצִית

HTV: **"O Jerusalem, Jerusalem - you who are killing the prophets - and stoning those who are sent to you. How many times did I desire to gather your children - as the hen gathers her chicks under her wings - but you were not willing!"**

KJV: O Jerusalem, Jerusalem, *thou* that killest the prophets, and stonest them which are sent unto thee, how often would I have gathered thy children together, even as a hen gathereth her chickens under *her* wings, and ye would not!

Matthew 23:38

Freiburg Hebrew Manuscript

הִנֵּה יֵעָזֵב לָכֶם בֵּיתְכֶם מֵחָרָב

HTV: **"Behold, your house will be left desolate!"**

Note: Yeshua is saying that destruction is coming upon Israel for their sins - past and present – 'You will lose your house, Temple, nation! All will be in ruins.' Within 40 years, the Temple was destroyed and the nation of Isreal disbanded, destroyed or enslaved! See Matthew 24:2.

KJV: Behold, your house is left unto you desolate.

Matthew 23:39

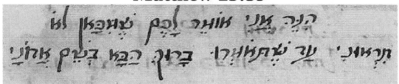

Freiburg Hebrew Manuscript

הִנֵּה אֲנִי אוֹמֵר לָכֶם שֶׁמִכָּאן לֹא תִרְאוּנִי עַד שֶׁתֹּאמְרוּ בָּרוּךְ הַבָּא בְּשֵׁם אֲדוֹנָי

HTV: **"Behold, I tell you that you will not see me again - until you say, 'Blessed is he that comes in the name of Yehovah!' "**

Note: Psalm 118:26, "Blessed be he that cometh in the name of Yehovah: We have blessed you from the house of Yehovah." ASV

KJV: For I say unto you, Ye shall not see me henceforth, till ye shall say, Blessed *is* he that cometh in the name of the Lord.

Matthew Chapter 24
Hebrew Text Version (HTV)

¹ Yeshua went out - departing from the Temple. His disciples drew near - to show him the temple buildings.

² Yeshua responded and said to them, "Do you see all of these buildings? Truly I say to you - there will not be left one stone upon another - that will not be torn down."

³ When Yeshua was seated upon the Mount of Olives his disciples; Peter, John and Andrew - came to him privately. They said, "Tell us when these things shall be? What is the sign of your coming - and of the end of the world?"

⁴ Yeshua answered and said to them, "Take heed that no one deceives you"

⁵ "Because many shall come in my name! They will say - 'I am the Messiah!' - and they will deceive many."

⁶ "When you hear of wars and rumors of wars - do not be troubled - Because all these things must happen - But the end is not yet."

⁷ "For nation will rise against nation, and kingdom against kingdom. There will also be plagues, famine, and earthquakes - in all lands and places."

⁸ "All these things are the beginning of sorrows!"

⁹ "They will kill you - and you will be hated in the sight of all nations - for my name's sake."

¹⁰ "At that time many will fall into a trap. Each man will betray his neighbor - And each man will hate his brother."

¹¹ "Many false prophets will arise - and they will deceive many!"

¹² "It (*the falsehood of the prophets*) will multiply transgression (*of the Torah*) - and *thus* the love of many will grow cold."

¹³ "Whosoever perseveres until the end - that one will be saved!"

14 "The Gospel of the Kingdom will be declared in all the world - for a testimony to all nations. Then comes the end!"

¹⁵ "When you see the abomination of desolation standing in the holy place (*of the Temple*) - which was spoken of by the prophet Daniel - Whoever reads *Daniel* will understand."

¹⁶ "Then those who are in Judea will flee to the mountains."

¹⁷ "Whoever will be upon the roof - should not come down to take anything from his house."

¹⁸ "The one who is in the field should not return to get his coat!"

¹⁹ "Woe to pregnant women and to nursing mothers in those days!"

²⁰ "Pray therefore that your flight will not be in winter - nor on the Sabbath."

²¹ "For at that time - there shall be great distress - such as has not been *seen* from the beginning of the world until now - nor shall be *ever again*."

²² "So unless Yehovah cuts short those days - no flesh will be saved! However, because of the chosen of Yehovah - those days will be cut short."

²³ "So, at that time if anyone will say to you, 'Behold, the Messiah is here!' - or – 'There *he is*!' - Do not believe *it*."

²⁴ "For false messiahs and false prophets will rise up. They will give great signs and wonders until people fall into deception - if possible - even the chosen."

²⁵ "Behold, I have forewarned *you*!"

²⁶ "Therefore if they say to you, 'Look, he is in the wilderness' - do not go out *there* - and 'Behold, he is in the chambers' - do not believe *it*."

²⁷ Yeshua said to his disciples, "As the lightning comes forth from the east *flashing* as far as the west - so will the coming of the Son of Man be."

²⁸ "For wherever there is a corpse - there shall the vultures be gathered."

²⁹ "Immediately after the anguish of those days - the sun will be eclipsed - the moon will not give her light - the stars will fall from the heavens - and the firmament of the heavens will falter."

³⁰ "Then the sign of the Son of Man will be seen in the heavens. At that time all the tribes of the earth will mourn. They shall see The Son of Man coming in the clouds with great victory and glory."

³¹ "He will send his angels with the sound of a great shofar. They will gather his chosen ones - from the four corners of the earth - from one end of the heavens to the other."

³² "Now learn a proverb from the fig tree - for when its branches become tender and blossom - then you know that summer is near."

³³ "Likewise you also - when you will see these things - you will know that it is near - at the gates."

³⁴ "Truly I say to you that this generation will not pass away - until all of these things have come to pass."

³⁵ "The heavens and the earth will pass away - but my words will not pass away."

³⁶ "In truth - of that day and of that hour - no one knows - not even the angels of heaven - except for the Father alone."

³⁷ Again, Yeshua said to his disciples, "Just as it was in the days of Noah - so it will it be at the coming of the Son of Man."

³⁸ "For as in the years before the flood - they were eating and drinking - taking wives and giving wives - until the day that Noah entered the ark."

³⁹ "They did not understand - until the flood came and destroyed all of them! So shall it be at the coming of the Son of Man."

⁴⁰ "At that time there will be two ploughing in a field - one righteous and the other wicked - the one will be taken and the other will be left."

⁴¹ Two *women* will be grinding at the millstones - the one will be taken and the other will be left. And two in a bed - the one will be taken and the other will be left.

⁴² Then Yeshua said to his disciples, "Therefore, watch with me - because you do not know at what hour your lord is coming."

⁴³ "But you should know this: If the owner of the house knew at which hour the thief would come - truly he would stay awake. He would not allow his house to be broken into."

⁴⁴ "Therefore, you should be ready - because you do not know at which hour the Son of Man shall come."

⁴⁵ "Who *among you* is the wise and faithful servant - whom his lord has appointed over those of his household - to give them (spiritual) sustenance in due season?"

⁴⁶ "Blessed is that servant who - when his lord shall come -

The Hebrew Book of Matthew

will find him doing so!"

⁴⁷ "Truly - I say to you, that Yeshua will appoint him over all that is his."

⁴⁸ "But if the wicked servant says in his heart, 'Indeed my lord delays in coming' "

⁴⁹ "And he begins to do violence to his fellow servants - and eat with gluttons - and drink with drunkards!"

⁵⁰ "Behold, the master of that servant shall come on the day that he was not expecting - and at an hour that he (the evil servant) knows not."

⁵¹ "They (the angels) will sever him (the evil servant) and set his portion with the deceivers. There will be weeping and gnashing of teeth!"

Matthew Chapter 24

HTV with translator notes and KJV comparison

Matthew 24:1

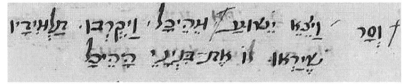

Freiburg Hebrew Manuscript

וַיֵּצֵא יֵשׁוּעַ וְסָר מֵהֵיכָל וַיִּקְרְבוּ תַלְמִידָיו שֶׁיַּרְאוּ לוֹ אֶת-בִּנְיָנֵי הַהֵיכָל

HTV: Yeshua went out - departing from the Temple. His disciples drew near - to show him the temple buildings.

KJV: And Jesus went out, and departed from the temple: and his disciples came to *him* for to shew him the buildings of the temple.

Matthew 24:2

וְהוּא עָנָה וַיֹּאמַר לָהֶם הַאַתֶּם רוֹאִים כֹּל הָאֵלֶה בִנְיָנִים בֶּאֱמֶת אֲנִי אוֹמֵר לָכֶם לֹא תֵעָזֵב שָׁם אֶבֶן עַל הָאֶבֶן אֲשֶׁר לֹא תְנֻתַּץ

Chapter 24

HTV: **Yeshua responded and said to them, "Do you see all of these buildings? Truly I say to you - there will not be left one stone upon another - that will not be torn down."**

KJV: And Jesus said unto them, See ye not all these things? verily I say unto you, There shall not be left here one stone upon another, that shall not be thrown down.

Matthew 24:3

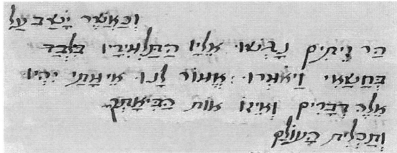

Freiburg Hebrew Manuscript

וְכַאֲשֶׁר יָשַׁב עַל הַר זֵיתִים נִגְשׁוּ אֵלָיו הַתַּלְמִידָיו בְּחַשָּׁאי וַיֹּאמְרוּ אֱמוֹר לָנוּ אֵימָתַי יִהְיוּ אֵלֶּה דְבָרִים וְאֵיזוֹ אוֹת הַבִּיאָתְךָ וְתַכְלִית הָעוֹלָם

HTV: **When Yeshua was seated upon the Mount of Olives his disciples; Peter, John and Andrew - came to him privately. They said, "Tell us when these things shall be? What is the sign of your coming - and of the end of the world?"**

Note: The Shem Tov Manuscript (STM) says Peter, John, and Andrew spoke with him privately. If it had included all of the disciples, as it says in the Greek, then it would not have been privately.

KJV: And as he sat upon the mount of Olives, the disciples came unto him privately, saying, Tell us, when shall these things be? and what *shall be* the sign of thy coming, and of the end of the world?

Matthew 24:4

וַיַּעַן יֵשׁוּעַ וַיֹּאמַר לָהֶם רְאוּ שֶׁלֹּא שׁוּם יַשִּׂיא אֶתְכֶם

HTV: **Yeshua answered and said to them, "Take heed that no one deceives you"**

KJV: And Jesus answered and said unto them, Take heed that no man deceive you.

Matthew 24:5

Freiburg Hebrew Manuscript

כִּי רַבִּים יָבוֹאוּ בִשְׁמִי וְיֹאמְרוּ אֲנִי הַמָּשִׁיחַ וְיַשִּׁיאוּ רַבִּים

HTV: "Because many shall come in my name! They will say - 'I am the Messiah!' - and they will deceive many."

Note: This is a crucial caution for our times especially. Not all those who proclaim the name of Jesus (or Yeshua) are legitimate. Many are deceivers. Beware! It is for the Holy Spirit to separate the evil from the good.

KJV: For many shall come in my name, saying, I am Christ; and shall deceive many.

Matthew 24:6

וְכַאֲשֶׁר תִּשְׁמְעוּ מִלְחָמוֹת וּשְׁמוּעוֹת הַמִּלְחָמוֹת רְאוּ שֶׁלֹא תִבָּהֲלוּ כִּי צָרִיךְ לִהְיוֹת אֵלֶּה דְבָרִים כֻּלָּם אֲבָל עוֹד לֹא תַכְלִית

HTV: "When you hear of wars and rumors of wars - do not be troubled - Because all these things must happen - But the end is not yet."

KJV: And ye shall hear of wars and rumors of wars: see that ye be not troubled: for all *these things* must come to pass, but the end is not yet.

Matthew 24:7

כִּי יָקוּם הַגּוֹי כְּנֶגֶד הַגּוֹי גַּם הַמַּלְכוּת כְּנֶגֶד הַמַּלְכוּת וְיִהְיוּ דֶבֶר וְרָעָב וְרַעַשׁ אֶרֶץ בְּכֹל מְקוֹמוֹת

HTV: "For nation will rise against nation, and kingdom against kingdom. There will also be plagues, famine, and earthquakes - in all lands and places."

Chapter 24

KJV: For nation shall rise against nation, and kingdom against kingdom: and there shall be famines, and pestilences, and earthquakes, in diverse places.

Matthew 24:8

כֹּל אֵלֶּה דְבָרִים הֵם רֵאשִׁית הַיִּגוֹנִים

HTV: **"All these things are the beginning of sorrows!"**

KJV: All these *are* the beginning of sorrows.

Matthew 24:9

וְיַהַרְגוּ אֶתְכֶם וְתִהְיוּ לְשִׂנְאָה בְּעֵינֵי כֹל גּוֹיִם בַּעֲבוּר שְׁמִי

HTV: **"They will kill you - and you will be hated in the sight of all nations - for my name's sake."**

KJV: Then shall they deliver you up to be afflicted, and shall kill you: and ye shall be hated of all nations for my name's sake.

Matthew 24:10

Freiburg Hebrew Manuscript

וְאָז רַבִּים יִפְּלוּ בְּמוֹקֵשׁ וְיִמְסְרוּ אִישׁ אֶת־רֵעֵהוּ וְיִשְׂנְאוּ אִישׁ אֶת־אָחִיו

HTV: **"At that time many will fall into a trap. Each man will betray his neighbor - And each man will hate his brother."**

KJV: And then shall many be offended, and shall betray one another, and shall hate one another.

Matthew 24:11

וְיָקוּמוּ רַבִּים נְבִיאִים שֶׁקְרָנִים וְיַשִּׁיאוּ רַבִּים

HTV: **"Many false prophets will arise - and they will deceive many!"**

KJV: And many false prophets shall rise, and shall deceive many.

Matthew 24:12

Freiburg Hebrew Manuscript

וְיִתְרָבֶּה הַפֶּשַׁע וְאַהֲבַת הָרַבִּים תִּתְכַּבֶּה

HTV: "It (*the falsehood of the prophets*) will multiply transgression (*of the Torah*) - and *thus* the love of many will grow cold."

Note: "Sin is the transgression of Torah!" 1st John 3:4. This must remain our understanding of wickedness in the biblical sense. The modern world operates on a very different system. See also Numbers 15:31. "Because he has despised the Word of Yehovah, and has broken His commandments, that soul shall be utterly cut off. His iniquity shall be upon him!"

KJV: And because iniquity shall abound, the love of many shall wax cold.

Matthew 24:13

וַאֲשֶׁר יַתְמִיד עַד הַסּוֹף הַהוּא יִוָּשַׁע

HTV: "Whosoever perseveres until the end - that one will be saved!"

Note: See Daniel 12:1-12.

KJV: And because iniquity shall abound, the love of many shall wax cold.

Matthew 24:14

וְתָגֵּד הַבְּשׂוֹרָה הַזֹּאת שֶׁל מַלְכוּת בְּכֹל הָעוֹלָם לְעֵידַת כֹּל גּוֹיִם וְאָז יָבוֹא הַסּוֹף

HTV: "The Gospel of the Kingdom will be declared in all the world - for a testimony to all nations. Then comes the end!"

KJV: And this gospel of the kingdom shall be preached in all the world for a witness unto all nations; and then shall the end come.

Matthew 24:15

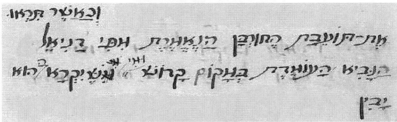

Freiburg Hebrew Manuscript

וְכַאֲשֶׁר תִּרְאוּ אֶת-תּוֹעֲבַת הַחוּרְבָּן הַנֶּאֱמֶרֶת מִפִּי דָּנִיֵּאל הַנָּבִיא
הָעוֹמֶדֶת בְּמָקוֹם קָדוֹשׁ וּמִי שֶׁיִּקְרָא הַהוּא יָבִין

HTV: "When you see the abomination of desolation standing in the holy place (*of the Temple*) - which was spoken of by the prophet Daniel - Whoever reads *Daniel* will understand."

Note: See Daniel 9:27 and 12:1-12 for an in-depth description of the abomination and end times.

KJV: When ye therefore shall see the abomination of desolation, spoken of by Daniel the prophet, stand in the holy place, (whoso readeth, let him understand:)

Matthew 24:16

וְאָז שֶׁיִּהְיוּ בִּיהוּדָה יִבְרְחוּ עַל הָרִים

HTV: "Then those who are in Judea will flee to the mountains."

KJV: Then let them which be in Judaea flee into the mountains:

Matthew 24:17

וּמִי שֶׁיִּהְיֶה עַל הַגַּג אַל יֵרֵד לִטּוֹל מְאִימָה מִבֵּיתוֹ

HTV: "Whoever will be upon the roof - should not come down to take anything from his house."

KJV: Let him which is on the housetop not come down to take anything out of his house:

Matthew 24:18

וּמִי שֶׁבַּשָּׂדֶה הוּא לֹא יָשׁוּב לָקַחַת אֶת-כְּתוֹנֶת שֶׁלּוֹ

HTV: **"The one who is in the field should not return to get his coat!"**

KJV: Neither let him, which is in the field, return back to take his clothes.

Matthew 24:19

הוֹי לִמְעֻבָּרוֹת וְלַמֵּינִיקוֹת בְּאוֹתָם הַיָּמִים

HTV: **"Woe to pregnant women and to nursing mothers in those days!"**

KJV: And woe unto them that are with child, and to them that give suck in those days!

Matthew 24:20

Freiburg Hebrew Manuscript

הִתְפַּלְלוּ נָא שֶׁמִּבְרָחֲכֶם לֹא יִהְיֶה בְחוֹרֶף אוֹ בְשַׁבָּת

HTV: **"Pray therefore that your flight will not be in winter - nor on the Sabbath."**

> Note: Almost every army that has opposed the Israelites from the Greeks, to the Romans, to the Arabs - has been aware they are not vigilant during the Sabbath. Does this indicate the abomination of desolation will occur under attack from a foreign adversary like in the past?

KJV: But pray ye that your flight be not in the winter, neither on the sabbath day:

Matthew 21:21

כִּי אָז תִּהְיֶה צוּקָה גְדוֹלָה אֲשֶׁר כָּזֹאת לֹא הָיְתָה מֵרֵאשִׁית הָעוֹלָם עַד עַתָּה וְלֹא תִהְיֶה

HTV: **"For at that time - there shall be great distress**

- such as has not been *seen* from the beginning of the world until now - nor shall be *ever again.*"

KJV: For then shall be great *tribulation*, such as was not since the beginning of the world to this time, no, nor ever shall be.

Matthew 24:22

Freiburg Hebrew Manuscript

וְלוּלֵי הַיָּמִים נִקְצְרוּ לֹא יִוָּשַׁע כֹּל בָּשָׂר אַךְ בַּעֲבוּר הַנִּבְחָרִים יִקָּצְרוּ הָאוֹתָם יָמִים

HTV: "So unless Yehovah cuts short those days - no flesh will be saved! However, because of the chosen of Yehovah - those days will be cut short."

Note: Because of the Greek text this verse is consistently misread. It is because of the intervention in prayer and action of Yehovah's remnant that the devastation is lifted.

KJV: And except those days should be shortened, there should no flesh be saved: but for the elect's sake those days shall be shortened.

Matthew 24:23

וּבָעֵת הַהוּא אִם מִי יֹאמַר לָכֶם הִנֵּה הַמָּשִׁיחַ הוּא שָׁם אוֹ שָׁם אַל תַּאֲמִינוּ

HTV: "So, at that time if anyone will say to you, 'Behold, the Messiah is here!' - or – 'There *he is*!' - Do not believe *it.*"

KJV: Then if any man shall say unto you, Lo, here *is* Christ, or there; believe *it* not.

The Hebrew Book of Matthew

Matthew 24:24

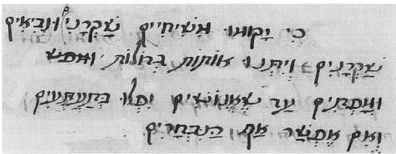

Freiburg Hebrew Manuscript

כִּי יָקוּמוּ מְשִׁיחִיִּים שַׁקְרָנִים וּנְבִיאִים שַׁקְרָנִים וְיִתְּנוּ אוֹתוֹת גְּדוֹלוֹת וּמֶפְתִים עַד שֶׁאֲנוּשִׁים יִפְּלוּ בְּתַעֲתָעִים וְאִם אֶפְשָׁר אַף הַנִּבְחָרִים

HTV: "For false messiahs and false prophets will rise up. They will give great signs and wonders until people fall into deception - if possible - even the chosen."

> Note: We all know righteous people who are deceived into following a wrong path of belief. This should not be a surprise. We should all be vigilant in the Spirit to know what is false. "Surely our fathers have inherited lies, vanity, and things wherein there is no profit." Jer 16:19.

KJV: For there shall arise false Christs, and false prophets, and shall shew great signs and wonders; insomuch that, if *it were* possible, they shall deceive the very elect.

Matthew 24:25

הִנֵּה אֲנִי אָמַרְתִּי

HTV: "Behold, I have forewarned *you!*"

KJV: Behold, I have told you before.

Matthew 24:26

Freiburg Hebrew Manuscript

Chapter 24

לְפִיכָךְ אִם יֹאמְרוּ לָכֶם הִנֵּה הוּא בַמִּדְבָּר אַל תֵּצֵאוּ וְהִנֵּה הוּא בַחֲדָרִים אַל תַּאֲמִינוּ

HTV: "Therefore if they say to you, 'Look, he is in the wilderness' - do not go out *there* - and 'Behold, he is in the chambers' - do not believe *it*."

Note: Other translations, such as the KJV, mention "the secret chambers." Most religions claim exclusive authority of God himself - He is in their "secret chambers" and nowhere else. God is in heaven not the exclusive possession of any church. In the end times many will claim authority they do not have. Let the Spirit lead you.

KJV: Wherefore if they shall say unto you, Behold, he is in the desert; go not forth: behold, *he is* in the secret chambers; believe *it* not.

Matthew 24:27

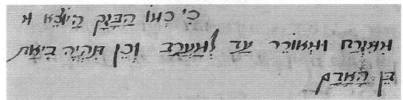
Freiburg Hebrew Manuscript

כִּי כְמוֹ הַבָּזָק הַיּוֹצֵא מִמִּזְרָח וּמֵאוֹרֵר עַד לְמַעֲרָב וְכֵן תִּהְיֶה בִּיאַת בֶּן הָאָדָם

HTV: Yeshua said to his disciples, "As the lightning comes forth from the east *flashing* as far as the west - so will the coming of the Son of Man be."

Note: See 1st Corinthians 15:21-22, 45-48, for Paul's discussion of the first Man, Adam who brought sin and death into the world so that it required the second Man, the Son of Adam (Man), the Man without sin to sacrifice himself "so that we might bear the image of the heavenly."

KJV: For as the lightning cometh out of the east, and shineth even unto the west; so shall also the coming of the Son of man be.

Matthew 24:28

כִּי בְּכֹל מָקוֹם שֶׁבּוֹ הַפֶּגֶר לְשָׁם יִקָּבְצוּ הַנְּשָׁרִים

The Hebrew Book of Matthew

HTV: **"For wherever there is a corpse - there shall the vultures be gathered."**

Note: With the return of the conquering-king Messiah, the Son of Adam (Man), who is the Son of God - given all authority in heaven and earth - there will be vast destruction of the evil ones who control this fallen world. **The end of evil will be the feast of vultures.**

KJV: For wherever the carcass is, there will the eagles be gathered together.

Matthew 24:29

וּמִיָּד אַחֲרֵי הַצָּרַת הָאוֹתָם יָמִים יִלְקֶה הַשֶּׁמֶשׁ וְהַלְּבָנָה לֹא תִתֵּן אֶת-אוֹרָהּ וְכוֹכָבִים יִפְּלוּ מִשָּׁמַיִם וְכוֹחוֹת הַשָּׁמַיִם תְּמוֹטַטְנָה

HTV: **"Immediately after the anguish of those days - the sun will be eclipsed - the moon will not give her light - the stars will fall from the heavens - and the firmament of the heavens will falter."**

Note: See Joel 2:10,31 for this prophecy in the Old Testament.

KJV: Immediately after the tribulation of those days shall the sun be darkened, and the moon shall not give her light, and the stars shall fall from heaven, and the powers of the heavens shall be shaken:

Matthew 24:30

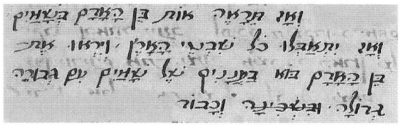
Freiburg Hebrew Manuscript

וְאָז תֵּרָאֶה אוֹת בֶּן הָאָדָם בְּשָׁמַיִם וְאָז יִתְאַבְּלוּ כֹּל שִׁבְטֵי הָאָרֶץ וְיִרְאוּ אֶת-בֶּן הָאָדָם בּוֹא בַּעֲנָנִים שֶׁל שָׁמַיִם עִם גְּבוּרָה גְּדוֹלָה וְכָבוֹד

HTV: **"Then the sign of the Son of Man will be seen in the heavens. At that time all the tribes of the earth will mourn. They shall see The Son of Man coming in the clouds with great victory and glory."**

Chapter 24

Note: This corresponds to Acts 1:9-11, "Shall so come in like manner - as you have seen him go into heaven."

KJV: And then shall appear the sign of the Son of man in heaven: and then shall all the tribes of the earth mourn, and they shall see the Son of man coming in the clouds of heaven with power and great glory.

Matthew 24:31

וְיִשְׁלַח אֶת-מַלְאָכָיו בְּשׁוֹפָר וּבְקוֹל גָּדוֹל וְיִקְבְּצוּ אֶת-נִבְחָרָיו מֵאַרְבַּע פְּאוֹת הָעוֹלָם מִצֵּית הַשָּׁמַיִם עַד גְּבוּלֵיהֶם

HTV: "He will send his angels with the sound of a great shofar. They will gather his chosen ones - from the four corners of the earth - from one end of the heavens to the other."

Note: This verse corresponds to the description in 1st Thessalonians 4:16.

KJV: And he shall send his angels with a great sound of a trumpet, and they shall gather together his elect from the four winds, from one end of heaven to the other.

Matthew 24:32

לִמְדוּ נָא מָשָׁל מֵאִילוֹן הַתְּאֵנָה כִּי כַּאֲשֶׁר עֲנָפָהּ יִהְיֶה רַכִּיךְ וְהוֹצִיא אֶת-עָלֶיהָ אָז אַתֶּם יוֹדְעִים אֲשֶׁר קַיְטָא קָרוֹב

HTV: "Now learn a proverb from the fig tree - for when its branches become tender and blossom - then you know that summer is near."

KJV: Now learn a parable of the fig tree; When his branch is yet tender, and putteth forth leaves, ye know that summer *is* nigh:

Matthew 24:33

וְכֵן גַּם אַתֶּם כַּאֲשֶׁר תִּרְאוּ אֵלֶּה דְבָרִים תֵּדְעוּ אֲשֶׁר הוּא קָרוֹב לִפְנֵי הַפֶּתַח

HTV: "Likewise you also - when you will see these things - you will know that it is near - at the gates."

KJV: So likewise ye, when ye shall see all these things, know that it is near, *even* at the doors.

Matthew 24:34

בֶּאֱמֶת אֲנִי אוֹמֵר לָכֶם שֶׁלֹּא יַעֲבוֹר הַדּוֹר הַזֶּה עַד שֶׁאֵלֶּה דְבָרִים נֵעָשׂוּ כֻלָּם

HTV: "Truly I say to you that this generation will not pass away - until all of these things have come to pass."

KJV: Verily I say unto you, This generation shall not pass, till all these things be fulfilled.

Matthew 24:35

הַשָּׁמַיִם וְהָאָרֶץ יַעֲבְרוּ אֲבָל דְּבָרַי לֹא יַעֲבְרוּ

HTV: "The heavens and the earth will pass away - but my words will not pass away."

Note: This corresponds to Matthew 5:18 "Not a yod or even the tip of a yod shall pass away until all these things have come to pass."

KJV: Heaven and earth shall pass away, but my words shall not pass away.

Matthew 24:36

אָמְנָם מֵאוֹתוֹ הַיּוֹם וּמֵאוֹתָהּ הַשָּׁעָה אֵין יוֹדֵעַ שׁוּם אָדָם וְאֵין הַמַּלְאָכִים שֶׁל שָׁמַיִם כִּי אִם הָאָב לְבַדּוֹ

HTV: "In truth - of that day and of that hour - no one knows - not even the angels of heaven - except for the Father alone."

KJV: But of that day and hour knoweth no *man*, no, not the angels of heaven, but my Father only.

Matthew 24:37

Freiburg Hebrew Manuscript

Chapter 24

וּכְמוֹ יִהְיֶה בִּימֵי נוֹחַ וְכֵן תִּהְיֶה הַבִּיאַת בֶּן הָאָדָם

HTV: Again, Yeshua said to his disciples, "Just as it was in the days of Noah - so it will it be at the coming of the Son of Man."

KJV: But as the days of Noe *were,* so shall also the coming of the Son of man be.

Matthew 24:38

כִּי כַּאֲשֶׁר בְּיָמִים לִפְנֵי הַמַּבּוּל יִהְיוּ אוֹכְלִים וְשׁוֹתִים וּמִתְחַתְּנוֹת וּמְאָרְשִׂים אִשּׁוֹת עַד הָאוֹתוֹ הַיּוֹם שֶׁבּוֹ נוֹחַ נִכְנַס בַּתֵּיבָה

HTV: "For as in the years before the flood - they were eating and drinking - taking wives and giving wives - until the day that Noah entered the ark."

KJV: For as in the days that were before the flood they were eating and drinking, marrying and giving in marriage, until the day that Noe entered into the ark,

Matthew 24:39

Freiburg Hebrew Manuscript

וְלֹא יָדְעוּ עַד שֶׁבָּא הַמַּבּוּל וַיִּקַּח כֻּלָּם וְכֵן תִּהְיֶה בִּיאַת בֶּן הָאָדָם

HTV: "They did not understand - until the flood came and destroyed all of them!   So shall it be at the coming of the Son of Man."

Note: Man cannot understand that all of his world can be gone in an instant. God has that power. The coming of the Son of Man is a part of the great tribulation sent by Yehovah.

KJV: And knew not until the flood came, and took them all away; so shall also the coming of the Son of man be.

The Hebrew Book of Matthew

Matthew 24:40

Freiburg Hebrew Manuscript

וְאָז יִהְיוּ שְׁנַיִם בְּשָׂדֶה הָאֶחָד יְקַבֵּל וְהָאַחֵר יַעֲזֹב

HTV: "At that time there will be two ploughing in a field - one righteous and the other wicked - the one will be taken and the other will be left."

Note: This verse is critical to the interpretation of the modern theology of the Rapture. The Hebrew text denotes one as righteous and the other as wicked, an understanding not specified in the Greek.

This is also reflected by literal translations from the Greek. For example, "received" is used in Young's Literal Version and the Standard Literal Version. It can also mean "caught up" or "trapped." Matthew 13:47-50. It is not clear whether the righteous or the wicked is taken.

KJV: Then shall two be in the field; the one shall be taken, and the other left.

Matthew 24:41

Freiburg Hebrew Manuscript

וּשְׁתַּיִם תִּהְיֶינָה טוֹחֲנוֹת בָּרֵחַיִים הָאַחַת תְּקַבֵּל וְהָאַחֶרֶת תַּעֲזֹב וּשְׁנַיִם בְּמִשְׁכָּב הָאֶחָד יְקַבֵּל וְהָאַחֵר יַעֲזֹב

HTV: Two *women* will be grinding at the millstones - the one will be taken and the other will be left. And two in a bed - the one will be taken and the other will be left.

Note: It is not entirely clear whether this is instantaneous, natural or supernatural. These two verses along with Thessalonians 4:17 and 1st Corinthians 15:51-52, are the entire scriptural basis for the Rapture. So these verses need to be critically examined.

KJV: Two *women shall be* grinding at the mill; the one shall be taken, and the other left.

Matthew 24:42

Freiburg Hebrew Manuscript

לְפִיכָךְ תְּשָׁקְדוּ כִּי אַתֶּם אֵין יוֹדְעִים אֶת-הַשָּׁעָה אֲשֶׁר בָּה הָאָדוֹן שֶׁלָּכֶם יָבוֹא

HTV: Then Yeshua said to his disciples, "Therefore, watch with me - because you do not know at what hour your lord is coming."

Note: The Hebrew text conveys the sense of "keeping vigil" with Yeshua during the end time. "Truly - of that day and of that hour - there is no one *who* knows - not even the angels of heaven - except for the Father alone." Matthew 24:36.

KJV: Watch therefore: for ye know not what hour your Lord doth come.

Matthew 24:43

אֲבָל הַזֹּאת יֵשׁ לָכֶם לָדַעַת שֶׁאִם בַּעַל הַבַּיִת יָדַע בְּאֵיזוֹ שָׁעָה יָבוֹא הַגַּנָּב בֶּאֱמֶת הוּא הָיָה שׁוֹקֵד וְלֹא יָנִיחַ לְהֵחָפֵר אֶת-בֵּיתוֹ

HTV: "But you should know this: If the owner of the house knew at which hour the thief would come - truly he would stay awake. He would not allow his house to be broken into."

KJV: But know this, that if the goodman of the house had known in what watch the thief would come, he would have watched, and would not have suffered his house to be broken up.

Matthew 24:44

לְפִיכָךְ אַתֶּם תִּהְיוּ נְכוֹנִים כִּי אֵינְכֶם יוֹדְעִים בְּאֵיזוֹ שָׁעָה יָבוֹא בֶן הָאָדָם

HTV: "Therefore, you should be ready - because you do not know at which hour the Son of Man shall come."

KJV: Therefore be ye also ready: for in such an hour as ye think not the Son of man cometh.

Matthew 24:45

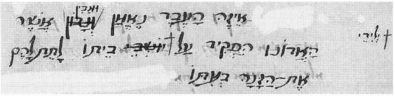

Freiburg Hebrew Manuscript

אֵיזֶה הָעֶבֶד נֶאֱמָן וּמֵבִין אֲשֶׁר הָאָדוֹנוּ הִפְקִיד עַל יְלִידֵי בֵיתוֹ לָתֵת לָהֶם אֶת-הַזָּנָה בְּעִתּוֹ

HTV: "Who *among you* is the wise and faithful servant - whom his lord has appointed over those of his household - to give them (spiritual) sustenance in due season?"

Note: *Hazanah* "nourishment" by extension refers to spiritual sustenance as well as physical sustenance. See John 4:32, "I have meat to eat that you know not of." "in due season" refers not to daily bread but the spiritual sustenance and strength that will be needed in the end times.

KJV: Who then is a faithful and wise servant, whom his lord hath made ruler over his household, to give them meat in due season?

Mathew 24:46

אַשְׁרֵי הָעֶבֶד הַהוּא אֲשֶׁר אִם יָבוֹא הָאָדוֹן יִמְצָאֵהוּ כֵן עוֹשֶׂה

HTV: "Blessed is that servant who - when his lord shall come - will find him doing so!"

KJV: Blessed *is* that servant, whom his lord when he cometh shall find so doing.

Matthew 24:47

Freiburg Hebrew Manuscript

Chapter 24

בֶּאֱמֶת אֲנִי אוֹמֵר לָכֶם כִּי יַפְקִידֵהוּ עַל כֹּל שֶׁלּוֹ

HTV: "Truly - I say to you, that Yeshua will appoint him over all that is his."

Note: Is the wise and faithful servant to be appointed over all the earth, "and the fullness thereof?" Psalm 24:1. See also Revelation 3:21, "He who overcomes I will grant dominion to sit with me at my throne, even as I also overcame and sat with my Father."

KJV: Verily I say unto you, That he shall make him ruler over all his goods.

Matthew 24:48

אֲבָל אִם הָעֶבֶד הָרַע יֹאמַר בְּלִבּוֹ הִנֵּה הָאֲדוֹנִי מִתְאַחֵר לָבוֹא

HTV: "But if the wicked servant says in his heart, 'Indeed my lord delays in coming' "

KJV: But and if that evil servant shall say in his heart, My lord delayeth his coming;

Matthew 24:49

Freiburg Hebrew Manuscript

וְיָתְחִיל לְהַכּוֹת אֶת-הָעוֹבְדִים עִמּוֹ וְיֹאכַל וְיִשְׁתֶּה עִים שְׁכּוֹרִים

HTV: "And he begins to do violence to his fellow servants - and eat with gluttons - and drink with drunkards!"

Note: As the evil servant in charge comes to believe God has no more presence or authority over him his true evil nature begins to run riot. Power corrupts - Absolute power corrupts absolutely!

Note: In the Hebrew, the word לְהַכּוֹת refers to serious violence including beating, devastating, and slaying those good servants over whom the evil servant has been given authority. See John 16:2, "The time will come - when whosoever kills you will think he is doing a service to God!"

The Hebrew Book of Matthew

KJV: And shall begin to smite *his* fellow servants, and to eat and drink with the drunken;

Matthew 24:50

הִנֵּה יָבוֹא הָאָדוֹן הָאוֹתוֹ עֶבֶד בַּיּוֹם שֶׁלֹּא יִהְיֶה מְחַכֶּה וּבְשָׁעָה שֶׁלֹּא יָדַע

HTV: **"Behold, the master of that servant shall come on the day that he was not expecting - and at an hour that he (the evil servant) knows not."**

KJV: The lord of that servant shall come in a day when he looketh not for *him*, and in an hour that he is not aware of,

Matthew 24:51

Freiburg Hebrew Manuscript

וְיַפְרִידֵהוּ וְחָלְקוֹ יָשׂוּם עִם חֲנֵפִים שָׁם יִהְיֶה בְּכִי וְחֵרוּק שִׁנַּיִם

HTV: **"They (the angels) will sever him (the evil servant) and set his portion with the deceivers. There will be weeping and gnashing of teeth!"**

> Note: The angels mentioned in Matthew 24:41 are those doing the severing. They are separating good from evil. The Greek says **"him"** - The Hebrew agrees that Yeshua will send his angels to do the cutting asunder - **severing the evil servant** from his authority, his household, and the righteous.

KJV: And shall cut him asunder, and appoint *him* his portion with the hypocrites: there shall be weeping and gnashing of teeth.

Matthew Chapter 25

Hebrew Text Version (HTV)

1 Again, Yeshua said to his disciples, "The Kingdom of Heaven is like ten virgins who took their lamps and went out to meet the groom."

2 "Five of them were foolish and five of them were wise."

3 "The five foolish *ones* took their lamps - but brought no oil."

4 "But the wise *ones* took oil - along with their lamps."

5 "Since the bridegroom was late - they all dozed off and fell asleep."

6 In the middle of the night - the cry was renewed: "Behold the bridegroom has come! - Go out to meet him."

7 "Then all of the virgins rose up and readied their lamps."

8 "The foolish virgins said to the wise *ones* - 'Give us some of your oil - because our lamps have gone out!'"

9 "The wise *ones* answered, saying, 'There is not enough for us and for you *both*. Therefore, go to the seller - and buy *some* for yourselves.'"

10 "While they were gone - behold, the bridegroom came! Those who were prepared entered with him for the wedding - and the door was closed."

11 "At last, the foolish virgins returned. And they said, 'Lord, Lord please open for us!'"

12 "He answered and said, 'Truly, I say to you - I do not know you.'"

13 "Therefore, you should watch most diligently - since you cannot know the day or the hour when the bridegroom will return."

14 Yeshua told his disciples another parable. "The kingdom of heaven is like a man traveling to a distant land - who calls his servants to turn over to them his money!"

15 HTV: "To one he gave five talents of gold - to another he gave two talents of gold - and to one he gave one talent of gold

- each according to his ability - then he went on his journey!"

16 "The one who received five talents went and traded them and earned another five talents."

17 "Likewise, the one who received two talents earned another two talents."

18 "However, the one who received one talent went and buried it in the ground and hid his lord's money."

19 "After a long time, the lord of those servants came and reckoned with them."

20 "And the one who received the five talents approached and brought another five talents, and said, 'My lord, you gave me five talents - behold, I gained five more!'"

21 "And the Lord said unto him, 'Good and faithful servant! - You have been faithful over a few things - I will appoint you over many things. Enter now into the joy of your Lord.'"

22 "And the one who had received two talents came near, saying, 'My Lord, you gave unto me two talents; behold, I have gained two more talents.'"

23 "And the Lord said unto him, 'Aha! - Good and faithful servant! - You have been faithful over a few things - I will appoint you over many things - Enter into the joy of your Lord.'"

24 "And the one who had received one talent came near saying, 'Lord I knew that you are a hard man - you reap in a place where you have not sowed - and gather in a place where you did not pasture.'"

25 "For this reason, I feared - so I went and hid your talent in the ground. Here is what is yours!"

26 "And his Master answered and said to him, 'Wicked and lazy servant, you knew I reap where I did not sow - and gather what I did not pasture.'"

27 "Therefore, what would have been worthwhile - *was* to give my money to the bankers - so when I returned - I would surely have what is mine with interest."

28 "Take then the talent from him - and give it to him who has ten talents."

29 "For the one who has much - even more abundance will be given to him. For the one who has nothing - behold, even what was intended for him may be taken away."

30 "Cast the wicked servant into the outer darkness - for there will be weeping and gnashing of teeth!"

31 Again, Yeshua said to his disciples, "When the Son of Man shall come in his majesty - and all the angels with him - then shall he sit on the throne of his glory."

32 "And all nations will be gathered unto Yeshua, - and he will separate this one from that one - as the shepherd separates the sheep from the goats."

33 "And he will set the sheep to his right and the goats to his left."

34 "And then the king will say to those on his right, 'Come, blessed ones of my Father - and receive your kingdom - *which was prepared from the creation of the world!*"

35 "For I was hungry, and you fed me - I was thirsty and you gave me drink - and I was a wayfarer and you welcomed me into your home."

36 "I was naked and you clothed me - I was sick and you cared for me - I was in prison and you visited me."

37 Then the righteous will answer him and say, "O Lord, when did we see you hungry and fed you - thirsty, and gave you drink?"

38 "When did we see you as a wayfarer, and took you to our home? *When did we see you* naked, and clothed you?"

39 "Or when did we see you sick, or in prison, and came to you?"

40 "And the king answered and said unto them, 'Truly I say unto you, whatsoever you have done - to one of the least of my brothers - you have done to me.'"

41 "Then he will also say to those that are on his left, 'Depart from me, you *who* are cursed - to the eternal fire that is *prepared from* long ago for Satan and his *fallen* angels!"

42 "Because I was hungry and you did not feed me - I was thirsty and you did not give me drink!"

43 "I was a wayfarer and you did not take me into your home - I was naked and you did not clothe me - I was sick and in prison and you did not visit me!"

44 Then they *again* spoke to him and said, "O Lord, when did we see you hungry or thirsty or a stranger or naked or in prison and did not serve you?"

45 Then he answered them and said, "Truly I say to you, whatever

you did not do - to the least of these - you did not do to me."

46 And these will go into the eternal punishment of the fire of Gei-Hinnom (Hell) - and the righteous *will go* into eternal life!

Matthew Chapter 25
HTV with translator notes and KJV comparison

Matthew 25:1

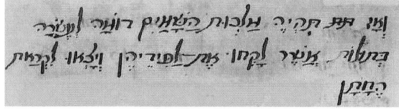
Freiburg Hebrew Manuscript

וְאָז תִּהְיֶה מַלְכוּת הַשָּׁמַיִם דּוֹמָה לְעֲשָׂרָה בְּתוּלוֹת אֲשֶׁר לָקְחוּ אֶת־לַפִּידֵיהֶן וְיָצְאוּ לִקְרַאת

HTV: **Again, Yeshua said to his disciples, "The Kingdom of Heaven is like ten virgins who took their lamps and went out to meet the groom."**

> Note: The separation of the Word into chapters (and verses) was done in the 13th century AD, more than a thousand years after they were written. So, this is a continuation from the themes in chapter 24. **The Hebrew usage of "Again, Yeshua said to his disciples" in the STM** - usually left out of the Greek/English translations to better separate this from the last chapter - when, in fact, it is a connected narrative. **This is a marker of the Hebrew origin of Matthew.**
>
> Shem Tov Hebrew Matthew (STM): **Again Yeshu said to his disciples:** The kingdom of heaven is like ten virgins who took their **lamps** and went forth to meet a **bridegroom** and a bride.

KJV: Then shall the kingdom of heaven be likened unto ten virgins, which took their lamps, and went forth to meet the bridegroom.

Matthew 25:2

וְחָמֵשׁ מֵהֶן תִּהְיֶינָה כְּסִילוֹת וְחָמֵשׁ חֲכָמוֹת

HTV: "Five of them were foolish and five of them were wise."

KJV: And five of them were wise, and five *were* foolish.

Matthew 25:3

וְהַחָמֵשׁ מֵהֶן אִתְּרֵי שֶׁלָּקְחוּ אֶת-לַפִּידֵיהֶן לֹא לָקְחוּ שֶׁמֶן

HTV: "The five foolish *ones* took their lamps - but brought no oil."

KJV: They that *were* foolish took their lamps, and took no oil with them:

Matthew 25:4

אֲבָל הַחֲכָמוֹת הֵלָּקְחוּ בִּכְלֵיהֶן שֶׁמֶן יַחַד עִם לַפִּידִים

HTV: "But the wise *ones* took oil - along with their lamps."

KJV: But the wise took oil in their vessels with their lamps.

Matthew 25:5

וְכַאֲשֶׁר הֶחָתָן הִתְאַחֵר כֻּלָּן יָשְׁנוּ וְרָדְמוּ

HTV: "Since the bridegroom was late - they all dozed off and fell asleep."

KJV: While the bridegroom tarried, they all slumbered and slept.

Matthew 25:6

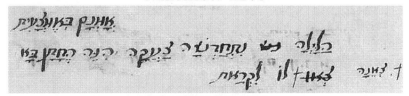

Freiburg Hebrew Manuscript

אָמְנָם בְּאֶמְצָעִית הַלַּיְלָה נִתְחַדְּשָׁה צְעָקָה הִנֵּה הֶחָתָן בָּא צְאֶנָה לוֹ לִקְרַאת

HTV: **In the middle of the night - the cry was renewed: "Behold the bridegroom has come! - Go out to meet him."**

KJV: And at midnight there was a cry made, Behold, the bridegroom cometh; go ye out to meet him.

Matthew 25:7

וְאָז קָמוּ הָאוֹתָן בְּתוּלוֹת כֻּלָּן וְתִקְּנוּ אֶת לַפִּידֵיהֶן

HTV: **"Then all of the virgins rose up and readied their lamps."**

KJV: Then all those virgins arose, and trimmed their lamps.

Matthew 25:8

וּכְסִילוֹת אָמְרוּ לַחֲכָמוֹת תְּנֶינָה לָנוּ גַם מִשֶּׁמֶן שֶׁלָּכֶן כִּי לַפִּידֵינוּ נִתְכְּבוּ

HTV: **"The foolish virgins said to the wise** ones **- 'Give us some of your oil - because our lamps have gone out!' "**

KJV: And the foolish said unto the wise, Give us of your oil; for our lamps are gone out.

Matthew 25:9

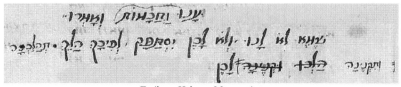
Freiburg Hebrew Manuscript

וַחֲכָמוֹת עָנוּ וְאָמְרוּ שֶׁמָּא לֹא לָנוּ וְלֹא לָכֶן יִסְתַּפֵּק לְפִיכָךְ הַלֵּךְ תְהַלֵּכְהָ וְתִקְנֶינָה לָכֶן

HTV: **"The wise** ones **answered, saying, 'There is not enough for us and for you** both**. Therefore, go to the seller - and buy** some **for yourselves.' "**

Note: As a metaphor Yeshua is saying the foolish ones have no spiritual bank account to draw upon. They have not readied themselves spiritually to enter the kingdom. They must draw closer to the Holy Spirit to get what they need. Then they may enter the Kingdom of Heaven.

KJV: But the wise answered, saying, *Not so*; lest there be not enough for us and you: but go ye rather to them that sell, and buy for yourselves.

Matthew 25:10

וּבְתוֹךְ שֶׁהָלְכוּ לִקְנוֹת הִנֵּה בָא הֶחָתָן וַאֲשֶׁר תִּהְיֶינָה נְכוֹנוֹת נִכְנְסוּ אִתּוֹ לַנִּשּׂוּאִים וּפֶתַח נִסְגַּר

HTV: **"While they were gone - behold, the bridegroom came! Those who were prepared entered with him for the wedding - and the door was closed."**

KJV: And while they went to buy, the bridegroom came; and they that were ready went in with him to the marriage: and the door was shut.

Matthew 25:11

Freiburg Hebrew Manuscript

וּבְאַחֲרוֹן בָּאוּ גַם בְּתוּלוֹת הַשְּׁאָרוֹת וְאָמְרוּ הוֹי הָאָדוֹן הָאָדוֹן פְּתַח נָא לָנוּ

HTV: **"At last, the foolish virgins returned. And they said, 'Lord, Lord please open for us!'"**

> Note: Yeshua is reinforcing lessons, in this case Matthew 7:21 "Not everyone who says to me, **'Lord, Lord,'** will enter the kingdom of heaven, but only the one who does the will of my Father who is in heaven."

KJV: Afterward came also the other virgins, saying, Lord, Lord, open to us.

Matthew 25:12

Freiburg Hebrew Manuscript

אֲבָל הוּא עָנָה וַיֹּאמַר בֶּאֱמֶת אֲנִי אוֹמֵר לָכֶן אֲשֶׁר אֵינִי מַכִּיר אֶתְכֶם

The Hebrew Book of Matthew

HTV: **"He answered and said, 'Truly, I say to you - I do not know you.'"**

Note: Again, Yeshua reiterates Matthew 7:23, "And then I myself shall profess to them, 'I never knew you! Get away from me - all you workers of iniquity!'" Assemblies are full of nominal believers who do not truly know Yehovah nor his Son Yeshua. It is a sobering truth.

KJV: But he answered and said, Verily I say unto you, I know you not.

Matthew 25:13

לְפִיכָךְ שְׁקוֹד תִּשְׁקַדְנָה כִּי אַתֶּן אֵין יוֹדְעוֹת לֹא אֶת-הַיּוֹם וְלֹא אֶת-הַשָּׁעָה

HTV: **"Therefore, you should watch most diligently - since you cannot know the day or the hour when the bridegroom will return."**

KJV: Watch therefore, for ye know neither the day nor the hour wherein the Son of man cometh.

Matthew 25:14

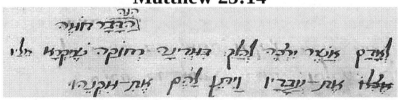
Freiburg Hebrew Manuscript

הִנֵּה הַדָּבָר דּוֹמֶה לְאָדָם אֲשֶׁר יִרְצֶה לָהֲלֹךְ בִּמְדִינָה רְחוֹקָה שֶׁיִּקְרָא אֵלָיו אֶת-עֲבָדָיו וַיִּתֵּן

HTV: **Yeshua told his disciples another parable. "The kingdom of heaven is like a man traveling to a distant land - who calls his servants to turn over to them his money!"**

Note: The word in Freiburg for "money" is וְהֲנָקָם which has a broader meaning of "substance, money, goods and/or property." In Matthew 25:23 - the parable is revealed "Well done, good and faithful servant: you have been faithful over a few things, I will make you ruler over many things!"

KJV: *For the kingdom of heaven is* as a man travelling into a far country, *who* called his own servants, and delivered unto them his goods.

Matthew 25:15

וְלָזֶה נָתַן חֲמִשָּׁה כִּכָּרִים וְלָזֶה שְׁנַיִם וּלְאַחֵר אֶחָד וְכָל אֶחָד וְאֶחָד לְפִי כוֹחוֹתָיו וּמִיָּד הָלַךְ

HTV: "To one he gave five talents of gold - to another he gave two talents of gold - and to one he gave one talent of gold - each according to his ability - then he went on his journey!"

KJV: And unto one he gave five talents, to another two, and to another one; to every man according to his several ability; and straightway took his journey.

Matthew 25:16

וַאֲשֶׁר לָקַח חֲמִשָּׁה כִּכָּרִים הָלַךְ וְסָחַר בָּהֶם וְהִרְוִיחַ עוֹד אֲחֵרִים חֲמִשָּׁה כִּכָּרִים

HTV: "The one who received five talents went and traded them and earned another five talents."

KJV: Then he that had received the five talents went and traded with the same, and made *them* other five talents.

Matthew 25:17

וּכְמוֹ כֵן גַּם שֶׁלָּקַח שְׁנַיִם כִּכָּרִים הִרְוִיחַ עוֹד אֲחֵרִים שְׁנַיִם כִּכָּרִים

HTV: "Likewise, the one who received two talents earned another two talents."

KJV: And likewise he that *had received* two, he also gained other two.

Matthew 25:18

אָמְנָם אֲשֶׁר לָקַח כִּכָּר אֶחָד הָלַךְ וַחֲפָרוֹ בָאָרֶץ וְהִסְתִּיר אֶת-כֶּסֶף הָאֲדוֹנוֹ

HTV: "However, the one who received one talent went and buried it in the ground and hid his lord's money."

KJV: But he that had received one went and digged in the earth, and hid his lord's money.

Matthew 25:19

וְאַחֲרֵי זְמָן הָאָרוּךְ בָּא הָאָדוֹן שֶׁל אוֹתָם הָעֲבָדִים וַיְחָשֵׁב עִם הָאוֹתָם עֲבָדִים

HTV: "After a long time, the lord of those servants came and reckoned with them."

KJV: After a long time the lord of those servants cometh, and reckoneth with them.

Matthew 25:20

וַיִּגַּשׁ אֲשֶׁר חֲמִשָּׁה כִּכָּרִים לָקַח וְהֵבִיא אֲחֵרִים חֲמִשָּׁה כִּכָּרִים וַיֹּאמַר הָאֲדוֹנִי אַתָּה נָתַתָּ לִי חֲמִשָּׁה כִּכָּרִים הִנֵּה הִרְוַיְחְתִּי חֲמִשָּׁה אֲחֵרִים כִּכָּרִים

HTV: "And the one who received the five talents approached and brought another five talents, and said, 'My lord, you gave me five talents - behold, I gained five more!'"

KJV: And so he that had received five talents came and brought other five talents, saying, Lord, thou deliveredst unto me five talents: behold, I have gained beside them five talents more.

Matthew 25:21

וַיֹּאמַר הָאֲדוֹנוֹ לוֹ הֶאָח הָעֶבֶד טוֹב וּנֶאֱמָן אֲשֶׁר הָיִיתָ בִמְעַטִים נֶאֱמָן אֲנִי אַפְקִידְךָ עַל דְּבָרִים רַבִּים בּוֹא נָא בְּשִׂמְחַת אֲדוֹנְךָ

HTV: "And the Lord said unto him, 'Good and faithful servant! - You have been faithful over a few things - I will appoint you over many things. Enter now into the joy of your Lord.'"

KJV: His lord said unto him, Well done, thou good and faithful servant: thou hast been faithful over a few things, I will make thee ruler over many things: enter thou into the joy of thy lord.

Matthew 25:22

וַיִּגַּשׁ אֲשֶׁר לָקַח שְׁנַיִם כִּכָּרִים וַיֹּאמַר הָאֲדוֹנִי אַתָּה נָתַתָּ לִי שְׁנַיִם כִּכָּרִים הִנֵּה אֲנִי הִרְוַיְחְתִּי שְׁנַיִם אֲחֵרִים כִּכָּרִים

Chapter 25

HTV: **"And the one who had received two talents came near, saying, 'My Lord, you gave unto me two talents; behold, I have gained two more talents.'"**

KJV: He also that had received two talents came and said, Lord, thou deliveredst unto me two talents: behold, I have gained two other talents beside them.

Matthew 25:23

וַיֹּאמֶר לוֹ הָאֲדוֹנוֹ הֶאָח הָעֶבֶד טוֹב וְנֶאֱמָן אֲשֶׁר הָיִיתָ בִמְעַטִים נֶאֱמָן אֲנִי אַפְקִידְךָ עַל רַבִּים בּוֹא נָא בְשִׂמְחַת אֲדוֹנֶךָ

HTV: **"And the Lord said unto him, 'Aha! - Good and faithful servant! - You have been faithful over a few things - I will appoint you over many things - Enter into the joy of your Lord.'"**

KJV: His lord said unto him, Well done, good and faithful servant; thou hast been faithful over a few things, I will make thee ruler over many things: enter thou into the joy of thy lord.

Matthew 25:24

Freiburg Hebrew Manuscript

וַיִּגַּשׁ אֲשֶׁר לָקַח כִּכָּר אֶחָד וַיֹּאמַר הָאֲדוֹנִי אֲנִי יָדַעְתִּי אֲשֶׁר אַתָּה אָדָם קָשֶׁה מְקַצֵּר בְּמָקוֹם אֲשֶׁר לֹא זָרַעְתָּ בּוֹ וְאַתָּה מְקַבֵּץ בְּמָקוֹם אֲשֶׁר לֹא פִּזַּרְתָּ בּוֹ

HTV: **"And the one who had received one talent came near saying, 'Lord I knew that you are a hard man - you reap in a place where you have not sowed - and gather in a place where you did not pasture.'"**

409

The Hebrew Book of Matthew

> Note: The final clause "gather where you did not put out to field" refers to animal husbandry, gathering up herds that you did not tend, nor disperse into the fields. In any case, the excuses of the lazy servant are essentially the same.

KJV: Then he which had received the one talent came and said, Lord, I knew thee that thou art an hard man, reaping where thou hast not sown, and gathering where thou hast not strawed:

Matthew 25:25

לְפִיכַךְ יָרֵאתִי וְהָלַכְתִּי וְהִסְתַּתַּרְתִּי אֶת־כִּכָּרְךָ בָּאָרֶץ הִנֵּה לְךָ מַה שֶּׁלְּךָ

HTV: **"For this reason I feared - so I went and hid your talent in the ground. Here is what is yours!"**

KJV: And I was afraid, and went and hid thy talent in the earth: lo, *there* thou hast *that is* thine.

Matthew 25:26

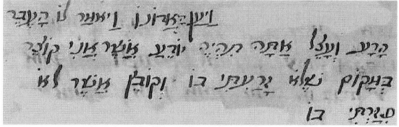
Freiburg Hebrew Manuscript

וַיַּעַן הָאָדוֹנוֹ וַיֹּאמֶר לוֹ הָעֶבֶד הָרַע וְעָצֵל אַתָּה תִהְיֶה יוֹדֵעַ אֲשֶׁר אֲנִי קוֹצֵר בְּמָקוֹם שֶׁלֹּא זָרַעְתִּי בוֹ וְקוֹבֵץ אֲשֶׁר לֹא פִּזַּרְתִּי בוֹ

HTV: **"And his Master answered and said to him, 'Wicked and lazy servant, you knew I reap where I did not sow - and gather what I did not pasture.'"**

> Note: Yeshua did not baptize anyone in the Gospels - he always had his disciples baptize others in the Holy Spirit to receive Salvation so that they would know they had the authority. Those who have received the Holy Spirit and do not or will not share it are the evil ones in this parable.

KJV: His lord answered and said unto him, *Thou* wicked and slothful servant, thou knewest that I reap where I sowed not, and gather where I have not strawed:

Matthew 25:27

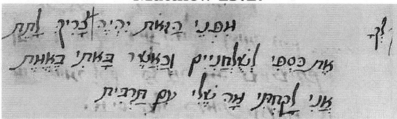

Freiburg Hebrew Manuscript

מִפְּנֵי הַזֹּאת יִהְיֶה לְךָ צָרִיךְ לָתֵת אֶת כַּסְפִּי לְשֻׁלְחָנִיִּים וְכַאֲשֶׁר בָּאתִי בֶּאֱמֶת אֲנִי לָקַחְתִּי מַה שֶּׁלִי עִם תַּרְבִּית

HTV: "Therefore, what would have been worthwhile - *was* to give my money to the bankers - so when I returned - I would surely have what is mine with interest."

Note: The modern equivalence of money changers would be bankers.

KJV: Thou oughtest therefore to have put my money to the exchangers, and *then* at my coming I should have received mine own with usury.

Matthew 25:28

שְׂאוּ נָא מִמֶּנּוּ אֶת-הַכִּכָּר וּתְנוּ לַאֲשֶׁר לוֹ עָשָׂר כִּכָּרִים

HTV: "Take then the talent from him - and give it to him who has ten talents."

KJV: Take therefore the talent from him, and give *it* unto him which hath ten talents.

Matthew 25:29

Freiburg Hebrew Manuscript

כִּי לְכֹל שֶׁלּוֹ כְּלוּם לְאוֹתוֹ יִנָּתֵן וְיוֹתִיר וַאֲשֶׁר אֵין לוֹ כְּלוּם הִנֵּה מַה שֶּׁבְּיָדוֹ יִקַּח מִמֶּנּוּ

HTV: **"For the one who has much - even more abundance will be given to him. For the one who has nothing - behold, even what was intended for him may be taken away."**

> Note: This same statement is almost exact to that in Matthew 13:12. Those who have been given of the Holy Spirit and done nothing with it are those that are wicked. The Spirit and the promise of eternal life will be taken away from them. Judas would be the best example of this. He received the Holy Spirit but then betrayed it. See 2nd Peter 2:21 "Those who have received and turned away…" Give of your Salvation to others.

KJV: For unto every one that hath shall be given, and he shall have abundance: but from him that hath not shall be taken away even that which he hath.

Matthew 25:30

וְאֶת-הָעֶבֶד הַבִּלְתִּי מוֹעִיל הַשְׁלִיכוּ בַּחֲשָׁכִים הַחִיצוֹנִים כִּי שָׁם יִהְיֶה בְּכִי וְחִרוּק הַשִּׁנַּיִם

HTV: **"Cast the wicked servant into the outer darkness - for there will be weeping and gnashing of teeth!"**

KJV: And cast ye the unprofitable servant into outer darkness: there shall be weeping and gnashing of teeth.

Matthew 25:31

וְכַאֲשֶׁר בֶּן הָאָדָם יָבוֹא בִּכְבוֹדוֹ וְכֹל מַלְאָכִים אִתּוֹ אָז יֵשֵׁב עַל כִּסֵּא הַכְּבוֹדוֹ

HTV: **Again, Yeshua said to his disciples, "When the Son of Man shall come in his majesty - and all the angels with him - then shall he sit on the throne of his glory."**

KJV: When the Son of man shall come in his glory, and all the holy angels with him, then shall he sit upon the throne of his glory:

Matthew 25:32

Freiburg Hebrew Manuscript

וְיִקָּבְצוּ אֵלָיו כֹּל גּוֹיִם וְיַפְרִידָם הַזֶּה מֵהַזֶּה כַּאֲשֶׁר הָרוֹעֶה הַמַּפְרִיד אֶת-הַצֹּאן מִתְּיָשִׁים

HTV: "And all nations will be gathered unto Yeshua, - and he will separate this one from that one - as the shepherd separates the sheep from the goats."

> Note: Yeshua said his sheep know his voice (John 10:27). Goats, notably, go their own way being rather stubborn and recalcitrant. Those followers of the Savior (symbolized as sheep) will be separated from those who will not submit (symbolized by goats).

KJV: And before him shall be gathered all nations: and he shall separate them one from another, as a shepherd divideth *his* sheep from the goats:

Matthew 25:33

וְיַעֲמִיד אֶת-הַצֹּאן לִימִינוֹ וְאֶת-תְּיָשִׁים לִשְׂמֹאולוֹ

HTV: "And he will set the sheep to his right and the goats to his left."

KJV: And he shall set the sheep on his right hand, but the goats on the left.

Matthew 25:34

וְאָז יֹאמַר הַמֶּלֶךְ לְאוֹתָם אֲשֶׁר לִימִינוֹ בּוֹאוּ נָא הַבְּרוּכֵי הָאָבִי וּקְנוּ אֶת-הַמַּלְכוּת שֶׁלָּכֶם נְכוֹנָה מִבְּרִיאַת הָעוֹלָם

HTV: "And then the king will say to those on his right, 'Come, blessed ones of my Father - and receive your kingdom - *which* was prepared from the creation of the world!"

KJV: Then shall the King say unto them on his right hand, Come, ye blessed of my Father, inherit the kingdom prepared for you from the foundation of the world:

Matthew 25:35

כִּי רָעַבְתִּי וְהֶאֱכַלְתֶּם אוֹתִי צָמֵאתִי וְהִשְׁקִיתֶם אוֹתִי וַאֲנִי אֶהְיֶה גֵּר וּקְבַלְתֶּם אוֹתִי לְבֵיתְכֶם

HTV: "For I was hungry, and you fed me - I was thirsty and you gave me drink - and I was a wayfarer and you welcomed me into your home."

KJV: For I was an hungred, and ye gave me meat: I was thirsty, and ye gave me drink: I was a stranger, and ye took me in:

Matthew 25:36

וְאֶהְיֶה עֵרוֹם וְכִסִּיתֶם אוֹתִי וְאֶהְיֶה חוֹלֶה וּפְקַתֶּם אוֹתִי וְאֶהְיֶה בְּבֵית אֲסִירִים וּבָאתֶם אֶצְלִי

HTV: "I was naked and you clothed me - I was sick and you cared for me - I was in prison and you visited me."

KJV: Naked, and ye clothed me: I was sick, and ye visited me: I was in prison, and ye came unto me.

Matthew 25:37

וְאָז יַעֲנוּ לוֹ הַצַּדִּיקִים וְיֹאמְרוּ הוֹי הָאָדוֹן אֵימָתַי רָאִינוּ אוֹתְךָ רָעֵב וְהֶאֱכַלְנוּךְ צָמֵא וְהִשְׁקִינוּךְ

HTV: Then the righteous will answer him and say, "O Lord, when did we see you hungry and fed you - thirsty, and gave you drink?"

KJV: Then shall the righteous answer him, saying, Lord, when saw we thee an hungred, and fed *thee*? or thirsty, and gave *thee* drink?

Matthew 25:38

וְאֵימָתַי רָאִינוּ אוֹתְךָ הֱיוֹת גֵּר וּלְקַחְנוּךָ לְבֵיתֵנוּ עֵרוֹם וְהִכְסִינוּךָ

HTV: "When did we see you as a wayfarer, and took you to our home? *When did we see you* naked, and clothed you?"

KJV: When saw we thee a stranger, and took *thee* in? or naked, and clothed *thee*?

Chapter 25

Matthew 25:39

אוֹ אֵימָתַי רָאִינוּ אוֹתְךָ חוֹלֶה אוֹ בְּבֵית אֲסִירִים וּבָאנוּ אֵלֶיךָ

HTV: "Or when did we see you sick, or in prison, and came to you?"

KJV: Or when saw we thee sick, or in prison, and came unto thee?

Matthew 25:40

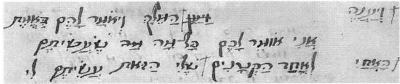
Freiburg Hebrew Manuscript

וְיָעֲנֶה הַמֶּלֶךְ וְיֹאמַר לָהֶם בֶּאֱמֶת אֲנִי אוֹמֵר לָכֶם כָּל מָה שֶׁעֲשִׂיתֶם לְאֶחָד הַקְּטַנִּים הָאַחִי שֶׁלִי הַזֹּאת עֲשִׂיתֶם לִי

HTV: "And the king answered and said unto them, 'Truly I say unto you, whatsoever you have done - to one of the least of my brothers - you have done to me.'"

Note: Yeshua is not being all encompassing here. He is referring to brothers and sisters in the faith. Galatians 6:10, "Let us do good to all, but especially to those of the household of faith."

KJV: And the King shall answer and say unto them, Verily I say unto you, Inasmuch as ye have done *it* unto one of the least of these my brethren, ye have done *it* unto me.

Matthew 25:41

וְאָז יֹאמַר גַּם לְאוֹתָם שֶׁלִּשְׂמֹאלוֹ סוּרוּ מִמֶּנִּי הַמְקֻלָּלִים לָאֵשׁ הָעוֹלָמִי שֶׁמְזֻמָּן לְשָׂטָן וּלְמַלְאָכָיו

HTV: "Then he will also say to those that are on his left, 'Depart from me, you *who* are cursed - to the eternal fire that is *prepared from* long ago for Satan and his *fallen* angels!"

KJV: Then shall he say also unto them on the left hand, Depart from me, ye cursed, into everlasting fire, prepared for the devil and his angels:

The Hebrew Book of Matthew

Matthew 25:42
כִּי רָעַבְתִּי וְלֹא הֶאֱכַלְתֶּם אוֹתִי צָמֵאתִי וְלֹא הִשְׁקִיתֶם אוֹתִי

HTV: "Because I was hungry and you did not feed me - I was thirsty and you did not give me drink!"

KJV: For I was an hungred, and ye gave me no meat: I was thirsty, and ye gave me no drink:

Matthew 25:43
וְאֶהְיֶה גֵר וְלֹא לְקַחְתֶּם אוֹתִי בְּבֵיתְכֶם וְעֵרוֹם וְלֹא כִסִּיתֶם אוֹתִי וְאֶהְיֶה
חוֹלֶה וּבְבֵית אֲסִירִים וְלֹא פְּקַדְתֶּם אוֹתִי

HTV: "I was a wayfarer and you did not take me into your home - I was naked and you did not clothe me - I was sick and in prison and you did not visit me!"

KJV: I was a stranger, and ye took me not in: naked, and ye clothed me not: sick, and in prison, and ye visited me not.

Matthew 25:44
וְאָז גַם הֵמָה יַעֲנוּ לוֹ וְיֹאמְרוּ הוֹי הָאָדוֹן אֵימָתַי רְאִינוּ אוֹתְךָ רָעֵב אוֹ
צָמֵא אוֹ גֵר אוֹ עֵרוֹם אוֹ בְּבֵית אֲסִירִים וְלֹא שֵׁרַתְנוּ לָךְ

HTV: Then they *again* spoke to him and said, "O Lord, when did we see you hungry or thirsty or a stranger or naked or in prison and did not serve you?"

KJV: Then shall they also answer him, saying, Lord, when saw we thee an hungred, or athirst, or a stranger, or naked, or sick, or in prison, and did not minister unto thee?

Matthew 25:45
וְאָז יַעֲנֶה לָהֶם וְיֹאמֶר לָהֶם בֶּאֱמֶת אֲנִי אוֹמֵר לָכֶם כֹּל מַה שֶּׁלֹּא
עֲשִׂיתֶם לְאֶחָד מֵאֵלֶּה הַקְּטַנִּים גַּם לִי לֹא עֲשִׂיתֶם

HTV: Then he answered them and said, "Truly I say to you, whatever you did not do - to the least of these - you did not do to me."

KJV: Then shall he answer them, saying, Verily I say unto you, Inasmuch as ye did *it* not to one of the least of these, ye did *it* not to me.

Matthew 25:46

וְאֵלֶּה יֵלְכוּ לְעוֹנֶשׁ עוֹלָמִי וְהַצַּדִּיקִים לְחַיִּים עוֹלָמִיים

HTV: **And these will go into the eternal punishment of the fire of Gei-Hinnom (Hell) - and the righteous** *will go* **into eternal life!**

KJV: And these shall go away into everlasting punishment: but the righteous into life eternal.

Matthew Chapter 26

Hebrew Text Version (HTV)

¹ When Yeshua had finished all of these parables - then he said to his disciples:

² "You know that after two days it will be Pesach (Passover) - and the Son of Man will be delivered over to be crucified."

³ Then the chief priests and elders of the people assembled together - in the courtyard of the high priest, who was called Caiaphas -

⁴ To conspire together - how to deceitfully trap Yeshua and kill him.

⁵ But they said, "Do not do *it* on a feast day so there will not be an uprising of the people."

⁶ At that time, Yeshua was in Bethany - in the home of Simon the leper.

⁷ There came to Yeshua a certain woman - who had a flask

of costly and precious oil - which she poured on *his* head as he reclined.

⁸ When his disciples saw this, they responded in anger at her - saying, "Why this waste?"

⁹ "Because this could have been sold for a lot of money - and given to the poor!"

¹⁰ When Yeshua knew of this matter, He said to them, "Don't blame this woman - because she has done me a good deed."

¹¹ "Because the poor will always be with you - However, I will not always be with you."

¹² She who anointed this oil upon my head did it to purify me.

¹³ "In truth I say to you all - that in every place you preach this gospel in all the world - this woman also will be remembered for what she has done."

¹⁴ Then, one of the twelve disciples, whose name *was* Judas Iscariot, went to the chief priests.

¹⁵ He said to them - what are you willing to give me to deliver him into your hands? - They promised to give him thirty pieces of silver.

¹⁶ And from then on - he sought an occasion to deliver Yeshua to them.

¹⁷ On the first day of the Festival of Unleavened Bread, the disciples approached Yeshua, and said unto him - "Where would you like us to prepare for you to eat the Pesach (Passover)?"

¹⁸ So, Yeshua said, "Go into the city to a certain man. Say to him, 'The Master says - My time is near. I will keep the Passover at your house with my disciples.'"

¹⁹ The disciples did as Yeshua had commanded them and prepared the Passover (Pesach).

²⁰ Afterwards - when it was evening - Yeshua reclined at the table with his twelve disciples.

²¹ As they were eating - Yeshua said, "Truly, I say to you that one of you will deliver me to die!"

²² They were very sorrowful - and they began - each and every one - to say, "Lord is it me?

²³ But Yeshua answered and said, "He who dips his hand with me - in this bowl - he will deliver me to die." - All of them were eating from one dish. Therefore, they did not recognize him; because

if they had recognized him, they would have destroyed him.

²⁴ "The Son of Man goes as it was written concerning him. Woe to the man by whose hand the Son of Man will be handed over to die. It would be better for that man if he had not been born."

²⁵ Judas, who handed Yeshua over to die said, "Is it I, my Rabbi?" - and Yeshua said to him, "You said *it!*"

²⁶ And while they were eating the evening meal, Yeshua took bread, he <u>blessed</u> it and broke it, then he gave it to his disciples and said, "Take and eat - this is my body!"

²⁷ And Yeshua also took the cup - and blessed it - and gave it to them saying, "Drink from this each of you!"

²⁸ "This is my blood of the New Covenant, which shall be poured out in exchange for many for the forgiveness of sins."

²⁹ Truly I say to you, "From now on - I will not drink from this fruit of the vine until the day when I will drink with you anew in the kingdom of my Father."

³⁰ And after Yeshua sang a psalm of thanksgiving *with them* - they went out to the Mount of Olives.

³¹ Then Yeshua said to his disciples, "All of you will flee (fall away) on account of me - a trap *is set* this night - for it is written -'Strike the shepherd and the sheep will be scattered!' "

³² "And when I rise from the dead - I will appear (go) before you into Galilee."

³³ And Peter said to Yeshua, "If everyone falls away - forsaking you - I myself will never fall away!"

³⁴ Yeshua said to him, "Truly, I say to you, this *very* night, before the rooster crows - you will deny me three times!"

³⁵ And Peter said to Yeshua, "Even if I must die with you - I will not deny you!" All the disciples likewise wholeheartedly said *the same*.

³⁶ Then Yeshua came with them to the valley of Gethsemane and said to his disciples, "Stay here while I go *over* there and pray."

³⁷ And he took with him Peter and the two sons of Zebedee (James & John), and began to be sorrowful and troubled.

³⁸ And Yeshua said to them, "My soul is sorrowful until death. Wait here and be vigilant with me."

³⁹ And Yeshua went a little further from here and fell on his face praying and said, "Father, if it is possible, remove this cup

from me. Nevertheless, it should not be as I will - but as you will!"

⁴⁰ And Yeshua came to his disciples and found them sleeping. He said to Peter, "Is it fitting to be *asleep*? Could you not spend one hour being vigilant with me?"

⁴¹ "Be vigilant now - and pray that you will not come into temptation (testing) - because the spirit is ready and willing - but the flesh is weak!"

⁴² And Yeshua again, for the second time, turned aside from them and prayed saying, "My father - if you are not able to turn this cup aside from me - and I drink it - may your will be done."

⁴³ And again, Yeshua came and found them asleep - because their eyes were heavy.

⁴⁴ And Yeshua left them again - and for the third *time* - prayed in the same way.

⁴⁵ And then Yeshua came unto his disciples and he said unto them, "Sleep now and rest, behold the hour draws near - when the Son of Man will be delivered into the hands of the ungodly."

⁴⁶ "Rise up, let us go from here - behold he is drawing near - he who will betray me."

⁴⁷ As Yeshua spoke *those* words - Behold! Here came Judas, one of the twelve disciples, and with him a great company with swords and clubs - sent forth from the chief priests and elders of the people.

⁴⁸ And when Judas betrayed Yeshua, he gave them a sign. He said, "The one whom I kiss - there is the one whom you shall arrest!"

⁴⁹ At once, he turned to Yeshua and said, "Peace be with you, Rabbi" and kissed him.

⁵⁰ Yeshua said to him, "Beloved, why have you come?" Behold, they then drew near - put their hands onto Yeshua - and seized him!

⁵¹ And behold, one of those who were with Yeshua stretched out his hand - drew his sword and struck the servant of the chief priest servant - and cut off his ear.

⁵² And Yeshua said to him, "Return your sword to its place! Everyone who takes *up* the sword shall perish by the sword!"

⁵³ "Do you think that I cannot ask my Father - and He will give me more than twelve legions of angels?"

⁵⁴ "But if so, how will the Scriptures be fulfilled? Because it

is necessary - *that* must be so."

⁵⁵ At that hour, Yeshua said to the company - "You have come out like this, as if to a thief, to attack me with swords and clubs and arrest me? Yet day after day, I sat with you teaching in the temple - and you did not arrest me."

⁵⁶ All this was so that the writings of the prophets would be fulfilled. - Then all the disciples abandoned Yeshua and ran away!

⁵⁷ And those who arrested Yeshua - they brought him unto Caiaphas the head of the priests. Where the scribes and elders of the people were assembled.

⁵⁸ However, Peter followed them from a distance - unto the courtyard of the high priest. He entered, and sat with the servants, to see what the outcome *would be*.

⁵⁹ The chief priests and all the assembly sought false witness against Yeshua - in order to put him to death,

⁶⁰ but none were found *credible*. After a great many false witnesses had come *forth* - finally two *more* false witnesses came forward.

⁶¹ They testified, "This one (Yeshua) said, 'I can destroy the Temple of Elohim - and in three days - I will rebuild it!'"

⁶² The chief priest arose and said to Yeshua, "Are you not going to say anything - about the words given as evidence against you?"

⁶³ Yeshua answered not a word. And the chief priest said to him, "I urge you to swear, in the Name of the living God - that you tell us if you are the Messiah, the Son of God!"

⁶⁴ Yeshua said to him, "You speak truth. I say to you, from here on you will see the Son of Man sitting at the right hand of Almighty God - and coming in the clouds of heaven."

⁶⁵ Then the high priest tore his clothes and said, "He cursed God! Why do we need more witnesses? - you have heard his blasphemy!"

⁶⁶ "How do you judge?" They answered and said, "He must be put to death!"

⁶⁷ Then they spat in his face - and struck him in the neck - and some of them beat him in the face with their fists!

⁶⁸ Saying, "Prophesy to us Messiah - which one is it who struck you?"

⁶⁹ Peter was sitting outside in the courtyard - and a slave-girl drew near and said, "You were with Yeshua the Galilean!"

⁷⁰ And Peter denied it before everyone saying, "I do not know what you are talking about!"

⁷¹ After he had gone outside - another slave-girl saw him and told those who were there - "This one was also with Yeshua of Nazareth."

⁷² And he again denied with an oath, "I do not know this man!"

⁷³ After a little while, those who were standing there said to Peter, "Surely you are also one of them - for your accent gives you away."

⁷⁴ Then Peter began to curse and swear, saying, "I do not know the man!" Immediately the rooster crowed.

⁷⁵ Peter remembered what Yeshua said to him, "Before the rooster crows - three times you will deny me." He went out and wept bitterly.

Matthew Chapter 26

HTV with translator notes and KJV comparison

Matthew 26:1

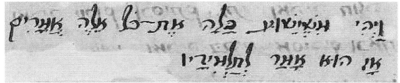

Freiburg Hebrew Manuscript

וַיְהִי מְשֶׁיֵּשׁוּעַ כַּלָּה אֶת-כֹּל אֵלֶּה אֲמָרִים אָז הוּא אָמַר לְתַלְמִידָיו

HTV: When Yeshua had finished all of these parables - then he said to his disciples:

KJV: And it came to pass, when Jesus had finished all these sayings, he said unto his disciples,

Chapter 26

Matthew 26:2

כִּי אַתֶּם יוֹדְעִים אֲשֶׁר אַחֲרֵי שְׁנֵי יָמִים יִהְיֶה הַפֶּסַח וּבֶן הָאָדָם יִמָּסֵר לְהִצָּלֵב

HTV: **"You know that after two days it will be Pesach (Passover) - and the Son of Man will be delivered over to be crucified."**

KJV: Ye know that after two days is the feast of the passover, and the Son of man is betrayed to be crucified.

Matthew 26:3

וְאָז נוֹסְדוּ יַחַד הָרָאשֵׁי הַכּוֹהֲנִים וְזִקְנֵי הָעָם בַּחֲצַר הָרֹאשׁ הַכּוֹהֲנִים אֲשֶׁר יִקָּרֵא קַיָּפָה

HTV: **Then the chief priests and elders of the people assembled together - in the courtyard of the high priest, who was called Caiaphas -**

KJV: Then assembled together the chief priests, and the scribes, and the elders of the people, unto the palace of the high priest, who was called Caiaphas,

Matthew 26:4

לְהִתְיָעֵץ אֵיכָה אֶת-יֵשׁוּעַ יִתְפְּשׂוּ בְּמִרְמָה וְיַהַרְגוּהוּ

HTV: **To conspire together - how to deceitfully trap Yeshua and kill him.**

KJV: And consulted that they might take Jesus by subtilty, and kill him.

Matthew 26:5

אָמְנָם אָמְרוּ לֹא בְיוֹם הֶחַג כְּדֵי שֶׁלֹא תִּתְוֹלֵד מְהוּמָה בָעָם

HTV: **But they said, "Do not do** *it* **on a feast day so there will not be an uprising of the people."**

KJV: But they said, Not on the feast day, lest there be an uproar among the people.

Matthew 26:6

אֲבָל כַּאֲשֶׁר יֵשׁוּעַ יִהְיֶה בְּבֵית-עַנְיָה בְּבֵית סִימוֹן הַצָּרוּעַ

HTV: **At that time, Yeshua was in Bethany - in the home of Simon the leper.**

KJV: Now when Jesus was in Bethany, in the house of Simon the leper,

Matthew 26:7

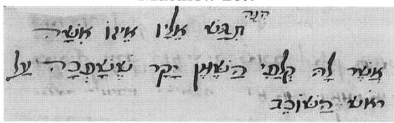

Freiburg Hebrew Manuscript

הִנֵּה תִגַּשׁ אֵלָיו אֵיזוֹ אִשָּׁה אֲשֶׁר לָהּ קְלָפִי הַשֶּׁמֶן יָקָר שֶׁשָּׁפְכָה עַל רֹאשׁ הַשּׁוֹכֵב

HTV: **There came to Yeshua a certain woman - who had a flask of costly and precious oil - which she poured on *his* head as he reclined.**

KJV: There came unto him a woman having an alabaster box of very precious ointment, and poured it on his head, as he sat at meat.

Matthew 26:8

אֲשֶׁר מִשֶּׁתַּלְמִידָיו רָאוּ הִנֵּה חָדָה אַפָּם בָּהּ וְאָמְרוּ מָה נָא אֲבֵדָה הַזֹּאת

HTV: **When his disciples saw this, they responded in anger at her - saying, "Why this waste?"**

KJV: But when his disciples saw it, they had indignation, saying, To what purpose is this waste?

Matthew 26:9

כִּי יוּכַל לְהִמָּכֵר בְּכֶסֶף גָּדוֹל וּלְהִנָּתֵן לְאֶבְיוֹנִים

HTV: **"Because this could have been sold for a lot of money - and given to the poor!"**

KJV: For this ointment might have been sold for much, and given to the poor.

Matthew 26:10

וּמִשֶּׁיֵּשׁוּעַ יָדַע אֶת-דָּבָר הַזֶּה אָמַר לָהֶם אַל תִּהְיוּ לָאִשָּׁה הַזֹּאת לְעָקְתָא כִּי הִיא פָּעֲלָה בִּי פֹּעַל טוֹב

HTV: When Yeshua knew of this matter, He said to them, "Don't blame this woman - because she has done me a good deed."

KJV: When Jesus understood it, he said unto them, Why trouble ye the woman? for she hath wrought a good work upon me.

Matthew 26:11

כִּי יִהְיוּ תָּמִיד אֶבְיוֹנִים אֶצְלְכֶם אֲבָל אֲנִי לֹא אֶהְיֶה תָּמִיד אֶצְלְכֶם

HTV: "Because the poor will always be with you - However, I will not always be with you."

KJV: For ye have the poor always with you; but me ye have not always.

Matthew 26:12

אֲשֶׁר הַזֹּאת שָׁפַךְ אֶת-שֶׁמֶן הַזֶּה עַל רֹאשִׁי עָשְׂתָה לְהִקָּבֵר אוֹתִי

HTV: She who anointed this oil upon my head did it to purify me.

KJV: For in that she hath poured this ointment on my body, she did it for my burial.

Matthew 26:13

בֶּאֱמֶת אֲנִי אוֹמֵר לָכֶם שֶׁבְּכֹל מָקוֹם אֲשֶׁר תְּבַשֵּׂר בּוֹ בְּכָל הָעוֹלָם הַבְּשׂוּרָה הַזֹּאת יְסֻפַּר גַּם מָה שֶׁעָשְׂתָה הַזֹּאת לְזִכָּרוֹנָהּ

HTV: "In truth I say to you all - that in every place you preach this gospel in all the world - this woman also will be remembered for what she has done."

KJV: Verily I say unto you, Wheresoever this gospel shall be preached in the whole world, there shall also this, that this woman hath done, be told for a memorial of her.

Matthew 26:14

וְאָז הָלַךְ אֶחָד מִשְׁנֵי עָשָׂר תַּלְמִידִים שְׁמוֹ יְהוּדָה אִישְׁכַּרְיוּת לְרָאשֵׁי הַכּוֹהֲנִים

HTV: **Then, one of the twelve disciples, whose name *was* Judas Iscariot, went to the chief priests.**

KJV: Then one of the twelve, called Judas Iscariot, went unto the chief priests,

Matthew 26:15

וַיֹּאמֶר לָהֶם מָה אַתֶּם רוֹצִים לָתֵת לִי וַאֲנִי אֶמְסוֹר אוֹתוֹ בְּיֶדֵיכֶם וְהֵמָּה הִבְטִיחוּהוּ לָתֵת שְׁלֹשִׁים כְּסָפִים

HTV: **He said to them - what are you willing to give me to deliver him into your hands? - They promised to give him thirty pieces of silver.**

KJV: And said unto them, What will ye give me, and I will deliver him unto you? And they covenanted with him for thirty pieces of silver.

Matthew 26:16

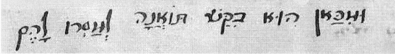

Freiburg Hebrew Manuscript

וּמִכָּאן הוּא בִּקֵּשׁ תּוֹאֲנָה לְמַסְרוֹ לָהֶם

HTV: **And from then on - he sought an occasion to deliver Yeshua to them.**

KJV: And from that time he sought opportunity to betray him.

Matthew 26:17

וּבְיוֹם רִאשׁוֹן הַמַּצּוֹת קָרְבוּ הַתַּלְמִידִים אֶל יֵשׁוּעַ וְאָמְרוּ אַיֵּה נָא אַתָּה רוֹצֶה שֶׁנָּכִין לְךָ לֶאֱכֹל אֶת-הַפֶּסַח

HTV: **On the first day of the Festival of Unleavened Bread, the disciples approached Yeshua, and said unto him - "Where would you like us to prepare for you to eat the Pesach (Passover)?"**

Chapter 26

KJV: Now the first day of the feast of unleavened bread the disciples came to Jesus, saying unto him, Where wilt thou that we prepare for thee to eat the passover?

Matthew 26:18

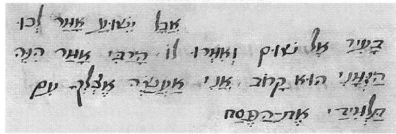
Freiburg Hebrew Manuscript

אֲבָל יֵשׁוּעַ אָמַר לְכוּ בָעִיר אֶל שׁוּם וְאָמְרוּ לוֹ הָרַבִּי אָמַר הִנֵּה הַזְמַנִּי הוּא קָרוֹב אֲנִי אַעֲשֶׂה אֶצְלְךָ עִם תַּלְמִידַי אֶת-הַפֶּסַח

HTV: **So, Yeshua said, "Go into the city to a certain man. Say to him, 'The Master says - My time is near. I will keep the Passover at your house with my disciples.'"**

Note: Luke 22:7-10, **"Say to the goodman of that house - The Teacher asks, Where is the guest hall, where I may eat the Passover with my disciples?"** Possibly this had all been pre-arranged. There is reason to believe it was the Essene guest house - in the Essene quarter of Jerusalem.

KJV: And he said, Go into the city to such a man, and say unto him, The Master saith, My time is at hand; I will keep the passover at thy house with my disciples.

Matthew 26:19

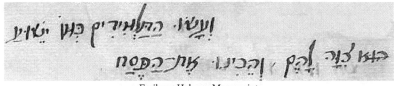
Freiburg Hebrew Manuscript

וְעָשׂוּ הַתַּלְמִידִים כְּמוֹ יֵשׁוּעַ צִוָּה לָהֶם וְהֵכִינוּ אֶת-הַפֶּסַח

HTV: **The disciples did as Yeshua had commanded them and prepared the Passover (Pesach).**

KJV: And the disciples did as Jesus had appointed them; and they made ready the passover.

427

Matthew 26:20

וְאַחֲרֵי שֶׁיִּהְיֶה עֶרֶב הוּא יִהְיֶה שׁוֹכֵב לְשֻׁלְחָן עִם שְׁנֵים עָשָׂר תַּלְמִידָיו

HTV: **Afterwards - when it was evening - Yeshua reclined at the table with his twelve disciples.**

KJV: Now when the even was come, he sat down with the twelve.

Matthew 26:21

וּבְאָכְלָם הוּא אָמַר בֶּאֱמֶת אֲנִי אוֹמֵר לָכֶם שֶׁאֶחָד מִכֶּם יִמְסְרֵנִי לְמִיתָה

HTV: **As they were eating - Yeshua said, "Truly, I say to you that one of you will deliver me to die!"**

KJV: And as they did eat, he said, Verily I say unto you, that one of you shall betray me.

Matthew 26:22

וְהֵמָה מְאוֹד נִתְעַצְּבוּ וְהִתְחִילוּ כֹּל אֶחָד וְאֶחָד לֵאמוֹר הַאִם אָנֹכִי הָאָדוֹן

HTV: **They were very sorrowful - and they began - each and every one - to say, "Lord is it me?**

KJV: And they were exceeding sorrowful, and began every one of them to say unto him, Lord, is it I?

Matthew 26:23

Freiburg Hebrew Manuscript

אֲבָל הוּא עָנָה וַיֹּאמַר אֲשֶׁר טוֹבֵל אֶת־יָדוֹ אִתִּי בַּקְּעָרָה הַזֶּה יִמְסְרֵנִי לְמִיתָה

HTV: **But Yeshua answered and said, "He who dips his hand with me - in this bowl - he will deliver me to die." - All of them were eating from one dish. Therefore, they did not recognize him; because if they had recognized him, they would have destroyed him.**

Chapter 26

Note: It is also a reference to the fact that all of them, who dipped with him, would flee upon his arrest - which is a betrayal. They all said that night they would die with Yeshua. (Mt 26:35). The second part of the verse comes from the Shem Tov Hebrew Matthew.

KJV: And he answered and said, He that dippeth his hand with me in the dish, the same shall betray me.

Matthew 26:24

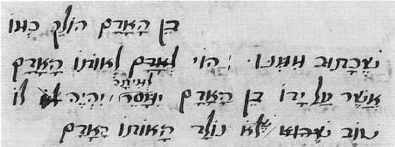

Freiburg Hebrew Manuscript

בֶּן הָאָדָם הוֹלֵךְ כְּמוֹ שֶׁכָּתוּב מִמֶּנּוּ הוֹי לְאוֹתוֹ הָאָדָם אֲשֶׁר עַל יָדוֹ בֶּן הָאָדָם יִמָּסֵר לְמִתָה יִהְיֶה לוֹ טוֹב שֶׁלֹּא נוֹלַד הָאוֹתוֹ הָאָדָם

HTV: "The Son of Man goes as it was written concerning him. Woe to the man by whose hand the Son of Man will be handed over to die. It would be better for that man if he had not been born."

Note: In the HGC, this verse speaks of the act of the betrayer (Judas) being written of, **"A man who walks with me will betray the Son of Eloah, as it was prophesied of him."** The prophecy about "30 pieces of silver" is found in Zechariah 11:13.

KJV: The Son of man goeth as it is written of him: but woe unto that man by whom the Son of man is betrayed! it had been good for that man if he had not been born.

Matthew 26:25

Freiburg Hebrew Manuscript

The Hebrew Book of Matthew

יְהוּדָה אֲשֶׁר מָסְרוֹ לְמִיתָה וַיֹּאמֶר הַאִם אָנוֹכִי רַבִּי וַיֹּאמֶר לוֹ אַתָּה אָמַרְתָּ

HTV: **Judas, who handed Yeshua over to die said, "Is it I, my Rabbi?" - and Yeshua said to him, "You said *it!*"**

KJV: Then Judas, which betrayed him, answered and said, Master, is it I? He said unto him, Thou hast said.

Matthew 26:26

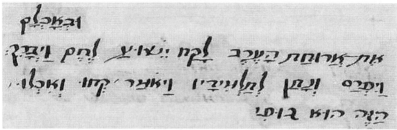

Freiburg Hebrew Manuscript

וּבְאָכְלָם אֶת-אֲרוּחַת הָעֶרֶב לָקַח יֵשׁוּעַ לֶחֶם וַיְבָרֵךְ וַיִּפְרֹס וְנָתַן לְתַלְמִידָיו וַיֹּאמֶר קְחוּ וְאִכְלוּ הַזֶּה הוּא גוּפִי

HTV: **And while they were eating the evening meal, Yeshua took bread, he blessed* it and broke it, then he gave it to his disciples and said, "Take and eat - this is my body!"**

*Note: The blessing given was from the ancient tradition, "Blessed are You, O Lord our Elohim, King of the universe, who gives the bread *of life* from the earth."

KJV: And as they were eating, Jesus took bread, and blessed it, and brake it, and gave it to the disciples, and said, Take, eat; this is my body.

Matthew 26:27

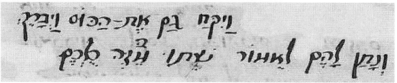

Freiburg Hebrew Manuscript

וַיִּקַּח גַּם אֶת-הַכּוֹס וַיְבָרֵךְ וְנָתַן לָהֶם לֵאמוֹר שְׁתוּ מֵהַזֶּה כֻּלְּכֶם

HTV: **And Yeshua also took the cup - and blessed it - and gave it to them saying, "Drink from this each of you!"**

Note: The blessing of the cup, "Blessed are You, O Lord our Elohim, King of the universe, who creates the fruit of the vine."

KJV: And he took the cup, and gave thanks, and gave it to them, saying, Drink ye all of it;

Matthew 26:28

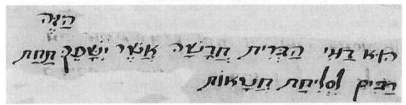
Freiburg Hebrew Manuscript

הִנֵּה הוּא דָמִי הַבְּרִית חֲדָשָׁה אֲשֶׁר יִשָּׁפֵךְ תַּחַת רַבִּים לִסְלִיחַת חֲטָאוֹת

HTV: "This is my blood of the New Covenant, which shall be poured out in exchange for many for the forgiveness of sins."

Note: In Jeremiah 31:31, Yehovah speaks of a New Covenant to come when the king (Messiah) comes. This is the dividing line between Christianity as a New (Greek) Religion - and Messianism as a Renewed Covenant with Yehovah. The Hebrew word *hadash* can mean either *new* or *renewed*. The word **Covenant** is typically replaced with the word **"Testament"** - in Greek & English texts. For example, The N.T. is called **"The New Covenant!"** in Hebrew.

KJV: For this is my blood of the new testament, which is shed for many for the remission of sins.

Matthew 26:29

אָמְנָם אֲנִי אוֹמֵר לָכֶם מֵעַתָּה לֹא אֶשְׁתֶּה מִזֶּה צֶמַח הַגֶּפֶן עַד הָאוֹתוֹ יוֹם אֲשֶׁר בּוֹ אֶשְׁתֶּה אִתְּכֶם חָדָשׁ בְּמַלְכוּת הָאָבִי

HTV: Truly I say to you, "From now on - I will not drink from this fruit of the vine until the day when I will drink with you anew in the kingdom of my Father."

KJV: But I say unto you, I will not drink henceforth of this fruit of the vine, until that day when I drink it new with you in my Father's kingdom.

The Hebrew Book of Matthew

Matthew 26:30

Freiburg Hebrew Manuscript

וְאַחֲרֵי שֶׁאָמַר אֶת-הַמִזְמוֹר יָצְאוּ בְהַר זֵיתִים

HTV: And after Yeshua sang a psalm of thanksgiving *with them* - they went out to the Mount of Olives.

Note: The Hallel Psalms are 113-118. It is one of these Psalms that are cited as the ones Yeshua and his disciples sang before leaving the last supper.

KJV: And when they had sung an hymn, they went out into the mount of Olives.

Matthew 26:31

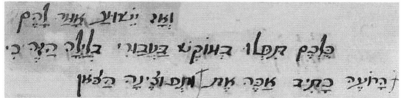

Freiburg Hebrew Manuscript

וְאָז יֵשׁוּעַ אָמַר לָהֶם כֻּלְכֶם תִּפְּלוּ בְּמוֹקֵשׁ בַּעֲבוּרִי בְּלַיְלָה הַזֶה כִּי כָתִיב אַכֶּה אֶת הָרוֹעֶה וּתְפוּצֶינָה הַצֹּאן

HTV: Then Yeshua said to his disciples, "All of you will flee (fall away) on account of me - a trap *is set* this night - for it is written - 'Strike the shepherd and the sheep will be scattered!'"

Note: In Zechariah 13:7, it says, "Strike the shepherd and the sheep will be scattered."

KJV: Then saith Jesus unto them, All ye shall be offended because of me this night: for it is written, I will smite the shepherd, and the sheep of the flock shall be scattered abroad.

Matthew 26:32

וְכַאֲשֶׁר אָקוּם מִמֵתִים אֲקַדֵּם לָכֶם בְּגָלִילָה

HTV: "And when I rise from the dead - I will appear (go) before you into Galilee."

KJV: But after I am risen again, I will go before you into Galilee.

Matthew 26:33

וַיַּעַן כֵּיפָא וַיֹּאמֶר לוֹ וְאִם כֻּלָּם יִפְּלוּ בְמוֹקֵשׁ בַּעֲבוּרְךָ אָנֹכִי לְעוֹלָם לֹא אֶפּוֹל בְּמוֹקֵשׁ

HTV: **And Peter said to Yeshua, "If everyone falls away - forsaking you - I myself will never fall away!"**

KJV: Peter answered and said unto him, Though all men shall be offended because of thee, yet will I never be offended.

Matthew 26:34

וַיֹּאמֶר לוֹ יֵשׁוּעַ בֶּאֱמֶת אֲנִי אוֹמֵר לָכֶם אֲשֶׁר בַּלַּיְלָה הַזֶּה קוֹדֶם שֶׁיָּשִׁיר הַתַּרְנְגוֹל אַתָּה שְׁלֹשָׁה פְּעָמִים תַּכְחִישֵׁנִי

HTV: **Yeshua said to him, "Truly, I say to you, this *very* night, before the rooster crows - you will deny me three times!"**

KJV: Jesus said unto him, Verily I say unto thee, That this night, before the cock crow, thou shalt deny me thrice.

Matthew 26:35

וַיֹּאמֶר לוֹ כֵּיפָא וְאִם יִצְטָרֵךְ לוֹ לָמוּת אִתְּךָ לֹא אַכְחִישֶׁךָ וּכְמוֹ כֵן אָמְרוּ כָּל תַּלְמִידִים

HTV: **And Peter said to Yeshua, "Even if I must die with you - I will not deny you!" All the disciples likewise wholeheartedly said** *the same.*

KJV: Peter said unto him, Though I should die with thee, yet will I not deny thee. Likewise also said all the disciples.

Matthew 26:36

וְאָז בָּא יֵשׁוּעַ אִתָּם לְגֵיא-שֶׁמֶן וַיֹּאמֶר לְתַלְמִידָיו שְׁבוּ שָׁם עַד שֶׁאֵלֵךְ לְשָׁם וְאֶתְפַּלֵּל

The Hebrew Book of Matthew

HTV: **Then Yeshua came with them to the valley of Gethsemane and said to his disciples, "Stay here while I go *over* there and pray."**

KJV: Then cometh Jesus with them unto a place called Gethsemane, and saith unto the disciples, Sit ye here, while I go and pray yonder.

Matthew 26:37

וַיִּקַח אִתּוֹ אֶת-כֵּיפָא וּשְׁנֵי בְנֵי זִבְדִי וְהִתְחִיל לְהִתְעַצֵּב וּלְהִתְדָּאֵג

HTV: **And he took with him Peter and the two sons of Zebedee (James & John), and began to be sorrowful and troubled.**

KJV: And he took with him Peter and the two sons of Zebedee, and began to be sorrowful and very heavy.

Matthew 26:38

וַיֹּאמֶר לָהֶם הַנַּפְשִׁי נִתְעַצְּבָה עַד הַמָּוֶת הַמְתִּינוּ שָׁם וְשִׁקְדוּ אִתִּי

HTV: **And Yeshua said to them, "My soul is sorrowful until death. Wait here and be vigilant with me."**

KJV: Then saith he unto them, My soul is exceeding sorrowful, even unto death: tarry ye here, and watch with me.

Matthew 26:39

וְהָלַךְ מִכָּאן מְעַט לְהַלְאָה וְנָפַל עַל פָּנָיו מִתְפַּלֵל וְאוֹמֵר בִּי הָאָבִי אִם אֶפְשַׁר יָסוּר מִמְּנִי הַכּוֹס הַזֶּה אָמְנָם אַל יְהִי כְּמוֹ אָנוֹכִי רוֹצֶה כִּי אִם כְּמוֹ אַתָּה רוֹצֶה

HTV: **And Yeshua went a little further from here and fell on his face praying and said, "Father, if it is possible, remove this cup from me. Nevertheless, it should not be as I will - but as you will!"**

KJV: And he went a little further, and fell on his face, and prayed, saying, O my Father, if it be possible, let this cup pass from me: nevertheless not as I will, but as thou wilt.

Chapter 26

Matthew 26:40

Freiburg Hebrew Manuscript

וּבָא אֶל תַּלְמִידָיו וּמְצָאָם יְשֵׁנִים וַיֹּאמֶר אֶל כֵּיפָא הַאִם רָאוּי לִהְיוֹת כֵּן הַאִם לֹא יָכלְתָּ שָׁעָה אַחַת לִשְׁקוֹד אִתִּי

HTV: And Yeshua came to his disciples and found them sleeping. He said to Peter, "Is it fitting to be *asleep*? Could you not spend one hour being vigilant with me?"

KJV: And he cometh unto the disciples, and findeth them asleep, and saith unto Peter, What, could ye not watch with me one hour?

Matthew 26:41

שְׁקְדוּ נָא וְהִתְפַּלְלוּ שֶׁלֹּא תָבוֹאוּ בְמַסָּה כִּי הָרוּחַ הוּא מְזֻמָּן וְהַבָּשָׂר הוּא חָלָשׁ

HTV: "Be vigilant now - and pray that you will not come into temptation (testing) - because the spirit is ready and willing - but the flesh is weak!"

KJV: Watch and pray, that ye enter not into temptation: the spirit indeed is willing, but the flesh is weak.

Matthew 26:42

וְהוֹסִיף בְּשֵׁנִית לָסוּר מֵהֶם וְהִתְפַּלֵּל לֵאמֹר בִּי הָאָבִי אִם לֹא יוּכַל הַכּוֹס הַזֶּה לָסוּר מִמֶּנִּי כִּי אִם שֶׁאֶשְׁתֶּה יְהִי רְצוֹנְךָ

HTV: And Yeshua again, for the second time, turned aside from them and prayed saying, "My father - if you are not able to turn this cup aside from me - and I drink it - may your will be done."

KJV: He went away again the second time, and prayed, saying, O my Father, if this cup may not pass away from me, except I drink it, thy will be done.

Matthew 26:43

וְעוֹד בָּא וּמְצָאָם יְשֵׁנִים כִּי עֵינֵיהֶם יִהְיוּ כְּבֵדִים

HTV: **And again, Yeshua came and found them asleep - because their eyes were heavy.**

KJV: And he came and found them asleep again: for their eyes were heavy.

Matthew 26:44

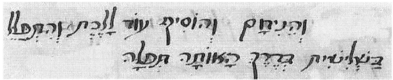
Freiburg Hebrew Manuscript

וְהֵנִיחָם וְהוֹסִיף עוֹד לָלֶכֶת וְהִתְפַּלֵּל בַּשְּׁלִישִׁית בַּדֶּרֶךְ הָאוֹתָהּ תְּפִלָּה

HTV: **And Yeshua left them again - and for the third *time* - prayed in the same way.**

KJV: And he left them, and went away again, and prayed the third time, saying the same words.

Matthew 26:45

וְאָז בָּא אֶל תַּלְמִידָיו וַיֹּאמֶר לָהֶם תִּישְׁנוּ כְבָר וְתָנוּחוּ הִנֵּה קָרְבָה הַשָּׁעָה וּבֶן הָאָדָם יִמָּסֵר בְּיַד חַטָּאִים

HTV: **And then Yeshua came unto his disciples and he said unto them, "Sleep now and rest, behold the hour draws near - when the Son of Man will be delivered into the hands of the ungodly."**

KJV: Then cometh he to his disciples, and saith unto them, Sleep on now, and take your rest: behold, the hour is at hand, and the Son of man is betrayed into the hands of sinners.

Matthew 26:46

קוּמוּ שֶׁנֵּלֵךְ מִשָּׁם הִנֵּה קָרֵב אֲשֶׁר יִמְסְרֵנִי

HTV: **"Rise up, let us go from here - behold he is drawing near - he who will betray me."**

Chapter 26

KJV: Rise, let us be going: behold, he is at hand that doth betray me.

Matthew 26:47

וְעוֹד דַּבְּרוֹ הִנֵּה יְהוּדָה אֶחָד מִשְׁנֵי עָשָׂר תַּלְמִידִים בָּא וְעַמּוֹ כַּת גָּדוֹל עִם חֲרָבוֹת וְעִם אַלּוֹת שֶׁיִּהְיוּ נִשְׁלָחִים מֵרָאשֵׁי הַכּוֹהֲנִים וְזִקְנֵי הָעָם

HTV: **As Yeshua spoke *those* words - Behold! Here came Judas, one of the twelve disciples, and with him a great company with swords and clubs - sent forth from the chief priests and elders of the people.**

KJV: And while he yet spake, lo, Judas, one of the twelve, came, and with him a great multitude with swords and staves, from the chief priests and elders of the people.

Matthew 26:48

וַאֲשֶׁר מְסָרוֹ הוּא נָתַן לָהֶם אוֹת וַיֹּאמַר אֲשֶׁר אֲנִי אֲנַשֵּׁק הַהוּא יֵשׁ הַחֲזִיקוּהוּ

HTV: **And when Judas betrayed Yeshua, he gave them a sign. He said, "The one whom I kiss - there is the one whom you shall arrest!"**

KJV: Now he that betrayed him gave them a sign, saying, Whomsoever I shall kiss, that same is he: hold him fast.

Matthew 26:49

Freiburg Hebrew Manuscript

וּמִיָּד הוּא קָרַב אֶל יֵשׁוּעַ וַיֹּאמַר שָׁלוֹם לְךָ הָרַבִּי וַיְנַשֵּׁק אוֹתוֹ

HTV: **At once, he turned to Yeshua and said, "Peace be with you, Rabbi" and kissed him.**

KJV: And forthwith he came to Jesus, and said, Hail, master; and kissed him.

Matthew 26:50

וַיֹּאמֶר לוֹ יֵשׁוּעַ הָאָהוּב לָמָה בָאתָ הִנֵּה וְאָז הֵמָּה קָרְבוּ וְהִשְׁלִיחוּ אֶת־יְדֵיהֶם בְּיֵשׁוּעַ וְהֶחֱזִיקוּהוּ

HTV: Yeshua said to him, "Beloved, why have you come?" Behold, they then drew near - put their hands onto Yeshua - and seized him!

KJV: And Jesus said unto him, Friend, wherefore art thou come? Then came they, and laid hands on Jesus, and took him.

Matthew 26:51

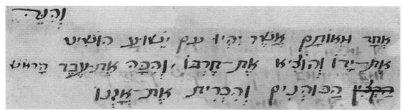

Freiburg Hebrew Manuscript

וְהִנֵּה אֶחָד מֵאוֹתָם אֲשֶׁר יִהְיוּ עִם יֵשׁוּעַ הוֹשִׁיט אֶת־יָדוֹ וְהוֹצִיא אֶת־חַרְבּוֹ וְהִכָּה אֶת־עֶבֶד הָרֹאשׁ הַכֹּהֲנִים וְהִכְרִית אֶת־אָזְנוֹ

HTV: And behold, one of those who were with Yeshua stretched out his hand - drew his sword and struck the servant of the chief priest servant - and cut off his ear.

> Note: In John 18:10 It says that it was the right ear of the priest's servant that was cut. This was a defect that would have prevented him from serving in the Temple.

KJV: And, behold, one of them which were with Jesus stretched out his hand, and drew his sword, and struck a servant of the high priest's, and smote off his ear.

Matthew 26:52

וְאָז אָמַר לוֹ יֵשׁוּעַ הָשֵׁיב הָשִׁיב אֶת־חַרְבְּךָ לִמְקוֹמוֹ כֹּל שֶׁיִּקַּח אֶת חֶרֶב הַהוּא יֹאבַד בְּחֶרֶב

HTV: And Yeshua said to him, "Return your sword to its place! Everyone who takes *up* the sword shall perish by the sword!"

KJV: Then said Jesus unto him, Put up again thy sword into his place: for all they that take the sword shall perish with the sword.

Matthew 26:53
הַאִם אַתָּה חוֹשֵׁב שֶׁלֹּא אוּכַל לִשְׁאוֹל אֶת-הָאָבִי וְיִתֵּן לִי יוֹתֵר מִשְׁנֵים עָשָׂר לִגְיוֹנִים שֶׁל מַלְאָכִים

HTV: **"Do you think that I cannot ask my Father - and He will give me more than twelve legions of angels?"**

KJV: Thinkest thou that I cannot now pray to my Father, and he shall presently give me more than twelve legions of angels?

Matthew 26:54
וְאִם כֵּן אֵיכָה נָא יִמָּלְאוּ הַכְּתוּבִים כִּי צָרִיךְ לִהְיוֹת כֵּן

HTV: **"But if so, how will the Scriptures be fulfilled? Because it is necessary -** *that* **must be so."**

KJV: But how then shall the scriptures be fulfilled, that thus it must be?

Matthew 26:55
וּבְאוֹתָהּ שָׁעָה אָמַר יֵשׁוּעַ לַכִּתִּים אַתֶּם יְצָאתֶם כְּאִלּוּ לִפְרִיץ עִם חֲרָבוֹת וְעִם אַלּוֹת לְהַחֲזִיקֵנִי כִּי מִיּוֹם לְיוֹם אֲנִי אֵשֵׁב אֶצְלְכֶם מְלַמֵּד בַּהֵיכָל וְלֹא הֶחֱזַקְתֶּם אוֹתִי

HTV: **At that hour, Yeshua said to the company - "You have come out like this, as if to a thief, to attack me with swords and clubs and arrest me? Yet day after day, I sat with you teaching in the temple - and you did not arrest me."**

KJV: In that same hour said Jesus to the multitudes, Are ye come out as against a thief with swords and staves for to take me? I sat daily with you teaching in the temple, and ye laid no hold on me.

Matthew 26:56

Freiburg Hebrew Manuscript

כֹּל הַזֹּאת הָיְתָה כְּדֵי שֶׁיִּמָּלְאוּ כְּתוּבֵי הַנְּבִיאִים וְאָז כֹּל תַּלְמִידִים עֲזָבוּהוּ וַיִּבְרְחוּ

HTV: **All this was so that the writings of the prophets would be fulfilled. - Then all the disciples abandoned Yeshua and ran away!**

> Note: This verse is from the prophecy in Zechariah 13:7, "Strike the shepherd and the sheep will be scattered."

KJV: But all this was done, that the scriptures of the prophets might be fulfilled. Then all the disciples forsook him, and fled.

Matthew 26:57

וַאֲשֶׁר הָיוּ מַחֲזִיקִים אֶת-יֵשׁוּעַ הֱבִיאוּהוּ אֶל קַיָּפָה הָרֹאשׁ כּוֹהֲנִים אֲשֶׁר אֶצְלוֹ נוֹסְדוּ סוֹפְרִים וְזִקְנֵי הָעָם

HTV: **And those who arrested Yeshua - they brought him unto Caiaphas the head of the priests. Where the scribes and elders of the people were assembled.**

KJV: And they that had laid hold on Jesus led him away to Caiaphas the high priest, where the scribes and the elders were assembled.

Matthew 26:58

אֲבָל כֵּיפָא יִרְדּוֹף מֵרָחוֹק עַד חֲצִיר רֹאשׁ הַכֹּהֲנִים וְנִכְנַס וַיֵּשֶׁב עִם מְשָׁרְתִים לִרְאוֹת אֶת-הַסּוֹף

HTV: **However, Peter followed them from a distance - unto the courtyard of the high priest. He entered, and sat with the servants, to see what the outcome *would be*.**

KJV: But Peter followed him afar off unto the high priest's palace, and went in, and sat with the servants, to see the end.

Matthew 26:59

אָמְנָם רֹאשׁ הַכּוֹהֲנִים וְכֹל עֵדָה יְבַקְשׁוּ עֵדוּת הַשֶּׁקֶר כְּנֶגֶד יֵשׁוּעַ לַהֲמִיתוֹ

HTV: **The chief priests and all the assembly sought false witness against Yeshua - in order to put him to death,**

KJV: Now the chief priests, and elders, and all the council, sought false witness against Jesus, to put him to death;

Matthew 26:60

Freiburg Hebrew Manuscript

וְלֹא מָצָאוּ וְכַאֲשֶׁר רַבִּים עֵדִים שְׁקָרִים קָרְבוּ בְאַחֲרִית בָּאוּ שְׁנֵי עֵדִים שְׁקָרִים

HTV: **but none were found** *credible*. **After a great many false witnesses had come** *forth* **- finally two** *more* **false witnesses came forward.**

Note: Apparently many false witnesses had no credible accusations - but at last two were found who could cite what Yeshua had said in order to build a case against.

KJV: But found none: yea, though many false witnesses came, yet found they none. At the last came two false witnesses,

Matthew 26:61

Freiburg Hebrew Manuscript

וְאָמְרוּ הָזֶה אָמַר אֲנִי יָכוֹל לִנְתוֹץ אֶת-הֵיכַל הָאֱלֹהִים וּבִשְׁלֹשָׁה יָמִים אֶבְנֶה אוֹתוֹ

The Hebrew Book of Matthew

HTV: **They testified, "This one (Yeshua) said, 'I can destroy the Temple of Elohim - and in three days - I will rebuild it!'"**

Note: The testimony is false, Yeshua did not say he could or would destroy the Temple. He spoke of the Temple of his body given up to Yehovah - he would be killed and rise from the dead in three days. John 2:19, "Destroy this Temple - and in three days I will raise it up!"

KJV: And said, This fellow said, I am able to destroy the temple of God, and to build it in three days.

Matthew 26:62

וַיָּקָם רֹאשׁ הַכּוֹהֲנִים וַיֹּאמֶר לוֹ הַאִם אַתָּה אֵין עוֹנֶה כְלוּם עַל דְּבָרִים אֲשֶׁר הָאֵלֶּה מְעִידִים כְּנֶגְדְּךָ

HTV: **The chief priest arose and said to Yeshua, "Are you not going to say anything - about the words given as evidence against you?"**

KJV: And the high priest arose, and said unto him, Answerest thou nothing? what is it which these witness against thee?

Matthew 26:63

וְיֵשׁוּעַ לֹא אָמַר כְּלוּם וְרֹאשׁ הַכּוֹהֲנִים אָמַר לוֹ אֲנִי מַשְׁבִּיעַ אוֹתְךָ בְּשֵׁם הָאֱלֹהִים חַי שֶׁתֹּאמַר לָנוּ אִם אַתָּה הַמָּשִׁיחַ הַבֵּן הָאֱלֹהִים

HTV: **Yeshua answered not a word. And the chief priest said to him, "I urge you to swear, in the Name of the living God - that you tell us if you are the Messiah, the Son of God!"**

KJV: But Jesus held his peace. And the high priest answered and said unto him, I adjure thee by the living God, that thou tell us whether thou be the Christ, the Son of God.

Matthew 26:64

Freiburg Hebrew Manuscript

Chapter 26

וַיֹּאמֶר לוֹ יֵשׁוּעַ אַתָּה אָמַרְתָּ בֶּאֱמֶת אֲנִי אוֹמֵר לָכֶם אֲשֶׁר מִכָּאן
תִרְאוּ אֶת-בֶּן הָאָדָם יוֹשֵׁב בִּימִין גְּבוּרַת הָאֱלֹהִים וּבָא בְּעַנְנֵי שָׁמַיִם

HTV: Yeshua said to him, "You speak truth. I say to you, from here on you will see the Son of Man sitting at the right hand of Almighty God - and coming in the clouds of heaven."

Note: The references in this verse come from Psalms 110:1 and Daniel 7:13 "The Son of Man came with the clouds of heaven unto the Ancient of Days."

KJV: Jesus saith unto him, Thou hast said: nevertheless I say unto you, Hereafter shall ye see the Son of man sitting on the right hand of power, and coming in the clouds of heaven.

Matthew 26:65

וְאָז קָרַע רֹאשׁ הַכֹּהֲנִים אֶת-לְבוּשָׁיו וְאָמַר הוּא נָאֵץ אֶת-הָאֱלֹהִים
מָה נָא עוֹד נִצְטָרֵךְ עֵדִים הִנֵּה עַתָּה שְׁמַעְתֶּם אֶת-נָאָצָתוֹ

HTV: Then the high priest tore his clothes and said, "He cursed God! Why do we need more witnesses? - you have heard his blasphemy!"

KJV: Then the high priest rent his clothes, saying, He hath spoken blasphemy; what further need have we of witnesses? behold, now ye have heard his blasphemy.

Matthew 26:66

מָה נִרְאֶה לָכֶם אָבָל הֵמָה עָנוּ וַיֹּאמְרוּ הוּא נִתְחַיֵּב לָמָוֶת

HTV: "How do you judge?" They answered and said, "He must be put to death!"

KJV: What think ye? They answered and said, He is guilty of death.

Matthew 26:67

וְאָז יָרְקוּ בְּפָנָיו וְהִכּוּהוּ בְצַוָּארוֹ וּקְצָתָם בְּאֶגְרֹפָם הִכּוּהוּ בְּפָנָיו

HTV: Then they spat in his face - and struck him in the neck - and some of them beat him in the face with their fists!

443

The Hebrew Book of Matthew

KJV: Then did they spit in his face, and buffeted him; and others smote him with the palms of their hands,

Matthew 26:68

Freiburg Hebrew Manuscript

לֵאמֹר נַבֵּא לָנוּ הַמָשִׁיחַ אֵיזֶה הוּא אֲשֶׁר הִכָּה אוֹתְךָ

HTV: Saying, "Prophesy to us Messiah - which one is it who struck you?"

> Note: Mark 14:65, says they covered his face in order to beat him and taunt him, "Which one struck you?"

KJV: Saying, Prophesy unto us, thou Christ, Who is he that smote thee?

Matthew 26:69

אָמְנָם כִּיפָא הָיָה יוֹשֵׁב בַּחוּץ בֶּחָצֵר וַתִּקְרַב אֵלָיו שִׁפְחָה אַחַת וַתֹּאמֶר לוֹ גַם אַתָּה תִהְיֶה עִם יֵשׁוּעַ הַגְלִילִי

HTV: Peter was sitting outside in the courtyard - and a slave-girl drew near and said, "You were with Yeshua the Galilean!"

KJV: Now Peter sat without in the palace: and a damsel came unto him, saying, Thou also wast with Jesus of Galilee.

Matthew 26:70

Freiburg Hebrew Manuscript

וְהוּא הִכְחִישׁ לִפְנֵי כֻלָּם לֵאמֹר אֵינִי יוֹדֵעַ מָה אַתְּ אוֹמֶרֶת

HTV: And Peter denied it before everyone saying, "I do not know what you are talking about!"

KJV: But he denied before them all, saying, I know not what thou sayest

Matthew 26:71

אַחֲרֵי שֶׁהוּא יָצָא תִרְאֶה אוֹתוֹ שִׁפְחָה אַחֶרֶת וַתֹּאמַר לְאוֹתָם שֶׁיִּהְיוּ שָׁם גַם הַזֶּה יִהְיֶה עִם יֵשׁוּעַ הַגְּלִילִי

HTV: **After he had gone outside - another slave-girl saw him and told those who were there - "This one was also with Yeshua of Nazareth."**

KJV: And when he was gone out into the porch, another maid saw him, and said unto them that were there, This fellow was also with Jesus of Nazareth.

Matthew 26:72

וְהוֹסִיף לְהַכְחִישׁ עִים שְׁבוּעָה לֹא יָדַעְתִּי אֶת-הָאָדָם הַזֶּה

HTV: **And he again denied with an oath, "I do not know this man!"**

KJV: And again he denied with an oath, I do not know the man.

Matthew 26:73

וְאַחֲרֵי מְעַט קָרְבוּ אֲשֶׁר יִהְיוּ שָׁם עוֹמְדִים וַיֹּאמְרוּ לְכֵיפָא בֶּאֱמֶת גַם אַתָּה מֵהֶם כִּי לְשׁוֹנְךָ מַגְלָה אוֹתְךָ

HTV: **After a little while, those who were standing there said to Peter, "Surely you are also one of them - for your accent gives you away."**

KJV: And after a while came unto him they that stood by, and said to Peter, Surely thou also art one of them; for thy speech bewrayeth thee.

Matthew 26:74

וְאָז הִתְחִיל לָאֲרוֹר וּלְהִשָּׁבֵעַ לֵאמֹר אֵינִי יָדַעְתִּי את-הָאָדָם וּמִיָּד יָשִׁיר הַתַּרְנְגוֹל

HTV: **Then Peter began to curse and swear, saying, "I do not know the man!" Immediately the rooster crowed.**

KJV: Then began he to curse and to swear, saying, I know not the man. And immediately the cock crew.

Matthew 26:75

וַיִּזְכּוֹר כֵּיפָא מָה שֶׁאָמַר יֵשׁוּעַ כֵּיצַד שֶׁאָמַר לוֹ קוֹדֶם שֶׁתַּרְנְגוֹל יָשִׁיר אַתָּה שָׁלֹשָׁה פְּעָמִים תַּכְחִישֵׁינִי וַיֵּצֵא וַיִּבְכֶּה בַּמְרִירוּת

HTV: **Peter remembered what Yeshua said to him, "Before the rooster crows - three times you will deny me." He went out and wept bitterly.**

KJV: And Peter remembered the word of Jesus, which said unto him, Before the cock crow, thou shalt deny me thrice. And he went out, and wept bitterly.

Matthew Chapter 27

Hebrew Text Version (HTV)

[1] And from that morning - behold - all the chief priests and elders were united to conspire against Yeshua - to put him to death.

[2] And they brought him bound - and they delivered him to Pontius Pilate, the Governor.

[3] And when Judas Iscariot saw they had delivered him - and that Yeshua was sentenced to death - behold, he repented and gave back to the chief priests and elders the thirty pieces of silver.

[4] And Judas said, "I have sinned in sending innocent blood to death." But they said, "What is that to us? You deal with that."

[5] And he cast the silver coins into the Temple - then went - and hung himself with a rope.

[6] The chief priests who took the silver said, "We will not accept that which you cast into the temple offering - because it is blood money!"

[7] And when they conspired together - they bought with the silver coins - the potter's field for the burial of sojourners.

[8] Therefore, *that* portion of the field is called the Field of

Chapter 27

Blood unto this day.

⁹ Then *was* fulfilled what *was* said according to Jeremiah the prophet, saying - "They took the thirty pieces of silver - a steep price - which the sons of Israel coveted." *(Jeremiah 19:1-13, Zechariah 11:12-13)*

¹⁰ And they gave them (the silver coins) in exchange for the Potter's field - as Yehovah had appointed it. *(Jeremiah 19:1-13)*

¹¹ And Yeshua stood before Pontius Pilate, the governor, and he asked him, "Are you the king of the Jews?" - Yeshua said to him, "So you say."

¹² When the chief priests and elders slandered him - Yeshua answered nothing.

¹³ And then Pilate said to him, "Do you not hear how many charges these *people* are bringing against you?"

¹⁴ Yeshua did not answer him a word - so that Pilate was greatly astonished.

¹⁵ On the day of the sacred feast of Passover, it was the custom for the *Roman* governor of the city to free to the people one of the prisoners - whomever they wish.

¹⁶ Pilate had a prisoner who was almost crazy - his name was Bar Rabban - *who* had been arrested for murder and put in the dungeon.

¹⁷ And after they were gathered, Pilate said to them all, "Who do you want released to you? Bar Rabban - or Yeshua - who is called the Messiah?

¹⁸ *He gave* this *choice* because Pilate knew that - due to hatred without cause - Yeshua had been arrested.

¹⁹ And when Pilate was sitting on the judgment seat (throne) - his wife sent to him a message saying, "Do not speak a word against this righteous man - For this night in a dream I suffered many things because of him."

²⁰ But the chief priest and elders coerced (deceived) the people - into asking for Bar Rabban *to be released* - and for Yeshua to perish!

²¹ And the governor replied to them saying, "Who do you want me to release to you?" And they said - "Bar Rabban!"

²² And Pilate said unto them, "What shall I do *with* Yeshua - called the Messiah?" - And they said to him, "Let him be crucified!"

²³ And the governor said to them, "What evil has he done?"

but still they cried even more saying, "Crucify *him*!"

²⁴ When Pilate saw that nothing would help - that the tumult would increase *even* more. He took water and washed his hands in the eyes of the people saying - You see - I am innocent of this righteous blood!

²⁵ And all the people replied, "His blood be upon us and upon our sons (our seed - our descendants)!"

²⁶ Then Pilate released Bar-Rabban to them. After Yeshua was scourged with a whip - he was given up to be crucified.

²⁷ Then the soldiers of Pilate took Yeshua to the House of Judgment (Beit Din) and *there* gathered a crowd of many peoples.

²⁸ And they stripped Yeshua and clothed him with a robe of scarlet.

²⁹ They wove a crown of thorns and put it on his head - and put a reed in his right hand - and bowed down on their knees before Yeshua and mocked him saying, "Hail to you - King of the Jews."

³⁰ And they spit in his face and took the reed and struck his head!

³¹ And after they had mocked Yeshua - they stripped him of the scarlet robe, clothed him in his own clothes - and took him away to be crucified.

³² When they went out, they found a man from Cyrene, his name was Simon, whom they compelled to carry his cross.

³³ They came to a place called Golgoltha - place of the skull.

³⁴ They gave him wine to drink - mixed with bitter *herbs* – and when he tasted it he would not drink it.

³⁵ After they crucified Yeshua, they divided his clothes and cast lots - to fulfill what was said by the prophet - "They divided my clothing unto themselves - and upon my clothing they cast lots." *(from Psalms 22:18)*

³⁶ And the inhabitants watched him there *(Psalm 22 and Isaiah 53)*

³⁷ They wrote over his head his accusation - "This is Yeshua - the King of the Jews!"

³⁸ And they crucified with him - two bandits - one at his right hand and one at his left.

³⁹ Those *who* passed by were cursing Yeshua and shaking their heads

Chapter 27

⁴⁰ Saying, "Alas, you who said - Destroy the Temple and in three days I will raise it up! Save yourself! - If you are the son of Elohim - descend from the cross!"

⁴¹ So, as the chief priests were mocking Yeshua - together with the scribes and elders - they said:

⁴² "He saved others - but he is not able to save himself. If he is the king of Israel - Let him come down from the cross now - and we will believe in him."

⁴³ "He trusted in Yehovah - now let Yehovah rescue him - If He wants him! For he said, 'I am the Son of Elohim.' "

⁴⁴ This they also did - the bandits who were crucified with him - in *the same* manner they were taunting Yeshua.

⁴⁵ And from the sixth hour until the ninth hour - darkness came over all the land.

⁴⁶ At about the ninth hour, Yeshua cried out in a loud voice saying, "My God, my God! Why have you spared me?"

⁴⁷ From among those standing there - and those hearing these words - they said, "This one is calling Elijah!"

⁴⁸ Immediately one of them ran and took a sponge. He soaked it in vinegar - put it on a reed - and gave it to Yeshua to drink.

⁴⁹ The others were saying, "Be quiet now! - That we may see if Elijah will come to deliver him."

⁵⁰ Yeshua again cried out in a loud voice - and sent his spirit up to his Father!

⁵¹ Behold, the Holy of Holies was broken from top to bottom, and the earth shook, and the stones were split in two!

⁵² The tombs were opened - and the bodies of the righteous - who were lying *there* - rose from death.

⁵³ They came out from the tombs and went into the holy city - after Yeshua's resurrection from the dead - and they appeared to many.

⁵⁴ Indeed, the centurion - and those who were with him guarding Yeshua - when they saw the earth shake violently and the other things that *happened*. Behold, they were very afraid and said, "Surely, this was the Son of God!"

⁵⁵ There were many women standing at a distance - *those* who followed after Yeshua from Galilee - in order to serve him.

⁵⁶ Among whom were Mary Magdalene - and Mary the mother of Jacob and Joseph - and the mother of the sons of Zebedee.

⁵⁷ And in the evening, there came a certain rich man from Arimathea, his name was Joseph, who was also a follower of Yeshua.

⁵⁸ This *same* one (Joseph of Arimathea) came to Pilate - and asked for Yeshua's body - and Pilate ordered the body to be given to him.

⁵⁹ And when he had taken away the body - he wrapped it in a garment of clean fine linen.

⁶⁰ And he put Yeshua in his *own* new tomb, which he carved from rock, and he rolled a large stone over the tomb's entrance - and he went away.

⁶¹ And there *came* Mary Magdalene and another Mary to sit in front of the tomb.

⁶² And on the day after Pesach (Passover), the chief priests and Pharisees gathered with Pilate.

⁶³ And they said, "My Lord, we remember that this deceiver said, while he was still alive, 'After three days I will rise from the dead.'"

⁶⁴ Command, therefore, that the tomb be guarded until the third day - lest his disciples come and steal his body and tell the people that he rose from the dead - If so, the last mistake will be worse than the first!

⁶⁵ Pilate said to them (chief priests), "You have a watch - go and guard (the tomb) as well as you know how."

⁶⁶ And with that, they went and secured the tomb - sealing the stone and placing guards.

Matthew Chapter 27

HTV with translator notes and KJV comparison

Matthew 27:1

וּמִשֶּׁיִּהְיֶה בַּבֹּקֶר הִנֵּה כָּל רָאשֵׁי הַכּוֹהֲנִים וְזִקְנֵי הָעָם נוֹסְדוּ לְהִתְוַעֵץ כְּנֶגֶד יֵשׁוּעַ לְמָסְרוֹ לָמָוֶת

HTV: **And from that morning - behold - all the chief priests and elders were united to conspire against Yeshua - to put him to death.**

KJV: When the morning was come, all the chief priests and elders of the people took counsel against Jesus to put him to death:

Matthew 27:2

וַיְבִיאוּהוּ אֲלֵיהֶם קָשׁוּר וַיִּמְסְרוּהוּ לְפוֹנְצִיּוּס פִּלָטוּס הַפָּקִיד

HTV: **And they brought him bound - and they delivered him to Pontius Pilate, the Governor.**

KJV: And when they had bound him, they led him away, and delivered him to Pontius Pilate the governor.

Matthew 27:3

וְאָז רָאָה יְהוּדָה אֲשֶׁר מְסָרוֹ לְמִיתָה שֶׁהוּא נִשְׁפַּט לְמִיתָה הִנֵּה הוּא נִתְחָרֵט וַיִּתֵּן לְרָאשִׁים שֶׁל כּוֹהֲנִים וְלַזְּקֵנִים אֶת-שְׁלֹשִׁים כְּסָפִים

HTV: **And when Judas Iscariot saw they had delivered him - and that Yeshua was sentenced to death - behold, he repented and gave back to the chief priests and elders the thirty pieces of silver.**

KJV: Then Judas, which had betrayed him, when he saw that he was condemned, repented himself, and brought again the thirty pieces of silver to the chief priests and elders,

Matthew 27:4

וַיֹּאמַר חָטָאתִי בְּמָסְרִי לְמִיתָה אֶת-הַדָּם הַנָּקִי אֲבָל הֵמָּה אָמְרוּ זֹאת אֵין לָנוּ לַחֲשָׁשָׁה אַתָּה תִרְאֶה

HTV: **And Judas said, "I have sinned in sending innocent blood to death." But they said, "What is that to us? You deal with that."**

KJV: Saying, I have sinned in that I have betrayed the innocent blood. And they said, What is that to us? see thou to that.

The Hebrew Book of Matthew

Matthew 27:5

וְהִשְׁלִיךְ אֶת-כְּסָפִים בְּהֵיכָל וַיֵּלֶךְ לוֹ וַיִּתְלֶה עַצְמוֹ בְּפַח

HTV: And he cast the silver coins into the Temple - then went - and hung himself with a rope.

KJV: And he cast down the pieces of silver in the temple, and departed, and went and hanged himself.

Matthew 27:6

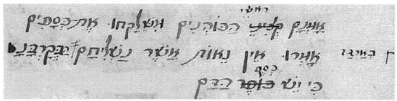

Freiburg Hebrew Manuscript

אָמְנָם רָאשֵׁי הַכּוֹהֲנִים מִשֶּׁלָּקְחוּ אֶת-כְּסָפִים אָמְרוּ אֵין נָאוֹת אֲשֶׁר נַשְׁלִיתָם בְּאַרְגַּז הַבְּקׇרְבָּנָא כִּי יֵשׁ כֶּסֶף הַדָּם

HTV: The chief priests who took the silver said, "We will not accept that which you cast into the temple offering - because it is blood money!"

Note: The chief priests cite it as unlawful to take blood money, see Ex 23:7 & Zech 11:12-13. None of them wanted to accept the blood money returned because it implicated them in a crime, so they describe it as an offering which they can not accept.

KJV: And the chief priests took the silver pieces, and said, It is not lawful for to put them into the treasury, because it is the price of blood.

Matthew 27:7

וּמִשֶּׁהִתְיַעֲצוּ קָנוּ בָהֶם שָׂדֵה הַיּוֹצֵר לִקְבִירַת הַגֵּרִים

HTV: And when they conspired together - they bought with the silver coins - the potter's field for the burial of sojourners.

KJV: And they took counsel, and bought with them the potter's field, to bury strangers in.

Chapter 27

Matthew 27:8

עַל מְנַת נִקְרָא הַשָׂדֶה הַזֶּה חֲקַלְדָּמָא עַד הַיּוֹם הַזֶּה

HTV: **Therefore, *that* portion of the field is called the Field of Blood unto this day.**

KJV: Wherefore that field was called, The field of blood, unto this day.

Matthew 27:9

וְאָז נִמְלָא מָה שֶׁנֶּאֱמַר עַל פִּי יִרְמְיָהוּ הַנָּבִיא הָאוֹמֵר וְלָקְחוּ אֶת־
שְׁלֹשִׁים כְּסָפִים אֶדֶר הַיְקָר אֲשֶׁר יָקְרוּ מִבְּנֵי יִשְׂרָאֵל

HTV: **Then *was* fulfilled what *was* said according to Jeremiah the prophet, saying - "They took the thirty pieces of silver - a steep price - which the sons of Israel coveted."** *(Jeremiah 19:1-13, Zechariah 11:12-13)*

KJV: Then was fulfilled that which was spoken by Jeremy the prophet, saying, And they took the thirty pieces of silver, the price of him that was valued, whom they of the children of Israel did value;

Matthew 27:10

Freiburg Hebrew Manuscript

וְנָתְנוּ אוֹתָם בְּעַד שָׂדֶה הַיּוֹצֵר כְּמוֹ תִקֵּן לוֹ יְהוָֹה

HTV: **And they gave them (the silver coins) in exchange for the Potter's field - as Yehovah had appointed it.**
(Jeremiah 19:1-13)

> Note: The Potter's field was in the Valley of Gehinnom where the Topeth statue, mentioned in Jeremiah 19:1-13, was used to sacrifice children unto Moloch. The first Temple was destroyed because of this abomination and the Israelites taken into exile and captivity.
>
> Now the Son of God has been slaughtered and the second Temple will be brought down only a few years later for this crime. Every Israelite would understand Matthew's reference to the Potter's field as a further condemnation of that abomination of sacrificing the innocent repeated yet again.

KJV: And gave them for the potter's field, as the Lord appointed me.

Matthew 27:11

אָמְנָם יֵשׁוּעַ עָמַד לִפְנֵי הַפָּקִיד וַיִּשְׁאָלֵהוּ הַפָּקִיד הָאִם אַתָּה הַמֶּלֶךְ הַיְּהוּדִים וַיֹּאמַר לוֹ יֵשׁוּעַ אַתָּה אוֹמֵר

HTV: **And Yeshua stood before Pontius Pilate, the governor, and he asked him, "Are you the king of the Jews?" - Yeshua said to him, "So you say."**

KJV: And Jesus stood before the governor: and the governor asked him, saying, Art thou the King of the Jews? And Jesus said unto him, Thou sayest.

Matthew 27:12

וְכַאֲשֶׁר רָאשֵׁי הַכּוֹהֲנִים וּזְקֵנִים יִהְיוּ מַלְשִׁינִים אוֹתוֹ הוּא לֹא עָנָה כְלוּם

HTV: **When the chief priests and elders slandered him - Yeshua answered nothing.**

KJV: And when he was accused of the chief priests and elders, he answered nothing.

Matthew 27:13

וְאָז אָמַר לוֹ פִּילָטוּס הָאִם אֵינְךָ שׁוֹמֵעַ כַּמָּה תְעוּדוֹת הָאֵלֶּה מוֹצִיאִים כְּנֶגְדְּךָ

HTV: **And then Pilate said to him, "Do you not hear how many charges these *people* are bringing against you?"**

KJV: Then said Pilate unto him, Hearest thou not how many things they witness against thee?

Matthew 27:14

וְלֹא עָנָה לוֹ לְשׁוּם דָּבָר עַד שֶׁיִּתְמַהּ הַפָּקִיד מְאוֹד

HTV: **Yeshua did not answer him a word - so that Pilate was greatly astonished.**

KJV: And he answered him to never a word; insomuch that the governor marvelled greatly.

Chapter 27

Matthew 27:15

וּבֶהָחַג יִתְנַהֵג הַפָּקִיד לָתֵת לָעָם אֶחָד אָסוּר חָפְשִׁי אֲשֶׁר הֵם יִרְצוּ

HTV: On the day of the sacred feast of Passover, it was the custom for the *Roman* governor of the city to free to the people one of the prisoners - whomever they wish.

KJV: Now at that feast the governor was wont to release unto the people a prisoner, whom they would.

Matthew 27:16

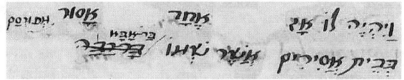

Freiburg Hebrew Manuscript

וַיְהִי לוֹ אָז אֶחָד אָסוּר מְפוּרְסָם בְּבֵית אֲסִירִים אֲשֶׁר שְׁמוֹ בַּר-אַבָּא

HTV: Pilate had a prisoner who was almost crazy - his name was Bar Rabban - *who* had been arrested for murder and put in the dungeon.

Note: Saint Jerome, who translated **Hebrew Matthew** into Greek and Latin, wrote in his **Commentary on Matthew** that Bar Abbas (son of the father), was called Bar Rabban (son of the teacher) in the **Gospel According to the Hebrews**. Bar Rabban is in the HGC.

KJV: And they had then a notable prisoner, called Barabbas.

Matthew 27:17

וְאַחֲרֵי שֶׁנִּתְקַבְּצוּ אָמַר פִּילָטוֹס כֹּל אֲשֶׁר אַתֶּם תִּרְצוּ אֲנִי אֶתֵּן לָכֶם חָפְשִׁי אֶת-בַּר-אַבָּא אוֹ אֶת-יֵשׁוּעַ הַנֶּאֱמָר מָשִׁיחַ

HTV: And after they were gathered, Pilate said to them all, "Who do you want released to you? Bar Rabban - or Yeshua - who is called the Messiah?

KJV: Therefore when they were gathered together, Pilate said unto them, Whom will ye that I release unto you? Barabbas, or Jesus which is called Christ?

The Hebrew Book of Matthew

Matthew 27:18

כִּי יִהְיֶה יוֹדֵעַ אֲשֶׁר בְּשִׂנְאָה מְסָרוּהוּ

HTV: **He gave** this *choice* **because Pilate knew that - due to hatred without cause - Yeshua had been arrested.**

KJV: For he knew that for envy they had delivered him.

Matthew 27:19

וְכַאֲשֶׁר הוּא יָשַׁב עַל הַבִּימָה שָׁלְחָה אֵלָיו הָאִשְׁתּוֹ אוֹמֶרֶת אֶל יִהְיֶה לְךָ אֵיזֶה עֵסֶק עִם הַצַּדִּים הַזֶּה כִּי רַבּוֹת צָרוֹת אֲנִי סָבַלְתִּי בַעֲבוּרוֹ הַיּוֹם בַּחֲלוֹם

HTV: **And when Pilate was sitting on the judgment seat (throne) - his wife sent to him a message saying, "Do not speak a word against this righteous man - For this night in a dream I suffered many things because of him."**

KJV: When he was set down on the judgment seat, his wife sent unto him, saying, Have thou nothing to do with that just man: for I have suffered many things this day in a dream because of him.

Matthew 27:20

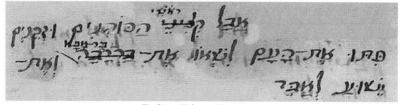
Freiburg Hebrew Manuscript

אֲבָל רָאשֵׁי הַכֹּוהֲנִים וּזְקֵנִים פִּתּוּ אֶת-הָעָם לִשְׁאוֹל אֶת-בַּר-אַבָּא וְאֶת-יֵשׁוּעַ לְאַבֵּד

HTV: **But the chief priest and elders coerced (deceived) the people - into asking for Bar Rabban** *to be released* **- and for Yeshua to perish!**

> Note: This was not a random crowd. It was composed of priests and their followers who were complicit in condemning Yeshua. But there were also a large number of agents of Herod Antipas' secret police. The Herods were famous for their secret police. They could manifest a riotous crowd anytime, anywhere. These thugs were there to coerce the crowd

into demanding the death of the Messiah. Herod wanted Yeshua dead. But he did not want to be implicated. It is strange that 2000 years later it is still assumed the Hebrew people demanded Yeshua's death rather than the major powerbrokers - Herod and the chief priests Caiaphas & Ananus and their followers.

KJV: But the chief priests and elders persuaded the multitude that they should ask Barabbas, and destroy Jesus.

Matthew 27:21

וַיַּעַן הַפָּקִיד וַיֹּאמַר לָהֶם אֵיזֶה אַתֶּם רוֹצִים לְשַׁלֵּחַ לָכֶם חוֹפְשִׁי וְהֵמָה אָמְרוּ אֶת-בַּר-אַבָּא

HTV: And the governor replied to them saying, "Who do you want me to release to you?" And they said - "Bar Rabban!"

KJV: The governor answered and said unto them, Whether of the twain will that I release unto you? They said, Barabbas.

Matthew 27:22

וַיֹּאמַר לָהֶם פִּילָטוֹס מָה נָא אֶעֱשֶׂה בְּעֵסֶק יֵשׁוּעַ שֶׁנִּקְרָא מָשִׁיחַ וְאָמְרוּ לוֹ הוּא יִצָּלֵב

HTV: And Pilate said unto them, "What shall I do *with* Yeshua - called the Messiah?" - And they said to him, "Let him be crucified!"

KJV: Pilate saith unto them, What shall I do then with Jesus which is called Christ? They all say unto him, Let him be crucified.

Matthew 27:23

וַיֹּאמַר לָהֶם הַפָּקִיד מָה הָרַע שֶׁהוּא עָשָׂה אֲבָל הֵמָה עוֹד יוֹתֵר צָעֲקוּ לֵאמוֹר יִצָּלֵב

HTV: And the governor said to them, "What evil has he done?" but still they cried even more saying, "Crucify *him*!"

KJV: And the governor said, Why, what evil hath he done? But they cried out the more, saying, Let him be crucified.

The Hebrew Book of Matthew

Matthew 27:24

וּמִשְׁפִּילָטוֹס רָאָה אֲשֶׁר לֹא יוֹעִיל מְאוּמָה כִּי אִם הַמְּהוּמָה עוֹד יוֹתֵר וְיוֹתֵר תִּתְרַבֶּה הוּא לָקַח אֶת-הַמַּיִם וְרָחַץ אֶת-יָדָיו בְּעֵינֵי הָעָם לֵאמוֹר אֲנִי נָקִי מִדַּם הַזֶּה הַצַּדִּיק אַתֶּם תֶּרְאוּ

HTV: When Pilate saw that nothing would help - that the tumult would increase *even* more. He took water and washed his hands in the eyes of the people saying - You see - I am innocent of this righteous blood!

KJV: When Pilate saw that he could prevail nothing, but that rather a tumult was made, he took water, and washed his hands before the multitude, saying, I am innocent of the blood of this just person: see ye to it.

Matthew 27:25

Freiburg Hebrew Manuscript

וַיַּעַן כֹּל הָעָם וַיֹּאמַר הַדָּמוֹ עָלֵינוּ וְעַל בָּנֵינוּ

HTV: And all the people replied, "His blood be upon us and upon our sons (our seed - our descendants)!"

Note: To the Hebrews this would be a horrendous thing to say. Believers would know this to plague all their descendants forever. Herod's thugs though had not such compunctions, and the priests felt secure in their self-righteousness. "It is better that one man die for the people than for the whole nation to perish." (John 11:50)

KJV: Then answered all the people, and said, His blood be on us, and on our children.

Matthew 27:26

וְאָז שָׁלַח לָהֶם אֶת-בַּר-אַבָּא וְאֶת-יֵשׁוּעַ אַחֲרֵי שֶׁהוּכָּה בְשׁוֹטִים נָתַן לָהֶם לְהִצָּלֵב

HTV: Then Pilate released Bar-Rabban to them. After Yeshua was scourged with a whip - he was given up to be crucified.

KJV: Then released he Barabbas unto them: and when he had scourged Jesus, he delivered him to be crucified.

Matthew 27:27

Freiburg Hebrew Manuscript

וּמִכַּאן אַנְשֵׁי הַמִּלְחָמָה שֶׁל הַפָּקִיד לָקְחוּ אֶת-יֵשׁוּעַ בְּבֵית הַדִּין וְקָבְצוּ אֵלָיו כֹּל כִּיתָא

HTV: **Then the soldiers of Pilate took Yeshua to the House of Judgment (Beit Din) and *there* gathered a crowd of many peoples.**

Note: The House of Judgment refers to the Beit Din, probably the Sanhedrin hall, where there were crowds of people from all nations come to Jerusalem for the Passover. The point was to humiliate and torment Yeshua before the Hebrew people.

KJV: Then the soldiers of the governor took Jesus into the common hall, and gathered unto him the whole band of soldiers.

Matthew 27:28

Freiburg Hebrew Manuscript

וְהִפְשִׁיטוּהוּ וְהִלְבִּישׁוּהוּ בַּחֲלוּק תּוֹלָע

HTV: **And they stripped Yeshua and clothed him with a robe of scarlet.***

*Note: The robe was dyed from the stain of the Scarlet worm which weaves a nest into the trunk of a tree and it is bright scarlet - called worm-wood. Scarlet dye comes from worm-wood. Referred to in Revelation 8:11 - the star that fell to earth called **Wormwood** whose stain turned the waters scarlet and bitter.

KJV: And they stripped him, and put on him a scarlet robe.

Matthew 27:29

וְאָרְגוּ עֲטֶרֶת מְקוֹצִים וְשָׂמוּ עַל רֹאשׁוֹ וְקָנֶה נָתְנוּ בִּימִינוֹ וְכָרְעוּ אֶת-בִּרְכֵּיהֶם לְפָנָיו וַיִּצְחֲקוּ בוֹ לֵאמֹר שָׁלוֹם לְךָ מֶלֶךְ הַיְּהוּדִים

The Hebrew Book of Matthew

HTV: **They wove a crown of thorns and put it on his head - and put a reed in his right hand - and bowed down on their knees before Yeshua and mocked him saying, "Hail to you - King of the Jews."**

KJV: And when they had platted a crown of thorns, they put it upon his head, and a reed in his right hand: and they bowed the knee before him, and mocked him, saying, Hail, King of the Jews!

Matthew 27:30

וַיָּרְקוּ בוֹ וַיִּקְחוּ אֶת-הַקָּנֶה וַיַּכּוּ אֶת-רֹאשׁוֹ

HTV: **And they spit in his face and took the reed and struck his head!**

KJV: And they spit upon him, and took the reed, and smote him on the head.

Matthew 27:31

וְאַחֲרֵי שֶׁצְּחָקוּהוּ הִפְשִׁיטוּ לוֹ אֶת-הֶחָלוּק שֶׁל תּוֹלָע וְהִלְבִּישׁוּהוּ בִּבְגָדָיו וְהוֹצִיאוּהוּ לְהַצְלֵב

HTV: **And after they had mocked Yeshua - they stripped him of the scarlet robe, clothed him in his own clothes - and took him away to be crucified.**

KJV: And after that they had mocked him, they took the robe off from him, and put his own raiment on him, and led him away to crucify him.

Matthew 27:32

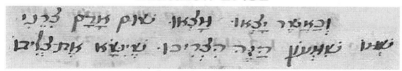
Freiburg Hebrew Manuscript

וְכַאֲשֶׁר יָצְאוּ מָצְאוּ שׁוּם אָדָם צָרְנִי שְׁמוֹ שִׁמְעוֹן הַזֶּה הִצְרִיכוּ שֶׁיִּשָּׂא אֶת-צְלִיבוֹ

HTV: **When they went out, they found a man from Cyrene, his name was Simon, whom they compelled to carry his cross.**

Chapter 27

Note: The words "cross, crucify, crucifixion" did not enter the Christian creed until the fourth century when Constantine made the Cross the symbol of the faith. It was not in the early texts of Scripture either in Hebrew or Greek. The Greeks used the word *stauros*, meaning "stake" for the cross. Hebrew texts later borrowed the weaver's term for crosswise - *shti va'erev* - for the cross and crucifixion.

KJV: And as they came out, they found a man of Cyrene, Simon by name: him they compelled to bear his cross.

Matthew 27:33

וַיָּבוֹאוּ לְמָקוֹם הַנִּקְרָא גּוּלְגּוֹלְתָּא

HTV: **They came to a place called Golgoltha - place of the skull.**

KJV: And when they were come unto a place called Golgotha, that is to say, a place of a skull,

Matthew 27:34

וְנָתְנוּ לוֹ לִשְׁתּוֹת יַיִן הַנִּמְזָג בִּמְרוֹרָה וּמִשֶּׁטְעָם לֹא יִרְצֶה לִשְׁתּוֹת

HTV: **They gave him wine to drink - mixed with bitter** *herbs* **– and when he tasted it he would not drink it.**

KJV: They gave him vinegar to drink mingled with gall: and when he had tasted thereof, he would not drink.

Matthew 27:35

וְאַחֲרֵי שֶׁהִצְלִיבוּהוּ חִלְּקוּ אֶת-מַלְבּוּשָׁיו בְּגוֹרָל שֶׁיִּמָּלֵא מַה שֶׁנֶּאֱמַר עַל פִּי הַנָּבִיא שֶׁאָמַר חִלְּקוּ בְגָדַי לָהֶם וְעַל לְבוּשִׁי הִפִּילוּ גוֹרָל

HTV: **After they crucified Yeshua, they divided his clothes and cast lots - to fulfill what was said by the prophet - "They divided my clothing unto themselves - and upon my clothing they cast lots."** *(from Psalms 22:18)*

KJV: And they crucified him, and parted his garments, casting lots: that it might be fulfilled which was spoken by the prophet, They parted my garments among them, and upon my vesture did they cast lots.

Matthew 27:36

וְהַיוֹשְׁבִים שָׁם יִשְׁמְרוּהוּ

HTV: **And the inhabitants watched him there.** *(Psalm 22 and Isaiah 53)*

> Note: In the Gospel of John it says the inhabitants mocked him at the spectacle of the cross.

KJV: And sitting down they watched him there;

Matthew 27:37

וְשָׂמוּ עַל רֹאשׁוֹ כְּתָב מִשְׁפָּטוֹ כֵּיצַד יֵשׁוּעַ הַמֶּלֶךְ הַיְהוּדִים

HTV: **They wrote over his head his accusation - "This is Yeshua - the King of the Jews!"**

KJV: And set up over his head his accusation written, THIS IS JESUS THE KING OF THE JEWS.

Matthew 27:38

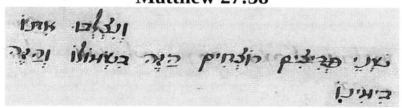

Freiburg Hebrew Manuscript

וְנִצְלְבוּ אִתּוֹ שְׁנֵי רוֹצְחִים הַזֶּה בִשְׂמֹאלוֹ וְהַזֶּה בִימִינוֹ

HTV: **And they crucified with him - two bandits - one at his right hand and one at his left.**

> Note: Different texts called them either "murderers or thieves." They were likely to be both since bandits murdered their victims so as not to leave witnesses to identify and accuse them.

KJV: Then were there two thieves crucified with him, one on the right hand, and another on the left.

Matthew 27:39

וְהָעוֹבְרִים הָיוּ מְחָרְפִים בּוֹ מוֹטִים אֶת-רָאשֵׁיהֶם

HTV: **Those *who* passed by were cursing Yeshua and shaking their heads**

KJV: And they that passed by reviled him, wagging their heads,

Matthew 27:40

Freiburg Hebrew Manuscript

לֵאמֹר הוֹי אֲשֶׁר מְנַתֵּץ אֶת-הֵיכַל אֱלֹהִים וּבְלֹשָׁה יָמִים יוֹסִיף עוֹד לִבְנוֹתוֹ הוֹשִׁיעַ עַצְמְךָ אִם אַתָּה הַבֵּן הָאֱלֹהִים רֵד נָא מִצְלִיבָה

HTV: **Saying, "Alas, you who said - Destroy the Temple and in three days I will raise it up! Save yourself! - If you are the son of Elohim - descend from the cross!"**

Note: The quotation cited from Yeshua is in John 2:19. Yeshua, however, was speaking of the Temple of his own body. After three days he rose up from death and destruction.

KJV: And saying, Thou that destroyest the temple, and buildest it in three days, save thyself. If thou be the Son of God, come down from the cross.

Matthew 27:41

וּכְמוֹ כֵן גַּם רָאשֵׁי הַכֹּהֲנִים הָיוּ מְצַחְקִים בּוֹ יַחַד עִם הַסּוֹפְרִים וּזְקֵנִים וַיֹּאמְרוּ׃

HTV: **So, as the chief priests were mocking Yeshua - together with the scribes and elders - they said:**

KJV: Likewise also the chief priests mocking him, with the scribes and elders, said,

Matthew 27:42

אֶת-הָאֲחֵרִים הוֹשִׁיעַ וְעַצְמוֹ אֵינוֹ יָכוֹל לְהוֹשִׁיעַ וְאִם הוּא הַמֶּלֶךְ יִשְׂרָאֵל יֵרֵד עַתָּה מִצְלִיבָה וְנַאֲמִין בּוֹ

The Hebrew Book of Matthew

HTV: **"He saved others - but he is not able to save himself. If he is the king of Israel - Let him come down from the cross now - and we will believe in him."**

KJV: He saved others; himself he cannot save. If he be the King of Israel, let him now come down from the cross, and we will believe him.

Matthew 27:43

הָיָה בוֹטֵחַ אֶל יְהֹוָה יְפַלְטֵהוּ עַתָּה כִּי אִם חָפֵץ בּוֹ כִּי אָמַר אֲנִי הַבֵּן הָאֱלֹהִים

HTV: **"He trusted in Yehovah - now let Yehovah rescue him - If He wants him! For he said, 'I am the Son of Elohim.' "**

Note: See Psalm 22:8.

KJV: He trusted in God; let him deliver him now, if he will have him: for he said, I am the Son of God.

Matthew 27:44

וְהַזֹּאת עָשׂוּ גַם הָרוֹצְחִים אֲשֶׁר יִהְיוּ נִצְלָבִים אִתּוֹ כֵּיצַד הָיוּ מְחָרְפִים בּוֹ

HTV: **This they also did - the bandits who were crucified with him - in *the same* manner they were taunting Yeshua.**

KJV: The thieves also, which were crucified with him, cast the same in his teeth.

Matthew 27:45

וּמִשָּׁעָה שִׁישִׁית עַד שָׁעָה תְּשִׁיעִית נִתְחַדְשׁוּ חֲשָׁכִים בְּכֹל הָאָרֶץ

HTV: **And from the sixth hour until the ninth hour - darkness came over all the land.**

KJV: Now from the sixth hour there was darkness over all the land unto the ninth hour.

Chapter 27

Matthew 27:46

Freiburg Hebrew Manuscript

וְכִמְעַט בְּשָׁעָה הַתְּשִׁיעִית צָעַק יֵשׁוּעַ בְּקוֹל גָּדוֹל לֵאמֹר אֵלִי אֵלִי לָמָה שְׁבַקְתַּנִי

HTV: At about the ninth hour, Yeshua cried out in a loud voice saying, "My God, my God! Why have you spared* me?"

> *Note: Yeshua is referring Psalm 22, "My God, my God, why have you forsaken me. Why are you so far from me." However, Yeshua is renowned for always putting a new spin on old verses. He says this in Aramaic - as acknowledged by every version of the N.T. - that is, "Eloi, Eloi - lama sabachtani!" - which has a different meaning. It means **"Why have you spared me?"** Within minutes, Yehovah takes Yeshua's spirit to him and he utters his final words, "It is finished!" So Yehovah did not forsake him.
>
> There is a very toxic theology often cited that Yehovah had to abandon His Son in his hour of greatest need because Yeshua had become sin. **There is no scriptural requirement that Yehovah need do this!** It is such a gross misjudgment of God's love for His Son and for us. It is a false theology. It is toxic. If Yehovah would abandon His own Son - the man without sin - why do we deserve any better?

KJV: And about the ninth hour Jesus cried with a loud voice, saying, Eli, Eli, lama sabachthani? that is to say, My God, my God, why hast thou forsaken me?

Matthew 27:47

וּקְצָת מְעוֹמְדִים שָׁם וְשׁוֹמְעִים הָאֵלֶּה דְבָרִים הָיוּ אוֹמְרִים הַזֶּה קוֹרֵא אֶת-אֵלִיָּה

HTV: From among those standing there - and those hearing these words - they said, "This one is calling Elijah!"

KJV: Some of them that stood there, when they heard that, said, This man calleth for Elias.

Matthew 27:48

וּמִיָּד רָץ אֶחָד מֵהֶם וַיִּקַּח סְפוֹג וַיְמַלֵּא בְחוֹמֶץ וַיָּשֶׂם עַל קָנֶה וַיִּתֵּן לוֹ לִשְׁתּוֹת

HTV: **Immediately one of them ran and took a sponge. He soaked it in vinegar - put it on a reed - and gave it to Yeshua to drink.**

KJV: And straightway one of them ran, and took a spunge, and filled it with vinegar, and put it on a reed, and gave him to drink.

Matthew 27:49

וְהָאֲחֵרִים הָיוּ אוֹמְרִים הֶרֶף נָא כְּדֵי שֶׁנִּרְאֶה הַאִם אֵלִיָה יָבוֹא לְהַצִּילוֹ

HTV: **The others were saying, "Be quiet now! - That we may see if Elijah will come to deliver him."**

KJV: The rest said, Let be, let us see whether Elias will come to save him.

Matthew 27:50

וְיֵשׁוּעַ הוֹסִיף לִקְרוֹא בְּקוֹל גָּדוֹל וַיִּשְׁלַח אֶת רוּחוֹ

HTV: **Yeshua again cried out in a loud voice - and sent his spirit up to his Father!**

KJV: Jesus, when he had cried again with a loud voice, yielded up the ghost.

Matthew 27:51

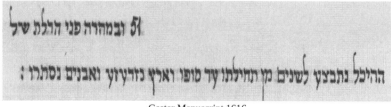

Gaster Manuscript 1616

HTV: **Behold, the Holy of Holies was broken from top to bottom, and the earth shook, and the stones were split in two!**

Chapter 27

Note: There was an earthquake at Yeshua's death that split the Temple stones. Jerome relates in his *Commentary upon Matthew* that in **The Gospel according to the Hebrews**, it is the large lintel stone at the entrance to the Holy of Holies that is split. The Greek versions say only that the veil of the sanctuary was split whereas in The Hebrew Gospels it is the stones of the Temple.

<u>**This is a huge difference between the Greek and Hebrew texts**</u>! The splitting of the stones is recorded in Matthew 27:51, Mark 15:38, and Luke 23:45 in *The Hebrew Gospels from Catalonia* (Vat Ebr 100), *The Cochin Gospels* (Cambridge Oo.1.32) and the Gaster 1616 manuscript, It is also in **The Ethiopian Gospels** in all three verses.

Jerome, in the fourth century, cites this from **The Hebrew Gospel** of the early first century Messianic church. The huge lintel stone was split in two. Greek texts do not have this.

KJV: And, behold, the veil of the temple was rent in twain from the top to the bottom; and the earth did quake, and the rocks rent;

Matthew 27:52

וּקְבָרִים נִפְתְּחוּ וְגוּפֵי קְדוֹשִׁים הַשּׁוֹכְבִים קָמוּ מִמִּיתָה

HTV: **The tombs were opened - and the bodies of the righteous - who were lying *there* - rose from death.**

KJV: And the graves were opened; and many bodies of the saints which slept arose,

Matthew 27:53

וְיָצְאוּ מִקְּבָרִים וְאַחֲרֵי קוּמָתוֹ מִמֵּתִים בָּאוּ בָעִיר קֹדֶשׁ וְנִרְאוּ לְרַבִּים

HTV: **They came out from the tombs and went into the holy city - after Yeshua's resurrection from the dead - and they appeared to many.**

KJV: And came out of the graves after his resurrection, and went into the holy city, and appeared unto many.

Matthew 27:54

אָמְנָם הַשַׂר מֵאוֹת וַאֲשֶׁר הָיוּ אִתּוֹ שׁוֹמְרִים אֶת-יֵשׁוּעַ מִשָּׁרָאוּ אֶת-רַעַשׁ אֶרֶץ וּדְבָרִים הָאַחֵרִים שֶׁהָיוּ הִנֵּה הֵמָּה יָרְאוּ מְאֹד וַיֹּאמְרוּ בֶּאֱמֶת הַזֶּה יִהְיֶה הַבֵּן הָאֱלֹהִים

The Hebrew Book of Matthew

HTV: **Indeed, the centurion - and those who were with him guarding Yeshua - when they saw the earth shake violently and the other things that** *happened.* **Behold, they were very afraid and said, "Surely, this was the Son of God!"**

KJV: Now when the centurion, and they that were with him, watching Jesus, saw the earthquake, and those things that were done, they feared greatly, saying, Truly this was the Son of God.

Matthew 27:55

וַתִּהְיֶינָה נָשִׁים רַבּוֹת עוֹמְדוֹת מֵרָחוֹק שֶׁרָדְפוּ אַחֲרֵי יֵשׁוּעַ מִגָּלִיל עוֹבְדוֹת לוֹ

HTV: **There were many women standing at a distance - *those* who followed after Yeshua from Galilee - in order to serve him.**

KJV: And many women were there beholding afar off, which followed Jesus from Galilee, ministering unto him:

Matthew 27:56

בֵּין אֲשֶׁר תִּהְיֶה מִרְיָם מַגְדְּלָנָה וּמִרְיָם יַעֲקוֹבִי וְאֵם יוֹסֵף וְאֵם בְּנֵי זְבְדִּי

HTV: **Among whom were Mary Magdalene - and Mary the mother of Jacob and Joseph - and the mother of the sons of Zebedee.**

KJV: Among which was Mary Magdalene, and Mary the mother of James and Joses, and the mother of Zebedee's children.

Matthew 27:57

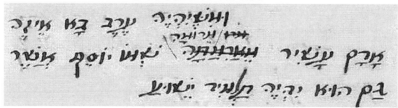
Freiburg Hebrew Manuscript

וּמְשֶׁיִּהְיֶה עֶרֶב בָּא אֵיזֶה אָדָם עָשִׁיר מֵרוּמָה שְׁמוֹ יוֹסֵף אֲשֶׁר גַּם הוּא יִהְיֶה תַּלְמִיד יֵשׁוּעַ

Chapter 27

HTV: And in the evening, there came a certain rich man from Arimathea, his name was Joseph, who was also a follower of Yeshua.

Note: What little we know about Joseph of Arimathea is intriguing. He was clearly wealthy and connected with the Romans, or he could not have gotten to see Pilate. Some sources say he was the "Minister of Mines," therefore, likely to be a Roman citizen.

He was Jewish - said to be the uncle of Myriam - Yeshua's mother - and therefore the uncle of Yeshua - or the Romans would not have released Yeshua's body to him. The story goes that Joseph owned mines in Canturbury, England and Yeshua went there while working and traveling for Joseph when he was a young man before starting his ministry. That legend is prevalent in Canturbury.

KJV: When the even was come, there came a rich man of Arimathaea, named Joseph, who also himself was Jesus' disciple:

Matthew 27:58

הַזֶּה בָּא לְפִילָטוֹס וַיִשְׁאַל אֶת-הַגּוּף יֵשׁוּעַ וְצִוָּה פִּילָטוֹס לָתֵת לוֹ אֶת-הַגּוּף

HTV: This *same* one (Joseph of Arimathea) came to Pilate - and asked for Yeshua's body - and Pilate ordered the body to be given to him.

KJV: He went to Pilate, and begged the body of Jesus. Then Pilate commanded the body to be delivered.

Matthew 27:59

Freiburg Hebrew Manuscript

וּמִשֶּׁלָקַח אֶת-הַגּוּף כִּירְבְּלוֹ בְּסָדִין טָהֹר

HTV: And when he had taken away the body - he wrapped it in a garment of clean fine linen.

Note: Some versions say "silk" which is certainly a fine garment. It is uncertain whether the word מֶשִׁי (meshi) means "fine cloth" or "silk."

Ezekiel 16:10 speaks of all types of fabric, specifying both linen and silk separately. However, traditional Hebrew wrapping is linen.

KJV: And when Joseph had taken the body, he wrapped it in a clean linen cloth,

Matthew 27:60

וַיָּשֶׂם אוֹתוֹ בְקִבְרוֹ הֶחָדָשׁ אֲשֶׁר חָצֵב בַּצּוּר וְגִלְגֵּל כֵּיפִי גָּדוֹל לְפוּם הַקֶּבֶר וְהָלַךְ מִכַּאן

HTV: **And he put Yeshua in his *own* new tomb, which he carved from rock, and he rolled a large stone over the tomb's entrance - and he went away.**

KJV: And laid it in his own new tomb, which he had hewn out in the rock: and he rolled a great stone to the door of the sepulchre, and departed.

Matthew 27:61

וְתִהְיֶה שָׁם מִרְיָם מַגְדְּלִינָה וּמִרְיָם אַחֶרֶת יוֹשְׁבוֹת מוּל הַקֶּבֶר

HTV: **And there *came* Mary Magdalene and another Mary to sit in front of the tomb.**

KJV: And there was Mary Magdalene, and the other Mary, sitting over against the sepulchre.

Matthew 27:62

וּבְיוֹם שֶׁהוּא אַחֵר בְּדִיקַת חָמֵץ נִקְבְּצוּ רָאשֵׁי הַכּוֹהֲנִים וּפְרוּשִׁים אֶל פִּילָטוּס

HTV: **And on the day after Pesach (Passover), the chief priests and Pharisees gathered with Pilate.**

KJV: Now the next day, that followed the day of the preparation, the chief priests and Pharisees came together unto Pilate,

Matthew 27:63

וַיֹּאמְרוּ אֲדוֹנִי אֲנַחְנוּ זוֹכְרִים אֲשֶׁר מַתְעֶה הַזֶּה אָמַר בִּהְיוֹת עוֹדֶנּוּ בַחַיִּים אַחֲרֵי שְׁלֹשָׁה יָמִים אֲנִי אָקוּם מִמֵּתִים

HTV: **And they said, "My Lord, we remember that this deceiver said, while he was still alive, 'After three days I will rise from the dead.'"**

KJV: Saying, Sir, we remember that that deceiver said, while he was yet alive, After three days I will rise again.

Matthew 27:64

לְפִיכָךְ תְּצַוֶּה לִשְׁמוֹר אֶת־הַקֶּבֶר עַד הַיּוֹם הַשְּׁלִישִׁי פֶּן יָבוֹאוּ תַלְמִידָיו וְיִגְנְבוּהוּ וְיֹאמְרוּ לָעָם הוּא קָם מִמֵּתִים וְתִהְיֶה הַטָּעוּת הָאַחֲרוֹנִית רָעָה מֵרִאשׁוֹנָה

HTV: **Command, therefore, that the tomb be guarded until the third day - lest his disciples come and steal his body and tell the people that he rose from the dead - If so, the last mistake will be worse than the first!**

KJV: Command therefore that the sepulchre be made sure until the third day, lest his disciples come by night, and steal him away, and say unto the people, He is risen from the dead: so the last error shall be worse than the first.

Matthew 27:65

וַיֹּאמֶר לָהֶם פִּילָטוֹס יֵשׁ לָכֶם מִשְׁמֶרֶת לְכוּ וְשִׁמְרוּ לְפִי מַה שֶׁאַתֶּם יוֹדְעִים

HTV: **Pilate said to them (chief priests), "You have a watch - go and guard (the tomb) as well as you know how."**

KJV: Pilate said unto them, Ye have a watch: go your way, make it as sure as ye can.

Matthew 27:66

Freiburg Hebrew Manuscript

וְהֵמָּה הָלְכוּ וְחִזְּקוּ אֶת-הַקֶּבֶר חוֹתְמִים אֶת-הָאֶבֶן עִם שׁוֹמְרִים

HTV: And with that, they went and secured the tomb - sealing the stone and placing guards.

Note: In this case, a cord would be stretched from one side to the other side sealed on both ends with wax and a royal signet seal - which made it a legal trespass to break it.

KJV: So they went, and made the sepulchre sure, sealing the stone, and setting a watch.

Matthew Chapter 28

Hebrew Text Version (HTV)

¹ On the evening of the Sabbath - which began the first of the Sabbaths - Mary Magdalene and the other Mary came to the grave.

² Behold a great shaking of the earth was renewed - because an angel of the Lord came down from heaven. He drew near - took away the stone and sat down upon it!

³ His appearance resembled lightning - and his clothing white as snow!

⁴ The guards trembled greatly - and became as dead men.

⁵ The angel spoke to the women saying, "Do not fear, for I know that you seek Yeshua - who was crucified."

⁶ "He is not there because he arose - as he said. Come! Come and see the place where he was laid!"

⁷ "Quickly go and say to his disciples that Yeshua has risen from the dead - and now he will go before you to Galilee. There you will see him. Behold! I have spoken this to you!"

⁸ So, they went out quickly from the sepulcher - with fear and great joy - running to tell his disciples!

⁹ And while they were going, Yeshua met them on the road, saying, "May Yehovah (El) save you!" And they kneeled at his feet - and they worshiped him.

¹⁰ Then Yeshua said to them, "Do not fear! Now go and tell my

brothers that they are to go into Galilee - and they will see me there."

¹¹ When they departed, behold - some of the guards went into the city and told the chief priests all of the things that were done.

¹² They (chief priests) gathered together with the elders - and they consulted - and gave a great quantity of silver to the guards!

¹³ Saying, "Now say that his disciples came in the night and they stole him (Yeshua) while we were sleeping."

¹⁴ And they said, "When Pilate comes to know this - we will persuade him – *so* that you will be safe!"

¹⁵ And when they took the silver - they did according to what they were instructed. And this word was spread amongst the Judeans up to this day.

¹⁶ So, *his* eleven disciples went unto Galilee to the mountain Yeshua had appointed.

¹⁷ And Yeshua appeared to them there. And when they saw him they worshipped him - but some of them *still* doubted.

¹⁸ And Yeshua came closer to speak, saying, "Behold, all authority in heaven and on earth has been given to me."

¹⁹ Go and teach all the nations - baptizing them in the name of the Father - and the Son - and the Holy Spirit.

²⁰ "Teach them to keep all the words - which I commanded you. Behold, I will be with you always - until the end of the world!"

Matthew Chapter 28

HTV with translator notes and KJV comparison

קפיטולו נד״ כפימטיאו

Chapter 54 according to Matthew

Note: Papias, in the second century, wrote that the *Gospel according to the Hebrews* was a collection of the Logia (Sayings) of the Messiah. This is reflected in the Shem Tov and the HGC where every time Yeshua speaks, they begin a new chapter. Thus there are 54 chapters in the HGC Hebrew Matthew. We have numbered them according to the modern chapter separation and designation that the reader is used to - but left the original chapter titles in the text for the sake of authenticity.

The Hebrew Book of Matthew

Matthew 28:1

Vat 100 Ebr Manuscript - Hebrew Gospel from Catalonia

קפיטולו נו̅ כפימטיאו

הראון יום אחד שנקרא (דוקמ־יי) דומיניגא באה מרימה מקדלינא
ואחרת מריאה ראו הקבר

HTV: **On the evening of the Sabbath - which began the <u>first of the Sabbaths</u> - Mary Magdalene and the other Mary came to the grave.**

> Note: This verse is typically misunderstood. It is the counting of the Omer, the seven Sabbaths from Passover (Pesach) until Shavuot (Pentecost). This is the meaning of "first of the Sabbaths." The counting of the Omer - 49 days - which is 7 Sabbaths - until Shavuot. This included counting every single day of the 49 days as a part of the "counting of the Sabbaths." It was still dark, the "*evening*" following the Sabbath. It was dawn Sunday - and according to the Angel in verse 6 - Yeshua was gone, having arisen from the grave at twiiight of the Sabbath the day before.

KJV: In the end of the sabbath, as it began to dawn toward the first *day* of the week, came Mary Magdalene and the other Mary to see the sepulchre.

Matthew 28:2

Freiburg Hebrew Manuscript

וְהִנֵּה רַעַשׁ הָאָרֶץ גָּדוֹל נִתְחַדֵּשׁ כִּי מַלְאַךְ אֲדֹנָי יָרַד מִשָּׁמַיִם וַיִּקְרַב
וְהֵסִיר אֶת-הָאֶבֶן וַיֵּשֶׁב עָלֶיהָ

HTV: **Behold a great shaking of the earth was renewed - because an angel of the Lord came down from heaven. He drew near - took away the stone and sat down upon it!**

Chapter 28

Note: There was an earthquake during Yeshua's crucifixion. This appears to be an aftershock, a renewal of the quaking, caused by the Angel descending from heaven to the earth.

KJV: And, behold, there was a great earthquake: for the angel of the Lord descended from heaven, and came and rolled back the stone from the door, and sat upon it.

Matthew 28:3

וַיְהִיֶה מַרְאֵה שֶׁלּוֹ דּוֹמֶה לְבָרָק וּלְבוּשׁוֹ לָבָן כְּשָׁלֶג

HTV: **His appearance resembled lightning - and his clothing white as snow!**

KJV: His countenance was like lightning, and his raiment white as snow:

Matthew 28:4

וּמֵרָעֲדוֹ נִתְרַעֲדוּ הַשּׁוֹמְרִים וַיִּהְיוּ כְּמֵתִים

HTV: **The guards trembled greatly - and became as dead men.**

KJV: And for fear of him the keepers did shake, and became as dead *men*.

Matthew 28:5

וַיַּעַן הַמַּלְאָךְ וַיֹּאמַר לַנָּשִׁים אַל תִּירָאֶנָה כִּי אֲנִי יוֹדֵעַ אֲשֶׁר אַתֶּן מְבַקְשׁוֹת אֶת-יֵשׁוּעַ אֲשֶׁר נִצְלַב

HTV: **The angel spoke to the women saying, "Do not fear, for I know that you seek Yeshua - who was crucified."**

KJV: And the angel answered and said unto the women, Fear not ye: for I know that ye seek Jesus, which was crucified.

Matthew 28:6

אֵינוֹ שָׁם כִּי הוּא קָם כְּמוֹ שֶׁאָמַר בּוֹאנָה וּרְאֶינָה אֶת-הַמָּקוֹם שֶׁיִּהְיֶה הוּשָׂם בּוֹ הָאָדוֹן

HTV: **"He is not there because he arose - as he said. Come! Come and see the place where he was laid!"**

475

KJV: He is not here: for he is risen, as he said. Come, see the place where the Lord lay.

Matthew 28:7

וּבִמְהֵרָה תֵלַכְנָה וְתֹאמַרְוֹת לְתַלְמִידָיו שֶׁהוּא קָם מֵמֵּתִים וְהִנֵּה יְקַדֵּם לָכֶם בְּגָלִילָה שָׁם תִּרְאוּהוּ הִנֵּה אָמַרְתִּי לָכֶן

HTV: **"Quickly go and say to his disciples that Yeshua has risen from the dead - and now he will go before you to Galilee. There you will see him. Behold! I have spoken this to you!"**

KJV: And go quickly, and tell his disciples that he is risen from the dead; and, behold, he goeth before you into Galilee; there shall ye see him: lo, I have told you.

Matthew 28:8

וַיָּצְאוּ בִמְהֵרָה מִקֶּבֶר עִם רַעַד וְשִׂמְחָה גְדוֹלָה רָצוֹת לְהַגִּיד לְתַלְמִידָיו

HTV: **So, they went out quickly from the sepulcher - with fear and great joy - running to tell his disciples!**

KJV: And they departed quickly from the sepulchre with fear and great joy; and did run to bring his disciples word.

Matthew 28:9

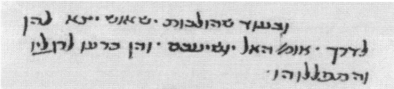

Vat 100 Ebr Manuscript - Hebrew Gospel from Catalonia

ובננוד שהולכות ישאוש יצא להן לדרך . אוז האן יצשיעכם יוהן כרעו לרגליו וה תפללוהו

HTV: **And while they were going, Yeshua met them on the road, saying, "May Yehovah (El) save you!" And they kneeled at his feet - and they worshiped him.**

Note: The HGC uses "May Yehovah (El) save you!" whereas the STM uses, "May Yehovah (Hashem) save you!"

This is a common Hebrew greeting to fellow believers in the faith. The Gentiles replaced this Hebrew greeting with a common Roman greeting, presumably to erase the Hebrew name of God in order to replace it with the Greek.

However, the substituted greeting "All Hail!" was the Roman military salute done by slamming the fist on the breastplate then thrusting it into the air. The Roman salute was adopted by Hitler 2000 years later as the Nazi salute. Now we know why one does not change the word of God. You never know.

KJV: And as they went to tell his disciples, behold, Jesus met them, saying, **All hail!** And they came and held him by the feet, and worshipped him.

Matthew 28:10

וְאָז אָמַר לָהֶן יֵשׁוּעַ אַל תִּירְאֶנָה לֵכְנָה נָא וְהַגֵּדְנָה לְאַחַי שֶׁיֵּלְכוּ בְּגָלִילָה שָׁם יִרְאוּנִי

HTV: **Then Yeshua said to them, "Do not fear! Now go and tell my brothers that they are to go into Galilee - and they will see me there."**

KJV: Then said Jesus unto them, Be not afraid: go tell my brethren that they go into Galilee, and there shall they see me.

Matthew 28:11

וּמִשֶּׁהָלְכוּ הִנֵּה קְצָת מִשּׁוֹמְרִים בָּאוּ בָעִיר וְהִגִּידוּ לְרָאשֵׁי הַכּוֹהֲנִים כֹּל דְּבָרִים אֲשֶׁר נֶעֱשׂוּ

HTV: **When they departed, behold - some of the guards went into the city and told the chief priests all of the things that were done.**

KJV: Now when they were going, behold, some of the watch came into the city, and shewed unto the chief priests all the things that were done.

Matthew 28:12

אֲשֶׁר נִקְבְּצוּ יַחַד עִם זְקֵנִים וְהִתְיָעֲצוּ וְנָתְנוּ הַרְבֵּה כְסָפִים לְאַנְשֵׁי מִלְחָמָה

HTV: **They (chief priests) gathered together with the elders - and they consulted - and gave a great quantity of silver to the guards!**

KJV: And when they were assembled with the elders, and had taken counsel, they gave large money unto the soldiers,

Matthew 28:13

לֵאמֹר אִמְרוּ נָא שֶׁתַּלְמִידָיו בָּאוּ בְלַיְלָה וַיִּגְנְבוּהוּ בִּזְמַן שֶׁאֲנַחְנוּ נִהְיֶה יְשֵׁנִים

HTV: **Saying, "Now say that his disciples came in the night and they stole him (Yeshua) while we were sleeping."**

KJV: Saying, Say ye, His disciples came by night, and stole him *away* while we slept.

Matthew 28:14

והם אמרו אם ידע פילאט אנחנו נשיג שתהיו בטוחים.

HTV: **And they said, "When Pilate comes to know this - we will persuade him – *so* that you will be safe!"**

KJV: And if this come to the governor's ears, we will persuade him, and secure you.

Matthew 28:15

וּמִשֶּׁלָּקְחוּ אֶת-הַכֶּסֶף עָשׂוּ לְפִי מָה שֶׁהָיוּ מְלֻמָּדִים וְהַדָּבָר הַזֶּה הָיָה פָּשׁוּט בֵּין הַיְהוּדִים עַד הַיּוֹם הַזֶּה

HTV: **And when they took the silver - they did according to what they were instructed. And this word was spread amongst the Judeans up to this day.**

KJV: So they took the money, and did as they were taught: and this saying is commonly reported among the Jews until this day.

Matthew 28:16

אֲבָל אֶחָד עָשָׂר תַּלְמִידִים הָלְכוּ בְגָלִילָה לְהַר אֲשֶׁר לָהֶם יֵשׁוּעַ יְקַבַּע

HTV: **So, *his* eleven disciples went unto Galilee to the mountain Yeshua had appointed.**

Chapter 28

KJV: Then the eleven disciples went away into Galilee, into a mountain where Jesus had appointed them.

Matthew 28:17

וְכַאֲשֶׁר רָאוּ אוֹתוֹ הִשְׁתַּחֲווּהוּ וּקְצָתָם מֵהֶם הָיוּ מִסְתַּפְּקִים

HTV: **And Yeshua appeared to them there. And when they saw him they worshipped him - but some of them *still* doubted.**

KJV: And when they saw him, they worshipped him: but some doubted.

Matthew 28:18

וַיִּגַּשׁ יֵשׁוּעַ וַיְדַבֵּר לֵאמֹר הִנֵּה נִתְּנָה לִי כֹל מֶמְשֶׁלֶת בַּשָּׁמַיִם וּבָאָרֶץ

HTV: **And Yeshua came closer to speak, saying, "Behold, all authority in heaven and on earth has been given to me."**

KJV: And Jesus came and spake unto them, saying, All power is given unto me in heaven and in earth.

Matthew 28:19

Freiburg Hebrew Manuscript

לְכוּ וְלַמְּדוּ אֶת כֹּל הַגּוֹיִם טוֹבְלִים אוֹתָם בְּשֵׁם הָאָב וְהַבֵּן וְהָרוּחַ קָדוֹשׁ

HTV: **Go and teach all the nations - baptizing them in the name of the Father - and the Son - and the Holy Spirit.**

> Note: This verse is missing in the earliest Greek texts - indicating it was added later to support the Trinity doctrine. It differs greatly from the baptism formula given seven times in the Gospels and Acts. Such as **Acts 2:38, "Be baptized every one of you in the name of Yeshua Ha Mashiach for the remission of sins - and you shall receive the gift of the Holy Spirit"** (from Yehovah).

KJV: Go ye therefore, and teach all nations, baptizing them in the name of the Father, and of the Son, and of the Holy Ghost:

Matthew 28:20
מְלַמְּדִים אוֹתָם לִשְׁמוֹר כֹּל דְּבָרִים שֶׁצִּוִּיתִיכֶם וְהִנֵּה אֲנוֹכִי אֶהְיֶה
אִתְּכֶם כֹּל יָמִים עַד תַּכְלִית הָעוֹלָם

HTV: **"Teach them to keep all the words - which I commanded you. Behold, I will be with you always - until the end of the world!"**

KJV: Teaching them to observe all things whatsoever I have commanded you: and, lo, I am with you alway, *even* unto the end of the world. Amen.

Editor's Final Comments

For those who wish to take a deeper dive into the Hebrew - we will be opening our archives to the public. All the information is there from all of the extant Hebrew manuscripts used, and the breakdown of each definition of each word. Whether you wish to agree or disagree, or make your own translation, all you need is there - from the manuscripts themselves to the interlinear charts and the historical and grammatical notes - everything you need is at your fingertips in one place.

For those who want more now - and who doesn't - join our **Revelation of the Month Club** and receive chapters of our latest research even before it is published. Also included in those offerings are videos from the Writing of God TV, interviews and other revelatory treasures of the **Word - and the world** of biblical archaeology. See our latest collection of treasures in **El Abba's Cave!** Put your email in Free Downloads and receive a free ebook and free Research Updates Newsletter. We want to give you as much of the Hebrew Word of the Gospel as we possibly can - so go to **www.WritingOfGod.com** and join our family.

Benai Emunah Institute
121 Mountain Way Drive
Kerrville, Texas 78028

830-257-7414